SOCIETY FOR NEW TESTAMENT STUDIES
MONOGRAPH SERIES
GENERAL EDITOR
MATTHEW BLACK, D.D., F.B.A.

3

THE THEOLOGICAL TENDENCY OF
CODEX BEZAE CANTABRIGIENSIS
IN ACTS

THE THEOLOGICAL TENDENCY OF
CODEX BEZAE CANTABRIGIENSIS
IN ACTS

BY

ELDON JAY EPP

CAMBRIDGE
AT THE UNIVERSITY PRESS
1966

Published by the Syndics of the Cambridge University Press
Bentley House, 200 Euston Road, London N.W.1
American Branch: 32 East 57th Street, New York, N.Y. 10022

Library of Congress Catalogue Card Number: 66-17055

Printed in Great Britain
at the University Printing House, Cambridge
(Brooke Crutchley, University Printer)

UXORI

CONTENTS

Acknowledgement	*page* viii
Preface	ix
List of Abbreviations	xi
Author's Note	xvi

I Introduction to the Study of Theological Tendency in the 'Western' Text   1

    A   The Problem   1

       1   The Problem and its Background   1

       2   The Problem and Present-day Textual Criticism   12

       3   The Problem and the Present Study   21

    B   Some Factors in the Study of Textual Variants for Dogmatic Tendency   35

       1   The Comparison of Textual Variants and its Ambiguity   35

       2   The Amount of Textual Variation and its Significance   37

       3   The Conservatism in Textual Variation and its Significance   38

II Anti-Judaic Tendencies in Acts   41

    A   The Jews and Jesus   41

    B   The Jews, Gentiles, and Christianity   64

    C   The Jews and the Apostles   120

III Conclusion   165

CONTENTS

Bibliography *page* 172

Index of Subjects 187

Index of Authors 195

Index of Passages 199

Index of Greek Words 205

Index of Latin Words 209

ACKNOWLEDGEMENT

Grateful acknowledgement is made to the editor of the *Harvard Theological Review*, Professor Krister Stendahl, for permission to quote extensively from 'The "Ignorance Motif" in Acts and Anti-Judaic Tendencies in Codex Bezae', vol. LV, copyright 1962 by the President and Fellows of Harvard College, and from 'Summaries of Dissertations', vol. LIV, copyright 1961 by the President and Fellows of Harvard College.

PREFACE

Those who look to the present study for an answer to the age-old question of what is the original text of Acts, whether the so-called 'Neutral' or the so-called 'Western' text, will be disappointed, for this question—important as it is—has in the last few decades shown itself to be, for us, a premature one. Although the textual theory of an earlier period may have allowed such a question and even the answer to it, today it is clear again that we must first re-analyse and re-evaluate our witnesses, utilizing every approach which will help us more accurately to understand them and their relationships to one another and to the early text-types which they may represent. Thus, the question of originality, whether it concerns the 'Western' text or any other, cannot be treated intelligently until the materials employed in such an inquiry are thoroughly understood. The present investigation is intended to contribute to this knowledge of the materials of textual criticism and specifically to a better understanding of the 'Western' text of Acts. If it succeeds in this aim, it may in turn be a contribution also to the final solution of the intractable problem of original text in Acts.

Recent discoveries and publications have added some significant 'Western' or partially 'Western' witnesses to the text of Acts, such as the Syriac fragment from Khirbet Mird (sy^{msK}), the extensively non-Vulgate León Palimpsest (l), and the extensive Coptic manuscript G67 in the Glazier Collection, Pierpont Morgan Library. Unfortunately, only a number of passages from this last manuscript have thus far been made available, and then only in English translation, but its close connections with other 'Western' witnesses at dozens of places indicate its great value as a 'Western' witness. The recent article, 'Coptic Manuscript G67 and the Rôle of Codex Bezae as a Western Witness in Acts', *JBL*, LXXXV (1966), 197–212, offers a preliminary, though detailed, analysis of its 'Western' character.

Evidence from discoveries such as these has served to strengthen the thesis originally argued in a Harvard University

PREFACE

Ph.D. dissertation (1961), which appears now in a thoroughly revised and considerably altered and augmented form. It is with pleasure that I record here my enduring indebtedness to the members of my Committee, Harvard professors Krister Stendahl, Helmut Koester, Amos Niven Wilder (now *emeritus*), and the late Arthur Darby Nock, and to Professor Henry M. Shires of the Episcopal Theological School. One is able perhaps to repay so large a debt for patient guidance and individual concern, for academic instruction, scholarly example, and intellectual inspiration only by attempting in some measure to transmit to one's own students that which in full measure was first given by these mentors.

Expressions of gratitude are due also to Principal Matthew Black for opening to the present work the *Monograph Series* of the Society for New Testament Studies, to the Syndics of the Cambridge University Press for undertaking the publication of the study, and to the editors, readers, and printers of the Press for their care, patience, and extraordinary skill in carrying through a most difficult publishing task. Moreover, a first prize award granted for an earlier form of this investigation by the Christian Research Foundation in its 1960–1 competition is gratefully acknowledged.

The footnotes and bibliography are sufficient indications of my immense obligation to researchers past and present in the field of textual criticism and more broadly in New Testament studies as a whole; more particularly for their sincere interest in the younger scholar, I wish to express my profound appreciation to Ernest Cadman Colwell and James M. Robinson. Finally, for the very considerable sacrifices, so selflessly made, which contributed to the present volume, I register my gratitude to my wife, to whom this book is inscribed.

E. J. E.

Redondo Beach, California
Whitsunday, 1966

LIST OF ABBREVIATIONS

I. TEXTUAL WITNESSES

Greek codices   Century or date

Papyri

$\mathfrak{P}^{29}$	Papyrus Oxyrhynchus 1597	(III)
$\mathfrak{P}^{38}$	Michigan Papyrus 1571	(c. A.D. 300)
$\mathfrak{P}^{41}$	Papyrus Wessely[237], Vienna K 7541–7548	(VIII)
$\mathfrak{P}^{48}$	Papyrus Società Italiana 1165	(end of III)
$\mathfrak{P}^{74}$	Papyrus Bodmer XVII	(VII)
$\mathfrak{P}^{75}$	Papyrus Bodmer XIV–XV	(beginning of III)

Uncials

ℵ	Codex Sinaiticus	(IV)
A	Codex Alexandrinus	(V)
B	Codex Vaticanus	(IV)
C	Codex Ephraemi rescriptus	(V)
D	Codex Bezae (Greek part)	(V/VI)
E	Codex Laudianus (Greek part) [Note: E usually stands for E*e*]	(VI/VII)
H	Codex Mutinensis	(IX)
L	Codex Angelicus	(IX)
P	Codex Porphyrianus	(IX)
S	Codex Athous	(VIII/IX)
Ψ	Codex Athous Laurae	(VIII/IX)

Minuscules

383	(=Tisch. 58) Oxford	(XIII)
614	(=Tisch. 137) Milan	(XIII)
1739	Athos	(X)

Latin codices

c	Codex Colbertinus	(XII)
d	Codex Bezae (Latin part)	(V/VI)
dem	Codex Demidovianus	(XII/XIII)
e	Codex Laudianus (Latin part) [Note: E usually stands for E*e*]	(VI/VII)
gig	Codex Gigas	(XIII)
g₂	Fragmenta Mediolanensia (Lectionary)	(X/XI)
h	Palimpsestus Floriacensis	(VI)
l	León Palimpsest (Codex 15, Cathedral of León)	(VII)

LIST OF ABBREVIATIONS

p	Codex Perpinianus (=Bibl. nat. Paris. lat. 321)	(XIII)
q	Codex Paris. 343	(XIII)
r	Lectionary, Schlettstadt, Stadtbibliothek, 1093	(VII/VIII)
s	Palimpsestus Bobbiensis	(V/VI)
t	Liber comicus (Lectionary)	(XI)
w	Codex Wernigerodensis	(XV)
cod.ard	Codex Ardmachanus *or* Book of Armagh *or* Codex Dublinensis (vg cod D)	(IX)
cor.vat	Correctorium vaticanum, Rome, Vat. 3466 (Vercellone N)	(XIII)

Versions

Latin

vg	Vulgate	[A.D. 384 ff.]
vg^s	Sixtina	[A.D. 1590]
vg^{cl}	Clementina	[A.D. 1592]
vg^{codd}	two or more Vulgate codices, but not the editions	
vg^{cod}	one codex, sometimes specified: e.g. vg^{cod}S	

Syriac

sy^p	Peshitta	[V]
sy^h	Harclean	[A.D. 616]
	MSS: Oxford, New College 333	(XI)
	Cambridge, Add. 1700	(XII)
sy^{h*}	Part of the Harclean apparatus: readings marked with asterisk (or obelus) and metobelus (in MS Oxford 333)	
sy^{hmg}	Harclean marginal notes (in MS Oxford 333) extracted by Thomas from a Greek MS in Enaton monastery near Alexandria	
sy^{msK}	Christian-Palestinian fragment from the Kastellion Monastery at Khirbet Mird	(VI)

Coptic

sa	Sahidic	[III]
bo	Bohairic	[IV]
cop	Coptic = Sahidic and Bohairic	
cop^{G67}	MS G. 67 in the Glazier Collection, Pierpont Morgan Library	(IV/V)

Others

arab	Arabic	[VI?]
arm	Armenian	[IV/V]

LIST OF ABBREVIATIONS

arm[osc]	Edition of Oscan	(A.D. 1666)
arm[zoh]	Edition of Zohrab	(A.D. 1789–1805)
bohem	Bohemian (from Latin)	[XIV]
dut	Medieval Dutch (Brit. Mus. Add. 26663)	(A.D. 1488)
eth	Ethiopic	[IV–VII]
geo	Georgian	[V]
prov	Provençal (from Latin)	(XIII)
tepl	Codex Teplensis (German version from Latin)	(XIV)

Fathers and Other Writings

Ado	Ado of Lyons and Vienne	(d. 875)
Ambr	Ambrose of Milan	(d. 397)
Ambst	Ambrosiaster	(IV)
Arist	Aristides	(II)
Aug	Augustine of Hippo	(d. 430)
Aug[a]	*Contra epistulam Manichaei quam vocant Fundamenti* 9	(A.D. 397?)
Aug[b]	*Contra Felicem Manichaeum*, i, 4–5	(A.D. 404)
Aug[c]	*De unitate ecclesiae* (*Epistola ad Catholicos de secta Donatistarum*), II (27)	(A.D. 405)
Bas	Basil	(d. 379)
Bede	Bede *or* Beda [Note: references to Bede usually signify that the reading was found by him in Greek]	(d. 735)
Cass	Cassiodorus	(d. 575)
Chr	Chrysostom of Byzantium	(d. 407)
Cl	Clement of Alexandria	(d. 212)
Const.Apost	*Constitutiones Apostolorum*	(IV?)
Cosm	Cosmas Indicopleustes	(fl. 547)
Cypr	Cyprian of Carthage	(d. 258)
Cyr	Cyril of Alexandria	(d. 444)
Cyr[hr]	Cyril of Jerusalem	(d. 386)
Didasc	*Didascalia Apostolorum*	(III)
Didy	Didymus the Blind of Alexandria	(IV)
Ephr	Ephrem of Syria [Note: Ephrem is cited by page number in Conybeare's Latin translation of the Armenian version of Ephrem's commentary on Acts, which is in Ropes, *Text*, pp. 373–453]	(d. 373)
Ephr[cat]	Sections of Ephrem's commentary drawn from the ancient Armenian catena [Page numbers refer to Conybeare's edition in Ropes]	

LIST OF ABBREVIATIONS

Epiph	Epiphanius of Cyprian Salamis	(d. 403)
Eus	Eusebius of Caesarea	(d. 340)
Faustin	Faustinus	(IV)
Ful	Fulgentius of Ruspe	(d. 533)
Gaud	Gaudentius of Brescia	(fl. 387)
Hier	Hieronymus *or* Jerome	(d. 420)
Hil	Hilary of Poitiers	(d. 367)
Ir	Irenaeus of Lyons [*Adversus haereses* unless otherwise noted]	(II)
Lcf	Lucifer of Cagliari	(d. 371)
Max[taur]	Maximus of Turin	(IV/V)
Or	Origen of Alexandria and Caesarea	(d. 254)
Pac	Pacianus of Barcelona	(IV)
Perpet	*Acts of Perpetua and Felicitas*	(II/III)
Petil	Petilianus	(V)
Prisc	Priscillian (d. 385) and the Priscillianist tract, *De trinitate*	
Prom	*Liber promissionum et praedictorum dei*	(V)
Proph	*Prophetiae ex omnibus libris collectae*	(IV)
Rebapt	*Liber de rebaptismate* (Cyprianic appendix)	(III?)
Spec	*Speculum* or *Liber de divinis scripturis* (Pseudo-Augustine)	(VIII/IX)
Tert	Tertullian of Carthage	(d. *c.* 240)
Thdot[anc]	Theodotus of Ancyra	(fl. 431)
Thdrt	Theodoret of Cyrus	(d. 466)
Thphyl	Theophylact of Bulgaria	(fl. 1077)
Vigil	Vigilius of Thapsus (V); *Contra Varimadum* (Pseudo-Vigilius)	
Zeno	Zeno of Verona	(fl. 350)

Note: many fathers are cited according to Tischendorf, *Novum Testamentum Graece*; see vol. III (by Gregory), pp. 1153–230, for editions used.

II. MISCELLANEOUS

( )	in textual apparatus: witnesses with minor variations
( )	within Greek words: necessary letters not found in the MS
[ ]	letters or words lacking in the MS
+	*addit, -unt* (adds, followed by)
*	original hand of a MS
B², D^A, D^B, etc.	correctors of a MS
add	*addit, -unt* (adds)
al	*alii* (others)

LIST OF ABBREVIATIONS

cett	*ceteri* (the others, the rest)
cod(d)	codex (codices)
def	*deficit* (is lacking)
mg	*in margine* (margin)
min(n)	minuscule(s)
MS(S)	manuscript(s)
om	*omittit, -unt* (omits)
praem	*praemittit, -unt* (precedes, i.e. the following is inserted before the quoted part of the text)
sim	*similiter, vel similia* (similar, -ly)
v(v)	verse(s)
vid	*videlicet* (apparently, evidently)

Note: unaccented words below the D column of Greek text indicate the exact reading of Codex Bezae for the corresponding words above.

III. JOURNALS AND SERIES

AngThR	*Anglican Theological Review*
BBC	*Bulletin of the Bezan Club* (1925–37)
CBQ	*Catholic Biblical Quarterly*
Class et Med	*Classica et Mediaevalia*
Coniect.neotest	*Coniectanea neotestamentica*
ET	*Expository Times*
Exp	*Expositor*
GGA	*Göttingische gelehrte Anzeigen*
HibbJ	*Hibbert Journal*
HTR	*Harvard Theological Review*
JBL	*Journal of Biblical Literature*
JRel	*Journal of Religion*
JTS	*Journal of Theological Studies*
LQHR	*London Quarterly and Holborn Review*
MKAWA	*Mededeelingen der Koninklijke Akademie van Wetenschappen te Amsterdam, Afdeeling Letterkunde*
NovTest	*Novum Testamentum*
NTS	*New Testament Studies*
ProcBrAc	*Proceedings of the British Academy*
RB	*Revue Biblique*
RBén	*Revue Bénédictine*
RSR	*Recherches de Science Religieuse*
SJT	*Scottish Journal of Theology*
StudTheol	*Studia Theologica*
ThSt	*Theological Studies*
TLZ	*Theologische Literaturzeitung*
TRu	*Theologische Rundschau*

LIST OF ABBREVIATIONS

TSK	*Theologische Studien und Kritiken*
TWNT	*Theologisches Wörterbuch zum Neuen Testament*, ed. G. Kittel and G. Friedrich
TZ	*Theologische Zeitschrift*
VigChr	*Vigiliae Christianae*
ZKT	*Zeitschrift für katholische Theologie*
ZNW	*Zeitschrift für die neutestamentliche Wissenschaft*
ZTK	*Zeitschrift für Theologie und Kirche*

AUTHOR'S NOTE

The critical apparatus for words and phrases in the textual tradition of Acts is intended to represent a full citation of extant witnesses which can be designated either as so-called 'pure' 'Western' or 'mixed' 'Western' witnesses (as outlined below, pp. 28–33), and includes as well much non-'Western' evidence.

Textual witnesses in languages other than Greek or Latin are, for convenience, variously quoted in Greek, Latin, or English.

Biblical quotations which are given in English are usually the author's own translation, though occasionally the Revised Standard Version has been followed.

CHAPTER I

INTRODUCTION TO THE STUDY OF THEOLOGICAL TENDENCY IN THE 'WESTERN' TEXT

A. THE PROBLEM

(1) *The Problem and its Background*

THE broad concern of the present investigation is the question of some theological motivation behind the textual variants in the so-called 'Western'[1] text of the New Testament. This kind of study has as its larger background the negative view of F. J. A. Hort regarding dogmatic influences upon the text of the New Testament. In his epoch-making *Introduction* to the Westcott–Hort edition of the Greek New Testament, he made these statements:

...Even among the numerous unquestionably spurious readings of the New Testament there are no signs of deliberate falsification of the text for dogmatic purposes.

Accusations of wilful tampering with the text are...not unfrequent in Christian antiquity: but, with a single exception [Marcion], wherever they can be verified they prove to be groundless, being in fact hasty and unjust inferences from mere diversities of inherited text.[2]

Although a few textual critics held that Hort, in the main, was correct at this point,[3] his view was effectively refuted soon after it was proposed, and the continually increasing evidence against

[1] On the use of the term 'Western', see A. C. Clark, *The Acts of the Apostles* (Oxford, 1933), pp. xv–xix. On the term 'Bezan text', see J. H. Ropes, *The Text of Acts* (London, 1926), p. lxxxiv, n. 2.

[2] B. F. Westcott and F. J. A. Hort, *The New Testament in the Original Greek*. Vol. II. Introduction, Appendix (London, 1002), pp. 282 f.; cf. 'Notes on Select Readings', pp. 64–8, in the same volume.

[3] E.g. B. B. Warfield, *An Introduction to the Textual Criticism of the New Testament* (New York, 1887), p. 96, though he does not mention Hort. C. R. Gregory, *Canon and Text of the New Testament* (Edinburgh, 1907), p. 504 (cf. p. 485), and A. T. Robertson, *An Introduction to the Textual Criticism of the New Testament* (Nashville, 1925), pp. 158–60, admit a few cases of dogmatic influence, but agree that it was rare.

it has rendered it completely untenable, though the extent and type of dogmatic influence may yet be long debated.

It is curious that Hort's position on this point was first 'refuted' by accusations of intentional (as well as accidental) corruption in the old uncial manuscripts, including the 'Neutral' text, by Dean Burgon and Edward Miller, who attempted a learned defence of the *textus receptus* in their studies on *The Traditional Text of the Holy Gospels Vindicated and Established* and *The Causes of the Corruption of the Traditional Text of the Holy Gospels* (1896).

Other scholars were more enlightened in their criticism of Hort and offered investigations (or at least lists) of some New Testament passages which showed dogmatic influence.[1] In the course of this criticism of Hort, some isolated instances of dogmatic bias were early identified in the 'Western' text, notably by J. Rendel Harris. One of Harris's chief conclusions in this area was that the 'Western' text had at some time been Montanized, but this view was not widely accepted.[2] Harris also emphasized Marcionite influence,[3] while Fr. Blass pointed to the sharpness against the Jews in the 'Western' text of Lk,[4]

[1] J. R. Harris, *Codex Bezae, A Study of the So-called Western Text of the New Testament* (Cambridge, 1891), pp. 148–53, 228–34; Idem, *Side-Lights on New Testament Research* (London, 1908), pp. 6, 29–35, 107–10; Idem, 'New Points of View in Textual Criticism', *Exp*, VIII, 7 (1914), 316–34; Idem, 'Was the Diatessaron Anti-Judaic?', *HTR*, XVIII (1925), 103–6; Idem, *BBC*, III (1926), 4–7; A. Harnack, *Studien zur Geschichte des Neuen Testaments und der alten Kirche*. Vol. I. *Zur neutestamentlichen Textkritik* (Berlin, 1931), pp. 86–104, 235–52; F. C. Conybeare, 'Three Early Doctrinal Modifications of the Text of the Gospels', *HibbJ*, I (1902/3), 96–113; K. Lake, *The Influence of Textual Criticism on the Exegesis of the New Testament* (Oxford, 1904), pp. 8–23; M. Goguel, *Le texte et les éditions du Nouveau Testament grec* (Paris, 1920), pp. 64–7; D. Plooij, *Tendentieuse Varianten in den Text der Evangeliën* (Leiden, 1926); Idem, 'The Ascension in the "Western" Textual Tradition', *MKAWA*, 67, A, 2 (1929), 39–58; W. F. Howard, 'The Influence of Doctrine upon the Text of the New Testament', *LQHR*, X (1941), 1–16; L. E. Wright, *Alterations of the Words of Jesus* (Cambridge, Mass., 1952), p. 7 n.; H. J. Vogels, *Handbuch der Textkritik des Neuen Testaments* (Bonn, 1955), pp. 178–82.

[2] Harris, *Codex Bezae*, pp. 148–53, 221–5. See the refutation by Ropes, *Text*, p. ccxxxiv; also A. F. J. Klijn, *A Survey of the Researches into the Western Text of the Gospels and Acts* (Utrecht, [1949]), p. 21.

[3] Harris, *Codex Bezae*, pp. 228–34.

[4] F. Blass, *Evangelium secundum Lucam sive Lucae ad Theophilum liber prior, secundum formam quae videtur Romanam* (Leipzig, 1897), pp. xlii, xlix.

and P. Corssen, in his review of Blass's edition of Acts, noted some anti-Jewish tendencies in the 'Western' text of Acts.[1] In spite of these suggestions, no large-scale motivation was successfully identified within the 'Western' text, and even the attempts of Harris were only incidental to his explanation of the distinctive 'Western' readings on the basis of Latinization.

Following this lead of Harris, others sought to explain the 'Western' text on the basis of a Semitic background. F. H. Chase in his two studies, *The Old Syriac Element in Codex Bezae* and *The Syro-Latin Text of the Gospels*, championed an explanation in terms of Syriac influence, and G. Zuntz also concerned himself with the Syriac background of the text of Acts.[2] C. C. Torrey explained the 'Western' text as a translation from Aramaic, and A. J. Wensinck suggested that it was influenced by the Aramaic tradition in the process of textual transmission.[3] The works of M. Black, *An Aramaic Approach to the Gospels and Acts*, and of M. Wilcox, *The Semitisms of Acts*, treat numerous 'Western' variants and are concerned with the general questions of Semitic influence and background. These matters are discussed below (pp. 24-6), but the warning of C. S. C. Williams (with reference to Acts) is pertinent here: 'The evidence of "Western" papyri in Egypt should be enough to warn us, however, against any theory that the whole of the "Western" text of Acts was written either in Syriac or in Latin.'[4]

Explanations of the 'Western' text along different lines include the theory of two versions by Luke himself, as presented by Fr. Blass and followed by Th. Zahn, E. Nestle, and others; the view of A. C. Clark and P. Glaue that the 'Western' text is original over against the 'Neutral'; and the common position that the 'Western' text is a free paraphrastic expansion of the

[1] P. Corssen, 'Acta Apostolorum ed. F. Blass', *GGA*, CLVIII (1896), 444.

[2] See also F. H. Chase, 'The Reading of Codex Bezae in Acts 1, 2', *Exp*, IV, 9 (1894), 314 17. Zuntz's work appeared in *Class et Med*, III (1940), 20-46. For criticisms of Chase, see Ropes, *Text*, pp. lxxiv-lxxvi; Klijn, *Survey*, pp. 25-31; M. Black, *An Aramaic Approach to the Gospels and Acts* (Oxford, 1954), pp. 29f.

[3] C. C. Torrey, *Documents of the Primitive Church* (New York, 1941), pp. 112-48; A. J. Wensinck, 'The Semitisms of Codex Bezae and their Relation to the Non-Western Text of the Gospel of Saint Luke', *BBC*, XII (1937), 11 48.

[4] C. S. C. Williams, *Alterations to the Text of the Synoptic Gospels and Acts* (Oxford, 1951), p. 82.

'true' text, championed by Westcott–Hort and, for Acts, especially by B. Weiss in his *Der Codex D in der Apostelgeschichte*, by J. H. Ropes, and by M. Dibelius.

But as far as dogmatic tendency in the 'Western' text is concerned, it must be stated, in short, that the position of James Hardy Ropes has been representative of the widely accepted view, and his statement may serve as a convenient point of departure for this study: 'Of any special point of view, theological or other, on the part of the "Western" reviser it is difficult to find any trace.'[1]

Along with this affirmation, however, Ropes himself listed several random variants which showed *possible* theological interests and which deserved further investigation.[2] He was followed by others (see below, pp. 21 f.) who added to the list of variants which were possibly of tendentious significance.

This question of some distinctive theological tendency or tendencies in the 'Western' text cannot, however, be treated conveniently by an indiscriminate reference to the 'Western' text as a whole, for, as Frederic Kenyon pointed out, '...there is so much discrepancy between the authorities for the δ text that the editor can make it longer or shorter to suit his own theory',[3] and, one might add, can select and organize the variants to support a given hypothesis.

The question naturally arises, then, as to whether the 'Western' text is a homogeneous text. Kenyon's statement, and the evidence which supports it, suggest that the answer must be negative. But Ropes took an opposite view, stating that the 'Western' text has 'an unmistakably homogeneous character' and is 'a definite integral text', whose variations 'show unmistakable signs of proceeding from a single hand with his own

---

[1] Ropes, *Text*, p. ccxxxiii. This view is repeated in H. Conzelmann, *Die Apostelgeschichte* (Tübingen, 1963), p. 2.

[2] Ropes, *Text*, p. ccxxxiii; see also pp. ccxxviii f.

[3] F. G. Kenyon, 'The Western Text in the Gospels and Acts', *ProcBrAc*, XXIV (1938), 303, cf. 297; and cf. Kenyon, *The Text of the Greek Bible* (London, 1949), pp. 214, 237f. See also H. A. Sanders, 'A Papyrus Fragment of Acts in the Michigan Collection', *HTR*, XX (1927), 18; F. W. Grosheide, 'Acts 18: 27, A Test Case', *BBC*, VIII (1930), 18; E. R. Smothers, 'Les Papyrus Beatty de la Bible grecque', *RSR*, XXIV (1934), 25. There was no uniformity even in a single geographical area: H. A. Sanders, 'The Egyptian Text of the Four Gospels and Acts', *HTR*, XXVI (1933), 77–98; Idem, *HTR*, XX (1927), 19.

characteristic method of work'.[1] Ropes did not, however, deny that our present evidence for this 'Western' text is found in corrupt and often fragmentary documents, or that there are considerable differences even among the 'Western' witnesses.[2] This makes it obvious that the line between the views represented by Kenyon and Ropes is a thin one.

The conclusion to be drawn on the question of homogeneity is twofold: (1) The general, overall effect of the bulk of 'Western' readings points to a type of text which, when compared with the so-called 'Neutral' text-type, shows a certain uniformity; the 'Western' readings frequently reveal a recognizably similar quality or character.[3] This might be referred to as an 'internal' or even a 'theoretical' homogeneity. This designation is justified by the fact that Ropes, for example, can argue for the existence of a definite 'Western' text, while admitting that it may never be completely recoverable in that original form. This theoretical homogeneity presupposes some sort of common factor or source to account for the general similarities. This could mean a single reviser (as Ropes thought), but sure knowledge about this common factor is not now available to us, and the question of revision in the 'Western' text is best left outside the discussion. (It may be noted, however, that Ropes viewed the 'Western' revision as the reworking of an ancient, pre-existing textual base of a 'Western' type, mainly by a single editor before, perhaps long before, A.D. 150. A. F. J. Klijn points out that one of the major gains of the past decade of study in the 'Western' text is the recognition that texts usually develop gradually, as opposed to undergoing radical revisions. Already Hort had felt that the 'Western' readings showed

[1] Ropes, *Text*, pp. viii, ccxxiif.; cf. A. D. Nock, '[Review of] Martin Dibelius: Aufsätze zur Apostelgeschichte. Göttingen, 1951', *Gnomon*, xxv (1953), 502; H. J. Cadbury, *The Book of Acts in History* (New York, 1955), p. 153. Ropes's view of revision is somewhat prejudiced by his conception of a 'Western' reviser working from the original Old Uncial type text (see pp. ccxxii–ccxxvi). The relation of 'Neutral' and 'Western' text-types cannot be discussed here.

[2] Ropes, *Text*, pp. viii, ccxv–ccxxi, cf. p. ccxxii, n. 1.

[3] See E. Jacquier, *Les Actes des Apôtres* (Paris, 1926), pp. cxxviiif. for a summary of the evidence for the unity of the 'Western' text. See also A. C. Clark, *Acts*, p. xxxii; Torrey, *Documents*, pp. 112–19 *passim*; J. Duplacy, 'Où en est la critique textuelle du Nouveau Testament?', *RSR*, XLVI (1958), 453 n.

'progressive change'; yet Ropes stresses the fact that the 'Western' variants arose within a brief time—about fifty years. These views do not necessarily exclude one another. Some, such as W. H. P. Hatch, followed Ropes in his view of revision; others, such as F. G. Kenyon, viewed the 'Western' text as the result of revision, though not by a single editor, but by many at many times and places. Still others opposed a revision in Ropes's sense, and A. C. Clark, of course, with his view of the originality of the 'Western' text, saw the B-text as the systematic work of an abbreviator, thus making the B-text a revision from the 'Western'.)[1] Incidentally, this homogeneity of which we have been speaking appears more clearly in Acts than elsewhere.

To return to the conclusion on homogeneity, (2) at the same time, however, practically speaking there is a lack of uniformity in the available witnesses to the 'Western' text (see Kenyon's statement above). This might be referred to in terms of 'external' or 'practical' homogeneity, since it concerns the various documents attesting the 'Western' text, and in this sense one cannot, in fact, speak about *the* 'Western' text, but only about 'Western' readings in various extant manuscripts and quotations. It goes without saying, then, that no one extant manuscript can be taken as even an approximation to the 'Western' text.[2] By the same token, reconstructions of the 'Western' text (such as those of Blass on Acts and Lk, and of Hilgenfeld, Zahn, and A. C. Clark on Acts) are bound to be synthetic abstractions which also are lacking even approximate representation in any one source.[3]

[1] For these views, see Ropes, *Text*, pp. ccxxvi, ccxliv, viii; Klijn, *NovTest*, III (1959), 3; Westcott and Hort, *New Testament*, II, 122, 128, xv; W. H. P. Hatch, *The 'Western' Text of the Gospels* (Evanston, 1937), pp. 12–15, 41–3; F. G. Kenyon, *Handbook to the Textual Criticism of the New Testament* (London, 1912), p. 357; Idem, *Recent Developments in the Textual Criticism of the Greek Bible* (London, 1933), p. 84; A. C. Clark, *Acts*, pp. xxxif., xlv. See also Torrey, *Documents*, pp. 114–17; E. Haenchen, *Die Apostelgeschichte* (Göttingen, 1961), pp. 53, 667; E. Fascher, *Textgeschichte als hermeneutisches Problem* (Halle (Saale), 1953), p. 5; and Sanders, *HTR*, xx (1927), 14.
[2] See Klijn, *NovTest*, III (1959), 4; and Kenyon, *Handbook*, p. 356.
[3] This, for example, is the assessment of Blass's reconstructions by D. W. Riddle, 'Textual Criticism as a Historical Discipline', *AngThR*, XVIII (1936), 226 n.; cf. Kenyon, *Text of Greek Bible*, pp. 237f. Cf. Ropes, *Text*, p. ccxlvi on Blass, Hilgenfeld, and Zahn; on Clark, cf. W. G. Kümmel, 'Textkritik und Textgeschichte des Neuen Testaments 1914–1937', *TRu*, XI (1939), 98.

To sum up, in the words of A. C. Clark, 'The evidence is scattered, but the text is homogeneous.'[1]

In an investigation of theological tendencies in the 'Western' text, it is preferable, therefore, to stay within the general limits of a single substantial manuscript which manifests many of what have become known as textual variants characteristic of the so-called 'Western' text. In this way one is relieved of the responsibility of constructing another tenuous and artificial 'Western' text from which to work, although one is required to show strong 'Western' support for the readings which are to be assessed in the selected manuscript. This procedure would at least provide a reasonable starting point for a further evaluation of the 'Western' text as a whole, as well as establish some manageable limitations for the investigation.

The obvious choice for a working basis is Codex Bezae Cantabrigiensis (D), a late fifth-century bilingual manuscript containing the four gospels and the Acts of the Apostles. This manuscript has always in modern textual criticism been regarded as the leading Greek representative of the 'Western' textual tradition;[2] it is the oldest Greek text containing many 'Western' readings and having anything like continuity.

Proposed dates for Codex Bezae range from the fourth century to the seventh. Successively, F. H. Scrivener adopted a sixth-century date; F. C. Burkitt, fifth century; J. Chapman, beginning of the fifth century; Ropes, fifth century; K. Sneyders de Vogel, seventh century; E. A. Lowe, fifth century; and most recently H. J. Frede defends a fourth-century date.[3] The present study stays with a date in the fifth century; the adoption of an earlier date would naturally have some interesting implications for this research but would not alter it materially.

[1] A. C. Clark, *Acts*, p. xlii.
[2] To the contrary, see Duplacy, *RSR*, XLVI (1958), 453.
[3] For these views, see F. H. Scrivener, *Bezae Codex Cantabrigiensis, Being an Exact Copy in Ordinary Type* (Cambridge, 1864), pp. xiv ff.; F. C. Burkitt, 'The Date of Codex Bezae', *JTS*, III (1901/2), 501–13; J. Chapman, 'The Order of the Gospels in the Parent of Codex Bezae', *ZNW*, VI (1905), 339–46; Ropes, *Text*, pp. lviif.; K. Sneyders de Vogel, 'Le codex Bezae est-il d'origine sicilienne?', *BBC*, III (1926), 10–13; E. A. Lowe, 'A Note on the Codex Bezae', *BBC*, IV (1927), 9–14; Lowe, *Codices Latini Antiquiores. A Palaeographical Guide to Latin Manuscripts Prior to the Ninth Century*, II, no. 140; H. J. Frede, *Altlateinische Paulus-Handschriften* (Freiburg, 1964), p. 18 and n. 4.

Codex Bezae has the following lacunae: Matt. i. 1–20; vi. 20–ix. 2; xxvii. 2–12; John i. 16–iii. 26; Acts viii. 29–x. 14; xxi. 2–10; xxii. 10–20; xxii. 29–end. Three leaves and eight quires are missing between the gospels and Acts. Their contents are a matter of conjecture,[1] but III John 11–15 in Latin still stand on the page preceding Acts.

The best descriptions of the codex itself and of the characteristics of its text and other matters are found in the editions of F. H. Scrivener, J. H. Ropes, and A. C. Clark.[2]

The Latin side of the bilingual codex requires special comment. In the present study the Latin side will command little attention compared with the Greek. The Latin (*d*) was once championed over the Greek, from as early as the seventeenth century and up through the defence of the Latinization of Codex Bezae by J. Rendel Harris in 1891. Harris concluded that 'so extensively has the Greek text of Codex Bezae been modified by the process of Latinization that we can no longer regard D as a distinct authority apart from *d*'.[3] This view has not found acceptance; Harris himself admitted later[4] that he had exaggerated the sphere of Latin influence (though at a still later time he spoke of the revival of the Latinization theory).[5] A cursory reading of Harris's examples, for instance, shows at once that in many cases the influence could have operated in either direction. In addition, papyrus fragments now prove that Greek texts of the type of D existed in Egypt in the third/fourth centuries, refuting Harris's view that the D-type text existed in Greek only as a translation of Latin.[6] Finally, A. C. Clark, in a

---

[1] See Ropes, *Text*, pp. lxviiif. and his references. On a more recent mutilation, see J. H. Ropes, 'Three Papers on the Text of Acts. I. The Reconstruction of the Torn Leaf of Codex Bezae', *HTR*, XVI (1923), 163–8; R. P. Casey, 'Two Notes: (1) Dickinson's Collation of Codex Bezae...', *HTR*, XVI (1923), 392–4; and G. D. Kilpatrick, 'Codex Bezae and Mill', *JTS*, VI (1955), 235–8.

[2] Scrivener, *Bezae*, pp. vii–lxiv; Ropes, *Text*, pp. lvi–lxxxiv; A. C. Clark, *Acts*, pp. 173–220.

[3] Harris, *Codex Bezae*, p. 114; cf. pp. 41–6 and his examples, pp. 53–114.

[4] J. Harris, *Four Lectures on the Western Text of the New Testament* (London, 1894), p. viii.

[5] Harris, *BBC*, VIII (1930), 4f.; cf. D. Plooij, 'The Bezan Problem', *BBC*, IX (1931), 15–17.

[6] Kenyon, *Text of Greek Bible*, p. 95.

detailed study, concluded that *d* in Acts is of little value, being a 'servile translation of D'.[1]

The Greek side has, of course, been influenced by the Latin at points (and *vice versa*); certainly Harris's study confirms this much.[2] Ropes summarized the history and treatment of this problem and concluded:

> That d has affected D seems beyond doubt...; but the proof is in most cases demonstrative only for details, many cases must remain doubtful, and in a great mass of instances, including most of the larger and more interesting readings, Codex Bezae has certainly preserved approximately the Greek text of the 'Western' recension.[3]

Finally, there are many differences between the Greek and Latin sides, so that D must often be distinguished from *d*.[4] J. A. Findlay made a count of the variations in the text of *d* and D, with the following result: Matthew 107, John 106, Lk 176, Mark 469, Acts 607. He suggested that 'possibly a corrector has been at work assimilating Greek to Latin in the Gospels, but has tired of his work by the time he reached Mark–Acts'.[5] These figures, incidentally, are of more than passing interest and draw special attention to Codex Bezae's text of Mark and Acts, especially if Findlay is correct that the assimilation in Matthew, John, and Lk was of Greek to Latin. In this case the importance of the Greek text in Mark and Acts would be enhanced, assuming however that *d* is not a translation of D, or, if it is a translation of D, that *d* had been conformed to another Latin text prior to the assimilation in Codex Bezae itself. But, as A. C. Clark has shown, at least in Acts *d* is a translation of D by a separate translator, and the assimilation, though it operated in both directions, was most predominantly of Latin to Greek, with *d* in addition being conformed, where it differs from D, to the 'Neutral' type of text by the use of a manuscript like

---

[1] A. C. Clark, *Acts*, p. 219; cf. pp. 192–220, xliiif.
[2] See Harris, *BBC*, III (1926), 2–9, VIII (1930), 4f.; H. J. Vogels, 'Codex Bezae als Bilingue', *BBC*, II (1926), 8–12; Idem, *Handbuch*, pp. 43f.; Klijn, *Survey*, pp. 22f.; Haenchen, *Apostelgeschichte*, p. 50.
[3] Ropes, *Text*, p. lxxx, cf. lxxii–lxxx; and Corssen, *GGA*, CLVIII (1896), 431.
[4] Vogels, *Handbuch*, p. 44.
[5] J. A. Findlay, 'On Variations in the Text of d and D', *BBC*, IX (1931), 11.

gig.[1] Thus, the Greek of D remains by far the more significant side of this bilingual codex, and the differences between D and *d* become less important because they are accounted for by the fact that it was largely *d* that suffered by assimilation. The Latin *d* is most valuable, however, when D is lacking (and *d* has not been conformed to a non-'Western' text-type) or when D itself (but not *d*) may have suffered conformation to another text-type.

The question now arises as to the relation of Codex Bezae to the 'Western' text as a whole, and specifically as to how accurately D reflects a genuine early 'Western' text. Ropes has emphasized 'the important distinction, not generally sufficiently noticed, between the text of D and the "Western" text', and that each is a problem in itself, and must be kept separate as much as possible. This means that D must be recognized as, after all, only one—though the most important—witness to the 'Western' text.[2]

That D not only has many scribal errors and textual corruptions,[3] but contains textual strata more recent than that of the early 'Western' tradition it presumably represents, is freely admitted. The two most important elements in this impurity of D are contamination from various non-'Western' texts and conformation of the Greek D to the parallel Latin *d* in details. Observe, however, that an agreement of D and the Antiochian text may be due to the adoption of 'Western' readings by the latter, and not to conformation of D to the Antiochian.[4]

The question of recent strata in D is now somewhat affected by the discovery of the Coptic manuscript G67. Assuming a late fifth-century date for D and a late fourth-century date for G 67, we can no longer attribute to the whim of the scribe of D those readings which previously were found only in Codex Bezae but which now appear in G67. Such readings are pushed back a

[1] A. C. Clark, *Acts*, pp. 205, 219f., xliiif. I have not seen the 1962 St Andrews Ph.D. thesis of R. S. MacKenzie, 'The Text of Codex Bezae in Acts: A Study of the Inter-relationship of the Greek and Latin Columns and of the Problem of the Longer Text.'

[2] Ropes, *Text*, pp. lxxxiiif.

[3] For lists of blunders in D, see H. von Soden, *Die Schriften des Neuen Testaments in ihrer ältesten erreichbaren Textgestalt hergestellt auf Grund ihrer Textgeschichte* (Göttingen, 1911–13), I, 1305–40, 1720–7, 1814–36. For Acts alone, see A. C. Clark, *Acts*, pp. 181–91; B. Weiss, *Der Codex D in der Apostelgeschichte. Textkritische Untersuchung* (Leipzig, 1897), pp. 17–52; and Ropes, *Text*, pp. lxix–lxxi. [4] *Ibid.* pp. lxxx–lxxxii, clxxi.

century in actual manuscript evidence, and farther when it is noted that G67 is not the working manuscript of the Coptic translator, but is a professional copy of an older manuscript.[1] How many such readings there are cannot be known until the Coptic manuscript is fully published, but T. C. Petersen's English translation of selected passages reveals at least four and possibly as many as eight readings of D which find their first additional support in G67: Acts iv. 24; v. 18; xiii. 44; part of the long D-variant in xi. 2; and perhaps also xiii. 29; v. 8; vii. 31; and vii. 54. G67 also attests, of course, a vast number of readings in Codex Bezae which are supported by the later manuscript witnesses; all that G67 demonstrates here is that these variants did not originate with the copyist of D. Thus, this early Coptic manuscript evidence by no means automatically carries us back to the 'Western' text of the second century, but at least it strengthens the case for the antiquity of even those readings peculiar to D, and it presents the earliest non-fragmentary *manuscript* evidence for the 'Western' text of Acts.[2]

The same question must now be asked about D which was raised earlier about the 'Western' text as a whole: is the text of D homogeneous or not? The answer is similar to that given on the 'Western' text: the character of D's variants strengthens the conviction of an underlying homogeneity—the variants are of a similar nature and quality,[3] though again it is a qualified homogeneity, since it has been obscured by an accumulation of heterogeneous elements which have attached themselves to the text of D throughout its history. This is why A. F. J. Klijn, for example, can call D 'a text with a rather heterogeneous character', and Ropes can refer to it as a mixed text.[4] This does not, however, remove it from its leading role among the 'Western' witnesses, but only makes imperative its proper use in that role. This right use involves, in brief, a testing of D's

[1] T. C. Petersen, 'An Early Coptic Manuscript of Acts: An Unrevised Version of the Ancient So-called Western Text', *CBQ*, xxvi (1964), 229 n.
[2] Further on recent strata in D, see Sanders, *HTR*, xx (1927), 13 f.; Ropes, *Text*, pp. lxxvf.; Haenchen, *Apostelgeschichte*, pp. 50, 667; now E. J. Epp, 'Coptic Manuscript G67 and the Rôle of Codex Bezae as a Western Witness in Acts', *JBL*, lxxxv (1966), 197–212.
[3] See Torrey, *Documents*, pp. 112, 115–17, 119; cf. Duplacy, *RSR*, xlvi (1958), 453 and n. 390 *bis*.
[4] Klijn, *Nov T est*, iii (1959), 172; Ropes, *Text*, p. lxxxiii.

reading in each case against other available 'Western' evidence. Such a procedure (described below, pp. 27–34) provides a measure of assurance that D-readings approved in this way can reasonably be assumed to represent that early 'Western' textual tradition which was current in perhaps the second century.[1]

In view of the close relationship of Codex Bezae to the 'Western' text as a whole, and in view of its special character and value within that relationship, it is surprising that Ropes's challenging statement regarding a viewpoint in the 'Western' text has not been answered by a comprehensive study of D with an assessment of theological motivation in mind. Much more recently, A. F. J. Klijn offers another challenge when, in speaking of accounting for the peculiarities of D, he says that 'dogmatic tendencies seem unlikely'.[2]

(2) *The Problem and Present-day Textual Criticism*

Codex Bezae has been an object of scholarly attention ever since it was presented to Cambridge University by Theodore Beza in 1581, but, with few exceptions, the question has been whether its text or particular variants have claim to greater or less originality or accuracy. A conspicuous example is B. Weiss, whose exhaustive examination of D in Acts led him to conclude that its variants, when compared with other manuscripts of Acts, nowhere change anything essential or bring forward anything of new significance touching the historical course of

[1] On the second-century currency of the 'Western' text, see Scrivener, *Bezae*, pp. xlv–lxiv; Westcott and Hort, *New Testament*, II, 148f.; Ropes, *Text*, pp. ccxxiiif.; also A. C. Clark, *Acts*, pp. xvf.; Kümmel, *TRu*, XI (1939), 101; Petersen, *CBQ*, XXVI (1964), 227. On a second-century orthography in D, see J. H. Moulton and W. F. Howard, *A Grammar of New Testament Greek* (Edinburgh, 1929), II, 51.

[2] Klijn, *Survey*, p. 21. (But now cf. Klijn, *NovTest*, III, 1959, 170.) Another direct challenge of Ropes, that a thorough linguistic investigation of D had never been made (*Text*, p. lxxi, n. 1), has only recently been answered by J. D. Yoder in his unpublished thesis, parts of which appear in 'The Language of the Greek Variants of Codex Bezae', *NovTest*, III (1959), 241–8, and 'Semitisms in Codex Bezae', *JBL*, LXXVIII (1959), 317–21. He does not attempt to deal with the thought behind the variants. See also Yoder, *Concordance*. The Latin had been investigated earlier by R. C. Stone, *The Language of the Latin Text of Codex Bezae* (Urbana, Illinois, 1946).

events in our picture of the early church.[1] Even when the theological interest of a variant has been discussed, it was often only with these considerations in mind. To cite but one example, Harris's vigorous attack upon Hort's view is within the framework of whether or not a given reading (in this case a dogmatically motivated reading) should be permitted to stand in the text.[2] Harris's brief chapter on 'The Codex Bezae a Montanist Manuscript' was an exception.[3]

This emphasis on accuracy and originality was natural, of course, when textual criticism was primarily, if not exclusively, concerned with the recovery of the 'original' text (notice the title of Westcott–Hort's edition: *The New Testament in the Original Greek*!), or with the reconstruction of the history of the transmission of the text. These endeavours certainly are the ultimate purposes and goals of textual criticism; its obvious aim is the restoration of the original text, or the closest possible approximation to what the author wrote. But when this is interpreted to mean that if the author's original manuscript had survived, 'it would of course be unnecessary to trouble about later and less accurate copies of it, or the work of revising editors',[4] and 'there would be no textual criticism of the New Testament',[5] then strong objection must be voiced. In such a case textual criticism would be unnecessary only if no variant texts of the autographs existed. But with variant texts, there would remain the valid tasks of tracing the development of the variants in the history of textual transmission and of attempting to uncover reasons for the deviations. After all, these variant texts were for some Christians at some time and place *the* 'original' text; it would be a denial of history to ignore them under any circumstances. Thus, textual criticism does not stand or fall with the search for the original text.

D. W. Riddle observes that the quest for the original text was followed by that for the history of the text, and he reminds us

[1] Weiss, *Codex D*, p. 105, see also pp. 17f., 51, 104. For a concise statement on D's place in recent studies, see Black, *Aramaic Approach*, pp. 25–31.
[2] Harris, *Exp*, VIII, 7 (1914), 323, 333.
[3] Idem, *Codex Bezae*, pp. 148–53.
[4] Kenyon, *Text of Greek Bible*, p. 12.
[5] A. Souter, *The Text and Canon of the New Testament* (London, 1954), p. 3; see the same view in J. H. Greenlee, *Introduction to New Testament Textual Criticism* (Grand Rapids, 1964), p. 17.

that the sub-title of H. von Soden's work first made explicit this change of emphasis (*Die Schriften des Neuen Testaments in ihrer ältesten erreichbaren Textgestalt hergestellt auf Grund ihrer Textgeschichte*) and that von Soden, especially in his work on the text of the Middle Ages, put it into practice.[1]

But again, the recovery of the original text and the historical reconstruction of the transmission of the text do not exhaust the tasks or the value of textual criticism. There is today, moreover, a measure of pessimism regarding the recovery of the original text,[2] and it is only natural that more than ever the interest of the textual critic should turn in other and new directions. Thus, as a development from the study of the history of the text, the comparatively recent emphasis on a theological approach to textual criticism, as an approach valid in its own right, even apart from any quest for an original text, provides a vigorous stimulus and a fresh environment in which to investigate the theological motivation(s) of the D-variants. As a matter of fact, the question of originality, whether it concerns D or not, cannot be treated intelligently until the materials employed in such an inquiry are thoroughly understood. This applies, naturally, to such matters as the date, language, place of origin, and text-type of a manuscript, and so forth. But, in addition, that a manuscript (or the text it represents) may have been affected by bias or show the influence of a controlling tendency is a fact of the highest importance in assessing not only its evidence, but also its status as a witness in the investigation. Klijn can go so far as to say that 'we cannot say anything with regard to the original text until each reading in it has been checked for its linguistic, tendentious or other peculiarities'.[3] Of course, such an assessment of all the readings is an ideal which

---

[1] Riddle, *AngThR*, XVIII (1936), 220f. On these two phases of text-critical work, see also M. M. Parvis, 'The Nature and Tasks of New Testament Textual Criticism: An Appraisal', *JRel*, XXXII (1952), 169f.; K. W. Clark, 'The Effect of Recent Textual Criticism upon New Testament Studies', *The Background of the New Testament and its Eschatology* (Cambridge, 1956), pp. 42–7; Lake, *Influence*, pp. 5f.; G. Zuntz, *The Text of the Epistles* (London, 1953), pp. 9–13; K. Aland, 'The Position of New Testament Textual Criticism', *Studia Evangelica* (Berlin, 1959), p. 731.

[2] See K. W. Clark, 'Effect', pp. 30f. *et passim*; Zuntz, *Text*, pp. 8f.; Aland, 'Position', pp. 717–31; for an older opinion, Goguel, *Le texte*, p. 67.

[3] Klijn, *Survey*, p. 168.

is for all practical purposes unattainable; naturally, then, the establishment of the best New Testament text cannot await the attainment of this goal. Real results, nevertheless, must be sought for along these lines at every opportunity.

This present-day understanding of textual criticism finds inchoate expression at least as far back as Kirsopp Lake's inaugural lecture at the University of Leiden in 1904 on 'The Influence of Textual Criticism on the Exegesis of the New Testament', in which he stated that a new period had begun in the textual criticism of the gospels. Because of the 'splendid failure' of Westcott and Hort ('...it was one of those failures which are more important than most successes'),[1] the textual critic could no longer suppose that he could immediately edit the original text; editing of local texts must come first. This, said Lake, complicated the task of the exegete, for he must now '...expound the meaning, not of Westcott and Hort's text, but of the ecclesiastical Bibles in use at different times....We need to know what the early Church thought [a passage] meant and how it altered its wording in order to emphasize its meaning.'[2] In addition, J. Rendel Harris emphasized the need for reading the history of the text side by side with the history of the church and in view of the various parties within it, stressing (over against Lake) that 'the study of personal texts (say, of Marcion and Tatian) is more likely to give definite results than the study of located texts'.[3] For example, in speaking of Tatian's treatment of documents, Harris says, '...What we really want to get at is not the local provenance of any particular group of MSS so much as the presiding genius of the scriptorium.'[4] No one would dispute the value and validity of these emphases.

But the full view in perhaps its boldest form was delineated by Donald W. Riddle:

[1] Lake, *Influence*, pp. 9f.

[2] *Ibid.* pp. 11f. Cf. K. Lake, R. P. Blake and S. New, 'The Caesarean Text of the Gospel of Mark', *HTR*, xxi (1928), 345 n.; Lake, *The Text of the New Testament* (London, 1928), p. 1.

[3] Harris, *BBC*, vi (1929), 2. (He says, however, that his own view and Lake's emphasis on local texts do not really conflict, but are supplementary.) See also Harris, *Exp*, viii, 7 (1914), 319f., 322; and for similar views, C. H. Turner, 'Historical Introduction to the Textual Criticism of the New Testament', *JTS*, x (1909), 13; Sanders, *HTR*, xxvi (1933), 77.

[4] J. R. Harris, 'The Mentality of Tatian', *BBC*, ix (1931), 8.

It is not enough to admit the propriety of investigating the history of the text, or of the study of the text-types in the later periods. The legitimate task of textual criticism is not limited to the recovery of approximately the original form of the documents, to the establishment of the 'best' text, nor to the 'elimination of spurious readings'. It must be recognized that every significant variant records a religious experience which brought it into being. This means that there are no 'spurious readings': the various forms of the text are sources for the study of the history of Christianity.[1]

As for the 'Western' text, explained Riddle, its qualities as a popular religious text (Riddle prefers 'texts'),[2] transmitted freely and apart from learned or ecclesiastical control, '... clearly demonstrate the unreality of that common abstraction..., the 'original' text from which all variants were derived'.[3] He continues:

Of course the New Testament writers wrote something. But what is the use of picturing this original copy? It had no status as a sacred document; no reverence for it as Scripture was accorded it until a century after its writing; it was valued only for its practical value; it was early and frequently copied.[4]

Riddle's assumption of textual transmission free and without controls is too loose a conception of the textual tradition. At the opposite extreme stand the view of H. Riesenfeld and the later detailed defence of the same general position by B. Gerhardsson.[5] Riesenfeld conceives of a rigid and fixed form of the tradition, handed down in a way analogous to the Palestinian conception of tradition and through special persons, the apostles. This procedure 'led to the written fixation of the text at a comparatively early date'; the words and deeds of Jesus were not improvised, nor was there any free narration or inventing. This

---

[1] Riddle, *AngThR*, xviii (1936), 221; cf. 231, also his examples, pp. 221–4.
[2] *Ibid.* p. 230. The general homogeneity of the 'Western' text would be against this view.
[3] *Ibid.* p. 227.
[4] *Ibid.* Much the same view finds forceful expression in Black, *Aramaic Approach*, pp. 214 f.
[5] H. Riesenfeld, 'The Gospel Tradition and its Beginnings', *Studia Evangelica* (Berlin, 1959), pp. 54–61; B. Gerhardsson, *Memory and Manuscript. Oral Tradition and Written Transmission in Rabbinic Judaism and Early Christianity* (Uppsala, 1961), especially chapter 16; Idem, *Tradition and Transmission in Early Christianity* (Lund/Copenhagen, 1964).

view could hardly, however, be applied beyond the first few generations and, more important for our purpose, even if the text were 'fixed' at an early date, it does not take into account the influence of scribes and early copyists (see on Fascher, below).

Furthermore, Riddle obviously goes too far when he says that 'every significant variant records a religious experience which brought it into being'. What does he mean by *significant*? If he means every *noteworthy* reading, he is surely wrong, for many striking readings can be accounted for on grounds other than religious experience, such as scribal error, influence of another language, or conviction as to better knowledge—whether geographical, historical, or grammatical, etc. If he means every *theologically significant* variant, his statement says little.

The main point remains, however, even if overstated: *many* variants reveal a religious viewpoint (and perhaps a religious 'experience') which accounts for their origin or (it should be added) which occasioned their retention in or deletion from a given text. Finally, if Riddle has too loose an attitude toward the original documents (see below), he none the less is certainly right in his high view of the variant texts as sources for the history of Christianity.

Merrill M. Parvis, building directly upon Riddle's work, demanded that textual criticism be reassessed within the framework of the changed theological climate of our times and reiterated Riddle's contention that there are no spurious readings, for all are products of the church's tradition, whether originating in the twelfth century or the first:

All are a part of the tradition; all contribute to our knowledge of the history of Christian thought. And they are significant contributions because they are interpretations which were highly enough thought of in some place and at some time to be incorporated into the Scripture itself.[1]

Even when we have approached the autographs, he adds, we still have only one form of the tradition. He almost laments the invention of printing, stating that prior to its use '...the Scripture was a living body of literature, which was constantly

[1] Parvis, *JRel*, xxxii (1952), 172. He is not speaking of obvious scribal errors.

being enriched as it was interpreted and reinterpreted by each succeeding generation'.[1] Thus, rather than asking what text-type a certain father used, it is more valuable, he suggests, to ask what particular interpretation he gave to a certain passage; relationships of manuscripts might better be traced through their reflections of particular doctrines; lectionaries should be seen as reflecting the worship of the church, and versions as mirroring the beliefs and worship of their times and places. After all, Parvis reminds us, our manuscripts may not have been reproduced as mechanically as we have thought; at any given time and place a manuscript could have been produced which reflected the particular theological interpretation which was prominent there.[2] Textual criticism, then, has ceased to be merely a search for the original text and has become also a historical discipline.[3]

Riddle and Parvis obviously represent an extreme position, which, while it adequately comprehends the religious factor in textual variation, nevertheless fails to appreciate the religious significance of the 'original' text in the church. For example, it neglects the importance of the church's possession of the *ipsissima verba* of Jesus or (on certain views of divine revelation) of God himself. In this sense the 'original' text may have (or have had) a unique value and meaning for the church, both in the earliest stages and at every point in its history. These matters, however, are not the primary concern of the present study, and the thoroughgoing positions of Riddle and Parvis serve to emphasize what is the present concern, namely, the significance and relevance of a theological approach to texts and textual variants.

A more moderate advocate of this general approach is Kenneth W. Clark. He does not so drastically minimize the importance of the original text or its quest, but recognizes the several tasks of textual criticism, evaluating their present progress, possibilities, and value. In the case of those variants

[1] Parvis, *JRel*, xxxii (1952), 173. For a similar view of the Old Latin version, see B. M. Metzger, 'The Evidence of the Versions for the Text of the New Testament', *New Testament Manuscript Studies* (Chicago, 1950), p. 54.
[2] Parvis, *JRel*, xxxii (1952), 173.
[3] M. M. Parvis, 'New Testament Criticism in the World-Wars Period', *The Study of the Bible Today and Tomorrow* (Chicago, 1947), p. 58; cf. Riddle, *AngThR*, xviii (1936), 233.

THE PROBLEM

which may have theological motivation, he suggests that the task is not only to determine the original reading, but also to ascertain how each reading played its part in the life of the church,[1] for throughout its history the New Testament has maintained its role as interpreter of doctrine; 'the freedom men assumed in altering its text was inspired by their understanding of Christian doctrine, and by their purpose to make it plain to others';[2] 'textual criticism pursues its research at the very centre of Christian faith and life'.[3]

Professor Clark has put this theory into practice with reference to the Pauline epistles, and others have done so in other areas,[4] but the volume of Erich Fascher, *Textgeschichte als hermeneutisches Problem*, published in 1953, is of special interest. Fascher is not so much concerned with the recovery of the original text or reading as to show how and to what extent certain theological and hermeneutical presuppositions gave rise to additions, alterations, and other textual variants in certain

[1] K. W. Clark, 'Effect', p. 45, cf. pp. 44–6; Idem, 'The Manuscripts of the Greek New Testament', *New Testament Manuscript Studies* (Chicago, 1950), pp. 11f.

[2] Idem, 'Textual Criticism and Doctrine', *Studia Paulina in honorem Johannis De Zwaan septuagenarii* (Haarlem, 1953), pp. 54f. See also K. W. Clark, 'Manuscripts', pp. 22–4, 175, n. 2; and Goguel, *Le texte*, p. 67. Howard, *LQHR*, x (1941), 12, seeks to illustrate the tendency of scribes to insert 'what they knew to be established in the belief and practice of the Church'. (See his examples.)

[3] K. W. Clark, 'The Textual Criticism of the New Testament', *Peake's Commentary on the Bible* (London/New York, 1962), p. 669.

[4] Idem, 'Textual Criticism and Doctrine', pp. 56–65; others include A. Bludau, *Die Schriftfälschungen der Häretiker. Ein Beitrag zur Textkritik der Bibel* (Münster i. W., 1925); E. L. Titus, 'The Motivation of Changes Made in the New Testament Text by Justin Martyr and Clement of Alexandria: A Study in the Origin of New Testament Variation' (unpublished Ph.D. thesis, University of Chicago, 1942); E. C. Blackman, *Marcion and his Influence* (London, 1948), especially pp. 42ff., 128ff.; E. W. Saunders, 'Studies in Doctrinal Influences on the Byzantine Text of the Gospel', *JBL*, LXXI (1952), 85–90; Wright, *Alterations*, especially pp. 58–71; H. J. Vogels, 'Der Einfluss Marcions und Tatians auf Text und Kanon des Neuen Testaments', *Synoptische Studien, Alfred Wikenhauser zum siebzigsten Geburtstag...* (München, 1953), pp. 278–89; Harnack and Pott, whose work on tendentious readings in Marcion is summarized in Klijn, *Survey*, pp. 61–7; and K. Stendahl, *The School of St Matthew* (Uppsala, 1954), pp. 183–202, 85f., 112, *et passim*, on theological interpretation of OT variants in both DSH and in the formula quotations in Matthew.

manuscripts and text-types. His view, similar to that of Riddle and Parvis, may be summarized in these sentences of his:

> These manuscripts come from men who have not merely copied a text mechanically, but who, on the basis of their own reflection, improved, elucidated, or made the text more understandable, as they thought.... The interpreting copyist moves between text and copy and forces his interpretation upon his later readers, since he has as yet no knowledge of an authoritative text.[1]

Thus, Fascher would affirm that the interpretation of the New Testament began, not with the writing fathers, but with the copyists of the text. This process, moreover, first took place not in connection with the great fourth- and fifth-century codices nor even the second-century papyri, but the copyists 'were involved already as unknown agents in the generation between 50 and 125 A.D.'[2]

The practical question which Fascher seeks to answer, then, is this: to what extent do textual variants reveal definite interpretations, which in turn indicate a definite understanding of the text on the part of the copyist? The remaining nine-tenths of his book is devoted to textual examples, with this question in mind.

Fascher undoubtedly has somewhat overestimated the importance of the copyist in this process and not given sufficient weight to other factors which could have produced the same results in the text. But the significance of his method and examples is not thereby lessened. For our purpose, it is noteworthy, however, that when Fascher comes to the variants of D in Acts he regards them as showing differences which are for the most part not theologically significant, but which represent different psychological explanations, or local accounts of historical scenes for the purpose of making the narrative vivid to the reader.[3]

Now it is along this very line that the textual variants of D are to be investigated, to see whether the variants do, in fact, involve some distinctive theological differences or are merely

---

[1] Fascher, *Textgeschichte*, p. 12. A similar approach is found in M. Karnetzki, 'Textgeschichte als Überlieferungsgeschichte', *ZNW*, XLVII (1956), 170–80; see Klijn's criticism, *NovTest*, III (1959), 161–3.
[2] Fascher, *Textgeschichte*, p. 12.
[3] *Ibid.* pp. 26f.

different conceptions of the events, expressed through more vivid narration, added local colour, etc. The investigation will be, then, within the broad context of a theological approach to textual criticism,[1] rather than within the older framework of assessing variants with respect to their claims for greater or less originality and/or accuracy. This latter procedure must, as a matter of fact, be set aside (at least temporarily) if D's account is to be understood; it is the inner consistency and meaning of the D-'version' which must be the primary concern. After all, why should an aberrant text of the New Testament not be studied with a view to ascertaining, for its own sake, the ideas or theological interests behind it? Need the dissident text be tried and judged only by the court of the 'standard' and 'established' text, without a chance to speak for itself?

(3) *The Problem and the Present Study*

Only occasionally, and then in a limited manner, have the textual variants of D been studied from the point of view of their possible theological motivation(s). They have recently been so treated in a partial way within such brief studies as those by C. S. C. Williams, *Alterations to the Text of the Synoptic Gospels and Acts* (1951), P. H. Menoud, 'The Western Text and the Theology of Acts' (1951), E. Fascher, *Textgeschichte als hermeneutisches Problem* (1953), Joseph Crehan, 'Peter according to the D-Text of Acts' (1957), and to some degree by Lucien Cerfaux (1950);[2] and earlier by J. Rendel Harris in his chapter on 'The Codex Bezae a Montanist Manuscript' and in his section on

[1] Others supporting this understanding of textual criticism include E. C. Colwell, 'Method in Locating a Newly-Discovered Manuscript within the Manuscript Tradition of the Greek New Testament', *Studia Evangelica* (Berlin, 1959), p. 769; Zuntz, *Text*, p. 10; Idem, 'A Textual Criticism of Some Passages of the Acts of the Apostles', *Class et Med*, III (1940), 21, 23. I. L. Seeligmann, *The Septuagint Version of Isaiah* (Leiden, 1948) (see p. 3), and D. H. Gard, *The Exegetical Method of the Greek Translator of the Book of Job* (Philadelphia, 1952) (see pp. 3 f., 91–3), apply a theological approach to the LXX over against the Hebrew, though recent OT textual developments would seem to cast some doubts on this particular enterprise.

[2] L. Cerfaux, 'Citations scripturaires et tradition textuelle dans le Livre des Actes', *Aux sources de la tradition Chrétienne, Mélanges offerts à M. Maurice Goguel*... (Neuchâtel, 1950), who approaches the textual problem 'through the bias' of the OT quotations in Acts (p. 43).

Marcionitism (1891)[1] and elsewhere (he repeats these views in several later articles), and to a limited extent by B. W. Bacon, 'Some "Western" Variants in the Text of Acts' (1928), where, in an attempt to illuminate the sources of Luke, he discusses the 'why' of the variants and recognizes that they have a story of their own to tell even though not part of the original text. In a similar way, K. Lake and H. J. Cadbury in their commentary on Acts in *The Beginnings of Christianity*, volume IV (1933), often attempt to understand the inner meaning of the 'Western' readings. When this is done, however, the results are often vitiated by a prejudgement regarding the relation of the B- and D-texts. Many of J. H. Ropes's explanations in volume III (1926) are subject to the same criticism. Finally, reference should be made to the tendencies of D noted and classified by M.-J. Lagrange (1935)[2] and reproduced by C. S. C. Williams, as well as to the treatment of individual variants by various writers in numerous places (often relegated to a footnote). Most of these studies were, of course, concerned not only with the variants of D, but with those of the 'Western' text in general. But no thorough investigation either of Codex Bezae or of the 'Western' text which assesses possible theological reasons for their distinctive readings has appeared.

The stimulating article of Professor Menoud does, indeed, make a forward step in that direction, especially as far as the text of Acts is concerned. He maintains that the chief intention of the 'Western' tradition was 'to emphasize the newness of the Christian faith as regards Judaism', and he stresses two elements in this emphasis, namely, condemning the unbelief of the Jews and insisting on the greatness of the church and the apostles over against them.[3] Nearly one-half of Menoud's article is devoted, however, to the 'apostolic decree' in Acts xv, leaving only five pages for treatment of theological tendencies in the rest of Acts.

Thus, it is the aim of the present study to investigate, in the manner described, the textual variants of Codex Bezae (remembering both the prominence and limits of its role as a

[1] Harris, *Codex Bezae*, pp. 148–53, 228–34.
[2] M.-J. Lagrange, *Critique textuelle*. Vol. II. *La critique rationnelle* (Paris, 1935), pp. 389–94, 54f.; cf. Williams, *Alterations*, pp. 56–79.
[3] P. H. Menoud, 'The Western Text and the Theology of Acts', *Studiorum Novi Testamenti Societas*, Bulletin II, pp. 27f.

witness to the 'Western' text in general), taking into account the limited work of this kind which has been done previously. The D-variants, prominent as they are in Acts and elsewhere, often receive notice in the commentaries and in other places, but it is only occasionally that an attempt is made to discern their possible basic motivation. Such a probing for underlying tendencies is necessary, however, and it can be most profitable, if only in terms of better understanding the materials of criticism, but more so if some positive conclusions can be reached which permit a given variant reading to be evaluated in the light of that known tendency which forms its background.

Certain emphases have on occasion been suggested as special interests of D, such as the full Christological titles, stress on the Holy Spirit, Gentile interests, something of an anti-Judaic spirit, and so forth, but usually these have been deduced only from the larger, more notable variants, while the smaller, less conspicuous ones have not been taken into account. These smaller variants will be treated more fully here—something not previously done adequately or on a large scale—in an effort to determine whether or not they support the interests discerned in the larger and better-known D-readings.

Preliminary investigation showed that what may *generally* be termed an anti-Judaic tendency was emerging as the clearest and broadest line of bias in the D-variants. Taking the clue from Menoud's limited but suggestive treatment, the present study takes this anti-Judaism as its focal point.

(The term 'anti-Judaic', rather than 'anti-Jewish', is preferable, since the latter can more easily be taken to mean 'anti-Semitic', that is, an opposition to the Jew as person, which is not in view here. Rather, the bias is primarily an opposition to Judaism, and to the Jews only inasmuch as they represent or are part of that system. Thus, the term 'anti-Judaic' is used here in a rather broad sense, with 'Judaic' and 'Judaism' describing that religious complex out of which Christianity arose and contemporary with the earliest period of the new faith. 'Judaic', then, both involves the concept of Israel as the distinctive and exclusive people of God and also, at times, refers to the official religious system, including the regulations, customs, and institutions of both 'Palestinian' and 'Diaspora' Judaism, though cult does not figure largely in this study. When the Jews as persons are singled out, they appear as the representatives and instruments and often as the leaders of this system. The very fact that the leaders are so often singled out supports this contention. Furthermore, 'anti-Judaic' is the term predominantly used in discussions of this kind, though 'anti-Jewish' and 'anti-Judaistic' occur occasionally. Properly understood, there is no point in abandoning the term 'anti-Judaic'.)

The method of approach has been inductive—a study of the wording, phrasing, and character of the variants themselves and an inquiry as to the significance, in the case of additional material or material lacking in D, of its presence or absence in its particular context, or, in the case of variation, the significance of these different readings for the meaning of the passage in question, obvious scribal errors excluded. Not all variants, of course, will be significant for assessing theological interest, for (apart from scribal errors) many will appear to have been motivated by the influence of another language, or by stylistic or grammatical preferences and other attempts to improve the text, or by assimilation, conflation, harmonization,[1] and so forth. It cannot, however, be stated in advance which even of these may or may not be motivated by some special interest which might be called, rather loosely, theological.

The influence of Latin or of the Semitic languages with reference to the 'Western' text has been mentioned more than once. Such discussion will be relevant at a number of points, and the work of Harris, Chase, Wensinck, Torrey, Black, Wilcox, and others must be taken into account. An example may be seen in a variant of Codex Bezae in Mark xv. 34, where a theological alteration in a Syriac milieu would explain the toning down of the harshness in Jesus' cry from the cross;[2] examples in Acts will appear later.

One aspect of this discussion concerns misunderstanding or mistranslation: a plausible linguistic explanation of this kind for an alleged tendentious variant can cast serious doubt on its value as evidence for the presumed bias. The proof of this

---

[1] On harmonizations in D, see H. J. Vogels, *Die Harmonistik in Evangelientext des Codex Cantabrigiensis* (Leipzig, 1910); von Soden, *Schriften*, I, 1311–19; Lagrange, *Critique textuelle*, pp. 51–4. Klijn, *Survey*, p. 164, deprecates the value of harmonizations.

[2] For details, see Stendahl, *School of St Matthew*, p. 85, n. 1.

influence, however, is very difficult of attainment. Professor Black, for example, doubts that mistranslation can ever be demonstrated unless both the translation and the original are extant, and he calls it a 'precarious method of approach'.[1] In cases having the appearance of mistranslation, other possibilities often exist to account for the same phenomenon. There is, for instance, the possibility of a deliberate theological interpretation of an original text; certainly in view of such dogmatic alterations as those of Marcion, one can no longer exclude the possibility that a scribe or an expositor of a text might, by a mental alteration even as slight as one letter in the text from which he works, change the sense to suit his distinctive purpose and view; and then he, or someone later, conveys the resultant meaning to a translation. Would such a person feel himself anything less than an astute interpreter of the scripture? Similar procedures were common enough as principles in Rabbinic and Qumran hermeneutic; why should they not be operative also in the history of the New Testament text? Such an alteration could, for example, lie behind the λαός/κόσμος variant in Acts ii. 47 (see below, pp. 76–9).

There is, in addition, something to be said for a tendentious copyist's or reviser's acceptance of the text which presents itself to him regardless of the origin of the readings in that text. That is to say, even if one assumes, for example, that a text was the result of Semitic confusion and interchange of words, the fact that the copyist or reviser retains this text may indicate an acceptance by him of the particular emphasis which it carries, or perhaps he adopts from another text a reading agreeable to his viewpoint and purpose. Proof in such cases would, naturally, be hard to document in detail.

Moreover, presumed instances of influence of a text in one language upon that in another, as of *d* upon D in Harris's view, can in many cases, as noted earlier, have worked just as well in the other direction, and many of Chase's examples of the assimilation of D to a Syriac version mean nothing more than that a Syriac translator employed a 'Western' type Greek text.[2] Also, A. F. J. Klijn, in his criticism of Wensinck, speaks of the 'numerous other ways of explaining the Aramaisms in D'.[3]

[1] Black, *Aramaic Approach*, pp. 6f., 11.
[2] *Ibid.* p. 30.
[3] Klijn, *Survey*, p. 166.

In summary, it is pertinent to recall the caution of E. C. Colwell regarding alleged cases of variants which may have been influenced by Latin, Syriac, or Aramaic. He refers to a conclusion of Dr Plooij that a reading in the Dura fragment of Tatian was due to the omission of a letter in a Syriac original. Colwell, with Lagrange, was convinced that the variant revealed apologetic interest, and he concludes: 'We sometimes conjecture technical reasons for variations that are better explained by vital interests in the church.'[1] Variants do, of course, arise from language influence, but these other possibilities cannot be overlooked.

The present study will be limited to the Acts of the Apostles. The reasons for this, apart from the obvious limits of space, are simple enough. First of all, the characteristic features of the 'Western' text and Codex Bezae are the most prominent and abundant in Acts. The presumption is that a pattern will emerge more clearly and more surely where the deviations are the sharpest; at least this is the likely place to look first. Any conclusions formed from this evidence can then be tested, and confirmed or modified, in the other areas, notably the gospels (but in view of the many points of contact between Codex Bezae and Codex Claromontanus, perhaps in the epistles also).

A second and very important reason for limitation to Acts is that here one avoids some of the difficulties encountered in dealing with the text of the gospels, such as harmonistic influence. Harris, for example, approves Chase's choice of Acts for this reason, and he adds that 'the probability of Aramaic elements in the sources is, to say the least, much smaller in the Acts than in the Gospels....'.[2] Then, too, Acts is concerned with more diverse subject-matter and a broader field of activity than are the gospels. For example, some of the items narrated in the gospels are repeated in speeches in Acts, which covers in addition a vast area of experience involving new people and places in early Christianity. All this makes Acts fertile ground for investigation and one which may reasonably be expected to yield more fruitful results than the gospels in an assessment for tendentious bias. Indeed, Kirsopp Lake stated that one who

[1] Colwell, 'Method', pp. 769f. See his notes for details of the example.
[2] Harris, *Four Lectures*, p. 17. See also H. Greeven, 'Erwägungen zur synoptischen Textkritik', *NTS*, VI (1959/60), 288.

proposed to study the 'Western' problems should begin with the Acts, applying the results to the study of the gospels.[1] It may be observed, finally, that by its very nature Acts is an appropriate place to study Jewish–Christian relations.

If the present study of Codex Bezae in Acts is to contribute to knowledge of the 'Western' text as a whole, it is necessary, as previously stated, to differentiate between readings which can reasonably be assumed to be ancient and part of the genuine 'Western' tradition and those which may have come into the tradition at a later time—in some cases perhaps at a date almost as recent as the date of Codex Bezae itself. (It goes without saying that scribal errors and other corruptions must be discounted.) In other words, the primary concern is not what theological tendencies may be determined for those who copied or used the late fifth-century Codex Bezae itself, or its immediately preceding archetypes; rather, the interest centres in the theological bias resident in the early (second century) text-type which is now (if imperfectly) represented by the text of D. Codex Bezae must not, then, as Ropes reminds us, be 'used, in a fashion which has been all too common, as in every respect a trustworthy witness, as it stands, to the "Western" text'.[2] Unfortunately, some of the works mentioned above which treat theological interest in D have thus misused the manuscript.

What then is the proper use of D as a 'Western' witness? If $\mathfrak{P}^{38}$, because of its earlier date, is *ipso facto* assumed more accurately to preserve the early 'Western' text, then a comparison of D with this papyrus shows, as H. A. Sanders concluded, that 'D is a very imperfect source for the "Western", or second-century, text'.[3] Granting this, however, it must also be emphasized that D and $\mathfrak{P}^{38}$ show such a degree of agreement over against the B-text that the papyrus can be used, *at the same time*, to show that 'the D text existed in Egypt shortly after A.D. 300'; A. C. Clark could call $\mathfrak{P}^{38}$ 'a text almost identical with that of D'.[4] Codex Bezae, then, at many points is an imperfect witness to the 'Western' text, and yet on this account it does not lose its leading place among those witnesses.

[1] Lake, *Text of NT* (1908⁴), p. 91 (not in 6th ed., 1928).
[2] Ropes, *Text*, p. lxxviii.
[3] Sanders, *HTR*, xx (1927), 13.
[4] A. C. Clark, *Acts*, pp. xv f., cf. Sanders, *HTR*, xx (1927), 8–12.

H. A. Sanders and Kirsopp Lake help to clear up this mystery: Sanders adds to his earlier conclusion the important statement that the evidence of apparent later accretions in D cannot be used against D 'when it has good Syriac or Latin support'.[1] Similarly, Kirsopp Lake says:

> The text of D, in many places, is an involved conflation of Western and Neutral readings, which can only be disentangled by a comparison with the purer forms of the Western text which survive in Latin and in Syriac. But, making allowance for this element of corruption, it is the most important extant witness to the continuous Greek Western text.[2]

This provides the key to the right use of D: the best and only practical way to ascertain which of D's variants may reasonably be taken as attesting the early 'Western' tradition is by comparison with those witnesses which, along with D, are recognized as the best 'Western' evidence.

In the case of Acts, the most weight would be given to readings in Codex Bezae (D and also d—see above, pp. 8–10) which share the support of the following:

Greek witnesses

Papyrus fragments

𝔓³⁸—Michigan Papyrus 1571, dating about A.D. 300, containing Acts xviii. 27–xix. 6; xix. 12–16, published by H. A. Sanders, 'A Papyrus Fragment of Acts in the Michigan Collection', *HTR*, xx (1927), 1–19, with the text also in A. C. Clark, *Acts*, pp. 220–5.

𝔓⁴⁸—Papyrus 1165 of Società Italiana, dating at the end of the third century, containing Acts xxiii. 11–17, 23–9, published in *Papiri della Società Italiana*, x (1932), 112–18.[3]

𝔓²⁹—Papyrus Oxyrhynchus 1597, dating in the third century, containing Acts xxvi. 7–8, 20, with the text printed in Ropes, *Text*, pp. 235, 237.

𝔓⁴¹—Papyrus Wessely²³⁷, Vienna K 7541–7548, dating in the eighth century, containing parts of Acts xvii–xxii, with the text printed in Ropes, *Text*, pp. 271–5.

---

[1] Sanders, *HTR*, xx (1927), 13; for a similar statement on D in the gospels, see C. H. Turner, 'A Textual Commentary on Mk 1', *JTS*, XXVIII (1926/7), 148f.

[2] Lake, *Text of NT*, p. 18.

[3] See also M.-J. Lagrange, 'Les Papyrus Chester Beatty pour les Évangiles', *RB*, XLIII (1934), 5–41.

Irenaeus—who used a Greek text of a thoroughly 'Western' type, but whose text is mostly available only in Latin.[1] His text of Acts is taken from *Adversus haereses* unless otherwise noted, and it is printed in Ropes, *ad loc.* That the Latin translation of Irenaeus represents the Greek text which he used, rather than an Old Latin text, is the conclusion of K. Th. Schäfer, 'Die Zitate in der lateinischen Irenäusübersetzung und ihr Wert für die Textgeschichte des Neuen Testamentes.'

Old African Latin witnesses

h—Codex Floriacensis (palimpsest), dating in the sixth century, containing about 203 verses of Acts, and constituting the most extensive, and thereby the most important of the 'pure' 'Western' Old Latin witnesses, with the text, wherever extant, printed in Ropes. (For varying collations, see Ropes, *Text*, pp. cccxivf.)[2]

Cyprian—whose text agrees closely with *h*. Cyprian used a version of Acts now represented in *h*; this judgement is based chiefly on Acts iii. 6 and iv. 8–12, almost the only passages available for comparison.[3] The text is in P. Corssen, *Der Cyprianische Text der Acta Apostolorum* (1892), pp. 8–14; also in Ropes, *ad loc.*

Augustine—where he uses a Cyprianic text, namely Aug[a] (*Contra epistulam Manichaei quam vocant Fundamenti* 9), containing Acts i. 1–8; ii. 1–13, and Aug[b] (*Contra Felicem Manichaeum* i, 4–5), containing Acts i. 1–ii. 11. The quotations are printed in Ropes, *ad loc.*[4]

Tertullian—whose quotations from Acts are printed in Ropes, *ad loc.*

Coptic witness

cop[G67]—a parchment codex of 107 leaves, containing Acts i. 1–xv. 3, written in Middle Egyptian and dating in the late fourth or early fifth century. Since the manuscript has not yet been published, we rely entirely upon the English translation of selected passages containing 'Western' variants offered by T. C. Petersen, 'An Early Coptic Manuscript of Acts: An Unrevised Version of the Ancient So-called Western Text', *CBQ*, xxvi (1964), 225–41. Confirmation of Petersen's speculation that this manuscript (along with a similar Matthew codex) may represent 'the earliest

[1] Ropes, *Text*, p. clxxxvii; see Souter in W. Sanday and C. H. Turner (eds.), *Novum Testamentum Sancti Irenaei Episcopi Lugdunensis* (Oxford, 1923), pp. clivf., clxivf.
[2] On *h*, see Ropes, *Text*, pp. cvi–cviii; A. C. Clark, *Acts*, pp. 247–55.
[3] *Ibid.* pp. 247, xvii.
[4] Further on Augustine, see *ibid.* pp. 256–62; Ropes, *Text*, p. cxv.

completely preserved and entirely unadulterated witnesses to what has hitherto been known as the 'Western' recension of the text of the NT'[1] must await the investigation of the fully published text, but the profusion of readings in close agreement with D, Irenaeus, *h*, Ephrem, sy^{hmg} and sy^{h}* suggests that Petersen's claim may not be much overdrawn. Should volume II turn up (the manuscript ends abruptly with xv. 3, the exact middle of Acts, with the next verso-leaf blank and a frontispiece on the following additional leaf),[2] our knowledge of the early 'Western' text of Acts would be vastly increased, since D breaks off at xxii. 29 and other 'pure' 'Western' witnesses are fragmentary.

Syriac witnesses

Ephrem—who is the source for the Old Syriac version of Acts. Ephrem's material on Acts was collected by F. C. Conybeare and appears in Ropes, *Text*, pp. 373–453. A collation of notable passages appears in A. C. Clark, *Acts*, pp. 293–6.

sy^{hmg} and sy^{h}*—the marginal notes to and asterisked passages in the Harclean Syriac, respectively. Readings of both are in Ropes, *ad loc*. The marginal notes of Thomas represent a Greek manuscript from which he took the readings indicated. A. C. Clark calls sy^{hmg} 'Codex Thomas' for the presumed Greek manuscript; Ropes denied that these marginalia were derived from a Greek manuscript,[3] but in Ropes's own copy of his book (now in the Andover-Harvard Theological Library, Harvard Divinity School), he wrote in a marginal note dated June, 1932: 'I...think it may be that Thomas found his "Western" readings now preserved in his margin, in a Greek MS, perhaps from Caesarea, and put them there in Syriac because they were *interesting*.'[4] A. C. Clark held that the asterisked words (which he calls sy^{ph}) were already present in the text Thomas used in his revision.[5]

sy^{msK}—a Christian-Palestinian fragment from the Kastellion Monastery at Khirbet Mird, dating from the sixth century, published with a detailed study by Charles Perrot, 'Un fragment christo-palestinien découvert à Khirbet Mird (Actes des Apôtres, x, 28–29; 32–41)', *RB*, LXX (1963), 506–55. (The symbol, sy^{msK}, is our own designation.)

---

[1] Petersen, *CBQ*, XXVI (1964), 226. Cf. Epp, *JBL*, LXXXV (1966), 197–212.
[2] Petersen, *CBQ*, XXVI (1964), 226, n. 4.
[3] A. C. Clark, *Acts*, pp. 226–33; Ropes, *Text*, pp. clxxviii–clxxx.
[4] *Ibid.* note to p. clxxx.
[5] A. C. Clark, *Acts*, pp. 320 ff. On the relation of Thomas to the Philoxenian text, see Ropes, *Text*, pp. clv–clxxx; A. C. Clark, *Acts*, pp. 305–29; A. Vööbus, *Early Versions of the New Testament* (Stockholm, 1954), pp. 103–21.

THE PROBLEM

The Syriac source, sy^{hmg} and sy^h*, was considered by Ropes to be 'next to Codex Bezae, the most important single witness to the "Western" text of Acts', and he viewed this Harclean apparatus, D, and the African Latin as constituting the chief witnesses to the 'Western' text.[1] A. C. Clark considered D, $\mathfrak{P}^{38}$, and Codex Thomas (i.e. sy^{hmg}) the outstanding 'Western' sources for Acts.[2] Now cop^{G67} will have to be added to this *élite* group.

Beyond the Greek, Latin, Coptic, and Syriac witnesses just enumerated, many witnesses show a mixed text containing 'Western' readings to a greater or smaller degree. The more important of these **mixed witnesses** are the following:[3]

Greek witnesses

614 and 383—minuscule codices with numerous 'Western' readings; they appear throughout Acts in 614, but in 383 they are limited almost entirely to chapters xiii–xxii. For the text of both, see A. V. Valentine-Richards, *The Text of Acts in Codex 614 (Tisch. 137) and its Allies* (1934).

Chrysostom

Const.Apost, with Didasc—*Apostolic Constitutions*, I–VI (with *Didascalia Apostolorum*). The *Apostolic Constitutions*, dating in the fourth century (?), is based on the third-century work, *Didascalia*. The Greek of the latter is lost (except for a few small fragments), and it is fully extant only in Syriac, and partly in Latin. The text of both was edited by F. X. Funk, *Didascalia et Constitutiones Apostolorum* (1905).

Old Latin witnesses: Latin codices, Latin versions, and Latin writers or writings which contain (wholly or partially) a text of Acts substantially non-vulgate are the following:

p—Codex Perpinianus, thirteenth century, which is Old Latin in Acts i. 1–xiii. 6; xxviii. 16–31, and thus is properly a divided text, rather than mixed, since the Old Latin is in clearly separate sections.

gig—Codex Gigas, thirteenth century.

*g*₂—Lectionary, Fragmenta Mediolanensia, tenth/eleventh century, containing Acts vi. 8–vii. 2, vii. 51–viii. 4, and with a text like *gig*.

[1] Ropes, *Text*, pp. clxvf., clxxi, ccxvf.
[2] A. C. Clark, *Acts*, pp. 226, 320.
[3] The witnesses listed below are discussed, often in great detail, by Ropes, *Text*, pp. cvi–cci, 276–371, and/or by A. C. Clark, *Acts*, pp. 263–335, as well as in standard handbooks, notably Vogels, *Handbuch*, and Vööbus, *Early Versions*.

Lcf—Lucifer of Cagliari, whose text is very close to *gig*. See A. M. Coleman, *The Biblical Text of Lucifer of Cagliari (Acts)* (1927).

t—*Liber comicus*, Lectionary, eleventh century, with a text similar to *gig*, though A. C. Clark thinks it is closer to *p* and *h*.[1]

e—the Latin side of Codex Laudianus, a sixth/seventh century bilingual manuscript containing Acts only, though lacking xxvi. 29–xxviii. 26. Although the Greek side, E, was formerly viewed as close to D in text-type, it is no longer considered an important 'Western' witness; the strikingly 'Western' readings were apparently translated from the Latin text at some stage in its history. Thus, Codex Laudianus, in so far as it is a 'Western' witness, attests the Latin text, not the Greek.[2] There are, however, very few distinctively African readings in *e*; its text resembles *gig* and vg. A. C. Clark concludes that a text like *h* may have been the basis for the distinctively 'Western' elements. Bede in the early eighth century used either E or a precisely similar manuscript.[3] *Note*. In the apparatus below, E usually stands for E*e*.

l—the León Palimpsest, Codex 15 of the Cathedral of León, seventh century, containing Acts viii. 27–xi. 13 (Old Latin); xiv. 21–xv. 5 (vg); xv. 6–12 (Old Latin); xv. 13–25 (vg); xv. 26–38 (Old Latin); and xv. 39–xvii. 25 (vg). The manuscript was published by B. Fischer, 'Ein neuer Zeuge zum westlichen Text der Apostelgeschichte'.[4]

cod.ard—Codex Ardmachanus or Book of Armagh or Codex Dublinensis (vg codex D), ninth century.

w—Codex Wernigerodensis, fifteenth century, containing a partial interlinear version in Bohemian. On its agreements with *p* and prov, see Fr. Blass, *TSK*, LXIX (1896), 436–71.

s—Codex Bobbiensis (Palimpsest), fifth/sixth century, containing only portions of Acts xxiii–xxviii.

q—Codex Paris. 343, thirteenth century, which was collated by A. C. Clark and designated *q* by him.

c—Codex Colbertinus, twelfth century.

dem—Codex Demidovianus, twelfth/thirteenth century.

r—Lectionary, Schlettstadt, Stadtbibliothek, 1093, seventh/eighth century, with fourteen New Testament lessons, all from Acts, with a text like *gig* and *p*.

---

[1] Ropes, *Text*, p. cx; A. C. Clark, *Acts*, p. 267.

[2] Ropes, *HTR*, XVI (1923), 175–86; Idem, *Text*, pp. lxxxv–lxxxviii; cf. A. C. Clark, *Acts*, pp. 234–46.

[3] *Ibid.* pp. 234, 246.

[4] See the review by E. J. Epp, 'Some Important Textual Studies', *JBL*, LXXXIV (1965), 173.

THE PROBLEM

vg—the Latin Vulgate preserves a considerable number of Old Latin readings, perhaps more in Acts than elsewhere.[1]

prov, tepl, bohem—the Provençal, German, and Bohemian versions, respectively, might be included here, since they were made from the Latin (vg) and contain many 'Western' readings of Old Latin origin.

Spec (or *m*)—the Pseudo-Augustine *Speculum*, with a text akin to *p*.

Rebapt—the Pseudo-Cyprianic tract, *De rebaptismate*.

Vigil—the Pseudo-Vigilius of Thapsus tract, *Contra Varimadum*.

Ambst—Ambrosiaster, whose text is almost identical with *gig*.

Hil—Hilary of Poitiers.

Cass—Cassiodorus.

and others.

Other versions: the following preserve a substantial number of 'Western' readings:

sa—the Sahidic Coptic (Egyptian) version. One manuscript may be as early as the fourth century.[2]

eth—the Ethiopic version. For the readings of Paris. Aeth. 26 and other Ethiopic manuscripts, see J. A. Montgomery, *HTR*, xxvii (1934), 169–205.

sy^p—Peshitta or Syriac Vulgate.[3]

sy^h—the Harclean Syriac, that is, the text of the Harclean Syriac which is *not* marked by any signs of the Harclean apparatus. A number of 'Western' readings are found. A. C. Clark calls sy^h and sy^h* 'Philoxenian' and takes the view that the text of sy^h is actually Philoxenus', and that only the marginal notes belong to Thomas.[4]

arm—the Armenian version.

geo—the Georgian version.

---

[1] Ropes, *Text*, p. cxxvii; Vööbus, *Early Versions*, p. 62. See the comparative tables in Ropes, *Text*, pp. 277–90; cf. J. H. Ropes and W. H. P. Hatch, 'The Vulgate, Peshitto, Sahidic, and Bohairic Versions of Acts and the Greek Manuscripts', *HTR*, xxi (1928), 72–80.

[2] See B. M. Metzger, *The Text of New Testament. Its Transmission, Corruption, and Restoration* (New York and London, 1964), p. 79, n. 1. On the 'Western' character of the Sahidic, see Ropes, *Text*, pp. cxliii f., ccxxi, 317 56; Ropes and Hatch, *HTR*, xxi (1928), 86–8; A. C. Clark, *Acts*, pp. 330–5; Vööbus, *Early Versions*, pp. 227 f.

[3] See Ropes, *Text*, pp. cxlviii f., ccxxi, 291–316; Ropes and Hatch, *HTR*, xxi (1928), 81–6; A. C. Clark, *Acts*, pp. 297–304.

[4] On the whole question, see the critical evaluation by A. Vööbus, 'New Data for the Solution of the Problem Concerning the Philoxenian Version', *Spiritus et Veritas* (Eutin, 1953); and Idem, *Early Versions*, pp. 105–21.

Not all of these witnesses, of course, will be available for a given variation-unit, but any agreement with other 'pure' 'Western' witnesses will command special attention for a D-variant. A division in the 'pure' witnesses will call for special study; such division could indicate, for example, either (1) more than one early 'Western' tradition,[1] or (2) conformation in one strain to the text of a non-'Western' tradition, or, obviously, (3) some other form of corruption on one side or the other. These problems will be dealt with as they arise.

It is important, on the one hand, to emphasize the fact that unsupported or extraordinary readings of D cannot automatically be written off as part of a more recent stratum in D. Naturally, however, some control is necessary, and such unsupported readings in D (or in any other 'pure' 'Western' witness) cannot carry the same weight as the more widely attested variants. On the other hand, in a passage where no other 'Western' witnesses are extant, D itself (or any other 'pure' 'Western' witness) must be given its due weight as a 'Western' witness, provided no influence from other text-types can be shown, and especially if the variant in question indicates a viewpoint similar to those already ascertained from the better-attested cases.

In some other instances, where D does not appear to represent the early 'Western' tradition, but where this tradition can quite clearly be determined from other witnesses, the discussion will centre in the resultant 'Western' text rather than D.

Finally, even though the broad limits of the discussion will be determined by Codex Bezae, due consideration must be given to variants which are quite clearly 'Western' but do not appear in D at all, and even to those 'Western' readings in Acts where D is not extant. There are two reasons for this. First, such variants naturally provide additional evidence, but secondly and more important they also serve as a sort of check on the 'Western' character of the distinctive readings of Codex Bezae under discussion: if the same tendencies appear in both places, there is added assurance that both the methodology and the conclusions are sound. Such 'Western' readings cannot, therefore, be excluded from an investigation of 'The Theological Tendency of Codex Bezae Cantabrigiensis in Acts'.

---

[1] See Sanders, *HTR*, xx (1927), 14, 18.

B. SOME FACTORS IN THE STUDY OF TEXTUAL VARIANTS FOR DOGMATIC TENDENCY

Texts or textual traditions do not always tell us quite so much when they agree as when they differ. Even a massive, unified tradition may, at its base, be biased, corrupt, or distorted, or may have suffered by assimilation or editing, and its many individual witnesses may together constitute but one witness, whereas another single variant-text may witness to and represent a whole tradition of a different kind. In short, it is precisely where texts differ that one may expect them to yield some information and to reveal some purpose, idea, or influence which would not easily be discernible from a case of textual agreement. Variants obviously caused by errors or corruptions of a purely mechanical nature must not, of course, be considered. It is often difficult, however, to distinguish accidental and mechanical transformations from intentional alterations, and further difficulty arises in determining the motivation for the resulting variant.

Maurice Goguel, in discussing cases of dogmatic alterations in the text, says that these can be brought to light only when there is a point of comparison which permits their disclosure.[1] Thus, in the present study, those places where the D- or 'Western' text differs from the main-line text will serve as the only approach and, more important, as the only control in an attempt to discern a distinctive viewpoint or 'theology' behind that 'Western' text. Agreements with the main-line text will tell us very little. Analysis of textual variation in a dissident text like Codex Bezae can, therefore, point the way to new knowledge, especially if the main-line text has overshadowed and obscured some other distinctive texts or traditions by the effects of editorial processes involving conflation, assimilation, or other forms of conformation to the main-line text.

(1) *The Comparison of Textual Variants and its Ambiguity*

Variants by nature exist only over against some other text. The selection of a standard text will in large measure determine what become the variants of the text under investigation (except

---

[1] Goguel, *Le texte*, p. 67; cf. Klijn, *Survey*, p. 163.

where readings are unique to the latter). Change the standard, and quite another list of variants may be produced, with a corresponding change in possible conclusions which can be drawn from them. For example, as Klijn remarks, 'it is evident that if Pott compares Marcion with his standard, the ιαη text, he will reach other conclusions than if Harnack compares him with the ℵ B text'.[1] An acceptable standard text, then, is indispensable, but difficulties multiply when one attempts to choose it. In assessing dogmatic alterations, a logical standard would be the text at hand to those who made such changes. Obviously, this ideal, desirable standard is not available, and this accounts for the basic ambiguity in work of this kind: 'There is no standard from which we can start.'[2]

A critical edition, such as Nestle, gives a text which never existed, and furthermore, 'the best critical text so far achieved now holds little assurance of being the original text'.[3] At the same time, any attempt to determine the exact reading of the 'original' text in each passage, using it as the standard in each case, would involve grave difficulties, and undoubtedly the results would differ with each investigator. On the other hand, while selection of such a text as the so-called 'Neutral' (basically B, with ℵ) would provide a real text, it would still be only *a* text, and in addition a text which itself may have undergone editorial revision.[4]

Some standard must, however, be selected even though it be—as it inevitably must—a somewhat arbitrary one. The generally conservative character of the 'Neutral' text ('it is not harmonistic, it does not cultivate smoothness of phrase, it does not seek additions')[5] justifies its choice for the present study. It has, indeed, been often so used.[6] Most suitable for the book of Acts is the text of Codex Vaticanus (B), as printed in Ropes's

---

[1] Klijn, *Survey*, p. 166.   [2] *Ibid.* p. 163.   [3] K. W. Clark, 'Effect', p. 30.

[4] This, contrary to Westcott–Hort and B. Weiss, is the currently general view: see Turner, *JTS*, xxviii (1926/7), 147; Hatch, '*Western*' *Text*, p. 44; Kenyon, *Text of Greek Bible*, pp. 207–10, 243, 249f.; Idem, *Recent Developments*, pp. 84f.; and especially K. W. Clark, 'Effect', p. 37. Porter's demonstration of the close tie of 𝔓75 and B [*JBL*, LXXXI (1962), 363–76] may mean merely that B represents a *very early* revision.

[5] Kenyon, *Recent Developments*, p. 85.

[6] Ropes used B; Yoder used Westcott–Hort; A. C. Clark used the agreement of ℵABC.

edition, and this has been used here, comparing other 'Neutral' witnesses whenever the 'Neutral' evidence is seriously divided or at those points where it may be questionable whether B represents the 'Neutral' tradition.

(2) *The Amount of Textual Variation and its Significance*

Kirsopp Lake's lecture in 1904 on 'The Influence of Textual Criticism on the Exegesis of the New Testament' laid down the principle that '...in doctrinal modifications of the text, which are almost sure to be very early, it is vain to ask for much manuscript evidence', since actual New Testament manuscripts are later than the period when changes of this kind were made and since quotations of the fathers, too, are often obscured by corruptions. 'So that quite a small amount of evidence is sufficient to establish the claim to consideration of readings which are likely to have been obnoxious to early doctrine.'[1] Elsewhere Lake says that the reason why so few variants can certainly be traced to dogmatic motivation is 'the vigilance with which the orthodox and heretics regarded each other's efforts in this direction'.[2] Maurice Goguel presents the same view in somewhat more detail and concludes that a number of corrections and adaptations are no longer recognizable in the New Testament text because no term of comparison remains.[3]

Lake's position that doctrinal alterations were very early is reinforced by Vogels, who says that most, if not all, deliberate textual alterations go back to the second century, and that none is later than the fourth.[4] This view of Vogels is defended in detail by G. D. Kilpatrick.[5] As far as the present study of the 'Western' text is concerned, this position certainly is applicable and valid, but the limitation of dogmatically motivated variants to the earliest period is too narrow and restrictive a view when turning, for example, to a study of Byzantine New Testament texts, to lectionaries, and to other areas.

Finally, Lake is surely correct that evidence of tendentious

---
[1] Lake, *Influence*, pp. 10f.
[2] Lake, *Text of NT*, p. 6; cf. Klijn, *Survey*, p. 164 for a similar view.
[3] Goguel, *Le texte*, p. 67; cf. Wright, *Alterations*, p. 58.
[4] Vogels, *Handbuch*, p. 162.
[5] G. D. Kilpatrick, 'Atticism and the Text of the Greek New Testament', *Neutestamentliche Aufsätze*, pp. 128–31.

variants is likely to be obscured and therefore meagre, but, as the ensuing study will demonstrate, Lake is excessively conservative as to the detectability of such variants.

(3) *The Conservatism in Textual Variation and its Significance*
In the investigation of dogmatically motivated variants, not only may one expect a relatively limited amount of evidence, but also one should not always demand consistency of evidence. The copying and editing of manuscripts necessarily involve a certain considerable degree of respect for the text; these procedures represent, after all, a basically conservative endeavour. Tendentious alterations are more likely, therefore, to be introduced with cautious subtlety than with rigid consistency. If, however, they should be introduced consistently, the conservative processes of harmonization and of conformation to prevailing texts are likely, if they do not eliminate the tendentious variant entirely, at least to destroy its consistency. Thus one finds that, while a manuscript may show a dissident reading in one synoptic passage, it may not appear in the parallel passage(s). Nor is there always consistency within a single book, and certain emphases present in one place may not be found at other expected points. In the gospels, for example, the 'Western' text often neglects this general consistency, but frequently maintains consistency in the context.[1] In the 'Western' text of Acts there are some striking cases where consistency is thoroughgoing, for example, the variants in the 'apostolic decree' (xv. 20, 29; xxi. 25) and those in Codex Bezae concerned with the 'ignorance motif' (iii. 17; xiii. 27; cf. xvii. 30). But to expect this at every point, even apart from the modifying influences of harmonization and assimilation, would be to expect too much. As for D, it can perhaps best be described as 'at once conservative and innovating'.[2]

Undoubtedly this ambivalent character of D has contributed to the point of view, represented by Ropes, that it is difficult to find any trace of a special viewpoint. But if Lake's principle of the relatively great significance of a little evidence is remembered, and if Codex Bezae's alternating conservatism and

---
[1] Hatch, '*Western*' *Text*, pp. 23, 30, 36, 40.
[2] Menoud, 'Western Text', pp. 28, 32.

innovation are kept in mind, some progress can certainly be expected.

Incidentally, this emphasis on conservatism in textual transmission does not contradict our previous emphasis (in discussing the views of Riddle, Parvis, and Fascher) that there was in this early period little scruple against verbal changes in copying or against improvement in style.[1] This is not quite an either/or situation; both emphases involve relative statements, for the sphere of textual change for dogmatic purposes is, in view of the whole process of textual transmission, a circumscribed one (with some striking exceptions, to be sure), 'for we are dealing, for the most part, with the efforts of men who themselves "abode in the teaching of Christ" and who sought earnestly to strengthen their brothers'.[2] Thus, there can be both an attitude of considerable freedom toward the text and, at the same time, a conservative tendency in the preservation of the basic tradition as a whole. Indeed, both attitudes may not always be present in one and the same person, but even that is not at all unlikely.

Finally, it must be stressed that Codex Bezae and the 'Western' text do not represent another (i.e. a different) work on primitive Christianity—these texts are not apocryphal gospels and acts, nor heretical writings—but merely another textual tradition of the New Testament gospels and Acts, with, to be sure, a larger than usual number of variants and noticeable readings, but a textual tradition which nevertheless preserves the bulk of the traditional text (omissions in D are relatively few, except in the last chapters of Lk).[3]

The procedure we have outlined does not, after all, differ in principle from current methods of discerning the theologies of Matthew, Luke, Paul, or the deutero-Pauline literature. In these cases differences from the theology known to and contemporary with them are utilized to determine the distinctive thrust or direction of their thought in relation to the great common theological stock of the time. That there may be agreement even to the extent of 90 or 95 per cent would not minimize the significance of the differences, no matter how few, for it is

[1] Nock, *Gnomon*, XXV (1953), 502.
[2] Wright, *Alterations*, p. 58. Seeligmann, *Isaiah*, p. 3, says much the same for translations.
[3] See the charts in Kenyon, *Text of Greek Bible*, pp. 216–30.

these deviations which reveal not only isolated variations in concept and opinion, but also the all-important directional pull or torsional strain which is being exerted by a Luke or a Paul upon that vast body of tradition common to all Christians of their times. Thus, the differences and only the differences reveal the distinctive driving force and direction of movement of a thinker closely related to a larger tradition.

The objection, then, that an emphasis on textual variants overlooks the overwhelming majority of textual agreement among all New Testament texts and textual traditions is not well founded. This extensive agreement is obvious enough, but what is not so obvious is that twist or torsional strain which a specific text or textual tradition is bringing to bear upon the common textual material being transmitted. And it is precisely the textual variants which can bring to light this distinctive thrust.

Thus, through a theological understanding of textual criticism and by following the principles stated here, it should be possible to gain a new picture of at least one aspect or point of view in the early church, that of the theological background of the textual variants of Codex Bezae and the 'Western' text in Acts. This, if only in a small way, would add both to our understanding of the primitive church and its ideas and development, and to our store of information with which to assess manuscripts, textual traditions, and text-types.

CHAPTER II

ANTI-JUDAIC TENDENCIES IN ACTS

THE evidence for anti-Judaic tendencies of Codex Bezae in Acts falls generally under three headings. The first concerns the D-text's portrayal of the Jews' attitude toward and treatment of Jesus, the second deals with the broad area of the relation of the Jews, the Gentiles, and Christianity in D, and the third involves the interplay between the Jews and the apostles in the D-text. A strict separation of these topics is not always possible nor desirable and would lead to undue repetition at points, but, in general, such an arrangement will facilitate a somewhat orderly presentation of the material.

A. THE JEWS AND JESUS

The incidence of passages in Acts which relate to the attitude of the Jews toward Jesus is necessarily limited by the nature of the book of Acts, but the kerygmatic speeches occasionally provide such a portrayal, and it is of interest to see how the D-text formulates these passages.

Several variants in D are found in verses which concern the 'ignorance motif' in Acts.[1] Hans Conzelmann has emphasized the tendency of the Lucan writings to place all the blame for the crucifixion of Jesus on the Jews.[2] This tendency is clearer in the Gospel of Luke than in Acts, and in fact, as Conzelmann admits, the book of Acts leaves room for the Jews to be excused on the grounds of ignorance. These contrasting views of Luke in Acts may be due, as Conzelmann suggested in his first two German editions (and in the English edition), to the fact that one, the guilt of the Jews, derives from Luke's source, while the

[1] This material was previously published: E. J. Epp, 'The "Ignorance Motif" in Acts and Anti-Judaic Tendencies in Codex Bezae', *HTR*, LV (1962), 51–62.
[2] H. Conzelmann, *Die Mitte der Zeit* (1962⁴), pp. 78–85; Eng. trans. *The Theology of St Luke*, pp. 85–93. (He confines himself to the B-text.)

41

other, that ignorance is a ground for excuse, is Luke's own interpretation, although in the third and fourth German editions he apparently is not so sure that the contrasting views are due to Luke's source and to Luke's own view, respectively.[1] Nevertheless, these contrasting views in Luke remain, and Luke uses the theme of the guilt of the Jews in polemic against Judaism, while that of ignorance as a ground for excuse arises out of missionary needs.[2] Thus, Luke's emphasis on the guilt of the Jews for the crucifixion of Jesus stands in opposition to his report of the offered pardon, extended even to their rulers, because of ignorance.

A text-critical examination of the passages in Acts concerned with this 'ignorance motif' discloses, however, that in Codex Bezae these two attitudes no longer stand in sharp conflict, for in D the element of excuse is virtually absent, while that of guilt finds more emphasis.

The passages in question all occur in speeches. The first of these, Acts iii. 17, is found in Peter's speech in Solomon's Portico (Acts iii. 12-26). Here, in both the B- and D-texts, the Jews are saddled with the responsibility for delivering up Jesus, denying him before Pilate, and finally killing him (iii. 13-15). There is for the Jews, however, an extenuating circumstance—they, as well as their rulers, 'acted in ignorance' (iii. 17).

The D-version of the speech retains this exonerative feature, but its textual variants reveal a different underlying conception, placing the Jews in quite another light.

Acts iii. 17

B	D
καὶ νῦν, ἀδελφοί,	καὶ νῦν, ἄνδρες ἀδελφοί,
οἶδα	ἐπιστάμεθα
ὅτι	ὅτι ὑμεῖς μὲν
κατὰ ἄγνοιαν	κατὰ ἄγνοιαν
ἐπράξατε,	ἐπράξατε πονηρόν,
ὥσπερ καὶ οἱ ἄρχοντες ὑμῶν.	ὥσπερ καὶ οἱ ἄρχοντες ὑμῶν.

---

[1] Idem, *Mitte der Zeit* (1957²), pp. 75, 77, 139f.; Eng. trans. pp. 90, 92, 162, n. 2. But cf. *Mitte der Zeit* (1960³ and 1962⁴), p. 83.
[2] Idem, *Mitte der Zeit*⁴, pp. 84f., 151; Eng. trans. pp. 92, 162, n. 2; cf. Idem, *Apostelgeschichte*, p. 34.

THE JEWS AND JESUS

ἄνδρες D *d* E *h p q w* prov cop^G67
ἐπιστάμεθα D *h* cop^G67 Ephr^(p398)] *om d* (*d*² scimus)]οἶδα *cett* Ir^iii.12,3
ὑμεῖς μέν D *d*; μέν *h* (but Blass: [vos q]uidem *h*)
κατὰ ἄγνοιαν] [no]n quidem per scientiam *h* (but Blass: [vos q]uidem per ⟨in⟩scientiam *h*)
πονηρόν D (*praem* τό D^c) *d gig h p q w cod.ard* vg^codd prov cop^G67 sy^hmg Ir^iii.12,3 Aug^qu 66 Ambst^86 *et* 118] *om* Ephr^(p398)
(iniquitatem *d*; nequam *h* Ir; hoc malum *gig p q w* vg^codd prov Aug Ambst; scelus hoc *cod.ard*; this evil cop^G67)
ὥσπερ... ὑμῶν] *om* Ir^iii.12,3

Notice, first of all, some minor variants, which set the tone for what is to follow. The ἐπιστάμεθα of D (where B reads οἶδα)[1] changes the affirmation from 'I, Peter, know...' to 'We, the apostles [the μάρτυρες, iii. 15] know...', thereby emphasizing the contrast between the Christians and the Jews in the ensuing discussion. Whether D's ὑμεῖς is emphatic, strengthening this contrast and pointing the finger more directly at the Jews and their rulers, or merely provides better balance in the Greek sentence, is difficult to say. The μέν, however, places the act of the Jews over against the action of God in the δέ-clause of the next verse (iii. 18).[2] Harnack viewed μέν as secondary, since (he claimed) there was no contrast here.[3] Once it is seen as an anti-Judaic passage, however, the contrast is both evident and meaningful. The result so far in D may be paraphrased as follows:

We, the apostles of Christ, know that *you*, the Jews, *on the one hand*, acted in ignorance, as did also your rulers, but, *on the other hand*, God in this way fulfilled that which he foretold..., that his Χριστός should suffer.

In the D-text, then, not only is the contrast sharpened between the Jews and Christians, but also the disparity between what the Jews did and what God did is more clearly emphasized.[4]

[1] Black, *Aramaic Approach*, p. 179, cites these variants as examples of synonyms which could be viewed as different attempts at translation from an original Aramaic, but, he adds, they could also have arisen in Greek texts 'in the process of διόρθωσις' at an early period.
[2] Th. Zahn, *Die Apostelgeschichte des Lucas* (Leipzig, 1922), I, 154, n. 62.
[3] A. Harnack, '[Review of] Blass, *Professor Harnack und die Schriften des Lukas—Papias bei Eusebius...*', *TLZ*, XXXII (1907), 399.
[4] Harnack (*ibid.*) thought that the introduction to this speech in D went back to that in Acts xv. 7 (B and D): ἄνδρες ἀδελφοί, ὑμεῖς ἐπίστασθε ὅτι... The function of ὑμεῖς, however, is quite different; μέν is not accounted for,

43

The most significant variant, D's πονηρόν, confirms all this. The presence of this word now leaves no doubt as to how Peter, according to the D-text, really viewed what the Jews did to Jesus; it may have been done κατὰ ἄγνοιαν, but it was no less a culpable deed: ὑμεῖς ἐπράξατε πονηρόν. Harnack and B. Weiss felt that πονηρόν was secondary because it stands in conflict with κατὰ ἄγνοιαν.[1] This, however, is just the point here: the Jews cannot, according to D, be guiltless because of their ignorance. In the D-text the responsibility for Jesus' death rests squarely on the Jews.[2]

These textual variants, like so many others in D, are small—there is, after all, a basic conservatism in all New Testament texts. These small variants, nevertheless, combine to reveal the calculated anti-Judaic sentiment from which they first sprang.

An interesting sideline is the occurrence of πονηρόν in the D-text of Lk xxiii. 41. One of the criminals crucified with Jesus says concerning him: οὗτος δὲ οὐδὲν ἄτοπον ἔπραξεν (B-text), 'But he did nothing amiss', for which the D-text has οὗτος δὲ οὐδὲν πονηρὸν ἔπραξεν, 'But he did nothing evil' [πονηρόν D lat Chr[2, 480 (but not 2, 492)]. Cf. inicum = iniquum d; nihil mali it[p1]; nihil male q]. When this D-version of Lk xxiii. 41 is compared with the D-version of Acts iii. 17, the parallelism seems too striking to be mere coincidence:

Acts: ὑμεῖς [i.e. the Jews] μὲν...ἐπράξατε πονηρόν.
Lk: οὗτος [i.e. Jesus] δὲ οὐδὲν πονηρὸν ἔπραξεν.

As far as the D-text is concerned, the Jews had done an evil thing to Jesus, who himself, in fact, had done nothing evil. The contrast is vivid and effective.

Incidentally, D, with d cop[G67] sa, reads πονηρόν also in Acts v. 4, in Peter's question to Ananias: τί ὅτι ἔθου ἐν τῇ καρδίᾳ σου ποιῆσαι πονηρὸν τοῦτο; (B om ποιῆσαι and reads τὸ πρᾶγμα for πονηρόν), and in Lk v. 22, in Jesus' reply to the scribes and Pharisees: τί διαλογίζεσθε ἐν ταῖς καρδίαις ὑμῶν πονηρά; (D it). The latter case is undoubtedly a harmonization with Matt. ix. 4,

and, if xv. 7 were the source, why did D not simply take over ὑμεῖς ἐπίστασθε ὅτι..., which would have made perfect sense in iii. 17 (and cf. x. 28; xix. 25), or why not ἐπίσταμαι? The first person plural is not accounted for from xv. 7.

[1] Harnack, *TLZ*, xxxii (1907), 399; Weiss, *Codex D*, p. 61.
[2] Menoud, 'Western Text', p. 28.

and the former was patterned after it, as is shown by the parallelism in Acts v. 4 D and Lk v. 22 D. No such relationship appears with reference to Acts iii. 17 or Lk xxiii. 41, so that they remain separate cases. Whether these additional occurrences of πονηρός in D are sufficient to indicate a preoccupation with this term by the D-text is not clear because of the evidence of harmonization. On the other hand, it is quite possible that the term was found or remembered in the parallels and used consciously according to a predilection for it. Lk xx. 23 D has πονηρίαν, but so does its parallel, Matt. xxii. 18. Thus, this is harmonization in D, as in the case of Lk v. 22 and Matt. ix. 4.

It is noteworthy that the idea of the Jews acting in ignorance with reference to Jesus' death is peculiar to Luke. The obvious parallel to Acts iii. 17 is Lk xxiii. 34,[1] the words of Jesus from the cross: Πάτερ, ἄφες αὐτοῖς· οὐ γὰρ οἴδασιν τί ποιοῦσιν. Of significance here is the well-known but revealing fact that D in Lk lacks this prayer of forgiveness [lacking in D* (*add* D^L) *d* $\mathfrak{P}^{75}$ ℵ^a B W Θ minn *a* sy^s sa bo^{codd}]. J. Rendel Harris has, indeed, argued vigorously that the prayer was excised from the text because of 'an early and violent anti-Judaic polemic..., involving an actual abrenuntiation of all fellowship with the Jews'.[2] Also, Harnack defended the originality of the prayer of forgiveness and its subsequent excision for dogmatic reasons— because of anti-Judaic feelings.[3] The refusal of Hort to admit any dogmatic alterations in the New Testament text has been mentioned earlier, but notice his comment on this particular passage: 'Wilful excision, on account of the love and forgiveness shown to the Lord's own murderers, is absolutely incredible: no various reading in the New Testament gives evidence of having arisen from any such cause.'[4] This view, here and elsewhere, cannot bear the weight of evidence against it.

[1] Menoud, 'Western Text', p. 28, n. 32, says that Lk xxiii. 34 is the only parallel, rightly rejecting I Cor. ii. 8, which speaks of heavenly powers, not Jews. He has, however, overlooked Acts xiii. 27, which is discussed below. Note that Ephrem brings together Acts iii. 17 and Lk xxiii. 34 (see Ropes, *Text*, p. 398).

[2] Harris, *Exp*, VIII, 7 (1914), 333f., cf. 324f., 331ff. See also B. H. Streeter, *The Four Gospels. A Study of Origins* (London, 1924), pp. 138f. (This view assumes that the αὐτοῖς refers to the Jews, not to the Romans.)

[3] Harnack, *Studien*, I, 91–8, especially 96–8.

[4] Westcott and Hort, *New Testament*, II, 'Notes on Select Readings', p. 68.

The variants in Acts iii. 17, then, bring to focus the fact that, for the D-text, the Jews could not so easily be excused on the basis of ignorance.

The 'ignorance motif' recurs in Acts xiii. 27, which relates part of Paul's speech at Pisidian Antioch:

Acts xiii. 27

B
οἱ γὰρ κατοικοῦντες
ἐν Ἱερουσαλὴμ
καὶ οἱ ἄρχοντες αὐτῶν
τοῦτον ἀγνοήσαντες
καὶ τὰς φωνὰς
τῶν προφητῶν
τὰς κατὰ πᾶν σάββατον ἀναγει-
νωσκομένας
κρείναντες ἐπλήρωσαν, . . .

D
οἱ γὰρ κατοικοῦντες
ἐν Ἱερουσαλὴμ
καὶ οἱ ἄρχοντες αὐτ[ῆ]ς
μ[ὴ συνιέν]τες
τὰς γρ[αφ]ὰς
τῶν προφητῶν
τὰς κατὰ πᾶν σάββατον ἀναγει-
νωσκομένας
καὶ κρείναντες ἐπλήρωσαν, . . .

line 4: μ[η συνιεν]ταις

αὐτῆς D*_vid_ d gig t vg
τοῦτον ἀγνοήσαντες] hunc Christum ignorantes _cod.ard_; hunc Iesum ignorantes _cor.vat_* cop^G67; hunc (_om_ vg^codS*) ignorantes Iesum vg^coddSU
μὴ συνιέντες τὰς γραφάς D*_vid_ [see note 1] (D^F: τοῦτον ἀγνοοῦντες καί); (D^H: φωνάς); non intelligentes scripturas _d_ (καὶ τὰς γραφάς E sy^p) καί _ante_ κρείναντες D _d_ (cf. sy^p and Zahn's opinion)[2]

Here it is not so clear whether the ignorance referred to (especially in the B-text) provides an excuse or involves guilt. Conzelmann argues that Luke here shares the view of Mark xii. 24 that ignorance of the scriptures incurs blame,[3] but this is hardly convincing when one compares the features of Acts iii. 17 with those of Acts xiii. 27. There is in both, first of all, the element of ignorance (ἄγνοια, ἀγνοεῖν), namely a failure to

---

[1] See Scrivener, _Bezae_, p. 444, note to fo. 468b; the editions of Blass, Hilgenfeld, Ropes, and A. C. Clark; F. H. Chase, _The Old Syriac Element in Codex Bezae_ (London, 1893), pp. 89 ff.; and Th. Zahn, _Die Urausgabe der Apostelgeschichte des Lucas_ (Leipzig, 1916), who says συνιέντες is assured through _d_.

[2] _Ibid._ p. 283.

[3] Conzelmann, _Mitte der Zeit_[4], p. 147, n. 4, cf. p. 83; Eng. trans. p. 158, n. 4, cf. p. 90; Idem, _Apostelgeschichte_, p. 76.

46

recognize God's Χριστός: see Acts iii. 13–18, and observe the τοῦτον in xiii. 27 and the Vulgate codices which read *hunc Christum/Iesum* here. This assumes the view that τοῦτον refers to the 'Ιησοῦν of *v.* 23: ὁ θεὸς...ἤγαγεν τῷ 'Ισραὴλ σωτῆρα 'Ιησοῦν[1] and not to ὁ λόγος τῆς σωτηρίας (*v.* 26).[2] Conzelmann's assumption that τὰς φωνὰς τῶν προφητῶν is the object of ἀγνοήσαντες is also questionable. The choice is whether the καί of the B-text is copulative or epexegetic, and thus whether both τοῦτον and τὰς φωνάς are objects of ἀγνοήσαντες, or only τοῦτον, with τὰς φωνάς as the object of ἐπλήρωσαν.[3] Compelling reasons for one choice over the other are lacking. M. Dibelius, however, excises τοῦτον, making 'the voices of the prophets' the only object of ἀγνοήσαντες.[4] He apparently follows Ropes,[5] but Ropes's view was based on his explanation of the D-text—that the 'Western' reviser wished to clarify the simple reading ἀγνοήσαντες *sine* τοῦτον and substituted μὴ συνιέντες. The B-text, says Ropes, supplied a new object, τοῦτον. Unfortunately for this view, there is no evidence for reading ἀγνοήσαντες *sine* τοῦτον except the reading of D *d* (i.e. μὴ συνιέντες *sine* τοῦτον), and the explanation about to be given for D's lack of τοῦτον and its reading of μὴ συνιέντες for ἀγνοήσαντες obviates the need for Ropes's elaborate explanation.

This is not, however, to gloss over the textual problem in xiii. 27–9. The texts of both B and D do offer difficulty, but reconstructions of the 'Western' text generally follow D (Hilgenfeld, Zahn, A. C. Clark, Ropes), though Ropes deletes καὶ κρείναντες in favour of the same word in the next line (*v.* 28).[6] The text of D, then, can be accepted (with this possible exception) as the early 'Western' reading.

To continue with the comparison of iii. 17 and xiii. 27, both passages, secondly, specify the fulfilment of the scriptures, within the divine decree, by the unknowing act of the Jews

[1] *Beginnings*, IV, 153; Haenchen, *Apostelgeschichte*, p. 352.
[2] As held by Zahn, *Apostelgeschichte*, II, 439, and O. Glombitza, 'Akta XIII. 15–41. Analyse einer Lukanischen Predigt vor Juden', *NTS*, V (1958/9), 310f.
[3] See Jacquier, *Actes*, p. 400.
[4] M. Dibelius, *Studies in the Acts of the Apostles* (London, 1956), p. 91 (*Aufsätze zur Apostelgeschichte* (Göttingen, 1951), p. 83).
[5] Ropes, *Text*, p. 262.   [6] *Ibid.* pp. 261–3.

(iii. 18; xiii. 27, 29, 32f.). (Already the fact that the death of Jesus conforms to the scriptures somewhat alleviates the severity of judgement on the Jews.)[1] Finally, both passages name the Jews, with their rulers, as the subjects of the action against Jesus. This close parallelism permits us to take these passages in the same way. Now in the B-text of iii. 17, ignorance clearly provides an excuse, and there is no reason why xiii. 27, in the same text, should not be taken in the same way.[2]

Turning, then, to the text of D, it is at once apparent that the D-text again has differently conceived the ignorance on the part of the Jews. D reads μὴ συνιέντες τὰς γραφάς... for B's τοῦτον [i.e. Jesus] ἀγνοήσαντες καὶ τὰς φωνὰς...ἐπλήρωσαν. Here, as in iii. 17, the tendency of the B-text to excuse the Jews by reason of ignorance for crucifying Jesus appears in a more subdued manner in D, which refuses to let the Jews off so lightly. The lack of τοῦτον and the reading of μὴ συνιέντες for ἀγνοήσαντες, divest D of any thought which might suggest a relative pardon from guilt because of a disregard for or non-recognition of Jesus as Χριστός—the D-text has no room for such a formula of excuse. Indeed, the only exonerative factor left to the Jews here in D is a lack of understanding (συνιέναι) their scriptures, an excuse hardly complimentary or acceptable to the Jews.

The only two other occurrences of ἀγνοεῖν and ἄγνοια in Acts [but see on Acts xvi. 39 D below] are in Paul's Areopagus speech in chapter xvii (vv. 23, 30). Notice verse 30:

Acts xvii. 30

B	D
τοὺς μὲν οὖν χρόνους	τοὺς μὲν οὖν χρόνους
τῆς ἀγνοίας	τῆς ἀγνοίας ταύτης
ὑπεριδὼν ὁ θεός	παριδὼν ὁ θεός

[1] Bo Reicke, *Glaube und Leben der Urgemeinde* (Zürich, 1957), p. 67.

[2] Nor does the fact that xiii. 27 is a speech of Paul require that ἄγνοια be interpreted in a Pauline fashion, for two reasons: (1) Though in Paul ἄγνοια is regularly guilt-laden, Acts iii. 17 and xiii. 27 alone in the New Testament use the term in quite another connection. Thus B. Gärtner, *The Areopagus Speech and Natural Revelation* (Uppsala, 1955), p. 234, n. 2, cf. pp. 229–40; see also E. Fascher, 'Gott und die Götter', *TLZ*, LXXXI (1956), 298. (2) The parallelism shown here between Acts iii. 17 and xiii. 27 (not to mention other evidence) reveals the hand of Luke in each, rather than providing evidence for the unity of the preaching of Peter and Paul (Haenchen, *Apostelgeschichte*, p. 352).

τὰ νῦν ἀπαγγέλλει τὰ νῦν παραγγέλλει
τοῖς ἀνθρώποις τοῖς ἀνθρώποις
πάντας πανταχοῦ μετανοεῖν,... ἵνα πάντες πανταχοῦ μετανοεῖν,...

ταύτης D* d vg (cf. geo)] om cett Ir^iii.12,9(11)
παριδών D*
παραγγέλλει D 𝔓⁴¹ 𝔓⁷⁴ ℵ^c A E H L P S 614 383 sa Ath Cyr^abac 573
ἵνα πάντες D* sy^p; ut...paenitentiam agent d gig vg] πᾶσιν H L P S
614 383 sy^h Ir^iii.12,9(11)
μετανοεῖν] +εἰς αὐτόν Ir^iii.12,9(11) (in ipsum)

Here, οἱ χρόνοι τῆς ἀγνοίας which God overlooked[1] refer back to the ἄγνωστος θεός which the Athenians worshipped ἀγνοοῦντες (v. 23). The 'times of ignorance' have reference here only to heathen religion.

Why, then, does D read ταύτης in v. 30, 'the times of *this* ignorance', unless it is to distinguish the ignorance in the present context ('this ignorance'), which has nothing to do with the Jews' treatment of Jesus,[2] from the D-text's other mention of ignorance in iii. 17? Since the presence of πονηρόν, etc., in the latter passage in D already afforded the excuse of ignorance a much smaller place, the D-text wished to be certain that no reader thought it was *that* ignorance which God had overlooked.[3] In other words, the D-text is saying that the times of ignorance spoken of here in Acts xvii. 30 refer to the Athenian worship, and God overlooks *this* ignorance. But, says the D-text, let no one think that God overlooks *that* ignorance, referred to in iii. 17, through which the Jews crucified Jesus; God overlooks *this* ignorance of the Athenians, but not *that* ignorance of the Jews.

[1] Dibelius, *Studies*, p. 56, n. 89, thinks ὑπεριδών is a stronger term than παριδών. However, Gärtner, *Areopagus*, p. 230, thinks the two terms give the same sense: that God does not intervene to change the situation.

[2] Gärtner, *Areopagus*, p. 234, n. 2, distinguishes carefully the use of ἄγνοια in iii. 17 (to be taken with xiii. 27) from its meaning in xvii. 30, and in the epistles, LXX, Philo, pagan philosophy, etc. See his excellent discussion of the 'ignorance' theme, pp. 229–40.

[3] A passage closely related to xvii. 30 and one to which the 'ignorance motif' might be applied is Acts xiv. 16, in the Lystra speech: (B and D) ὃς ἐν ταῖς παρῳχημέναις γενεαῖς εἴασεν πάντα τὰ ἔθνη πορεύεσθαι ταῖς ὁδοῖς αὐτῶν. The specific mention of ἔθνη, however, excludes any confusion as to Jewish or Gentile reference.

This variant of D in Acts xvii. 30 provides striking confirmation of the view taken here as to the meaning of the D-text's variants in Acts iii. 17, along with those in xiii. 27. The rather minute textual variations discussed here stand in contrast to the larger and more elaborate readings usually singled out for study in Codex Bezae. Both the large and small variants will be treated in the following pages. Moreover, the variants connected with the 'ignorance motif' are of special interest because they show an instance where the D-text's point of view is carried through consistently in the text.[1] As noted earlier, since texts may be corrected to and influenced by other texts, such consistency can neither always be found nor expected (see above, pp. 38f.). Consequently, the consistency evident in this instance lends added significance to the results and demands further attention to the theological tendency which motivated such constructions in the 'ignorance' passages.

An additional occurrence of the verb ἀγνοεῖν in Acts is found within a longer variant reading of D in xvi. 39. The context of xvi. 39 tells of the release of Paul and Silas from prison at Philippi. The magistrates had just learned that the apostles were Romans and, hearing this, they were afraid. The B-text then reads (xvi. 39): ...καὶ ἐλθόντες παρεκάλεσαν αὐτούς, καὶ ἐξαγαγόντες ἠρώτων ἀπελθεῖν ἀπὸ τῆς πόλεως. The D-text, however, is much fuller:

...καὶ παραγενόμενοι μετὰ φίλων πολλῶν εἰς τὴν φυλακὴν παρεκάλεσαν αὐτοὺς ἐξελθεῖν εἰπόντες· Ἠγνοήσαμεν τὰ καθ' ὑμᾶς ὅτι ἐστὲ ἄνδρες δίκαιοι. καὶ ἐξαγαγόντες παρεκάλεσαν αὐτοὺς λέγοντες· Ἐκ τῆς πόλεως ταύτης ἐξέλθατε μήποτε πάλιν συστραφῶσιν ἡμεῖν ἐπικράζοντες καθ' ὑμῶν.

παραγενόμενοι D
μετὰ φίλων πολλῶν D d
εἰς τὴν φυλακήν D d 614 383 vg^codR² syh*
ἐξελθεῖν εἰπόντες D d 614 383 vg^codR² syh*
ἠγνοήσαμεν...δίκαιοι D d 614 383 vg^codR² syh* Ephr^(p432) et cat(p433)
καὶ ἐξαγαγόντες...λέγοντες D d
ἐκ...ὑμῶν D d 614 383 syh* Ephr^(p432) et cat(p433) [with minor variations in each]

---

[1] Another notable case of consistency in D is the lack of καὶ πνικτοῦ (-όν) or καὶ πνικτῶν in xv. 20; xv. 29; and xxi. 25, and the additional negative 'Golden Rule' in xv. 20 and 29 (though not in xxi. 25). See below, pp. 107–12.

The significant part for the present point[1] is the statement of the magistrates, Ἡγνοήσαμεν τὰ καθ' ὑμᾶς ὅτι ἐστὲ ἄνδρες δίκαιοι. The word ἠγνοήσαμεν here is clearly in the context of excuse; the magistrates are excusing themselves for beating and imprisoning the apostles, and the basis of their excuse is ignorance—ignorance that Paul and Silas were, as they put it, 'righteous men' (i.e. Roman citizens). What is interesting is that the D-text allows this excuse of ignorance in the case of the Roman officials.

The word δίκαιοι reminds one immediately of the words of the centurion at the cross (Lk xxiii. 47): ὄντως ὁ ἄνθρωπος οὗτος δίκαιος ἦν (D has ὄντως δίκαιος ἦν ὁ ἄνθρωπος οὗτος).[2] Thus, D's account here in Acts xvi. 39 parallels the experience of the apostles with that of Jesus: a Roman centurion calls Jesus δίκαιος, and Roman magistrates call the apostles δίκαιοι; the Jews do not recognize Jesus for what he is (κατὰ ἄγνοιαν, Acts iii. 17) but, nevertheless, are not excused by D on these grounds, while the Roman magistrates, who acknowledge that they had been ignorant (ἠγνοήσαμεν) of the apostles' character (as 'righteous men' or as 'innocent')[3] are allowed the excuse of ignorance in D. Once again the D-text is hard on the Jews.

The larger context of Acts iii. 17 can be adduced in support of the tendency seen there:

Acts iii. 14

B	D
ὑμεῖς δὲ τὸν ἅγιον καὶ δίκαιον ἠρνήσασθε, καὶ ᾐτήσασθε ἄνδρα φονέα χαρισθῆναι ὑμῖν, ...	ὑμεῖς δὲ τὸν ἅγιον καὶ δίκαιον ἐβαρύνατε, καὶ ᾐτήσατε ἄνδρα φονέα χαρισθῆναι ὑμεῖν, ...

---

[1] Further on xvi. 39, see below, pp. 147–50.
[2] Δίκαιος is used of Jesus also in Matt. xxvii. 19, 24 (though not in B or D); Acts iii. 14; vii. 52; xxii. 14. Note also that in Acts xiv. 2 D δίκαιοι is used of the Christians.
[3] On δίκαιος meaning 'innocent' in Lk xxiii. 47, see G. D. Kilpatrick, 'A Theme of the Lucan Passion Story and Luke xxiii. 47', *JTS*, XLIII (1942), 34f. See also [W. Bauer], W. F. Arndt and F. W. Gingrich, *A Greek–English Lexicon of the New Testament and Other Early Christian Literature* (Chicago, 1957), s.v.

ANTI-JUDAIC TENDENCIES IN ACTS

ἐβαρύνατε D; gravastis (grabastis) d; adgravastis Ir[iii.12,3]; onerastis et negastis Aug[pec. mer. i, 52 [see note 1]]; cf. Ephr[(p398)]: sprevistis et negastis[see note 2]] ἠρνήσασθε h cett ᾐτήσατε D[see note 3]

Various explanations for the ἐβαρύνατε of the D-text have been offered. Is it used merely to avoid the repetition of ἠρνήσασθε in two successive verses (B-text, vv. 13, 14)?[4] This can hardly be an adequate explanation; for D to use ἠρνήσασθε here would not be exact repetition, since the D-text of the preceding verse already has ἀπηρνήσασθε.[5]

Harris explained the variants here as having arisen through a complex process involving the misreading of a Greek marginal note, translation of this misreading into Latin, and retranslation into another Greek word, which in turn gave rise to various succeeding Latin translations.[6] Certainly the suggestion of an alteration for tendentious reasons is simpler than all this!

Each of the various mistranslation or misreading explanations seems to have met its sufficient refutation, often at the hands of an exponent of another. On the Hebrew/Aramaic side, Nestle's view, followed by Blass,[7] that כִּפַרְתֶּם, 'you denied', was wrongly copied as כִּבַּרְתֶּם, 'you weighed down, oppressed',[8] was refuted by Torrey, who said that neither Hebrew word could plausibly be given the required meaning. Torrey's own explanation is that the (alleged) Aramaic editor rendered ἠρνήσασθε by

---

[1] Migne reads *inhonorastis*, but cf. *Corpus Scriptorum Eccl. Lat.* LX (August. VIII, 1), p. 49, for manuscript evidence for *onerastis*; and see A. Merk, 'Der heilige Ephraem und die Apostelgeschichte', *ZKT*, XLVIII (1924), 464; Zahn, *Urausgabe*, p. 38.

[2] See Merk, *ZKT*, XLVIII (1924), 462-4.

[3] On the distinction between αἰτεῖν and αἰτεῖσθαι, see J. H. Moulton, *A Grammar of New Testament Greek*, vol. I, *Prolegomena* (Edinburgh, 1908), pp. 106f.

[4] As it is explained by W. L. Knox, *St Paul and the Church of Jerusalem* (Cambridge, 1925), p. xxi, and Bruce, *Acts*'[52], p. 109.

[5] There is no difference in the meaning of the simple and compound forms: H. Riesenfeld, 'The Meaning of the Verb ἀρνεῖσθαι', *Coniect. neotest.* XI (1947), 208. [6] Harris, *Codex Bezae*, pp. 162f.

[7] F. Blass, *Philology of the Gospels* (London, 1898), pp. 194ff.

[8] E. Nestle, 'Einige Beobachtungen zum Codex Bezae', *TSK*, LXIX (1896), 103; Idem, 'Some Observations on the Codex Bezae', *Exp*, V, 2 (1895), 237f. Quoted, apparently with approval, by Williams, *Alterations*, p. 81.

כַּדְבְתּוּן, 'you denied, declared false', which was wrongly copied as כַּבְדתּוּן, which, he says, 'could only be translated (regarded as a Hebraism) by the Greek ἐβαρύνατε'.[1] F. F. Bruce says it is by no means certain that this last equivalent is a possible one, and suggests that the Aramaic 'Aph'el אַכְבֵּדְתּוּן would more likely translate ἐβαρύνατε.[2]

As to Syriac influence, W. W. Harvey suggested that ἠρνήσασθε was translated by ܟܦܪ which was misread as ܟܒܪ.[3] This was adopted by Chase[4] and, with modifications, by Nestle,[5] but rejected by Ropes as less probable than viewing ἐβαρύνατε as a retranslation from the Latin. Ropes confesses, however, that even then the origin of the reading (now in the Latin) is unexplained.[6] (He does not adopt the complex process put forth by Harris.)

Must, then, the conclusion of Ropes be final, that no good explanation can be given for ἐβαρύνατε? Perhaps so, but another suggestion will not be out of order. In view of the fact that the D-text does not so lightly excuse the Jews' evil deed in *v.* 17, could the D-text here be saying (through Peter) that the Jews not merely said 'no' (ἀρνεῖσθαι) to Jesus' release, as in B, but as if with a vengeance they took positive action against him, they 'weighed down', 'oppressed', or 'tormented' (βαρύνειν) him by their request for Barabbas and their killing of Jesus?[7]

---

[1] Torrey, *Documents*, pp. 114, 145.

[2] Bruce, *Acts*[52], p. 109. Black, *Aramaic Approach*, does not discuss this passage, but see M. Wilcox, *The Semitisms of Acts* (Oxford, 1965), pp. 139–41.

[3] W. W. Harvey, *Sancti Irenaei*... (Cambridge, 1857), II, 55, n. 3.

[4] Chase, *Old Syriac Element*, p. 38. Quoted, apparently with approval, by Klijn, *Survey*, p. 28.

[5] Nestle, *Exp*, v, 2 (1895), 238. Ropes, *Text*, pp. ccxliv (n. 1), 28, rejects Nestle's view as improbable.

[6] Ropes, *Text*, p. 28.

[7] Or 'overburdened' or 'overloaded', as the aorist active is used in Plutarch, *Moralia*, vol. II, 127 Q; cf. Ezek. xxvii. 25, etc for the passive in that sense. It is used of an injury in *Iliad* v, 664. See other references in H. G. Liddell and R. Scott, *A Greek-English Lexicon* (Oxford, 1940). In the New Testament βαρύνειν does not occur, except in a variant of Lk xxi. 34, where D H Methodius Bas Cyr have βαρυνθῶσιν instead of βαρηθῶσιν, and in a variant of Acts xxviii. 27, where ℵ* has ἐβαρύνθη instead of ἐπαχύνθη; cf. *gig* (D *def*). Βαρύνειν is replaced by βαρεῖν in later Greek; thus, while βαρύνειν is frequent in LXX (mostly passive), βαρεῖν is not (*bis*, both passive); in New Testament βαρεῖν is common, though always in the passive

In this connection, notice the small variants of D in the preceding verse:

Acts iii. 13

B	D
ὁ θεὸς Ἀβραὰμ καὶ Ἰσαὰκ	ὁ θεὸς Ἀβραὰμ καὶ θεὸς Ἰσαὰκ
καὶ Ἰακώβ,	καὶ θεὸς Ἰακώβ,
ὁ θεὸς τῶν πατέρων ἡμῶν,	ὁ θεὸς τῶν πατέρων ἡμῶν,
ἐδόξασεν τὸν παῖδα αὐτοῦ	ἐδόξασεν τὸν παῖδα αὐτοῦ
Ἰησοῦν,	Ἰησοῦν Χριστόν,
ὃν ὑμεῖς μὲν	ὃν ὑμεῖς
παρεδώκατε	παρεδώκατε εἰς κρίσιν
καὶ ἠρνήσασθε	καὶ ἀπηρνήσασθε αὐτὸν
κατὰ πρόσωπον Πειλάτου,	κατὰ πρόσωπον Πειλάτου,
κρείναντος	τοῦ κρείναντος,
ἐκείνου ἀπολύειν.	ἐκείνου ἀπολύειν αὐτὸν θέλοντος.

line 6: ημεις

θεός (second and third) D d 𝔓[74] ℵ A C pr vg cop geo Ir[iii.12,3] om h cett
Χριστόν D d eth[pp] h[vid[see note 1]]] om Ἰησοῦν Χριστόν cod.ard Ir[iii.12,3]
μέν cett h] om D d 1 33 69 383 sy[p] sa
εἰς κρίσιν (κριτήριον E) D d E h p sy[hmg] Ir[iii.12,3]
ἀπηρνήσασθε D; abnegastis gig p*; (negastis h)
αὐτόν D d E P 614 383 462 sy[p, h] sa Chr] om h
τοῦ D* (om D²) d; τοῦ κρείναντος ἐκείνου] om Ir[iii.12,3] (h)
αὐτὸν θέλοντος D (θέλοντος om D²) d h eth Ir[iii.12,3] Ephr[(p398) et cat(p399)]
Hier[esai 52] (cf. Chr[9, 80])

Χριστόν here may well be more than D's usual full form of Jesus' name. When the D-text gives a longer form of the name of Jesus, as it does some twenty-one times in Acts [in i. 21; ii. 38; iv. 33; v. 42; viii. 16; x. 48; xi. 20; xiii. 33; xv. 11; xvi. 31; xviii. 5; xix. 5; xx. 21; xxi. 13; and within larger D-variants only: vi. 8; xiv. 10; xvi. 4; xviii. 8; and in the 'Western' text (D def) of ix. 40; possibly viii. 35 (D def)], it always brings the

(except, of course, in Acts iii. 14 D). (See further, Schrenk, *TWNT*, I, 556 f., and nn. 1, 2.)

For uses of the word in the sense of treating someone harshly or being angry with him, see the classical and papyri references given by A. C. Clark, *Acts*, p. 339. For the sense of to torment, molest, or harass, trouble, cf. Nahum iii. 15; II Macc. ix. 9. (See Schrenk, *TWNT*, I, 557.)

[1] In h, a small lacuna follows ihm; it presumably read [xpm qu]em. Cf. iii. 20 in h, which has ihm xpm.

THE JEWS AND JESUS

title to its fullest expression, ὁ κύριος Ἰησοῦς Χριστός, with but two exceptions (iii. 13; vii. 55).[1] Verse 13 is one exception, and it is tempting to see in this variant some special purpose for the additional Χριστός alone. Moreover, in the two other places in Acts where ὁ ἅγιος παῖς Ἰησοῦς occurs, D has nothing additional to Ἰησοῦς (both instances occur in prayer to God: iv. 27, 30; cf. iii. 26).[2]

What, then, does this Χριστόν variant mean? It is apparent that the ignorance which excused the Jews was a failure to recognize that Jesus is Χριστός.[3] The D-text, however, minimizes the excuse based on this ignorance in the passages just discussed (iii. 17; xiii. 27; cf. xvii. 30). It is, moreover, precisely Jesus as Χριστός that D's reading in iii. 13 emphasizes. (That the messiahship of Jesus is the point in this section is clear also from iii. 18, 20, and from the messianic terms in iii. 14: τὸν ἅγιον καὶ δίκαιον.)[4] The Jews, therefore, says the D-text, did or should have recognized this fact of messiahship (in some sense), and if they did not, they are culpable.

Ὁ θεὸς...ἐδόξασεν τὸν παῖδα αὐτοῦ Ἰησοῦν Χριστόν in D should perhaps be read, then, 'God...exalted his servant Jesus *as* Christ (or *to be* Christ)', in the way that δοξάζειν is used in Hebrews v. 5, although there the copulative verb is retained: Οὕτως καὶ ὁ Χριστὸς οὐχ ἑαυτὸν ἐδόξασεν γενηθῆναι ἀρχιερέα...;[5] compare Acts iii. 20 (B and D): '...that he may send the Christ appointed for you, (namely) Jesus' (ἀποστείλῃ τὸν προκεχειρισμένον ὑμῖν Χριστὸν Ἰησοῦν). The εἰς κρίσιν of D merely explains more precisely the meaning of παρεδώκατε, emphas-

---

[1] vii. 55 is obviously a special case since here is a change from the usual order: (Stephen)...εἶδε δόξαν θεοῦ καὶ Ἰησοῦν **τὸν κύριον** ἐκ δεξιῶν τοῦ θεοῦ ἑστῶτα.... Shorter forms of the name do occur within material peculiar to the D-text, but these really do not apply because there is no point of comparison: see τοῦ κυρίου Ἰησοῦ in xviii. 4; Ἰησοῦ alone in xvii. 31; xix. 14; xx. 25; Ἰησοῦν Χριστόν occurs in the 'Western' text (D *def*) of viii. 37; cf. sy[h] of xxviii. 31.

[2] Incidentally, does D read νεανίσκον in Acts xx. 12 (instead of παῖδα) because παῖς is a *terminus technicus*?

[3] Jacquier, *Actes*, pp. 108f.; see above, pp. 47f.

[4] Bruce, *Acts*'52, p. 109; Haenchen, *Apostelgeschichte*, p. 166. The context of xiii. 27 reveals the same emphasis there.

[5] The word does not occur in the NT with a double accusative, though it does in classical literature with its usual meaning of 'think', 'suppose' (see Liddell-Scott-Jones, *ad loc.*).

izing the fact that the Jews delivered Jesus to Pilate's judgement,[1] that is, they delivered him to the Romans.[2] They thought this would be a judgement of death (cf. Lk xxiv. 20: ...παρέδωκαν αὐτὸν...εἰς κρίμα θανάτου...),[3] but Pilate wished to release him (D: ἐκείνου ἀπολύειν **αὐτὸν θέλοντος**).[4] Thus, the Jews were forced to more drastic action, and it is here that D's ἐβαρύνατε is pertinent—they *oppressed* Jesus.

The whole D-passage (iii. 13–14) would then mean:

God...exalted his servant Jesus *as Christ*, whom you delivered *to judgement*, and you denied *him* (i.e. God's Χριστός) before Pilate, who, when he had given judgement, wished to release him. But you (in contrast to Pilate's decision and wish to release Jesus)[5] *oppressed* the Holy and Righteous One.

Thus, the entire picture here of the Jews' relationship to Jesus' condemnation is sharper in D, with more emphasis on the Jews' responsibility, and on their more direct and hostile action against him.

The context of Acts xiii. 27 is of a similar nature:

Acts xiii. 28–9

B	D
...καὶ μηδεμίαν αἰτίαν θανάτου εὑρόντες ᾐτήσαντο Πειλᾶτον ἀναιρεθῆναι αὐτόν. ὡς δὲ ἐτέλεσαν πάντα τὰ γεγραμμένα περὶ αὐτοῦ,	28. ...καὶ μηδεμίαν αἰτίαν θανάτου εὑρόντες ἐν αὐτῷ, κρείναντες αὐτὸν παρέδωκαν Πειλάτῳ ἵνα εἰς ἀναίρεσιν·
	29. ὡς δὲ ἐτέλουν πάντα τὰ περὶ αὐτοῦ γεγραμμένα εἰσίν, ᾐτοῦντο τὸν Πειλᾶτον τοῦτον μὲν σταυρῶσαι καὶ ἐπιτυχόντες πάλιν καὶ
καθελόντες ἀπὸ τοῦ ξύλου ἔθηκαν εἰς μνημεῖον.	καθελόντες ἀπὸ τοῦ ξύλου καὶ ἔθηκαν εἰς μνημεῖον.

28. ἐν αὐτῷ D *d* 614 *gig c t* vg cop eth geo sy[h]*
κρείναντες (+autem *d*) D* *d*

[1] *Beginnings*, IV, 36.
[2] In Lk the *terminus technicus*, παραδιδόναι, means to deliver to men, to the Romans (Haenchen, *Apostelgeschichte*, p. 165).
[3] D here has τοῦτον before παρέδωκαν.
[4] Note that in both B and D the guilt is removed from Pilate and placed entirely upon the Jews (see Haenchen, *Apostelgeschichte*, p. 166, n. 1).
[5] *Beginnings*, IV, 36; Bruce, *Acts*'52, p. 108.

παρέδωκαν Πειλάτῳ D* d
ἵνα εἰς ἀναίρεσιν D* (ut interficeretur *gig d*; *sim* vg bohem sy^p)
29. ἐτέλουν D*
εἰσίν D* (*d*: omnia quae...scripta sunt)
ἠτοῦντο...μὲν (*om* μέν *d*) σταυρῶσαι D* *d* cop^G67] σταυρωθέντος δὲ ἠτοῦντο τὸν Πιλᾶτον ἀπὸ τοῦ ξύλου καθελεῖν αὐτόν sy^hmg
καὶ ἐπιτυχόντες πάλιν D* *d* (cf. cop^G67); ἐπέτυχον sy^hmg
καί *ante* καθελόντες D* *d* sy^hmg
καί *ante* ἔθηκαν D* *d*

The textual problem here is complex,[1] and it must be considered carefully before basing conclusions on a given variant. Apart from minor points, however, the view of A. C. Clark that D and sy^hmg supplement one another in *v.* 29 seems admirably to account for the available evidence and, at the same time, to provide a meaningful and consistent passage. His 'Western' text is as follows:

> 29. ὡς δὲ ἐτέλουν
> πάντα τὰ περὶ αὐτοῦ γεγραμμένα,
> ἠτοῦντο τὸν Πιλᾶτον τοῦτον μὲν σταυρῶσαι
> ....
> σταυρωθέντος δὲ ἠτοῦντο τὸν Πιλᾶτον
> ἀπὸ τοῦ ξύλου καθελεῖν αὐτόν·
> καὶ ἐπιτυχόντες πάλιν καὶ
> καθελόντες ἀπὸ τοῦ ξύλου
> ἔθηκαν εἰς μνημεῖον.

Clark is of the opinion that a δέ-clause has dropped out (line 4),[2] and he accepts Bornemann's conjecture: τὸν δὲ Βαραββᾶν ἀπολῦσαι.

The events mentioned in the B-text are these: (1) in *v.* 27*b*, the Jews condemned Jesus, thus fulfilling the scriptures; (2) though Jesus was innocent, the Jews asked Pilate to have him killed; (3) when they had fulfilled all that was written, they took him down from the tree and laid him in a tomb. The D-text is somewhat different: (1) though Jesus was innocent,

---
[1] For further details, see Ropes, *Text*, pp. 261–3; *Beginnings*, IV, 153; A. C. Clark, *Acts*, p. 356.
[2] *Ibid.*

the Jews condemned him;[1] (2) they delivered him to Pilate to be killed;[2] (3) when they had fulfilled all that was written, they asked Pilate to crucify him; (4) after Jesus had been crucified, they asked Pilate for his body and, obtaining this second request (πάλιν), they took him down from the tree and placed him in a tomb.[3]

Exactly how does the D-text differ? The D-text shows more clearly Jesus' trial before the Council, which then 'delivered him to Pilate' (v. 28). This reading of παρέδωκαν Πειλάτῳ εἰς ἀναίρεσιν shows that the Council already wanted to put Jesus to death, but could not (as in John xviii. 31) and so took him to Pilate for that end. This text, then, shows the Jews as more eager to handle this case themselves[4] (cf. the 'Western' text of Acts xxiv. 6 below, p. 152). The D-text next records the more concrete request to 'crucify him', recalling the scene of the violently fanatical mob in the Gospels. In D, Paul's speech clearly lays stress on the mode of Jesus' death: σταυρῶσαι, a word not used in B in this passage.[5] After this comes another mention of the crucifixion and the second request to Pilate.

The conclusion to be drawn is that the D-text shows the Jews in a more active role in the death of Jesus than does B, stressing the trial before the Council and their desire to kill Jesus, and their subsequent delivery of him to Pilate, asking that he be crucified. Fascher states that this is evidence of a tendentious interest in D (in the direction taken in the Fourth Gospel) which has in view a stress on the guilt of the Jews.[6]

[1] This is true whether one accepts the κρίναντες of v. 27, or the κρίναντες of v. 28 (as does Ropes, *Text*, pp. 262 f.) or both (as does A. C. Clark) as part of the 'Western' text.
[2] That παρέδωκαν Πειλάτῳ was 'Western' is not doubted. Ἵνα may represent ἵνα ἀναιρῶσιν, as attested by several versions, but the 'Western' text was probably εἰς ἀναίρεσιν (see Ropes, *Text*, p. 263). On Latin influence, see E. Haenchen, 'Schriftzitate und Textüberlieferung in der Apostelgeschichte', *ZTK*, LI (1954), 155, n. 1; on Aramaic influence, see Wilcox, *Semitisms*, pp. 118–20.
[3] In these last two events, Ropes, *Text*, pp. 261 f., follows sy[hmg] rather than D, so that his 'Western' text has only one request of Pilate. Πάλιν is, therefore, a problem to Ropes, and now it finds added support in cop[G67]. For a view similar to Ropes on v. 29, see Torrey, *Documents*, p. 144.
[4] Fascher, *Textgeschichte*, p. 43, n. 1.
[5] Σταυροῦν occurs in Acts only in ii. 36 and iv. 10.
[6] Fascher, *Textgeschichte*, p. 43, n. 1.

THE JEWS AND JESUS

Acts ii. 23

B	D
..., τοῦτον τῇ ὡρισμένῃ βουλῇ καὶ προγνώσει τοῦ θεοῦ ἔκδοτον διὰ χειρὸς ἀνόμων προσπήξαντες ἀνείλατε,...	..., τοῦτον τῇ ὡρισμένῃ βουλῇ καὶ προγνώσει τοῦ θεοῦ ἔκδοτον λαβόντες διὰ χειρὸς ἀνόμων προσπήξαντες ἀνείλατε,...

λαβόντες D *d* ℵ^c C³ E P 614 383 81 sa[see note 1] sy^h Eus^{ecl 78} Chr^{9, 57} Thdot^{anc 433} Cosm⁵⁰³ Cyr^{4, 403} Bede^{retr 105}] *om* Ir^{iii. 12, 2} *cett*

The guilt of the Jews in the crucifixion of Jesus is clear enough in both the B- and D-texts here: ...προσπήξαντες ἀνείλατε. The question, however, concerns the meaning of D's λαβόντες. In the B-text διὰ χειρὸς ἀνόμων is to be construed with προσπήξαντες:[2] 'This one, delivered up by the appointed will and foreknowledge of God, you did slay, having nailed (him) up through the hand(s) of lawless men.' Or, it would be possible also to take it with ἔκδοτον: 'This one, by the appointed will and foreknowledge of God, delivered over through the hand(s) of lawless men, you nailed up and did slay.' The phrase would then be parallel to that in Mark xiv. 41, παραδίδοται εἰς τὰς χεῖρας τῶν ἁμαρτωλῶν.[3] Ἄνομοι can mean 'wicked' or simply 'heathen', i.e. the Romans.[4] Conzelmann, however, has a suggestive interpretation of ἄνομοι. While affirming that originally, in Luke's source, ἄνομοι referred to the Gentiles, he thinks that Luke was unacquainted with this Jewish use of the term and gave it a new meaning. (This view is based partly on Luke's use of ἄνομοι in Lk xxii. 37, where it means criminals, not non-Jews.) Thus, in Luke's use of ἄνομοι in Acts ii. 23 it refers, he says, to the Jews.[5] On this view the phrase, διὰ χειρὸς ἀνόμων, would seem to allude to the leaders of the Jews. So much for the B-text.

[1] See Zahn, *Apostelgeschichte*, I, 112, n. 66, for the view that sa follows a text like D.
[2] Haenchen, *Apostelgeschichte*, p. 143, n. 11.
[3] Bruce, *Acts*'⁵², p. 91, notes that, according to Torrey, the Aramaic behind these two phrases would be the same.
[4] The corresponding Hebrew term is often used of the Romans in Jewish literature: see *Beginnings*, IV, 23; Haenchen, *Apostelgeschichte*, p. 143, n. 10; Bruce, *Acts*'⁵², pp. 91 f.
[5] Conzelmann, *Mitte der Zeit*⁴, p. 84; Eng, trans. pp. 90–2. See his further evidence there.

ANTI-JUDAIC TENDENCIES IN ACTS

Now, with D's λαβόντες, the text *would seem* to say: 'This one...you laid hold of and, having nailed (him) up by the hand(s) of lawless men, you did slay.'[1] Or, perhaps διὰ χειρὸς ἀνόμων should now be construed with the added λαβόντες: 'This one...you took (*or possibly* received) through the hand(s) of lawless men...and did slay.' In either case the difference between B and D is not great, though λαβόντες does place some added emphasis on the direct action of the Jews against Jesus.

However, in 1715 Georgius Raphelius cited a passage from Josephus and one from Polybius to illustrate the ἔκδοτον λαβόντες of Acts ii. 23 in Greek writers,[2] and these two parallels illuminate the meaning of the D-reading here. Modern commentators have overlooked these passages, though Lake and Cadbury refer to the Josephus passage in connection with the ἔκδοτον of the B-text, but fail to mention its further parallel to the λαβόντες of the D-text.[3]

Polybius, *Histories*, XXVI, 2. 13 (Loeb, XXIV, 9. 13)

[οἱ 'Αχαιοί]...οὐ μόνον τὴν χώραν αὐτῶν καταφθεῖραι πᾶσαν ἀδίκων, ἀλλὰ καὶ τοὺς ἐπιφανεστάτους τῶν πολιτῶν, οὓς μὲν φυγαδεῦσαι, τινὰς δ' αὐτῶν **ἐκδότους λαβόντας**, αἰκισαμένους πᾶσαν αἰκίαν, ἀποκτεῖναι, διότι προεκαλοῦντο περὶ τῶν ἀμφισβητουμένων ἐπὶ 'Ρωμαίους.

The Achaeans...not only most unjustly devastated the whole of Messenia, but sent into exile some of its most distinguished citizens; and, *when others were delivered up to them*, put them to death after inflicting every variety of torture on them, just because they had appealed to Rome to judge the dispute.   (Loeb)

[1] Following such passages as John xviii. 31, xix. 6: λάβετε αὐτὸν ὑμεῖς..., or Ev Petri 3: οἱ δὲ λαβόντες τὸν κύριον.... See Zahn, *Apostelgeschichte*, I, 112, n. 66. Chase, *Old Syriac Element*, p. 19, says John xix. 6 is the source (through the Syriac) of D's reading; Chase's method of argument here is one of many which make Harnack's statement understandable: 'Verunglückt ist die Untersuchung von Chase' (*Studien*, I, 32).

[2] G. Raphelius, *Annotationes philologicae in Novum Testamentum ex Polybio & Arriano collectae* (Hamburg, 1715), p. 305. Raphelius has ἔκδοτον λαβόντες in his reading of Acts ii. 23. His only comment, after quoting Josephus and Polybius here, is: Bene graeca ergo sunt haec ἔκδοτον λαβόντες. J. J. Wettstein, Η ΚΑΙΝΗ ΔΙΑΘΗΚΗ, *Novum Testamentum Graecum* (Amsterdam, 1751–2), II, 467, also cites these passages.

[3] *Beginnings*, IV, 23.

60

Josephus, *Antiquities*, VI, 13. 9 (*or* VI, 316)

Σαοῦλος δὲ γνωρίσας τὴν τοῦ Δαυίδου φωνὴν καὶ μαθὼν ὅτι **λαβὼν αὐτὸν ἔκδοτον** ὑπὸ τοῦ ὕπνου καὶ τῆς τῶν φυλασσόντων ἀμελείας οὐκ ἀπέκτεινεν, ἀλλ' ἐφείσατο δικαίως ἂν αὐτὸν ἀνελών,...

Then Saul, when he recognized the voice of David and learned that *though he had had him at his mercy*, being asleep and neglected by his guards, he had yet not slain him but spared the life which he might justly have taken,... (Loeb)

...and understood, that *when he had him in his power*... (Whiston)

The combination, λαβὼν αὐτὸν ἔκδοτον, in Josephus (cf. τινὰς...ἐκδότους λαβόντας in Polybius) is exactly that in Acts ii. 23: τοῦτον...ἔκδοτον λαβόντες.[1] In Josephus it means 'to have had him in a position of having been delivered over', or, as we would say, 'to have had him at his mercy'. D in Acts should then be read: 'By the appointed will and foreknowledge of God you had this one [Jesus] at your mercy (*or* in your power) and you crucified and killed (him) through the hand(s) of lawless men', or, construing διὰ χειρὸς ἀνόμων with λαβόντες, '...you had this one at your mercy through the hand(s) of lawless men and you crucified and killed (him)'. The D-text, consequently, places a greater responsibility upon the Jews, emphasizing the fact that they (like David in Josephus, or like Pilate) had a choice, and that they exercised this freedom and decided to have Jesus crucified.

A reading of some interest in Acts x. 39, though not found in D or Irenaeus, also emphasizes the role of the Jews in the crucifixion of Jesus: Peter, in his speech before Cornelius, reportedly refers to all that which Jesus did, ἔν τε τῇ χώρᾳ τῶν Ἰουδαίων καὶ Ἱερουσαλήμ· ὃν καὶ ἀνεῖλαν κρεμάσαντες ἐπὶ ξύλου (B and D, with Ir). Some 'Western' witnesses, however, read 'whom *the Jews rejected and* put to death...' (ὅν] + ἀπεδοκίμασαν οἱ Ἰουδαῖοι καὶ *l l* cop^G67 sy^h* sy^msK; cf. *p**; *p*² and sy^p have *Iudei*). The witness now of *l*, cop^G67, and sy^msK added to sy^h*, with *t* and *p**, allows a more confident assertion that the early 'Western' reading is preserved in these manuscripts.

There is another side to the D-text's portrayal of a more hostile Jewish attitude toward Jesus, namely, that the D-text at

---

[1] Notice the ἀνείλατε in Acts and the ἀνελών in Josephus; also the ἀποκτεῖναι in both Polybius and Josephus.

the same time devotes greater attention to the person of Jesus. This is evident in the frequency with which the fullest form of the name (or better, title), ὁ κύριος Ἰησοῦς Χριστός, is found deeply rooted in the early 'Western' tradition. The instances are as follows, showing in each case only the additional words of the D-text, with their attestation, which are necessary to bring the title to its full form of expression:

(1) Acts i. 21 Χριστός D *d* cop[G67] sy[h] eth Aug[b]

(2) ii. 38 τοῦ κυρίου D *d* E 614 minn *p r* cop[G67] sa eth arm geo dut sy[p] (but sy[p] *om* Χριστοῦ) sy[h] Aug Ambr Bas[2,114] Cypr[ep 73, 17] Cyr[4, 893] Cyr[hr 47] Lcf Thdrt[ter] Epiph[27] Vigil] *om gig* Ir[iii. 12, 2] (Ir also *om* Χριστοῦ) Aug $\frac{2}{11}$ Hier *al*

(3) iv. 33 Χριστοῦ D *d* E א A *r* vg eth[ro] arm geo] *om* B P S 614 *gig p q t* sa sy[h] Ir[iii. 12, 5(6)] Aug[serm 356] Thphyl (Note: whether Χριστοῦ is a 'Western' reading here is not clear from the evidence.)

(4) v. 42 κύριον (+ἡμῶν Lcf) D *d gig h p* sa eth[pp] sy[p] Lcf[234]] *om* bo Ir[iii. 12, 5(6)] (but Ir reads τὸν Χριστὸν Ἰησοῦν τὸν υἱὸν τοῦ θεοῦ)

(5) vi. 8 τοῦ (*om* D) κυρίου Ἰησοῦ Χριστοῦ D *d* E 614 minn g_2 *gig p t* sa Aug Gaud Bede[retr 123]; Ἰησοῦ Χριστοῦ *h*; τοῦ κυρίου sy[h]*

(6) viii. 16 Χριστοῦ D *d* (H L P S) 383 vg[codd] cop[G67] eth (but eth *om* κυρίου) dut Didy[tri 3, 41]

(7) Possibly viii. 35, where no 'Western' witnesses are extant except cop[G67], which, with sa, reads 'the Lord Jesus Christ' for B's 'Jesus' (*p om* Iesum).

(8) ix. 40 (D *def*) τοῦ κυρίου ἡμῶν Ἰησοῦ Χριστοῦ *gig l p* (*cod.ard*) vg[cod] sa cop[G67] arm sy[h]* Ambr[jos 3, 489] Spec; Ἰησοῦ Χριστοῦ geo vg[cod] Cypr[op et eleem 6] Cass (cf. Acta Ioannis[22])

(9) x. 48 τοῦ κυρίου D *d* minn *p* vg[s, cl] arm[codd] geo sy[p] dut

(10) xi. 20 Χριστόν D *d* minn *c w* eth[pp]

(11) xiii. 33 τὸν κύριον...Χριστόν D *d* sa Ambr[fid]; τὸν κύριον ἡμῶν Ἰησοῦν 614 sy[h]* Hil[27 et 42]

(12) xiv. 10 τοῦ κυρίου Ἰησοῦ Χριστοῦ D *d* C E 614 383 minn sa arm geo cop[G67] sy[p] sy[hmg] Ambr Ir[iii. 12, 9(12)] Cass Bede[63] (Thphyl[b]); (*h*: ihu nostri dni fili di); (Ἰησοῦ Χριστοῦ minn *p w* vg[codd] prov)

(13) xv. 11 Χριστοῦ D *d* C minn *gig l* vg[s, cl] bo arm eth[pp] geo sy[p] Ir[iii. 12, 14(17)] Aug[pec. mer]] *om* Tert[pud 21]

(14) xvi. 4 τὸν κύριον Ἰησοῦν Χριστόν D *d* sy[hmg] (Ephr[(p428)]?)

(15) xvi. 31 Χριστόν D *d* C E H L P S 614 383 sa arm eth geo sy[p, h] Chr[9, 305 et 3, 186] Thdrt[5, 1150]

(16) xviii. 5 κύριον D *d* 383] *om* 614 *gig* sa

(17) xviii. 8 τοῦ κυρίου ἡμῶν (*om* ἡμῶν 614 383 sy[h]*) Ἰησοῦ Χριστοῦ D *d* 614 383 sy[h]*] *om* κυρίου *h*

(18) xix. 5 Χριστοῦ D d (𝔓³⁸?) 614 383 gig sa arab eth^pp sy^p sy^h* Hier^lucif Petil Ambr^spir 1, 3

(19) xx. 21 Χριστοῦ D d 𝔓⁷⁴ℵ A C E minn vg bo arm eth^pp geo sy^p Chr⁹, ³⁶⁹ Thphyl^b] om gig sa eth^ro sy^h Lcf²⁴¹ cett

(20) xxi. 13 Χριστοῦ D d C minn gig arm sy^p Tert^fug 6 et scorp ¹⁵ = ⅔ Ambst Aug^ps Cyr^bis Thdrt^bis Hier

Many of these passages appear in the discussion at various points, and only a summary treatment is necessary here. It is at least of interest to observe the context of these variants: i. 21 refers to the ministry of Jesus; xiii. 33 and iv. 33 speak of his resurrection; ii. 38, viii. 16, x. 48, xix. 5 concern baptism in the name of the Lord Jesus Christ (ii. 38 and xix. 5 refer to the remission of sins, while the contexts of viii. 16 and x. 48 involve the Holy Spirit); xvi. 31, xviii. 8, xx. 21 refer to faith and xv. 11 to salvation through grace; v. 42, viii. 35, xi. 20, xviii. 5, xxi. 13 concern apostolic preaching and witnessing; and vi. 8, ix. 40, xiv. 10 have reference to signs and wonders done by the apostles. Several of these (ii. 38; viii. 16; x. 48; xix. 5; xxi. 13) involve 'the name of our Lord Jesus Christ', with the D-text providing some seven more instances of this phrase than does B, namely vi. 8, ix. 17 (ἐν τῷ ὀνόματι Ἰησοῦ Χριστοῦ h vg²ᶜᵒᵈᵈ cop^G67 Chr); ix. 40, xiv. 10, xviii. 4 (ἐντιθεὶς τὸ ὄνομα τοῦ κυρίου Ἰησοῦ D d gig h cod.ard q w prov sy^hmg); xviii. 8, and xix. 14 (ἐπικαλεῖσθαι τὸ ὄνομα D d 𝔓³⁸ w tepl sy^hmg Cass), which indicates that the 'name of the Lord Jesus Christ' was of special significance for the D-text.

The contexts of other so-called Christological variants in D show that they can be understood as emphasizing the messiahship of Jesus: iii. 13 (Χριστόν D d h? eth^pp) and ix. 20 (D def; ὁ Χριστός h l sa cop^G67 Ir^iii. 12, 9(11) et cat Spec); or as emphasizing Jesus as Son of God: viii. 37 (D def; πιστεύω τὸν υἱὸν τοῦ θεοῦ εἶναι τὸν Ἰησοῦν Χριστόν with variation E minn gig l p r t cod.ard w vg^cl tepl cop^G67 arm geo sy^h* Aug Spec Ambst Ir^iii. 12, 8(10) et cat Thphyl^b Bede⁴²); or his future role as judge: xvii. 31 (Ἰησοῦ D d cod.ard Ir^iii. 12, 9(11)] om Aug); or as both Son of God and judge: xxviii. 31 ('saying that this is Christ Jesus the Son of God, through whom the whole world begins to be judged' with variation p q w dem tepl sy^h Spec; 'he alleged that Jesus Christ is the Son of God' Ephr^(p453)); or Jesus in his exaltation: vii. 55 (τὸν κύριον D d 614 h p cop^G67 sa] om Ir^iii. 12, 13(16)).

Others emphasize the forgiveness of sins *in him*: v. 31 (ἐν αὐτῷ D *d h p q* sa eth^ro Aug] *om* Ir^iii.12, 5(6)); or his exclusive power to heal: iv. 10 (ἐν ἄλλῳ δὲ οὐδενί with variation E *h* Cypr^test ii.16 Bede^retr sy^hmg] *om* D); or Jesus as one *in whom God is well pleased*: ix. 22 (D *def*; *gig h l p*); or in some other way: xx. 25 (τοῦ Ἰησοῦ D *d* sa; τοῦ κυρίου Ἰησοῦ *gig* Lcf).

A list of variants of this kind, with such strong 'Western' support in most cases, certainly reveals the central place which 'the Lord Jesus Christ' held in the thought of the D-text. Although Menoud surely understated the case when he said that these variants mentioning Jesus were 'neither numerous nor important', his suggestion that the D-text's titles for Jesus would be 'most offensive to the Jews, who considered Jesus neither as Christ nor as Lord',[1] is of definite interest. This statement provides a clue as to what very well may have been the motivation behind the heavy emphasis on Christology in the D-text—a dramatic affirmation of faith in Jesus as Christ over against Judaism.[2]

The portrayal of Jewish hostility toward Jesus and of Jewish responsibility for his death in the D-text reveals a clearly anti-Judaic attitude. On the other hand, the strong positive emphasis on Jesus as Lord and Christ turns the sword in the wound (so to speak), for by presenting Jesus in bold and heightened tones the heinousness of the Jews' action against him is even more strongly emphasized.

B. THE JEWS, GENTILES, AND CHRISTIANITY

The D-text of Acts contains numerous readings which concern the interplay between Judaism and Christianity, and the formulation of passages describing this confrontation, especially when Gentiles are involved, is the focal point of this part of the investigation. Variants portraying distinct attitudes of one of these groups toward another also are of major interest.

The very first textual variant in the book of Acts in Codex Bezae offers a hint of much that is to follow of the characteristic viewpoint of the D-text:

---

[1] Menoud, 'Western Text', p. 31.

[2] 'The basic factors in the existence of the Church are Christ and the Spirit' (Conzelmann, *Mitte der Zeit*⁴, p. 127; Eng. trans. p. 135).

THE JEWS, GENTILES, AND CHRISTIANITY

Acts i. 2

B	D
ἄχρι ἧς ἡμέρας	ἄχρι ἧς ἡμέρας
	ἀνελήμφθη
ἐντειλάμενος τοῖς ἀποστόλοις	ἐντειλάμενος τοῖς ἀποστόλοις
διὰ πνεύματος ἁγίου	διὰ πνεύματος ἁγίου
οὓς ἐξελέξατο	οὓς ἐξελέξατο
ἀνελήμφθη·	
	καὶ ἐκέλευσε κηρύσσειν τὸ εὐαγγέλιον·

ἀνελήμφθη *ante* ἐντειλάμενος D *d* sa sy^p sy^hmg] *om* ἀνελήμφθη *gig t**
Aug^abc Vigil^var Eplu^(p004)
καὶ ἐκέλευσε D *d* sy^hmg Aug^abc Ephr^(p384)
κηρύσσειν τὸ εὐαγγέλιον D *d gig t cod.ard* sa cop^G67 sy^hmg Aug^abc
Vigil^var 733 Ephr^(p384) (Cf. Epistle of Barnabas v. 9; Tert^apol 21)

The additional words in D give content to the preceding ἐντειλάμενος τοῖς ἀποστόλοις, which has no direct object unless it is given in *v.* 4: '...not to depart from Jerusalem, but to wait for the promise..., the Holy Spirit'. The D-text, however, explains the verb sooner and differently; for D the content of the command is 'to preach the gospel'. This emphasis on the command to preach the gospel is present in the 'Western' text, moreover, whether one follows D or those witnesses which omit ἐντειλάμενος (or, in Latin, the first *praecepit*), for this word is really superfluous in D and could easily have entered by conflation. Thus, Corssen[1] took the text of Aug^ab(c) Vigil^var as representative of the original 'Western' tradition: *in die quo (qua) apostolos elegit per spiritum sanctum et praecepit* (Vigil *om et praecepit) praedicare euangelium.* Cf. Ephrem.

What is significant is that the setting here in Acts is similar to that in Lk xxiv. 43-53 (compare Lk xxiv. 47-52 with Acts i. 1-12: in both Jesus is instructing the disciples before he was taken from them; comparison particularly of Lk xxiv. 47-9 and Acts i. 4-5, 8, will show the connection). The many parallels (e.g. remain in Jerusalem, await the promise, power, witnesses,

---

[1] P. Corssen, *Der Cyprianische Text der Acta Apostolorum* (Berlin, 1892), p. 19, followed by Ropes, *Text*, pp. 256f.; *Beginnings*, IV, 3; V, 2f. Further on the textual problem in i. 2, see Ropes, *Text*, pp. 256-61; A. C. Clark, *Acts*, p. 336, Lake in *Beginnings*, V, 1-3; J. M. Creed, 'The Text and Interpretation of Acts i. 1-2', *JTS*, XXXV (1934), 176-82.

taken from them, returned to Jerusalem, etc.)[1] suggest that the D-text's καὶ ἐκέλευσε κηρύσσειν τὸ εὐαγγέλιον is an allusion to the κηρυχθῆναι of Lk xxiv. 47. Notice the context there (D): ...καὶ κηρυχθῆναι ἐπὶ τῷ ὀνόματι αὐτοῦ μετάνοιαν καὶ (B reads εἰς for καί) ἄφεσιν ἁμαρτιῶν ὡς (om B) ἐπὶ πάντα τὰ ἔθνη ἀρξαμένων (-μενοι B) ἀπὸ Ἱερουσαλήμ. On the basis of the allusion, the ἐπὶ πάντα τὰ ἔθνη here more fully interprets the meaning of the D-variant in Acts i. 2, so that the D-text already had in view the Gentile mission long before it becomes a reality in the B-text of Acts (where it begins with Cornelius).

This connection of universalism with prophecy, as here in Lk xxiv. 46-7, is good Lucan theology (cf. Lk ii. 32; Acts x. 42-3; xiii. 47).[2] D's ἐκέλευσε κηρύσσειν τὸ εὐαγγέλιον in Acts i. 2, when seen in its relation to Lk xxiv. 47, has as its background, then, this same connection, and its presence in the D-text reveals an even more intense universalism than is to be found in the B-text of Acts generally. This is an instance where the D-text seems to 'out-Luke' Luke[3] in its emphasis on universalism— a universalism which, in D, will be brought into sharp relief over against the exclusivism of Judaism by the Jewish opposition it creates. This, however, is to anticipate somewhat the argument of the present section, but it will serve to clarify the approach taken, although the proof obviously must await the detailed evidence and be judged alone on its merits.

A similarly dual tendency—at once a positive and a negative emphasis—is much in evidence in the D-version of Peter's speech on Pentecost (Acts ii. 14-40), and Acts ii. 17 provides the focal point for it:

Acts ii. 17

LXX (Joel ii. 28)	B	D
καὶ ἔσται	καὶ ἔσται	ἔσται
μετὰ ταῦτα	μετὰ ταῦτα,	ἐν ταῖς ἐσχάταις ἡμέραις,
	λέγει ὁ θεός,	λέγει κύριος,

[1] See *Beginnings*, IV, 3, 5f.; V, 3.
[2] J. M. Creed, *The Gospel according to St Luke* (London, 1930), p. 301.
[3] The whole of the preceding section on 'The Jews and Jesus' provides another instance: while Luke already shows an inclination to blame the Jews for Jesus' death (thus Conzelmann), the D-text heightens this responsibility and also attributes to the Jews an even greater hostility toward Jesus.

THE JEWS, GENTILES, AND CHRISTIANITY

ἐκχεῶ ἀπὸ τοῦ πνεύ-	ἐκχεῶ ἀπὸ τοῦ πνεύ-	ἐκχεῶ ἀπὸ τοῦ πνεύ-
ματός μου	ματός μου	ματός μου
ἐπὶ πᾶσαν σάρκα,	ἐπὶ πᾶσαν σάρκα,	ἐπὶ πάσας σάρκας,
καὶ προφητεύσουσιν	καὶ προφητεύσουσιν	καὶ προφητεύσουσιν
οἱ υἱοὶ ὑμῶν	οἱ υἱοὶ ὑμῶν	οἱ υἱοὶ αὐτῶν
καὶ αἱ θυγατέρες ὑμῶν,	καὶ αἱ θυγατέρες ὑμῶν,	καὶ θυγατέρες αὐτῶν,
καὶ οἱ πρεσβύτεροι ὑμῶν	καὶ οἱ νεανίσκοι ὑμῶν	καὶ οἱ νεανίσκοι
ἐνύπνια ἐνυπνιασθήσονται	ὁράσεις ὄψονται,	ὁράσει ὄψονται,
καὶ οἱ νεανίσκοι ὑμῶν	καὶ οἱ πρεσβύτεροι ὑμῶν	καὶ οἱ πρεσβύτεροι
ὁράσεις ὄψονται.	ἐνυπνίοις ἐνυπνιασθήσονται.	ἐνυπνιασθήσονται,...

ἐν ταῖς ἐσχάταις ἡμέραις   D d ℵ A E P S 096 81 462 *gig* vg bo sy[p] Chr[9, 48] Ir[iii.12,1] Rebapt[369] Hil[962] Or Aug[ep 199] Tert[mcion v. 8] μετὰ ταῦτα LXX B 076 (sa) eth[pp] Aug ½ Cyr[lu]; μετὰ ταῦτα ἐν ταῖς ἐσχάταις ἡμέραις C minn arm
κύριος   D d E 242 *gig p* vg Ir[iii.12,1] Rebapt Hil
πάσας σάρκας   D* (πᾶσαν σάρκα D[A])
αὐτῶν (first)   D d *gig* Tert[mcion v. 8] Perpet Rebapt Hil Prisc
αὐτῶν (second)   D d *gig* Tert Rebapt Hil Prisc
ὑμῶν (third)]   eorum Prisc] *om* D d prov Rebapt
ὑμῶν (fourth)]   *om* D d E C*[vid] *p** Rebapt Prisc

The biblical quotation from Joel ii. 28 is altered by the D-text in a significant way in Peter's address to the Jews (cf. Acts ii. 5, 14, 22; proselytes are also mentioned, ii. 10). Incidentally, Lake and Cadbury's statement that the 'Western' text apparently assumes that the crowd at Pentecost consisted of pious foreigners, not Jews,[1] certainly is not the case; on the contrary, D's variants acquire their sharpness precisely because the address is to Jews. The first alteration, the change from μετὰ ταῦτα to ἐν ταῖς ἐσχάταις ἡμέραις (perhaps taken over, in D, from *v*. 18), may be only an attempt to adapt the quotation to the present situation,[2] but the other variants reveal another motive.

---

[1] *Beginnings*, iv, 21.
[2] It also reveals that D has an eschatology different from that of the B-text: see Haenchen, *ZTK*, LI (1954), 162. Note that in ii. 20 in D the sun was already darkened (D's μεταστρέφεται for μεταστραφήσεται *cett d*) (J. C. O'Neill, 'The Use of "Kyrios" in the Book of Acts', *SJT*, VIII, 1955, 160 and n. 5). Also, Acts in the 'Western' version may have ended on an eschatological note rather than an apologetic one: see *Beginnings*, IV, 349.

ANTI-JUDAIC TENDENCIES IN ACTS

As D. Plooij pointed out, the D-text did not want the promise of the Spirit's gifts to apply to the Jews, whom Peter was addressing, but wished to reserve them for Christians. It therefore twice alters ὑμῶν (first and second) to αὐτῶν and twice omits ὑμῶν (third and fourth). Thus, it is no longer 'your [i.e. the Jews'] sons and daughters' who will prophesy, but 'their sons and daughters'.[1] The gifts in this way are promised only to those who are baptized ἐν τῷ ὀνόματι τοῦ κυρίου ᾽Ιησοῦ Χριστοῦ (ii. 38).

F. H. Chase suggested that the ὑμῶν/αὐτῶν change arose from the confusion of ܒܢܝܟܘܢ (your-sons) and ܒܢܝܗܘܢ (their-sons). He cites an instance of the confusion of these two words in syp of I Cor. vii. 14 which reads 'their children', whereas the Greek has τὰ τέκνα ὑμῶν, and he gives another example from Acts xiv. 17, where syp has 'to them...their hearts' for the Greek ὑμῖν...τὰς καρδίας ὑμῶν.[2] To return to our case, observe, however, that no Syriac manuscript reads 'their sons' in Acts ii. 17, and that the examples, while showing that such confusion between suffixes is certainly a possible explanation, cannot be taken as proof in the case of Acts ii. 17. (See also on Acts ii. 47 below, pp. 77f.)

Those who read farther in Codex Bezae may think that this anti-Judaic position of the D-text is contradicted by a variant in ii. 33, where Peter, in referring to the Holy Spirit, says that the Lord 'has poured out *for you* [i.e. the Jews] that which you see and hear'. But the textual evidence is instructive:

B: ἐξέχεεν τοῦτο ὃ ὑμεῖς καὶ βλέπετε καὶ ἀκούετε.
D: ἐξέχεεν ὑμεῖν ὃ καὶ βλέπετε καὶ ἀκούετε.

τοῦτο 614 383 *gig* vg sy^{hmg} geo *cett*; + τὸ δῶρον E *c p r q t dem cor.vat* cod.ard* vg^s prov tepl sa arab sy^{p,h} Ir^{iii.12,2} Aug Hier Ambr Bede^{retr}] *om* D* *d*
ὑμεῖν ὃ D* *d*] in nos *p* prov] ὃ ὑμεῖς ℵ A B C E 614 383 *p r t* vg sa sy^{p,h} Ir^{iii.12,2} Aug Ambr *cett*

[1] Plooij, 'Ascension', p. 43. Ropes, *Text*, p. ccxxxiii, and Haenchen, *ZTK*, LI (1954), 162, and others (see below) also view this D-passage as indicative of universalistic and Gentile interests.
[2] Chase, *Old Syriac Element*, p. 18; Idem, *Exp*, IV, 9 (1894), 316. For other examples, see Chase, *The Syro-Latin Text of the Gospels* (London, 1895), pp. 85f. and n. 1.

The variant in question, ὑμεῖν ὅ, is attested alone by D *d*; in this case, unlike others in this section, there is strong 'Western' support against D, so that there is no need to regard D here as representing the 'Western' text.

To return to Acts ii. 17, the text of D is even more specific in identifying the recipients of the promise and in another variant has given it a universal scope. The original hand of D in ii. 17 reads πάσας σάρκας instead of πᾶσαν σάρκα, as in LXX and B. (The D-reading has been altered to πᾶσαν σάρκα by Corrector *A*.)[1] This plural form in Codex Bezae leaves no doubt that the D-text intends Peter to say that the promise is to all men, not only to the Jews; the outpouring of the Spirit is upon all races. It is *their* sons and *their* daughters who will benefit from the universal gift.[2] Moreover, both P. H. Menoud and M.-J. Lagrange (apparently independently) go so far as to say that D thus makes Peter a Paulinist, '...the preacher of the Pauline gospel, giving salvation to all mankind'.[3] And this is not to say too much, for D's conception of Peter's address as envisioning Gentiles is contradictory to the Lucan conception that the sermon here was directed only toward Jews (though they were Jews from all over the world) and that the Gentile mission first began later with Cornelius.[4] For the D-text, on the other hand, 'Peter's speech was really the beginning of the mission to the Gentiles'.[5]

The significance of the D-variants is clear: the D-text is here far more universalistic and, in by-passing Judaism, more anti-

[1] See Scrivener, *Bezae*, p. 440, note to fo. 420b.

[2] Lagrange, *Critique textuelle*, p. 392; *Beginnings*, IV, 21; Menoud, 'Western Text', p. 29; Ropes, *Text*, p. ccxxxiii; Haenchen, *Apostelgeschichte*, p. 142, n. 2; Idem, *ZTK*, LI (1954), 161 f.; Conzelmann, *Apostelgeschichte*, p. 29.

[3] Menoud, 'Western Text', p. 29; cf. Lagrange, *Critique textuelle*, p. 392.

[4] Haenchen, *ZTK*, LI (1954), 162; Idem, *Apostelgeschichte*, p. 142; see M. Simon, *St Stephen and the Hellenists in the Primitive Church* (London, 1958), pp. 130–3. It is possible, however, to see an adumbration of the Gentile mission in ii. 39(B) by comparing the OT allusions (see *Beginnings*, IV, 25 f.; Haenchen, *Apostelgeschichte*, p. 147; Bruce, *Acts*'[54], p. 68), but even if this is true, the picture is not basically changed, for D still stresses a full-blown universalism much earlier and much more clearly. For a strong argument that ii. 39 need not refer to Gentiles, see J. Munck, *Paul and the Salvation of Mankind* (Richmond, Va., 1959), p. 213, n. 2 (German, p. 208, n. 2).

[5] *Beginnings*, IV, 21.

Judaistic than the B-text. Plooij's strong conclusion deserves quotation in full:

> It is clear that the reviser wants to say that the promises belong to the spiritual Israel, the new people of God and not to the Israel κατά σάρκα to which he is speaking. The anti-judaic tendency is, it seems to me, so self-evident and convincing that we cannot avoid the conclusion that the Western reviser was not merely a stylistic redactor but a man of distinct dogmatic convictions, and that he did not hesistate to correct the text according to what he thought to be the truth.[1]

L. Cerfaux did not think, however, that so much could be drawn from πάσας σάρκας, especially since it is a reading peculiar to D.[2] If πάσας σάρκας stood alone, Cerfaux would have a point, but the αὐτῶν/ὑμῶν variants and the further evidence of universalism in the D-text more than justify the position taken by Menoud, Lagrange, Plooij, and others.

Finally, *De rebaptismate* has carried this anti-Judaic tendency one step farther in the omission of μου after δούλους and δούλας in ii. 18, thus eliminating the possibility that 'my slaves' might be taken to mean Jews.[3]

This intention of the D-text both to by-pass Judaism and to emphasize universalism is confirmed by some additional variants in this part of Acts. First, notice ii. 39:

Acts ii. 39

B	D
ὑμῖν	ἡμεῖν
γάρ ἐστιν ἡ ἐπαγγελία	γάρ ἐστιν ἡ ἐπαγγελία
καὶ τοῖς τέκνοις	καὶ τοῖς τέκνοις
ὑμῶν...	ἡμῶν...

ἡμεῖν...ἡμῶν D *d* Aug[c et fid et op 171]] ὑμῖν...ὑμῶν *cett* Cypr[ep 73,17]; (*p*[c]: nobis...vestris)

In the B-text the promise is 'to you and your children', presumably referring to the Jews who are being addressed. In the D-text, however, there is no specific reference to Jews, but

---
[1] Plooij, 'Ascension', p. 43.
[2] Cerfaux, 'Citations', p. 47.
[3] *Beginnings*, IV, 21. See Haenchen, *ZTK*, LI (1954), 161, for the meaning of Acts' addition (B and D) of μου to Joel's text.

the promise seems to be to Christians and to those who would become Christians.[1] Lake and Cadbury thought that this variant in D was probably accidental, but they suggested that it could, on the other hand, be connected with the changes in ii. 17,[2] and this suggestion is undoubtedly correct.

Variants such as these in the first and second person plural are frequent in D; there are some nineteen cases where the first person plural takes the place of the second, or *vice versa*, when D is compared with B. Can anything, then, be based on such a variant? The answer is 'Yes', if it can be shown to be a genuine 'Western' variant. In the case of ἡμεῖς/ὑμεῖς variants, the likelihood of accidental alteration or of correction to another text is great, since only one letter is involved. By the same token, such a simple variant could easily be produced for dogmatic reasons.

An analysis of all the ἡμεῖς/ὑμεῖς variants in Acts has been made, but a summary must suffice here: (1) In some cases (iv. 12; xvii. 28) it is B's reading which stands apart from the larger textual tradition; hence D's reading need not be considered a real variant at all. (2) Frequently the form is unique to D^gr and is obviously due to conformation to one or more similar pronominal forms in juxtaposition (iii. 13; iii. 15; iii. 22 [*post* ἀδελφῶν]; x. 39 [also in A]; xv. 25; xv. 28; perhaps also vii. 38, where D is supported by A C 81 *al*), or, often for the same reason, is a case of patent absurdity as far as the sense goes (ii. 14; iv. 11; xx. 27). These can therefore be eliminated—they most likely are part of a recent stratum in manuscript D itself. Other cases are unique to D (vii. 45) or have meagre support (xiii. 26: D *d* A 81) and may be grouped with those due to mechanical error. (3) This leaves the following cases: (*a*) ii. 22, where D* *d cod.ard* geo Eus read ὑμᾶς, but Tert Ir have ἡμᾶς. An anti-Judaic bias could be read from this and other variants in ii. 22, but this divided 'Western' witness renders it precarious. (*b*) ii. 39, the case just discussed. Here ἡμῶν is read by D *d* and two places in Aug, enough to outweigh Cypr perhaps, though ii. 39 D must be taken only as confirmatory evidence for a view already established on better grounds (here ii. 17 D). (*c*) xv. 7, where the 'Western' support is divided. (*d*) iii. 25, where ἡμῶν is

---
[1] See Plooij, 'Ascension', p. 43; Lagrange, *Critique textuelle*, p. 392.
[2] *Beginnings*, IV, 27.

a 'Western' variant. These last four, then, are the only ones to be considered in assessing theological motivation.

Secondly, the D-text reveals a universalistic outlook in ii. 38:

Acts ii. 38

B	D
Μετανοήσατε, καὶ βαπτισθήτω	Μετανοήσατε, καὶ βαπτισθήτω
ἕκαστος ὑμῶν ἐν τῷ ὀνόματι	ἕκαστος ὑμῶν ἐν τῷ ὀνόματι
Ἰησοῦ Χριστοῦ	τοῦ κυρίου Ἰησοῦ Χριστοῦ
εἰς ἄφεσιν τῶν ἁμαρτιῶν	εἰς ἄφεσιν ἁμαρτιῶν, ...
ὑμῶν, ...	

τοῦ κυρίου (+ἡμῶν p cop[G67] sy[h] geo dut. Aug[c] et $\frac{5}{11}$ Lcf[2] Epiph Cyr Bas[2codd] Thdrt[ter]) D d E 614 minn p r cop[G67] sa eth arm geo dut sy[p] (but sy[p] om Χριστοῦ) sy[h] Aug Ambr Bas[2,114] Cypr[ep 73,17] Cyr[4,893] Cyr[hr 47] Lcf* Thdrt[1, 305 et 2, 155 et 4, 1269] Epiph[27] Vigil] om gig Ir[iii.12,2] (Ir also om Χριστοῦ) Aug $\frac{2}{11}$ Hier al
εἰς ἄφεσιν ἁμαρτιῶν D d E P S 614 383 462 gig p* arm sy[p, h] Rebapt Ir[iii.12,2] Aug[c] Ambr Cypr[ep 73,17] Bas[2,114] Cyr[hr 47] Chr Lcf] + ὑμῶν p[2] t vg sa Aug Hier cett

The lack of ὑμῶν in D has been explained by Ropes as 'conformation to the solemn formula of the Gospels'.[1] It is true that in four of the five occurrences of ἄφεσις ἁμαρτιῶν in the gospels, there is no pronominal modifier. In Lk i. 77 (B and D), however (a case not mentioned by Ropes), the phrase is followed by αὐτῶν.[2]

In view of the transparently dogmatic purpose in twice omitting and twice altering ὑμῶν in v. 17, and in accordance with the D-text's other tendentious variants in this context, there is good reason to take this one in a similar way. The variant then reveals a universalistic bent: D has made forgiveness general.[3]

[1] Ropes, Text, p. 22. This is indicated, he says, by the complete absence of tendency to expand in Matt. xxvi. 28; Mark i. 4; Lk iii. 3. Ropes has this from Constantinus Tischendorf, Novum Testamentum Graece (Leipzig, 1869–72), II, 19.

[2] It would be better to argue that D lacks ὑμῶν in Acts ii. 38 in the interest of consistency in Acts, for then all five (D adds one more, xix. 5) occurrences of ἄφεσις ἁμαρτιῶν would agree in form. Cf. Acts v. 31; x. 43; xiii. 38; xxvi. 18; xix. 5 D.

[3] Lagrange, Critique textuelle, p. 397; Williams, Alterations, p. 75.

THE JEWS, GENTILES, AND CHRISTIANITY

Finally, observe Acts ii. 37:

                                    Acts ii. 37

B	D
	τότε πάντες οἱ συνελθόντες
ἀκούσαντες δὲ	καὶ ἀκούσαντες
κατενύγησαν τὴν καρδίαν,	κατενύγησαν τῇ καρδίᾳ,
εἶπόν τε	καί τινες ἐξ αὐτῶν εἶπαν
πρὸς τὸν Πέτρον	πρὸς τὸν Πέτρον
καὶ τοὺς λοιποὺς ἀποστόλους·	καὶ τοὺς ἀποστόλους·
Τί ποιήσωμεν, ἄνδρες ἀδελφοί;	Τί οὖν ποιήσομεν, ἄνδρες ἀδελφοί; ὑποδείξατε ἡμεῖν.

τότε. . . συνελθόντες D *d* sy[hmg]
τινὲς ἐξ αὐτῶν D* *d* Ephr[(p398)]
λοιπούς] *om* D *d* 241 *gig r* Aug[c]
οὖν D *d gig* sa Ir[iii.12,2] Aug[ter]] *om* Aug[c]
ποιήσομεν D *d* minn Cyr[hr 47]
ὑποδείξατε ἡμῖν D *d* E *gig p t cod.ard q r w* prov tepl cop[G67] sy[hmg]
Aug[c et bis] Bede[retr 110] Prom] *om cett* Ephr[(p398)]

Is τινὲς ἐξ αὐτῶν read by D merely because the whole crowd cannot speak to the apostles, as Haenchen says,[1] or is it not more likely that the D-text has this and the opening words, τότε πάντες οἱ συνελθόντες, in order to make a distinction between the whole crowd which was cut to the heart and the τινὲς ἐξ αὐτῶν who were ready to follow conviction with action (ὑποδείξατε ἡμεῖν)? In this latter case, the text of D minimizes the response from the Jewish audience and does not expect the repentance of all the Jews then listening.

D. Plooij characterizes D's τότε πάντες οἱ συνελθόντες as an instance of the paraphrastic nature of the 'Western' text, but adds the interesting comment that the phrase occurs several times in the Liège Diatessaron, for example, chapter xv (Lk ii. 38), *al dat volk dat daer versament was*, 'in which place it is an anti-Judaistic variant which we may safely ascribe to Tatian'.[2] Plooij elsewhere[3] explains the anti-Judaic character of the variant: the usual text in Lk ii. 38 reads that Anna, the prophetess, 'gave thanks to God and spoke of him to all who

[1] Haenchen, *Apostelgeschichte*, p. 146, n. 7.
[2] Plooij, *BBC*, VIII (1930), 25; IX (1931), 14.
[3] Idem, *Tendentieuse Varianten*, p. 23.

were looking for the redemption of Jerusalem'. The Liège Harmony, however, wishing to avoid any connection of Christianity with Jewish nationalism and Jerusalem, reads instead that Anna 'began to give testimony to him and to speak openly of him before *all the people that was gathered there*'. Plooij also remarks that other manuscripts tried to obviate the difficulty by substituting either Ἰσραήλ or ἐν Ἱερουσαλήμ (as does D) for Ἱερουσαλήμ. The phrase, τότε πάντες οἱ συνελθόντες, here in the D-text of Acts does not in itself, of course, carry any anti-Judaic sentiment, but it is of interest to point out that the Liège Harmony 'shows the same character of stylistic expansion and paraphrase as the Bezan Acts', and at the same time reveals an anti-Judaic colouring at several points.[1]

The anti-Judaic interpretation of Acts ii. 37 in the D-text above is supported by the D-text's use of τινὲς...αὐτῶν in Acts xvii. 12:

Acts xvii. 12

B	D
πολλοὶ μὲν οὖν ἐξ αὐτῶν ἐπίστευσαν,	τινὲς μὲν οὖν αὐτῶν ἐπίστευσαν, τινὲς δὲ ἠπίστησαν,
καὶ τῶν Ἑλληνίδων γυναικῶν τῶν εὐσχημόνων καὶ ἀνδρῶν	καὶ τῶν Ἑλλήνων καὶ τῶν εὐσχημόνων ἄνδρες καὶ γυναῖκες
οὐκ ὀλίγοι.	ἱκανοὶ ἐπίστευσαν.

τινές (first) D
τινὲς δὲ ἠπίστησαν D *d* 614 383
Ἑλλήνων καὶ D* *d*
ἱκανοὶ ἐπίστευσαν D* *d* (ἐπίστευσαν 383)
(Note: no other leading 'Western' witnesses are available at this point.)

The immediately preceding context (xvii. 11) describes the Jews of Beroea as εὐγενέστεροι (εὐγενεῖς D) τῶν ἐν Θεσσαλονίκῃ, etc., and in xvii. 12 B reports that **πολλοὶ** μὲν οὖν ἐξ αὐτῶν ἐπίστευσαν. The D-text, however, states that **τινὲς** μὲν οὖν αὐτῶν ἐπίστευσαν, and has the additional negative comment,

[1] Plooij, *BBC*, IX (1931), 14; Idem, *Tendentieuse Varianten*, pp. 23 f.; Idem, *A Further Study of the Liège Diatessaron* (Leyden, 1925), pp. 67, 84 f.; Harris, *BBC*, IX (1931), 10.

τινὲς δὲ ἠπίστησαν, which suggests that the D-text divides the Jews into two more or less equal parties.[1] This already indicates a different conception of the Jews on the part of the D-text; while reading the description of these 'noble' Jews as those who 'received the word with all eagerness, examining the scriptures daily...', the D-text has at the same time minimized their response to the gospel, thus placing them in an unfavourable light over against the heathen (of whom ἱκανοὶ ἐπίστευσαν).[2]

Moreover, the slight variations in the last part of the verse further broaden the group of recipients in D over against the Jews: in B, in addition to the Jews, τῶν Ἑλληνίδων γυναικῶν τῶν εὐσχημόνων καὶ ἀνδρῶν οὐκ ὀλίγοι believed. The stress here falls on the prominent women. The D-text states that τῶν Ἑλλήνων καὶ τῶν εὐσχημόνων ἄνδρες καὶ γυναῖκες ἱκανοὶ ἐπίστευσαν. Here there is no emphasis at all on the women,[3] and the group has been divided into two: the Greeks and the prominent men and women.[4] Assuming that this latter group were also Gentiles, the τινὲς Jews in D, viewed over against the ἱκανοί of Gentiles in D, become even less significant (cf. πολλοί in B).

To summarize, Peter's speech in Acts ii. 14–36 and its immediate context, as conceived in the D-text, reveal universalistic and anti-Judaic tendencies. Instead of a proclamation to the people of Israel, with possible adumbrations of a future universalism, as in the B-text, the D-text makes the Gentile mission clear from the very beginning of the address, revealing universalistic touches through small textual variations. The net result is that the importance of the Jews and Judaism to the new faith is effectively minimized in the D-text's representation.

This emphasis on universalism, especially when seen as a bypassing of Judaism as the sphere within and through which Christianity is propagated, and when seen as a development from Jewish opposition to this propagation, assumes a definite

---

[1] Jacquier, *Actes*, p. 518. For both phrases, cf. Acts xxviii. 24 (D def).
[2] Corssen, *GGA*, CLVIII (1896), 444.
[3] On the possibility of an anti feminist bias in D, see Menoud, 'Western Text', pp. 30f. and n. 42; on such a tendency in xvii. 12, see Ropes, *Text*, p. ccxxxiv; Bruce, *Acts*[54], p. 346, n. 13; W. Thiele, *Die lateinischen Texte des 1. Petrusbriefes* (Freiburg, 1965), p. 52, n. 2; and in Acts i. 14 and elsewhere, see Thiele, 'Eine Bemerkung zu Act 1, 14', *ZNW*, 53 (1962), 110f.
[4] Whether they were σεβόμενοι or pagans is not clear, Bruce, *Acts*[52], p. 329.

anti-Judaic character. Such an emphasis finds further exemplification in the D-text, and some instances follow.

The summary statement (Acts ii. 42-7) following the portion of Acts just discussed contains a well-known variant of Codex Bezae which is pertinent at precisely this point:

Acts ii. 47

B	D
...αἰνοῦντες τὸν θεὸν	...αἰνοῦντες τὸν θεὸν
καὶ ἔχοντες χάριν	καὶ ἔχοντες χάριν
πρὸς ὅλον τὸν λαόν.	πρὸς ὅλον τὸν κόσμον.

κόσμον D *d* (Note: no other leading 'Western' witnesses are available at this point.)

Λαός in Acts always refers to the Jewish people, with two exceptions (xv. 14; xviii. 10).[1] Observe that λαός, with these two exceptions, is carefully avoided in those parts of Acts dealing with Paul's missionary activity among the Gentiles (xiii. 31 to xxi. 28; in xix. 4 it is used in a description by Paul of the ministry of John the Baptist), and is only resumed when Paul returns to Jerusalem (see xxi. 28-40). After this it occurs only in Paul's addresses to the Jews, in Old Testament quotations, or in describing Paul's experience as a Jew, etc. (cf. xxiii. 5; xxvi. 17, 23; xxviii. 17, 26, 27). In these Gentile areas, Acts uses such terms as πλῆθος, ὄχλος, and δῆμος for 'people'. It is of interest that λαός always has the article when referring to the Jews, except in v. 37 and in the only two places where it is plural (iv. 25, 27). The two remaining anarthrous uses are the two references to Gentiles who become Christians (xv. 14; xviii. 10). That λαοί in iv. 25 (=Ps. ii. 1-2) refers to Israel (against Harnack)[2] is clear from iv. 27.[3]

In the two cases where λαός does not refer to the Jews, it is, though including Gentiles, actually describing the new people of God, the New Israel: xv. 14, 'Symeon has related how God first visited the Gentiles to take out of them a people for his name'; xviii. 10, 'The Lord said to Paul..., "Do not be afraid,

[1] N. A. Dahl, '"A People for His Name" (Acts xv. 14)', *NTS*, IV (1957/8), 324.
[2] A. Harnack, *The Acts of the Apostles* (London, 1909), pp. 50f.
[3] *Beginnings*, IV, 47; *TWNT*, IV, 51.

but speak..., for I have many people in this city'".[1] The result, then, is that the term λαός in Acts represents in every case a technical term for Israel, the people of God,[2] including the two instances in which it assumes the new sense of that designation.

In view of this technical usage of λαός, the variant κόσμον in D is all the more significant. One must not, however, prejudge the case by assuming that a D-reviser had the B-text before him and consciously avoided the use of the technical term because he did not want the believers to appear to enjoy the favour of the Jewish people (presumably in Jerusalem). Rather, looking only at the account of D itself, it is apparent that the D-text wishes to emphasize the fact that the believers enjoyed the favour of everyone,[3] of the whole world. The D-text thus enhances the prestige of the new faith and shows that it cannot be confined within Judaism.[4] This variant reveals itself as both universalistic and anti-Judaic[5] in intent.

E. Nestle, F. H. Chase, and C. C. Torrey[6] have argued for the Semitic origin of the λαόν/κόσμον variant: λαός = Hebrew עַם, and = Syriac ܥܡܐ; and κόσμος = Hebrew עֹלָם, and = Syriac ܥܠܡܐ. What makes this case one of the more impressive few is the fact that this substitution may be actually observable in several cases: Chase and others cite e.g. Lk ii. 10 where, for the

[1] Harnack, *Acts*, p. 51, thinks that only xv. 14 refers to Christians, but see *TWNT*, IV, 53.

[2] But see Dahl, *NTS*, IV (1957/8), 324, who says that 'λαός has not always the full theological meaning "the people of God" in its contrast to the Gentiles; in many cases Luke simply uses it as a synonym for ὄχλος, = "people" in the collective, unspecified sense of this word. But this "vulgar" usage is only found in contexts where the people in question is a crowd of Israelites.'

[3] Κόσμος in the sense of *le monde = les hommes* (Blass, *Acta*'95, p. 62).

[4] Ropes, *Text*, p. ccxxxiii.

[5] Corssen, *GGA*, CLVIII (1896), 444. The universalistic and anti-Judaic emphasis of the D-reading would not be altered if one adopted the suggestion of F. P. Cheetham that ἔχοντες χάριν πρός should be rendered 'favourably disposed toward', on the ground that 'to, towards' is the normal NT meaning of πρός ('Acts ii. 47: ἔχοντες χάριν πρός ὅλον τὸν λαόν', *ET*, LXXIV, 1962/3, 214f.).

[6] Nestle, *Exp*, V, 2 (1895), 235-7; Idem, *TSK*, LXIX (1896), 102f.; Idem, *Introduction to the Textual Criticism of the Greek New Testament* (London, 1901), p. 292 (note that Ropes, *Text*, p. ccxliv, n. 1, rejects his explanation as improbable); Chase, *Old Syriac Element*, p. 28; Idem, *Exp*, IV, 9 (1894), 317; Torrey, *Documents*, pp. 114, 145.

Greek παντὶ τῷ λαῷ, sy^p has '...world', and Matt. i. 21 where the Greek reads σώσει τὸν λαὸν αὐτοῦ, but sy^c has '...world'. In John xviii. 20, on the other hand, for the Greek λελάληκα τῷ κόσμῳ, sy^p has '...people'. No other manuscripts offer these variants which appear in the Syriac.[1]

These examples may show that such confusion and interchange of similar terms could occur. It is noteworthy, however, that the changes are reflected in no known Greek manuscript and that, moreover, no known Syriac text reads 'world' in Acts ii. 47. Far more decisive, though, against a purely linguistic explanation is a closer study of the interchange alleged in Matt. i. 21. H. J. Vogels points out that a mistake in writing is excluded here by the suffix (represented in Greek by αὐτοῦ) which the Syriac word 'people' must have had. This shows, he says, that the change was dogmatically motivated—Jesus was not the saviour only of the Jews.[2]

This case should warn us against excluding explanations other than those affirming accidental language influence on the reading of D in Acts ii. 47. (Harris's suggestion of Latin influence[3] is hardly compelling; the Latin could more easily have arisen from the Greek. This is one example of many in Harris in which the argument could as easily be turned the other way.) This evidence, in fact, provides warrant for seeking an explanation of D's κόσμον similar to that of Vogels for the Syriac variant of Matt. i. 21: it was dogmatically motivated in the interest of universalism.[4]

Observe, finally, that some modern writers quite often accept a reading as tendentious in character and also quote with apparent favour the evidence for a Semitic or Latin origin for the reading. Usually these writers are reluctant either to applaud or censure this evidence, perhaps because the question of language influence is so difficult of demonstrable proof in a given case.[5]

[1] Chase, *Exp*, IV, 9 (1894), 317; cf. Idem, *Old Syriac Element*, p. 28. For more examples, see Nestle, *Exp*, v, 2 (1895), 236f.
[2] Vogels, *Handbuch*, p. 178. Note that Vogels also takes the case of Lk ii. 10 to be a tendentiously motivated alteration. See Harris's discussion of Vogel's treatment (that would be in Vogel's first edition, 1923) of both of these: *HTR*, XVIII (1925), 106–8.
[3] Harris, *Codex Bezae*, pp. 103f.
[4] See Vogels, *Handbuch*, p. 178, n. 2.
[5] See e.g. the remarks of Williams, *Alterations*, pp. 57, 80–2.

An interesting result, applicable to the question of original text in Acts ii. 47, is derived from a study of the phrase ὅλος ὁ λαός/κόσμος in the New Testament. Ὅλος ὁ λαός is an expression *never* to be found in the New Testament (except, of course, in the B-text of Acts ii. 47); the usual expression is πᾶς ὁ λαός, which in fact is found twenty times in Lk–Acts (thirteen times in Lk, seven times in Acts) and only seven times in the other New Testament writings (Matt. xxvii. 25; John viii. 2; Rom. xv. 11, plural; Heb. ix. 19 *bis*; and Rev. xiii. 7 and xiv. 6, where the sense is somewhat different: 'every people'). Ὅλος ὁ κόσμος is a common enough phrase, occurring eight times (Matt. xvi. 26; xxvi. 13; Mark viii. 36; xiv. 9; Lk ix. 25; Rom. i. 8; I John ii. 2; v. 19); πᾶς ὁ κόσμος does occur, but only three times (Mark xvi. 15; Rom. iii. 19; Col. i. 6), and never in Lk–Acts. [Note that the only time this latter expression occurs in Codex Bezae (Mark xvi. 15), the πᾶς (ἅπαντα) is lacking, with the result that the phrase never occurs in D.]

All of this would seem to indicate that the D-expression, ὅλος ὁ κόσμος, might be the expected Lucan usage, rather than ὅλος ὁ λαός, as in B. Perhaps D *d* alone have preserved the original Lucan text here. This would mean that the D-text has not heightened but simply maintained the Lucan emphasis on universalism. The point remains, however, that the D-reading is more universalistic than that of B.

The mission of Paul and Barnabas in Pisidian Antioch (Acts xiii. 14–52) is the occasion for their decision to turn to the Gentiles because of the Jews' rejection of the word of God and their opposition to the apostles (see *vv*. 45–7). The D-text's treatment of these matters is illuminating. The first variant in this connection introduces universalistic interest even before Jewish opposition has begun, providing not only an indication but a scriptural backdrop for what is to happen in the ensuing narrative:

	Acts xiii. 33	
LXX (Ps. ii. 7–8)	B	D
	..., ὡς καὶ ἐν τῷ ψαλμῷ γέγραπται τῷ δευτέρῳ·	οὕτως γὰρ ἐν τῷ πρώτῳ ψαλμῷ γέγραπται·

7. Υἱός μου εἶ σύ,   Υἱός μου εἶ σύ,   Υἱός μου εἶ σύ,
   ἐγὼ σήμερον   ἐγὼ σήμερον   ἐγὼ σήμερον
   γεγέννηκά σε·   γεγέννηκά σε.   γεγέννηκά σε·
8. αἴτησαι παρ' ἐμοῦ,   αἴτησαι παρ' ἐμοῦ
   καὶ δώσω σοι ἔθνη   καὶ δώσω σοι ἔθνη
   τὴν κληρονομίαν σου,   τὴν κληρονομίαν σου,
   καὶ τὴν κατάσχεσίν σου   καὶ τὴν κατάσχεσίν σου
   τὰ πέρατα τῆς γῆς·   τὰ πέρατα τῆς γῆς·

line 7: αιμου

οὕτως γάρ D *d*
πρώτῳ D *d gig* Or[2, 538] Hil[27 *et* 42] Tert[mcion iv. 22] Bede[61, 62]
αἴτησαι...γῆς LXX D *d cod.ard* cop[G67] sy[hmg]

The variant πρώτῳ for τῷ δευτέρῳ is not pertinent to the present point.[1] What is striking is that Ps. ii. 8, the additional verse in D, is an extension of the quotation to include reference to the Gentiles. Sir Frederic Kenyon stated that 'the continuation of the quotation from Ps. ii. 8 is pointless'.[2] But the realization that this variant reveals once again the universalistic interest of the D-text makes it significant and meaningful and shows how wrong Kenyon was. For the D-text the promise (*v.* 32) is broader: it includes not only the declaration of Jesus as Son, which was fulfilled by the resurrection, but also a universal fulfilment by embracing the ἔθνη; the heathen here become the inheritance of Christ who takes possession of the ends of the earth.[3] This universalistic outlook is parallel to that of Isa. xlix. 6, which is quoted in Acts xiii. 47 (B and D), just *after* the actual announcement of the decision to turn to the

[1] Ropes, *Text*, pp. 263-5, argues for πρώτῳ; against Ropes, see E. R. Smothers, 'Les Papyrus Beatty. Deux leçons dans les Actes', *RSR*, XXIV (1934), 467-70.
[2] Kenyon, *ProcBrAc*, XXIV (1938), 312.
[3] Haenchen, *ZTK*, LI (1954), 158. Haenchen effectively refutes Cerfaux, 'Citations', p. 45, who thought that D's additional Psalm verse was intended to correct the B-text view that the promise referred to the Holy Spirit; D, then, according to Cerfaux, strengthens the quotation to bring it into harmony with the primitive theology which viewed the resurrection, rather than the Holy Spirit, as constituting Jesus as Saviour and Christ. Haenchen points out that there is no distinction here between B and D— in Acts the resurrection fulfils the promise to the fathers. (Note that Haenchen views the D-text here as secondary.)

THE JEWS, GENTILES, AND CHRISTIANITY

Gentiles. But, as already stated, the D-text has anticipated this emphasis. This outreach beyond Judaism is made clear also by the variants in xiii. 38f.:

Acts xiii. 38-9

B	D
γνωστὸν οὖν ἔστω ὑμῖν, ἄνδρες ἀδελφοί, ὅτι διὰ τούτου ὑμῖν ἄφεσις ἁμαρτιῶν καταγγέλλεται, καὶ ἀπὸ πάντων ὧν οὐκ ἠδυνήθητε ἐν νόμῳ Μωυσέως δικαιωθῆναι ἐν τούτῳ πᾶς ὁ πιστεύων δικαιοῦται.	38. γνωστὸν οὖν ἔστω ὑμεῖν, ἄνδρες ἀδελφοί, ὅτι διὰ τούτου ὑμεῖν ἄφεσις ἁμαρτιῶν καταγγέλλεται 39. καὶ μετάνοια ἀπὸ πάντων ὧν οὐκ ἠδυνήθητε ἐν νόμῳ Μωσέως δικαιωθῆναι, ἐν τούτῳ οὖν πᾶς ὁ πιστεύων δικαιοῦται παρὰ θεῷ.

---

38. τοῦτο B*, but τούτου ℵ A B² C D *cett*

38, line 4: αφεσεις
39, line 5: δικαιουτε

---

38. τούτου ℵ A B² C D *cett*] Iesum *gig*; hunc Iesum *cod.ard* vg^{cod Θ} cop^{G67} sa

39. καί] *om* ℵ A C* Aug
μετάνοια D *d* (*ante* καταγγέλλεται cop^{G67} sy^{h*}; *ante* ὑμῖν *cod.ard*)
οὖν D *d* 614 *dem* sy^{hmg}
παρά (+τῷ 614) θεῷ D *d* 614 383 sy^{hmg}; παρὰ κυρίῳ *t*

The D-text's μετάνοια and οὖν change the entire construction of these verses. The B-text reads:

(38) Let it be known therefore to you, brethren, that through this one forgiveness of sins is proclaimed to you. (39) and by this one every one who believes is justified from all things from which you could not be justified by the law of Moses.

The D-text, however, reads:

(38) Let it be known therefore to you, brethren, that through this one forgiveness of sins is proclaimed to you (39) and repentance from all things from which you could not be justified by the law of Moses. By this one therefore every one who believes is justified before God.

The μετάνοια[1] draws the first part of v. 39 to the sentence of v. 38, and the οὖν (which is more decisive and better attested) further divides the second part of v. 39 into a separate and *more clearly universalistic* sentence, to which παρὰ θεῷ is appended. Compare Acts iv. 31, where B and D read ...καὶ ἐλάλουν τὸν λόγον τοῦ θεοῦ μετὰ παρρησίας, after which the D-text has παντὶ τῷ θέλοντι πιστεύειν, D *d* E *q r w cod.ard* vg[codd] Ir[iii.12, 5(6) et]cat cop[G67] Ephr[(p400)] Bede[retr 118]; cf. Aug[serm 356(5, 1384f)] which *om* πιστεύειν.

The καὶ ἐσείγησαν which D reads at the end of Acts xiii. 41 follows Paul's warning from the prophets (Hab. i. 5 LXX):

Behold, you scoffers, and wonder, and vanish away; for I do a deed in your days, a deed you will never believe, if one declares it to you.

The unexpected deed is a reference by Paul (in both B and D) to the inclusion of the Gentiles, upon the rejection of the gospel by the Jews.[2] The question is whether καὶ ἐσείγησαν (D *d*; καὶ ἐσίγησεν 614 cop[G67] syh*) refers to Paul and Barnabas or to their hearers. If it refers to the hearers, it reveals the impression produced on the audience,[3] and would drive home Paul's victory[4]—he had effectively made his point regarding God's wonderful deed, the acceptance of the Gentiles, and they had no answer. If it refers to Paul and Barnabas, then it may suggest that this LXX quotation was the high point of Paul's address, and having stated it he was silent. On either view the variant highlights the Gentile interests of this context and supports the other similar emphases of the D-text here. While the reading of 614 cop[G67] syh* (ἐσίγησεν)[5] favours the latter alternative, the Lucan usage makes the former preferable.

---

[1] In place of B's reading of Lk xxiv. 47, μετάνοιαν εἰς ἄφεσιν ἁμαρτιῶν, D has μετάνοιαν καὶ ἄφεσιν ἁμαρτιῶν, again dividing the two terms.

[2] Haenchen, *Apostelgeschichte*, p. 355. The warning is against unbelief, and refers to punishment which God will visit on them, as he did through the Chaldeans at an earlier time. In the present situation, this punishment could take the form of the election of the Gentiles in place of the Jews, if they did not believe. See Jacquier, *Actes*, pp. 407–8. D could have strengthened its universalistic outlook had it known the Hebrew OT, which reads here, 'Look *among the nations*, and see; wonder and be astounded...'. No LXX text follows this.

[3] Thus Harnack, *Studien*, I, 40, n. 1.

[4] W. L. Knox, *St Paul and the Church of Jerusalem* (Cambridge, 1925), p. xx.

[5] Bruce, *Acts*'[54], p. 270, n. 40, suggests that D's reading is probably a corruption of this. Thus also Haenchen, *ZTK*, LI (1954), 161.

How is σιγᾶν used elsewhere in the New Testament? It is found, in fact, only in Lk–Acts and Paul. Three of the six[1] uses in Lk–Acts are similar to that in Acts xiii. 41 D, namely, summary statements after a declaration or speech: (1) In Lk xx. 26, after Jesus' answer to the crafty question of the scribes, the text reads: καὶ θαυμάσαντες ἐπὶ τῇ ἀποκρίσει αὐτοῦ ἐσίγησαν (D: ἐσείγησαν). (2) Lk ix. 36. At the transfiguration, words of Ps. ii. 7 (and Isa. xlii. 1) are quoted, as in Acts xiii. 33, and immediately following are the words: καὶ αὐτοὶ ἐσίγησαν (D has αὐτοὶ δὲ ἐσείγησαν). Finally (3) Acts xv. 12. In xv. 7–11 Peter makes a vigorous defence of the Gentile mission (cf. xv. 14), and, when he had finished, the text (xv. 12) has ἐσίγησεν δὲ πᾶν τὸ πλῆθος (B and D). The D-text, however, is anxious here to make clear that the others approved Peter's words about the Gentile mission and has the additional passage, συνκατατεθεμένων δὲ τῶν πρεσβυτέρων τοῖς ὑπὸ τοῦ Πέτρου εἰρημένοις, before ἐσείγησεν πᾶν τὸ πλῆθος. The significance of this usage of σιγᾶν for that in xiii. 41 D is obvious: not only is the expression used by Luke to set off important utterances (especially Lk ix. 36; cf. xx. 26), but in Acts xv. 12 (and also xv. 13) it adds solemnity to an important statement involving the mission to the Gentiles, where the D text shows an even greater Gentile interest by reporting the elders' agreement with Peter's words; and 'then the whole multitude was silent'. Now in Acts xiii. 41, following a speech in which the D-text again has shown its distinctive universalistic emphases, and following a prophetic statement referring to Gentile inclusion, the D-text also concludes with this significant phrase, καὶ ἐσείγησαν!

Finally, notice the reading of D at the end of Acts xiii. 43: ἐγένετο δὲ καθ' ὅλης τῆς πόλεως διελθεῖν τὸν λόγον,[2] D d and with variations E p q w vg^codd prov tepl cop^G67 sy^hmg Bede^retr 142. This may only be anticipatory of v. 44 (B and D): σχεδὸν πᾶσα (ὅλη D) ἡ πόλις συνήχθη.... (Cf. also v. 49.) It is of significance, however, since 'the whole city' in v. 44 means 'the whole Gentile population'.[3] The D-text, then, has an evangeliz-

---
[1] The others are Lk xviii. 39; Acts xii. 17; xv. 13; (also Lk xix. 40 D). Cf. Acts xxi. 40.
[2] Add τοῦ θεοῦ D, domini d.
[3] Bruce, Acts'⁵ᵃ, p. 273; Idem, Acts'⁵⁴, p. 281. Note the reading of L P S, etc. in v. 42: παρεκάλουν τὰ ἔθνη εἰς τὸ μεταξὺ σάββατον.

ation of the Gentiles already in *v.* 43, whereas in the B-text it does not begin until *v.* 47.

Acts xviii. 4–8 describes the events immediately surrounding Paul's decision and his announcement to the Corinthian synagogue that he is turning to the Gentiles (xviii. 6). It is of interest to see how the D-text handles these events:

Acts xviii. 4–6a

B	D
διελέγετο δὲ ἐν τῇ συναγωγῇ κατὰ πᾶν σάββατον,	4. εἰσπορευόμενος δὲ εἰς τὴν συναγωγὴν κατὰ πᾶν σάββατον διελέγετο, καὶ ἐντιθεὶς τὸ ὄνομα τοῦ κυρίου Ἰησοῦ,
ἔπειθέν τε	καὶ ἔπιθεν δὲ οὐ μόνον
Ἰουδαίους καὶ Ἕλληνας.	Ἰουδαίους ἀλλὰ καὶ Ἕλληνας.
ὡς δὲ κατῆλθον ἀπὸ τῆς Μακεδονίας ὅ τε Σείλας καὶ ὁ Τιμόθεος, συνείχετο τῷ λόγῳ ὁ Παῦλος, διαμαρτυρόμενος τοῖς Ἰουδαίοις εἶναι τὸν Χριστὸν Ἰησοῦν.	5. παρεγένοντο δὲ ἀπὸ τῆς Μακεδονίας τότε Σίλας καὶ Τιμόθεος. συνείχετο τῷ λόγῳ Παῦλος, διαμαρτυρόμενος τοῖς Ἰουδαίοις εἶναι τὸν Χριστὸν κύριον Ἰησοῦν. πολλοῦ δὲ λόγου γεινομένου καὶ γραφῶν διερμηνευομένων
ἀντιτασσομένων δὲ αὐτῶν καὶ βλασφημούντων ἐκτιναξάμενος τὰ ἱμάτια εἶπεν πρὸς αὐτούς·	6. ἀντιτασσομένων δὲ αὐτῶν καὶ βλασφημούντων ἐκτιναξάμενος ὁ Παῦλος τὰ εἱμάτια αὐτοῦ εἶπεν πρὸς αὐτούς·

5, line 5: διαμαρτυρουμενος
6, line 1: [ε]τι τασσομενων

---

4. εἰσπορευόμενος... διελέγετο D *d h cod.ard* (vg^codT)
   ἐντιθεὶς...Ἰησοῦ (*praem* καί D *d*) D *d gig h q w cod.ard c dem* vg^cl tepl sy^hmg; *post* Ἕλληνας prov
   οὐ μόνον Ἰουδαίους ἀλλὰ D *d h cod.ard*
   τότε D*; tunc *ante* supervenerunt *h*
5. συνείχετο...Ἰησοῦν] *om h*
   λόγῳ] πνεύματι H L P S 383 minn arm geo sy^hmg Chr^9,328

84

THE JEWS, GENTILES, AND CHRISTIANITY

Χριστὸν κύριον Ἰησοῦν D *d*; κύριον Ἰησοῦν Χριστὸν 383]
Χριστὸν Ἰησοῦν cett gig sy[h]*
πολλοῦ...διερμηνευομένων D *d h* sy[hmg]
6. ἀντιτασσομένων δὲ αὐτῶν] contr[adicebant] Judaei quidam *h*
ὁ Παῦλος D *d h w* prov
αὐτοῦ D *d* minn *c* dem gig *h* cod.*ard* vg[cl] eth geo sy[p] Thphyl[b]

Acts xviii. 4–6 *a*
Codex *h*

4. et cum introiret in syna[gogam, per]
omnem sabbatum disputabat, interponen[s nomen]
dni ihu suadebat autem non tantum Judae[is sed et Gre]cis.
5. tunc supervenerunt a Macedonia [Sileas et]
Timotheus. atque iterum, cum multis fier[et verbum]
et scripturae interpraetarentur 6. contr[adicebant]
Judaei quidam, et maledicebant. tunc exc[ussit ves]tem
suam Paulus, et dixit ad eos:...[1]

The textual problem in the D-text of *v.* 5 is complex. Since *h* does not have the sentence, συνείχετο τῷ λόγῳ Παῦλος, διαμαρτυρόμενος τοῖς Ἰουδαίοις εἶναι τὸν Χριστὸν κύριον Ἰησοῦν, it has been considered an interpolation into D from B.[2] Thus, Corssen, reading D without these words, held that it was probably the judgement of the D-text that Paul's strife was with his own adherents, Silas and Timothy (he cites xiii. 13; xv. 37 as other cases). This is unlikely, however, since the αὐτῶν of *v.* 6 obviously does not refer to Timothy and Silas, but to the Jews,[3] and this is what *h* reports explicitly: *contradicebant Judaei quidam*. Yet the reason for introducing the arrival of Silas and Timothy at this point is still somewhat unclear on any reading, although, as A. C. Clark suggested, their coming may have stimulated Paul to renewed efforts.[4] What is clear, however, is that in *h* the report of the arrival of Silas and Timothy is really a parenthetical statement which serves to mark an interval between what for *h* were two debates between Paul and the Jews: *atque* **iterum**, *cum multis fieret verbum, et scripturas interpraetarentur, contradicebant Judaei quidam*... (*vv.* 5–6). But to return to the alleged interpolation in D, the simple excision of

---
[1] Text from Ropes, *Text*, p. 173. Cf. A. C. Clark, *Acts*, p. 368.
[2] Corssen, *GGA*, CLVIII (1896), 431 f.; Ropes, *Text*, p. 172, followed by *Beginnings*, IV, 223, and Haenchen, *Apostelgeschichte*, p. 471, n. 3.
[3] Ropes, *Text*, p. 172.   [4] A. C. Clark, *Acts*, p. 368.

the sentence seems to remove some element essential to the passage; the presence in *h* of the words *Judaei quidam* attests this, and some specific reference to the Jews (as found in both B and *h*, as well as the present form of D) seems necessary to D, but exactly what form it took is now difficult to say, for what now stands in D has no doubt suffered to some degree from conformation to the B-type text.

The additional phrase in the D-text of *v.* 4, ἐντιθεὶς τὸ ὄνομα τοῦ κυρίου Ἰησοῦ, is of special interest. This must be read along with *v.* 5 (B and D), of which it is a parallel version, and with the D-variant there, especially the phrase, γραφῶν διερμηνευομένων. According to the D-text, the name of the Lord Jesus was introduced (*v.* 4), and subsequently there was a great discussion and the scriptures were interpreted. Ἐντιθεὶς τὸ ὄνομα τοῦ κυρίου Ἰησοῦ seems, therefore, to imply that Paul explained the Old Testament scripture by introducing or inserting the name of Jesus where appropriate (in the way that 'Messiah' was added to 'my servant' in the Targum of Jonathan ben Uzziel in Isa. xlii. 1; lii. 13).[1] The D-text in this way makes more explicit the terms of disagreement between Paul and the Jews, stressing that it was in the area of scripture interpretation, especially with reference to Jesus. And, more important, the D-text indicates a long debate and a heated battle[2] over this matter by the πολλοῦ δὲ λόγου γεινομένου καὶ γραφῶν διερμηνευομένων which precedes ἀντιτασσομένων δὲ αὐτῶν καὶ βλασφημούντων.... In fact, according to D, it was this discussion, along with the opposition and blasphemy of the Jews, which provided the immediate occasion for Paul's separation from the synagogue and from the Jews.

The other D-variants in this passage fill out the picture already sketched. The οὐ μόνον...ἀλλὰ καί construction in D (*v.* 4) emphasizes the contrast between the Jews and the Greeks (here they are Greeks who frequented the synagogue) and places special stress upon the Greeks whom Paul persuaded. In this way the D-text minimizes the importance of the Jews (cf. ii. 37 D and xvii. 12 D, above, pp. 73–5): it was not merely that he persuaded 'both Jews and Greeks' (as the B-text has it); rather, he persuaded '*not only* Jews', which might have been

---

[1] Bruce, *Acts*'52, pp. 343, 107; Idem, *Acts*'54, pp. 369f. and n. 15.
[2] Fascher, *Textgeschichte*, p. 44.

expected, 'but also Greeks'. The D-text thus 'betrays a Gentile's feeling that any statement is inadequate which implies that Christianity in the Apostolic age was limited to Jewry'.[1]

Moreover, the D-text here is preparing for and strengthening the reasons behind Paul's separation from the synagogue in Corinth and his turning to the Gentiles (xviii. 6). Over against the more intense disagreement and unresponsiveness of the Jews, the D-text has stressed the favourable response of the Gentiles to Paul's message. Observe, now, how the D-text words Paul's announcement of his decision in xviii. 6:

Acts xviii. 6b

B

καθαρὸς ἐγώ·
ἀπὸ τοῦ νῦν
εἰς τὰ ἔθνη πορεύσομαι.

D

καθαρὸς ἐγώ·
ἀ[φ' ὑμῶ]ν νῦν
εἰς τὰ ἔθνη πορεύομαι

ἀφ' ὑμῶν νῦν. πορεύομαι D d h (nunc vado ad gentes ab vobis h)

In B Paul goes to the Gentiles 'from this present time', but in D he specifies that now he goes 'from you', i.e. the Jews, to the Gentiles. (Note the emphatic position of ἀφ' ὑμῶν.)

The stichoi in D are arranged in this manner:

καθαρος εγω α[φ υμω]ν
νυν εις τα εθνη πορευομαι

Since D is written in sense-lines, this could be taken to mean 'I am clean from you'. This would change the meaning, but the anti-Judaic tone would remain. D, in this case, would be emphasizing Paul's innocence of the unresponsiveness of the Jews. This view is attractive, but is to be rejected (for the 'Western' text) because it is impossible in h.

Verse 8 tells of the first converts after this decision:

Acts xviii. 8

B

Κρεῖσπος δὲ ὁ ἀρχισυνάγωγος
ἐπίστευσεν τῷ κυρίῳ
σὺν ὅλῳ τῷ οἴκῳ αὐτοῦ,
καὶ πολλοὶ τῶν Κορινθίων

D

ὁ δὲ ἀρχισυνάγωγος Κρίσπος
ἐπίστευσεν εἰς τὸν κύριον
σὺν ὅλῳ τῷ οἴκῳ αὐτοῦ,
καὶ πολλοὶ τῶν Κορινθίων

[1] Ropes, *Text*, p. ccxxxiii, see n. 2.

ANTI-JUDAIC TENDENCIES IN ACTS

ἀκούοντες ἐπίστευον   ἀκούοντες ἐπίστευον
καὶ ἐβαπτίζοντο.   καὶ ἐβαπτίζοντο πιστεύοντες
                               τῷ θεῷ διὰ τοῦ ὀνόματος
                               τοῦ κυρίου ἡμῶν Ἰησοῦ Χριστοῦ.

εἰς τὸν κύριον D *d h* sa sy[p, h] ἐπίστευον καί] *om h* πιστεύοντες τῷ θεῷ D *d h* (*ante* καὶ ἐβαπτίζοντο arm sy[p] add τῷ θεῷ) διὰ τοῦ ὀνόματος τοῦ κυρίου ἡμῶν (*om* ἡμῶν 614 383 sy[h]*) Ἰησοῦ Χριστοῦ D *d* 614 383 sy[h]* (in nomine Iesu Christi *h*) (614 sy[h]* read διὰ τοῦ ὀνόματος...Χριστοῦ *ante* καὶ ἐβαπτίζοντο)

In the simple statement of the B-text the πολλοὶ τῶν Κορινθίων could be taken to mean Gentiles,[1] though it is at least ambiguous. The additional phrase in D, πιστεύοντες τῷ θεῷ διὰ τοῦ ὀνόματος τοῦ κυρίου ἡμῶν Ἰησοῦ Χριστοῦ,[2] removes any ambiguity and emphasizes the fact that for the D-text they are Gentiles, and Gentiles having no intimate connection with the synagogue. How is this indicated in the D-text? The clue is given in the verse itself, which reports that Crispus (with his whole house) ἐπίστευσεν εἰς τὸν **κύριον** (D), but that the πολλοὶ τῶν Κορινθίων were baptized, πιστεύοντες τῷ **θεῷ** through the name of our Lord Jesus Christ. There is, in fact, a definite pattern in the usage of πιστεύειν τῷ θεῷ/κυρίῳ (or πιστεύειν ἐπὶ/εἰς τὸν θεόν/κύριον) in Acts. Both the B-text and D, almost without exception, use πιστεύειν (1) with κύριος as object when the context indicates believers with Jewish or synagogue backgrounds, and (2) with θεός when pure Gentile background is in view. A summary of all these passages follows:

Πιστεύειν with θεός as object[3] occurs only in passages where the reference is clearly to Gentile believers or is spoken to Gentiles, namely, xiii. 12, where B states simply that the proconsul, Sergius Paulus, ἐπίστευσεν, but D *d* read ἐθαύμασεν καὶ ἐπίστευσεν τῷ θεῷ; xvi. 34 (B and D), referring to the jailer at

---

[1] Thus Jacquier, *Actes*, p. 548.

[2] This makes the preceding ἐπίστευον καί superfluous. It is rightly omitted in *h*. It probably arose by conflation with the B-text (Ropes, *Text*, p. 173).

[3] In the gospels, κύριος is never used as object to πιστεύειν or πίστις. Θεός is so used (B and D) only in John xiv. 1; cf. also Mark xi. 22 (B and D): ἔχετε πίστιν θεοῦ.

Philippi; and xxvii. 25 (D *def*), where Paul speaks to Gentile sailors.[1]

On the other hand, πιστεύειν with κύριος as object, where the reference is clearly to believing Jews, occurs in v. 14 (B and D),[2] ix. 42 (D *def*), xviii. 8*a* (B and D), and xxii. 19 (B and *d*; D *def*). xiv. 22–3 is a summary statement (cf. xv. 41) referring to the churches in Antioch, Iconium, and Lystra. Paul had a synagogue audience in Antioch of Pisidia (xiii. 14, 16, 42–4) and Iconium (xiv. 1), but in Lystra the apostles presumably faced a purely heathen audience. Thus, the subject of πεπιστεύκεισαν εἰς (τὸν κύριον) in xiv. 23 is a mixed group, though perhaps the reference would include mostly synagogue-related people. Moreover, a certain looseness of expression must be allowed to a general summary statement. Passages which refer to believing in the Lord Jesus (Christ), and are therefore unambiguous, are not discussed here.[3]

The only real difficulty is found in xvi. 15, where, assuming Lydia is synagogue-related, B follows the pattern: εἰ κεκρίκατέ με πιστὴν τῷ κυρίῳ εἶναι..., but D reads θεῷ (but only D; *d* has *domino*) instead of κυρίῳ. D has no support, but no other 'Western' authorities are available here. Is it possible that the D-text assumes that, though Paul and his companions 'supposed' (xvi. 13: ἐνομίζομεν[4] B *al*; ἐδόκει D *d e gig l* vg) there was a synagogue[5] by the river in Philippi, actually they were

---

[1] An additional case (though it is somewhat ambiguous) occurs in xi. 17D, where B has ἐγὼ τίς ἤμην δυνατὸς κωλῦσαι τὸν θεόν; after which D has the additional words, τοῦ μὴ δοῦναι αὐτοῖς πνεῦμα ἅγιον πιστεύσασιν ἐπ' αὐτῷ; Both Jewish and Gentile believers are under discussion, and the ἐπ' αὐτῷ could refer to κύριον Ἰησοῦν Χριστόν, but perhaps it should be taken with θεόν. Gentiles are the chief concern of *v*. 17*b*.

[2] Τῷ κυρίῳ may be taken with πιστεύοντες (as in xviii. 8; cf. xvi. 34; xiii. 12D) or προσετίθεντο (as in xi. 24). *Beginnings*, IV, 54; Haenchen, *Apostelgeschichte*, p. 199 and n. 2; and W. Bieder, 'Der Petrusschatten, Apg. 5, 15', *TZ*, XVI (1960), 409, n. 7, prefer the latter, but Bruce, *Acts*'[52], p. 138, says that formally it probably goes with πιστεύοντες.

[3] See xi. 17 (B and D); xvi. 31 (B and D, but D *add* Χριστόν); xx. 21 where B has πίστιν εἰς τὸν κύριον ἡμῶν Ἰησοῦν, but D has πίστιν διά..., and *add* Χριστοῦ; xxiv. 24 (D *def*); cf. x. 43.

[4] On νομίζειν also in the sense of 'to suppose' in this passage, see Zuntz, *Class et Med*, III (1940), 25, n. 2.

[5] On προσευχή as a Jewish-Hellenistic word for synagogue, see Zuntz (*ibid.*); *Beginnings*, IV, 191. But Bruce, *Acts*'[52], p. 314, thinks it simply means 'prayer' here.

mistaken, but spoke to the women there anyway? After all, how could there have been a synagogue service with only women present?[1] The D-text, on this view, takes Lydia to be a Gentile not connected with the synagogue. The difficulty, of course, is the σεβομένη τὸν θεόν (v. 14).[2] If this difficulty is insuperable, then xvi. 15 must be taken as the exception which proves the rule, or else must be considered a special, later reading of D. The evidence on this latter point is insufficient for a decision.

Such a distinction in the use of πιστεύειν τῷ θεῷ/κυρίῳ, etc. is perhaps to be expected, since the Jews (as well as proselytes) already believed in God, and to specify their Christian faith it would be natural to say that they believed in the Lord, i.e. in Jesus who had become both Lord and Christ.

The D-text's πιστεύοντες τῷ θεῷ in xviii. 8b indicates, then, that the πολλοὶ τῶν Κορινθίων who were baptized were pagans.[3] The rest of the variant, διὰ...Χριστοῦ, emphasizes again that this belief in God was mediated *through the name of our Lord Jesus Christ*'[4] and, in fact, needed no other mediation, not the synagogue nor adhesion to Judaism, etc. The D-text also is intimating, as Fascher[5] points out, that between Paul and the heathen here, there was no hindering dispute about the interpretation of scripture, as with the Jews in vv. 4ff., so that it was easier for the Gentiles to be moved to faith in *God*, since it proceeded directly out of faith in the κύριος, than it was for the Jews to overcome their previous bias and add to their faith in God the faith in Jesus Christ.

The variant is therefore anti-Judaic in the sense that it by-passes and, consequently, minimizes the importance of Judaism in the propagation of the new faith—Christianity could get along without Judaism and its institutions, notably the synagogue.

Subsequent to the announcement that he is going to the

---

[1] Bruce, *Acts*'52, p. 314.
[2] Even the non-technical, general use of σεβομένη (*Beginnings*, v, 87f.) would not eliminate this difficulty.
[3] See Ropes, *Text*, p. 173; O'Neill, *SJT*, VIII (1955), 170.
[4] Note that in xx. 21, where both Jews and Greeks are mentioned, B has πίστιν εἰς τὸν κύριον ἡμῶν Ἰησοῦν, while D has πίστιν διὰ τοῦ κυρίου ἡμῶν Ἰησοῦ Χριστοῦ.
[5] Fascher, *Textgeschichte*, p. 45.

Gentiles, Paul, according to the B-text, transfers his locale of teaching (xviii. 7). The D-text gives a different picture:

Acts xviii. 7

B	D
καὶ μεταβὰς	μεταβὰς
ἐκεῖθεν	[ἀπὸ τοῦ] Ἀκύλα
ἦλθεν	[καὶ] ἦλθεν
εἰς οἰκίαν	εἰς τὸν [ο]ἶ[κό]ν
τινὸς ὀνόματι Τιτίου Ἰούστου	τινος ὀνόματι Ἰούστου
σεβομένου τὸν θεόν,...	σεβομένου τὸν θεόν,...

καί *d h* cett] *om* D
ἀπὸ τοῦ Ἀκύλα D (or [δὲ ἀπὸ] Ἀκύλα D) *d h*; *praem* ἐκεῖθεν 614
καὶ ἦλθεν D?, et abiit *h*; or εἰσῆλθεν D? 𝔓[74] ℵ A minn, introivit *d gig p*
vg sa arm eth[vid] sy[p] sy[hmg] Thphyl[b]; ἦλθεν *sine* καί B E H L P 614
383 bo sy[h] Chr[9, 328] Thphyl[a]
τὸν οἶκον D*
Ἰούστου D* *d* A H L P *h*[vid] *p* 614 383 eth Chr Thphyl[a]] Τίτου sa sy[p]
Cass; Τίτου (Τιτίου) Ἰούστου *cett*

The text here is obscured in places. Blass inspected the manuscript and offered corrections to Scrivener's edition of D. Whereas Scrivener read only [ ]...λα following μεταβάς, Blass reported that Ἀκύλα can be read in its entirety. Nothing, however, is recognizable between these words; hence either [ἀπὸ τοῦ] or [δὲ ἀπό] is possible.[1] The evidence of 614, though it is conflate, is the only Greek 'Western' evidence besides D, and it supports the reading ἀπὸ τοῦ.[2] As to [εἰσ]ῆλθεν or [καὶ] ἦλθεν, Blass thought he could discern an ε before ἦλθεν:[3] thus εἰσῆλθεν. This is supported by *d* sy[hmg] (*introivit*). Blass, however, requested J. Rendel Harris to re-examine the manuscript of D precisely at this point, and Harris found traces of καί more likely. The reading of *h, et abiit*, is strong support for this reading of Harris, and Blass himself seems inclined toward it.[4] With D

[1] F. Blass, 'Zu Codex D in der Apostelgeschichte', *TSK*, LXXI (1898), 541; see Ropes, *Text*, p. 172.
[2] Note Harnack's remark, *Studien*, I, 51, that ἀπὸ τοῦ Ἀκύλα is excellently attested. On the importance of 614 for restoring the Greek of 'Western' readings, see Ropes, *Text*, p. clxxii.
[3] Blass, *TSK*, LXXI (1898), 541.
[4] *Ibid*. Note that Zahn, *Urausgabe*, p. 307, thought that D perhaps read ἀπῆλθεν, with *h*, though without καί (*et*).

uncertain and with h and sy[hmg] divided, the choice must be made on the basis of the best meaning in the context (see below).

Τὸν οἶκον is even more difficult. The versions are of no help here. The article is clearly in D; Blass felt sure that οἶκον, rather than οἰκίαν, was D's reading,[1] and he is followed by Hilgenfeld, Ropes, and A. C. Clark; hence the reading of these editors is followed here.

The καὶ μεταβὰς ἐκεῖθεν of the B-text suggests only that Paul 'withdrew from there', i.e. from the synagogue[2] (see xviii. 4f.), whereas the D-text reports that he 'withdrew from Aquila' (ἀπὸ 'Ακύλα or ἀπὸ τοῦ 'Ακύλα), that is, from the house of Aquila,[3] a Jew (xviii. 2), and entered the house of (Titius) Justus, a born pagan (though he was a σεβόμενος τὸν θεόν). This separation from the synagogue and surrender of house-fellowship with Aquila would be the clearest demonstration of Paul's break with the Jews and his turning to the Gentiles.[4]

Incidentally, the account in Acts of Paul's subsequent association with Aquila (xviii. 18) would hardly suggest that the D-version is original here, unless Paul's removal from Aquila's house was coincidental (and thus for other reasons), or unless it was an 'acted parable'. F. F. Bruce is probably right: the D-reading reflects a misunderstanding, and Paul moved his preaching headquarters rather than his private lodgings.[5] But this does not affect or remove the anti-Judaic intent in the D-text; regardless of how the reading suggested itself, this is how D accepted and interpreted it. In a similar manner, the D-text in xviii. 2 pictures Aquila and Priscilla as settling permanently in Achaia[6] (οἳ καὶ κατῴκησαν εἰς τὴν 'Αχαΐαν D d h sy[hmg] Ado), whereas in xviii. 18-19, cf. 26, they leave Achaia with Paul and apparently stay at Ephesus. Also, the D-text

---

[1] Blass, *TSK*, LXXI (1898), 541; cf. Scrivener, *Bezae*, p. 445, note to fo. 490b, line 30.

[2] Corssen, *GGA*, CLVIII (1896), 428; Haenchen, *Apostelgeschichte*, p. 471. Ἐκεῖθεν could be temporal, meaning 'after this' (cf. xiii. 21) (*Beginnings*, IV, 225), which would agree with the ἀπὸ τοῦ νῦν of v. 6, but there is no reason to abandon the more common meaning here.

[3] Harris, *BBC*, IX (1931), 4.

[4] Blass, *TSK*, LXXI (1898), 541; cf. Fascher, *Textgeschichte*, p. 45.

[5] Bruce, *Acts*'[54], p. 320, n. 17.

[6] Fascher, *Textgeschichte*, p. 44.

seems to regard Aquila as a non-Christian, while B is more ambiguous but perhaps implies the opposite.[1]

There is, moreover, the intriguing possibility, based on the reading μεταβάς ἀπὸ τοῦ Ἀκύλα καὶ ἦλθεν..., that the D-text intends to include the first four of these words in the announcement of Paul,[2] who then would say (vv. 6-7): 'I am clean. From you [i.e. the Jews] I now go to the Gentiles, *having withdrawn from Aquila*.' Καὶ ἦλθεν would begin the next sentence: 'And he went into the house....' Or, following the *stichoi* of D (but see above, p. 87): '"I am clean from you [Jews]. Now I, having withdrawn from Aquila, go to the Gentiles." And he went into the house....' To adopt this very suggestive interpretation would mean, however, to assert that D represents the 'Western' text at this point, against the evidence (though a divided evidence) of *h* (καὶ ἦλθεν) and sy[hmg] (εἰσῆλθεν). The real difficulty lies with the *et recessit* of *h* (v. 7); since it is not certain whether D had δέ *post* μεταβάς, it is preferable to stay with *h* (and *d*): 'And he withdrew from Aquila and went into the house....'

The D-text's emphasis, of course, is still clear: Paul's transfer of residence sharpens up his break with the Corinthian Jews and his turning to the Gentiles.

While οἶκος frequently means 'household' or 'family' as well as 'dwelling', οἰκία in the New Testament seldom means 'family'. Its usual meaning is 'dwelling'. If the D-text here wanted to reinforce its contention that Paul moved his residence from the house of Aquila to that of Justus, it could be done by saying that Paul 'entered the family of Justus', and οἶκος would more likely be understood in this way than would οἰκία. (Cf. xvi. 31-2: πίστευσον... καὶ σωθήσῃ σὺ καὶ ὁ **οἶκός** σου. καὶ ἐλάλησαν αὐτῷ... σὺν πᾶσιν τοῖς ἐν τῇ **οἰκίᾳ** αὐτοῦ.)

That the D-text intends this difference between the two words in xviii. 7 is shown by the presence of the article, εἰς **τὸν** οἶκον, whereas B has εἰς οἰκίαν. In B the article is unnecessary because the first οἰκία is identified in the next clause as identical to the second οἰκία—he entered *a* house, namely the house (ἡ οἰκία) adjoining the synagogue. In D he enters *the family* of Justus, whose house (ἡ οἰκία) adjoined the synagogue.[3]

---

[1] *Beginnings*, IV, 222.
[2] Blass makes this suggestion, *TSK*, LXXI (1898), 541.
[3] *Ibid.*

In summary of the D-text's handling of xviii. 4-8, it is clear that throughout this section the D-text is intent on stressing the sharpness of Paul's break with the recalcitrant Jews and on minimizing both their response and the importance of Judaism itself to the new faith.

In Acts xix Paul has a similar break with the synagogue:

Acts xix. 9a

B	D
ὡς δέ τινες	τινὲς μὲν οὖν αὐτῶν
ἐσκληρύνοντο καὶ ἠπείθουν	ἐσκληρύνοντο καὶ ἠπίθουν
κακολογοῦντες τὴν ὁδὸν	κακολογοῦντες τὴν ὁδὸν
ἐνώπιον τοῦ πλήθους,	ἐνώπιον τοῦ πλήθους τῶν ἐθνῶν.
ἀποστὰς ἀπ' αὐτῶν...	τότε ἀποστὰς ὁ Παῦλος ἀπ' αὐτῶν...

τινὲς μὲν οὖν D sy^p] +τῶν ἐθνῶν (+τότε 614) 614 383
αὐτῶν D *d gig* sy^p
τῶν ἐθνῶν D *d* E 103 sy^p sy^h* arab^e; populi *gig r*
τότε D *d* arab^e sy^p sy^h*
ὁ Παῦλος D *d* arab^e eth sy^p

In B πλῆθος refers to the congregation of Jews in the synagogue,[1] including, of course, some believers from among them.[2] B, then, relates that some Jews spoke evil of 'the Way' before this synagogue group. The D-text, however, reports that these Jews spoke evil of 'the Way' before the multitude *of the Gentiles*, showing that according to D the Jews sought to hinder the spread of the new faith also among the Gentiles,[3] opposing the universalism which Paul's preaching involved. A Gentile reader would not be kindly disposed toward the Jews upon reading this version.

This D-text reading shows, moreover, that Paul's transfer to the hall of a certain (τινός D *d* E H L P S 614 383 *c dem gig* vg^{s, cl} arm sy^h Bede^retr Chr^{9, 343}) Tyrannus in xix. 9*b* was an attempt especially directed to reaching Gentiles, for they were the ones, according to D, who were in danger of being turned away by the unbelieving Jews. These Gentiles would, however, be much less likely to come under adverse Jewish influence if they gathered to hear Paul in a public lecture hall.

---

[1] Ropes, *Text*, p. 182; *Beginnings*, IV, 239, see pp. 47f.
[2] Verse 9*b*; Haenchen, *Apostelgeschichte*, p. 188, n. 1.
[3] Thus Corssen, *GGA*, CLVIII (1896), 444.

The additional notice of the D-text (xix. 9*b*), that Paul lectured there ἀπὸ ὥρας ε ἕως δεκάτης (D *d* 614 383 *gig w cod.ard* sy[h]*; cf. Ambst[on IIC. xi. 23]), may indicate that Paul's discourses would not normally conflict in time with other sessions in the hall.[1] This is likely because Paul would probably occupy it during the midday meal and rest! That the D-text specifies this improbable hour for instruction may suggest the intensity of Paul's efforts to reach those Gentiles whom the Jews had attempted to predispose against 'the Way'.

In Acts vi. 1, the D-text specifies that it is the 'Hebrews' (i.e. Judaizing Jews) who were at fault in the dispute between these 'Hebrews' and the 'Hellenists' (i.e. Graecizing Jews) in the church: ὑπὸ τῶν διακόνων τῶν Ἑβραίων *h* (cop[G67]) or ἐν τῇ διακονίᾳ τῶν Ἑβραίων D* *d*] om D² 614 *gig cett*. Also, *h* and cop[G67] state specifically that it is the widows *of the Greeks* who were being neglected (*viduae*] + *Graecorum*).

The D-text of Acts vii. 52 provides an unusual confirmation of an anti-Judaic thrust already present in both the B- and D-texts. This point depends on a study of the usage of οἱ πατέρες ἡμῶν/ὑμῶν in Acts. The twenty-odd occurrences reveal a general agreement between the B- and D-texts in this usage. Both use οἱ πατέρες ἡμῶν whenever the fathers are referred to in a positive or neutral way; these comprise all but two of the instances: iii. 13; iii. 22 D; iii. 25 (where 𝔓[74] B A E sa geo Chr[9, 82] Thphyl read ὑμῶν but ℵ* C D *d* P 614 *gig h* vg[s, cl] bo sy[p, h] arm eth Ir Chr Cosm read ἡμῶν); v. 30; vii. 4 D); vii. 11, 12, 15, 38, 39,[2] 44, 45 *bis* (though in the second case D alone has ὑμῶν, obviously a scribal error; *d h* have ἡμῶν); xiii. 17; xiii. 32 D; xv. 10; xxii. 14 (D *def*, but *d* has ἡμῶν); xxvi. 6 (D *def*); xxviii. 25 (D *def*; ὁ θεὸς τῶν πατέρων σου in vii. 32, B and D, is a direct quotation from prophecy and does not apply here).

The two exceptions are found at the end of Stephen's speech, following eight occurrences of οἱ πατέρες ἡμῶν, and they appear suddenly, just when the tone of the speech changes and

---

[1] See *Beginnings*, IV, 239; Metzger, *Text of New Testament*, p. 51.

[2] Though A. F. J. Klijn, 'Stephen's Speech—Acts vii. 2–53', *NTS*, IV (1957/8), 27, sees a pejorative reference to the fathers in *vv*. 38 and 39. He may be correct about *v*. 39, and it may be that Ir[iv. 15, 1] minn geo and now cop[G67] represent the 'Western' text in vii. 39 in reading 'your fathers', which would indicate an anti-Judaic feeling here.

Stephen confronts the Jews directly, fiercely castigating them for resisting the Holy Spirit and killing the prophets. Here the expression οἱ πατέρες ὑμῶν occurs (vii. 51, 52). Thus, where the fathers are referred to in a negative or pejorative manner, Stephen is represented as disassociating himself (and Christians) from them—they are now 'your fathers', the fathers of those Jews who are stiff-necked and uncircumcized in heart. This would indicate a Lucan bias against rebellious and unbelieving adherents of Judaism.

However, for the second οἱ πατέρες ὑμῶν of B (vii. 52), D *d h t* have ἐκεῖνοι instead: τίνα τῶν προφητῶν οὐκ ἐδίωξαν ἐκεῖνοι. The strong contrast of the terms ἐκεῖνοι, referring to the Jews, and ἡμεῖς, referring to the Christians, appears vividly in the Epistle of Barnabas (see ii. 9–10; iii. 6; iv. 6–7; viii. 7; ix. 6; x. 12; xiii. 1, 3; xiv. 4–5),[1] and this same anti-Judaic use of ἐκεῖνοι appears here in the D-text of Acts vii. 52.

In Acts xv the D-text utilizes the record of the conduct of Judaizing Christians and the controversy surrounding their views to show its own feeling toward Judaism itself.

Acts xv. 4 concerns the arrival in Jerusalem of Paul, Barnabas, and some others from Antioch. They had been criticized at Antioch by Judaizers from Judea who objected, apparently not to the Gentile mission itself, but to Paul's teaching concerning the relationship of Gentile converts to Judaism (xv. 1–3).

Acts xv. 4

B	D
παραγενόμενοι δὲ εἰς Ἱεροσόλυμα	παραγενόμενοι δὲ εἰς Ἱερουσαλὴμ
παρεδέχθησαν	παρεδέχθησαν μεγ(άλ)ως
ἀπὸ τῆς ἐκκλησίας	ὑπὸ τῆς ἐκκλησίας
καὶ τῶν ἀποστόλων	καὶ τῶν ἀποστόλων
καὶ τῶν πρεσβυτέρων,...	καὶ τῶν πρεσβυτέρων,...

line 2: παρεδοθησαν

μεγάλως D *d* C 614 383 sa sy[h]* Ambr[ps 118, 23] Cass
ὑπό D 𝔓[74] ℵ A E H L P S 614 minn Chr[9,274]

[1] Though Professor Robert A. Kraft, who directed me to Barnabas here, would rather refer to this contrast in Barnabas as 'anti-cultic' than as 'anti-Judaic'; see *HTR*, LIV (1961), 300, and now his *Barnabas and the Didache* (New York/London, 1965), pp. 51, 84.

THE JEWS, GENTILES, AND CHRISTIANITY

The Jerusalem church, with the apostles and elders, received Paul and Barnabas 'in great fashion' or 'heartily'. Here it is the cordial reception of apostles from Antioch (xv. 1–2) which is emphasized in D, in spite of the fact that the D-text has just made it clear that it was the Judaizing opponents of Paul who had charged them to go to the apostles and elders in Jerusalem, and that this group opposing Paul and Barnabas was a specifically Jerusalem group [Acts xv. 2D: ...οἱ δὲ ἐληλυθότες ἀπὸ Ἱερουσαλήμ... D d sy[hmg] Ephr[cat(p423)]], which had accompanied Paul and Barnabas to Jerusalem (or also arrived there about the same time) [xv. 5D: οἱ δὲ παραγγείλαντες αὐτοῖς ἀναβαίνειν πρὸς τοὺς πρεσβυτέρους D d sy[hmg] Ephr[cat(p423)]]. In xv. 4 the D-text, then, reveals its attitude toward this group by indicating that this divisive group, though itself from Jerusalem, was not significant enough adversely to influence the Jerusalem church's enthusiastic welcome (μεγάλως) of Paul and Barnabas, nor would it, therefore, be able to divide the church by causing Paul and Barnabas to be censured at Jerusalem [see xv. 2D: ὅπως κριθῶσιν ἐπ' αὐτοῖς D d 614 383 sy[h]* Ephr[cat(p423)]]. Clearly, then, the Judaizing position and, by implication, Judaism itself do not come out well in the D-text.

Incidentally, this phrase of D in xv. 2, ὅπως κριθῶσιν ἐπ' αὐτοῖς, has evoked the statement of C. S. C. Williams that it 'implies the incredible suggestion that St Paul was willing to be tried at Jerusalem on this point'.[1] Such an opinion only illuminates the D-text's emphasis here: the early church is one of unity, and Paul can be portrayed as willing to be examined at Jerusalem rather than risk a breach of that unity. 'The emphasis in the D reading of Acts xv. 2 is not against Paul but in favour of the authority and unity of the church.'[2] The D-text cannot, therefore, be viewed as favouring a Judaizing viewpoint; quite the contrary (as will appear in this very context), for the interest of D here is in early church unity and, most important, in a unity over against the viewpoint of Judaism.

This stress on unity is borne out by the D-reading in xv. 12a, συνκατατεθεμένων δὲ τῶν πρεσβυτέρων τοῖς ὑπὸ τοῦ Πέτρου εἰρημένοις... D d sy[h]* Ephr[(p424) et cat(p425)], which also makes it

---
[1] Williams, *Alterations*, p. 60; similarly, Knox, *Church of Jerusalem*, p. xxiii.
[2] Menoud, 'Western Text', p. 29. That any aspersion on Paul is precluded here, see further Dibelius, *Studies*, p. 93.

clear that the Jerusalem group of elders and apostles could not be divided by the Judaizing advocates.

These variants in Acts xv could be taken as showing the leadership and control of the Jerusalem church,[1] but other variants of D combine with those already discussed to make it abundantly clear that besides the idea of unity the really significant factor here for D is the Judaizing viewpoint, and the D-text's attitude toward it deserves fuller attention.

First, however, observe two additional variants in connection with the unity of the church:

Acts iv. 32

B	D
τοῦ δὲ πλήθους τῶν πιστευ-σάντων ἦν καρδία καὶ ψυχὴ μία,...	τοῦ δὲ πλήθους τῶν πιστευ-σάντων ἦν καρδία καὶ ψυχὴ μία, καὶ οὐκ ἦν διάκρισις ἐν αὐτοῖς οὐδεμία,...

καὶ οὐκ ἦν διάκρισις (χωρισμός E Bede) ἐν αὐτοῖς οὐδεμία (τις E but *e* Bede have ulla) D *d* E Cypr[test iii. 3 et de op 25] Ambr ⅔ Bede[retr 119] Zeno[1. 3, 33]] om cett Aug

(*d*: et non erat accusatio [separatio *e* Bede] in eis ulla...; Cypr Zeno: nec fuit inter illos discrimen ullum...)

Although διάκρισις (D) and *discrimen* (Cypr) could be taken to mean 'distinction' and be given a social interpretation—there was no distinction among the believers—in accord with what follows regarding community of goods, etc., it is easier to take D's variant with what precedes, allowing διάκρισις (as well as *discrimen*) its other meaning of 'division' or 'separation', specifically 'dispute' or 'quarrel'.[2] In this case the phrase follows naturally upon the statement that the believers were of one heart and soul, and is in accord with the other readings for διάκρισις: χωρισμός E, *separatio e, accusatio* ('complaint') *d*. The direct statement that there was no division or dispute at all among them emphasizes the unity of the community.

Is it possible that D's reading here anticipates a parallel expression in xv. 9 (B and D) which refers to the unity of Jewish

[1] *Beginnings*, IV, 169; Ropes, *Text*, pp. 138f.
[2] W. Bauer, *Griechisch-deutsches Wörterbuch*[5] (Berlin, 1958), *ad loc.*

and Gentile believers: καὶ [ὁ θεὸς] οὐδὲν διέκρεινεν μεταξὺ ἡμῶν καὶ αὐτῶν?

As for relations between churches, consider Acts xi. 27:

Acts xi. 27

B
Ἐν αὐταῖς δὲ ταῖς ἡμέραις
κατῆλθον ἀπὸ Ἱεροσολύμων
προφῆται εἰς Ἀντιόχειαν.

D
Ἐν ταύταις δὲ ταῖς ἡμέραις
κατῆλθον ἀπὸ Ἱεροσολύμων
προφῆται εἰς Ἀντιόχειαν,
ἦν δὲ πολλὴ ἀγαλλίασις.

ἦν δὲ πολλὴ ἀγαλλίασις D d p q w vg^codd prov τερl cop^G67 Aug^serm dom ii.37 Proph

The rejoicing occasioned by the coming of prophets from the Jerusalem church to that at Antioch suggests that only the most pleasant and harmonious relationship existed between the churches. The reality of the joy described by the D-text is certified by the words of D which follow (verse 28D): συνεστραμμένων δὲ ἡμῶν... D d p q w vg^codd prov Aug^serm dom ii.37 Proph Ado (cf. cop^G67). This 'we'-statement of D implies that the church at Antioch itself could attest the accuracy of this report.

E. Haenchen says that this additional 'we'-passage in D does not belong to the oldest stock of the 'Western' text, though R. Bultmann disagrees.[1] Haenchen supports his own judgement by appealing to Irenaeus (III. 14, 1), who, he says, first has Luke accompany Paul in the 'we'-passage at xvi. 10. Irenaeus, says Haenchen, would not have overlooked a 'we'-passage in xi. 28 had he known it, as is shown by the carefulness with which he employed Acts. But Haenchen's argument, though impressive, is weakened by the fact that while 'we' elsewhere in Acts means 'Paul and his companions', here it refers to 'the church at Antioch'.[2]

Admittedly, this variant does not have the strongest 'Western' attestation; p is, however, Old Latin in Acts i. 1 to xiii. 6, and Hilgenfeld, Zahn, and A. C. Clark include the variant in their editions of the 'Western' text.

[1] Haenchen, *Apostelgeschichte*, p. 11, n. 7; R. Bultmann, 'Zur Frage nach den Quellen der Apostelgeschichte', *New Testament Essays. Studies in Memory of Thomas Walter Manson, 1893–1958* (Manchester, 1959), p. 77.
[2] Ropes, *Text*, p. 108.

Incidentally, does the plural in the 'Western' text of ix. 31 (D *def*), αἱ μὲν οὖν ἐκκλησίαι (+πᾶσαι E)...εἶχον εἰρήνην E H L P S 614 383 *gig cod.ard p* arab geo sy[h] Chr[9,181] Thphyl[a] Aug[c] (with the corresponding plural verbs), instead of B's ἡ...ἐκκλησία...εἶχεν εἰρήνην, indicate a similar emphasis on unity among individual churches?

Returning to the D-text's attitude toward the Judaizing viewpoint, notice, first of all, that in Acts xv. 1 the D-text shows the position of the men who came down from Judea to be a more rigid one than that represented in B:

Acts xv. 1

B	D
καί τινες κατελθόντες	καί τινες κατελθόντες
ἀπὸ τῆς Ἰουδαίας	ἀπὸ τῆς Ἰουδαίας
ἐδίδασκον τοὺς ἀδελφοὺς ὅτι	ἐδίδασκον τοὺς ἀδελφοὺς ὅτι
Ἐὰν μὴ περιτμηθῆτε	Ἐὰν μὴ περιτμηθῆτε
τῷ ἔθει τῷ Μωυσέως,	καὶ τῷ ἔθει Μωσέως περιπατῆτε,
οὐ δύνασθε σωθῆναι.	οὐ δύνασθε σωθῆναι.

Ἰουδαίας] +τῶν πεπιστευκότων ἀπὸ τῆς αἱρέσεως τῶν Φαρισαίων 614 383 sy[hmg] (cf. *v.* 5, B D etc.)
καί (second) D *d* sa sy[hmg]
Μωσέως] +καὶ τοῖς ἄλλοις ἔθεσιν οἷς διετάξατο (Didasc[vi.12,3]) Const.Apost[vi.12,2]
περιπατῆτε D *d* sa sy[hmg] Didasc[vi.12,3] Const.Apost[vi.12,2]

The B-text describes the Judaizing teaching as, 'Unless you are circumcised according to the custom of Moses...', whereas D has, 'Unless you are circumcised *and walk* in the custom of Moses...'. (This variant brings *v.* 1 D into harmony with *v.* 5 B and D; in B *v.* 1 and *v.* 5 each designate a different group with slightly different demands, but in D these two groups are one, with the same views expressed in each case.)[1]

It is interesting that in the apostolic letter in Acts xv. 24, this same Judaizing teaching is the explanation, in the 'Western' text, of the phrase ...ἐξετάραξαν ὑμᾶς λόγοις ἀνασκευάζοντες τὰς ψυχὰς ὑμῶν, οἷς οὐ διεστειλάμεθα (B and D). The 'Western' text here (though not D) after ψυχὰς ὑμῶν has λέγοντες

[1] See Williams, *Alterations*, p. 60, who says D failed to see that *v.* 5 spoke of the different demands of the Pharisees; but see Ropes, *Text*, p. 140, for evidence that the 'Western' text contained no mention of Pharisees here.

περιτέμνεσθαι (+ δεῖ E Bede) καὶ τηρεῖν τὸν νόμον C E H L P S Ψ 614 383 arm eth^pp geo sy^{p, h} Bede^{retr 143} Thphyl, sim Chr^{9, 281}; or after διεστειλάμεθα has λέγοντες περιτέμνεσθε καὶ τηρεῖτε τὸν νόμον gig vg^{cod} Ir^{iii. 12, 14(17)}] om D d cett.
At the same time, the D-text of xv. 2 makes explicit the contrary position of Paul:

Acts xv. 2

B

γενομένης δὲ στάσεως καὶ
ζητήσεως οὐκ ὀλίγης τῷ Παύλῳ
καὶ τῷ Βαρνάβᾳ πρὸς αὐτοὺς

ἔταξαν
ἀναβαίνειν Παῦλον καὶ Βαρνάβαν
καί τινας ἄλλους ἐξ αὐτῶν
πρὸς τοὺς ἀποστόλους καὶ
πρεσβυτέρους εἰς Ἱερουσαλὴμ

περὶ τοῦ ζητήματος τούτου.

D

γενομένης δὲ στάσεως καὶ
ζητήσεως οὐκ ὀλίγης τῷ Παύλῳ
καὶ Βαρνάβᾳ σὺν αὐτοῖς,
ἔλεγεν γὰρ ὁ Παῦλος μένειν
οὕτως καθὼς ἐπίστευσαν
διϊσχυριζόμενος, οἱ δὲ ἐληλυθότες
ἀπὸ Ἱερουσαλὴμ
παρήγγειλαν αὐτοῖς
τῷ Παύλῳ καὶ Βαρνάβᾳ
καί τισιν ἄλλοις ἀναβαίνειν
πρὸς τοὺς ἀποστόλους καὶ
πρεσβυτέρους εἰς Ἱερουσαλὴμ
ὅπως κριθῶσιν ἐπ' αὐτοῖς
περὶ τοῦ ζητήματος τούτου.

line 1: εκτασεως

ἔλεγεν... ἐπίστευσαν D d gig (+ αὐτοὺς post μένειν gig) q (w) vg^{codd} prov tepl cop^{G67} sy^{hmg} (ἐπίστευσεν sy^{hmg}) Ephr^{(p420)}
διϊσχυριζόμενος D sy^{hmg} (adverb); cf. cop^{G67} Ephr^{(p420)}] om d gig cett
οἱ δὲ ἐληλυθότες...καί τισιν ἄλλοις D d sy^{hmg} (τότε for αὐτοῖς sy^{hmg}) Ephr^{cat (p423)} (cop^{G67}: then they who had come)
ὅπως κριθῶσιν ἐπ' αὐτοῖς (-οἷς D*; -ῶν 614 383) post Ἱερουσαλὴμ D d; post τούτου 614 383 sy^{h*}; Ephr^{(p422) et cat (p423)}

Both the B- and D-texts indicate that Paul and Barnabas 'had no small dissension and debate with them', but the D-text continues: 'For Paul spoke maintaining firmly[1] that they [Gentile converts] should remain just as when they believed.' Thus, the D-text has sharpened up the issues in the controversy, and in xv. 2 b it specifies, as noted earlier, that the men of Judea who came down to Antioch are *from Jerusalem* and, moreover,

[1] Διϊσχυριζόμενος occurs in NT only in Lk xxii. 59 and Acts xii. 15.

101

that they are the ones who order Paul and Barnabas and some others to go to the apostles and elders in Jerusalem (in B ἔταξαν has no stated subject) *in order that they might be judged before them* (ὅπως κριθῶσιν ἐπ' αὐτοῖς) concerning this question. Notice, now, that in xv. 5, the D-text has these very same persons [οἱ δὲ παραγγείλαντες αὐτοῖς ἀναβαίνειν πρὸς τοὺς πρεσβυτέρους D *d* sy^hmg Ephr^cat(p423)] reaffirm, in the course of the disputation in Jerusalem, the obligation to be circumcised and to keep the law of Moses.

It becomes clear, then, that in the D-text there is only one group which represents the Judaizing point of view, whereas in the B-text there are at least two. B has one group from Judea (xv. 1–2), another in Jerusalem (xv. 5), and possibly a third if it is understood that in xv. 2 it is the Antiochian church which urges Paul *et al.* to go to Jerusalem,[1] and that some local Antiochian believers held or were persuaded to adopt the Judaizing view. Regardless of this last point, however, the D-text is very precise in stating that it is one and the same group which came from Judea with Judaizing teachings (*v.* 1), which ordered Paul *et al.* to go to Jerusalem (*v.* 2), and which reiterated Judaizing teaching in Jerusalem (*v.* 5). Three points emerge from this construction in D: (1) As already noted, the unity of the church is maintained and enhanced because this opposition to Paul and Barnabas comes from only one quarter—from this one small group of Judaizers. (2) The D-text minimizes not only the number of Judaizers—a single group—but, by the same token, minimizes the significance of the Judaizing viewpoint itself when seen in relation to the church as a whole. Already the D-text reveals an interest in playing down the seriousness of the whole dispute, a point which becomes even clearer as the narrative in chapter xv D proceeds.[2] (3) Along with this tendency to devalue the Judaizing viewpoint, the D-text has, however, both sharpened up the issues involved (xv. 1–2) and portrayed an increased intensity of opposition to Paul and Barnabas on the part of that Judaizing group, for the group not only accuses them at Antioch and drives them to Jerusalem to be judged, but the group also appears again in

---

[1] Thus Ropes, *Text*, pp. ccxxx, 138f.; see *BBC*, IX (1931), 3; Fascher, *Textgeschichte*, pp. 31f.; Williams, *Alterations*, p. 60.

[2] See also Dibelius, *Studies*, p. 93 and n. 3.

THE JEWS, GENTILES, AND CHRISTIANITY

Jerusalem as the opponent of Paul and Barnabas,[1] as if further to press its charges against them. It is not unnatural to think that these opponents themselves conducted Paul and Barnabas to Jerusalem to ensure their arrival there to give account.

Acts xv. 6ff. relates to the apostles and elders' consideration of the Gentile Christian matter and includes the speeches of Peter and James. Peter's speech here defends the Gentile mission and the validity of the Gentiles' faith and salvation, and takes the Pauline viewpoint—more or less—regarding regulations for Gentile believers (*vv*. 7–11), while the speech of James presents a more compromising position.

In view of this, it is noteworthy that the D-text, at the conclusion of Peter's speech (xv. 12), reports that 'the elders consented to what had been said by Peter' (συνκατατεθεμένων, literally 'putting down the same vote as'):

Acts xv. 12 a

B	D
	συνκατατεθεμένων δὲ τῶν πρεσβυτέρων τοῖς ὑπὸ τοῦ Πέτρου εἰρημένοις
ἐσείγησεν δὲ πᾶν τὸ πλῆθος, ...	ἐσείγησεν πᾶν τὸ πλῆθος, ...

συνκατατεθεμένων ... εἰρημένοις D *d* sy^h* Ephr^(p424) *et* cat (p425)

Thus, D once again supports the Pauline viewpoint in the debate, and all in all, the Judaizers come out rather poorly in the D-text.

A more striking indication of this attitude of the D-text, however, is found by comparing the introductory formulas to the speeches of Peter and of James in the two text-types:

Acts xv. 7

B	D
... ἀναστὰς	... ἀνέστ[η]σεν ἐν πνεύματι
Πέτρος	Πέτρος
εἶπεν πρὸς αὐτούς·	καὶ εἶπεν πρὸς αὐτούς·

ἀνέστησεν (=ἀνέστη) D* *d* sy^p?
ἐν πνεύματι (+ἁγίῳ 257 614 sy^hmg Cass) D* *d* 257 614 *l* sy^hmg Tert^pud 21 Cass Ephr^(p425)] *om* Ir^iii.12,14(17)
καί D *d* sy^p

[1] Fascher, *Textgeschichte*, p. 99.

103

ANTI-JUDAIC TENDENCIES IN ACTS

With this compare xv. 13:

Acts xv. 13

B
...ἀπεκρίθη Ἰάκωβος λέγων·

D
...ἀναστὰς Ἰάκωβος εἶπεν·

ἀναστὰς...εἶπεν D *d* sy^p

In xv. 7 the formula introducing Peter's speech in the B-text is ἀναστὰς Πέτρος εἶπεν πρὸς αὐτούς, while in xv. 13 the formula used for the speech of James runs ἀπεκρίθη Ἰάκωβος λέγων. In the D-text, however, Peter's speech is introduced by ἀνέστη [ἀνέστησεν] ἐν πνεύματι Πέτρος καὶ εἶπεν πρὸς αὐτούς, while that of James has ἀναστὰς Ἰάκωβος εἶπεν. Thus, the B-text formulates the two introductory statements differently, while the D-text employs the same basic formula for both speeches: ἀνέστη...Πέτρος καὶ εἶπεν, and ἀναστὰς Ἰάκωβος εἶπεν. Notice, now, that the remarks of Peter, which are essentially Pauline in their view of the Judaizing deliberations, are characterized as pneumatic: Peter rose up ἐν πνεύματι (+ἁγίῳ in some witnesses), while the remarks of James, who presents a compromising position, are not accorded this dignity, even though D uses the same formula in introducing the two speeches. Indeed, this very similarity in style certainly calls attention to the *lack* of ἐν πνεύματι in the case of James and seems more than coincidental.[1]

Of interest in this connection also is the remark of J. Dupont[2] that Ir[iii.12,14(17)] and Ephr[(p426) *et* cat(p427)] witness to a text of Acts xv. 19 which is anxious to diminish the importance of the intervention of James: Ir: *propterea ego* **secundum me** *judico*...; Ephr: *et de hoc* [*quantum stat in potentia*] *mea confirmo verba Shmavonis*...; Ephr[cat]: 'and so far as it lies in my power...'.

Turning for the moment from the situation portrayed in Acts xv, notice another situation (in Acts xi. 1–2) involving Peter and bearing similarities to the problem in Acts xv. B. W. Bacon, in fact, felt that Acts xi. 2 D showed a heightened parallelism between 'what is here described as Peter's journey to Jerusalem to vindicate his mission to gentiles and what is

---

[1] Fascher, *Textgeschichte*, pp. 36f.
[2] In L. Cerfaux and J. Dupont, *Les Actes des Apôtres* (Paris, 1953), p. 138.

THE JEWS, GENTILES, AND CHRISTIANITY

described in 15, 1-5 as a journey of Paul and Barnabas from Antioch to Jerusalem with the same object'.[1] This D-version of Acts xi. 2 is typical of the subtlety with which the D-text often makes its point. The context here relates that the apostles and elders in Judea heard that Gentiles had believed (v. 1) and that when Peter (who was in Caesarea) went to Jerusalem, he was assailed by 'those of the circumcision' (v. 2) for associating and eating with uncircumcised men (v. 3). Notice v. 2:

Acts xi. 2

B	D
ὅτε δὲ	ὁ μὲν οὖν Πέτρος
	διὰ ἱκανοῦ χρόνου ἠθέλησε
ἀνέβη Πέτρος εἰς Ἰερουσαλήμ,	πορευθῆναι εἰς Ἱεροσόλυμα·
	καὶ προσφωνήσας τοὺς ἀδελφοὺς
	καὶ ἐπιστηρίξας αὐτούς,
	πολὺν λόγον ποιούμενος,
	διὰ τῶν χωρῶν διδάσκων αὐτούς·
	ὃς καὶ κατήντησεν αὐτοῖς
	καὶ ἀπήγγιλεν αὐτοῖς
	τὴν χάριν τοῦ θεοῦ.
διεκρείνοντο πρὸς αὐτὸν	οἱ δὲ ἐκ περιτομῆς ἀδελφοὶ
οἱ ἐκ περιτομῆς...	διεκρίνοντο πρὸς αὐτόν...

line 2: ηθελησαι

[Add to verse 1: καὶ ἐδόξαϡον τὸν θεόν gig l p² q w dem vg^codd prov tepl cop^G67 sy^h* (dut)]
ὁ μὲν οὖν...προσφωνήσας (-ῆσαι sy^h*)...ἐπιστηρίξας αὐτούς (om αὐτούς p w sy^h*) D d p q w vg^codd prov tepl cop^G67 sy^h*
post ἐπιστηρίξας αὐτούς: ἐξῆλθεν or ἐπορεύθη p q w vg^codd cop^G67 sy^h*] om D d
πολὺν (+τε p q w)...διδάσκων αὐτούς D p q w vg^codd prov tepl cop^G67; καὶ ἐδίδασκεν αὐτούς sy^h* [see note 2]
ὃς καὶ...τοῦ θεοῦ D d (cop^G67)
ἀδελφοί D d l p w cop^G67

---

[1] Bacon, *HTR*, xxi (1928), 127f. This technique of paralleling in D has been illustrated above, pp. 51f., and will appear again: see below, pp. 124, 126, 162-4.
[2] On this reading in sy^h*, see W. D. McHardy, 'The Text of Acts in James of Edessa's Citations and in the Cambridge Add. MS. 1700', *JTS*, L (1949), 186, who confirms it from Cambridge Add. MS. 1700.

The B-text shows a close connection between the conversion of Gentiles, Peter's journey to Jerusalem, and his dispute with 'those of the circumcision' about fellowship with Gentiles. It could easily be inferred from the B-text that Peter's trip to Jerusalem was for the specific purpose of dealing with this problem, or even that he was recalled to Jerusalem to answer to the church.[1]

The D-text is quite different. There is, to be sure, a direct connection between the fact that the report of Gentile converts had reached Judea and Peter's return to Jerusalem (ὁ μὲν οὖν Πέτρος), but Peter's return is so much more casual, with no great urgency or immediacy about it.[2] The D-text, in fact, seems to labour the point of the long interval between the report (v. 1) and his arrival: πολὺν λόγον ποιούμενος, διὰ τῶν χωρῶν, etc. Moreover, the material of D is somewhat repetitious and of such a general nature as to suggest that it is here for some reason beyond the significance of the material itself, and such a reason can readily be found in a desire to separate the events of xi. 1 and those of xi. 2–3[3] and thereby to minimize the significance of the Judaizing problem as well as any urgent concern about it on the part of both the Jerusalem church and Peter himself. In other words, as far as the D-text was concerned, Peter could take his time and finish his work, for this Gentile problem could wait until Peter himself decided (...ἠθέλησε πορευθῆναι...) to go to Jerusalem. The problem is, as a matter of fact, a sort of excuse for Peter to go there, something he had wanted to do for a long time.

C. C. Torrey, incidentally, makes just the opposite out of this verse: he says that the D-reading shows Peter concerned about the effect that the report of his Gentile mission will have on the church, and so he returns to Jerusalem *as soon as possible*, going through Judea reassuring the brethren and instructing them about the divine purpose for the Gentiles.[4] There is very little in the passage to commend this view!

It is significant that the 'Western' text[5] (though not D) of xi. 1, following mention of the fact that the apostles and

---

[1] For the possibility of the latter view, see *Beginnings*, IV, 124; Jacquier, *Actes*, p. 337, who quotes Loisy.   [2] Thus also Jacquier, *Actes*, pp. 337f.
[3] See O. Bauernfeind, *Die Apostelgeschichte* (Leipzig, 1939), p. 152, for this point.   [4] Torrey, *Documents*, p. 126.
[5] That the words quoted represent the 'Western' text, see Ropes, *Text*, p. 102.

brethren in Judea heard that the Gentiles received the word of God, remarks: καὶ ἐδόξαζον τὸν θεόν, *gig l p² q w dem* prov tepl cop^G67 sy^h*. This is a statement which, in the B-text, is reserved for xi. 18, that is, *after* Peter's explanation of how God had bestowed the gift of the Spirit also on Gentiles (cf. also xxi. 20 where the phrase occurs *after* a similar explanation by Paul). The phrase in xi. 1 indicates, then, that as far as the 'Western' text was concerned, any controversy over eating with Gentiles was overshadowed by God's divine activity among Gentiles, about which there was nothing but a positive reaction from the very beginning.

Returning to Acts xv, *vv.* 20 and 29, along with xxi. 25, offer what are undoubtedly the best known and most widely discussed variants of the D-text in Acts:[1]

Acts xv. 20

B	D
...ἀλλ' ἐπιστεῖλαι αὐτοῖς	...ἀλλὰ ἐπιστεῖλαι αὐτοῖς
τοῦ ἀπέχεσθαι	τοῦ ἀπέχεσθαι
τῶν ἀλισγημάτων τῶν εἰδώλων	τῶν ἀλισγημάτων τῶν εἰδώλων
καὶ τῆς πορνείας	καὶ τῆς πορνείας
καὶ πνικτοῦ	
καὶ τοῦ αἵματος.	καὶ τοῦ αἵματος,
	καὶ ὅσα μὴ θέλουσιν ἑαυτοῖς
	γείνεσθαι ἑτέροις μὴ ποιεῖτε.

καὶ πνικτοῦ] *om* D *d gig* Ir^iii.12,14(17) Ir^gk=cod 1739mg Ambr Ambst^gal 2, 2 Arist Aug Gaud? Hier^gal 5, 2 Ephr^(p426)] 'and dead' sa eth
καὶ ὅσα... μὴ ποιεῖτε (ποιεῖν *cod.ard* Ir) D *d cod.ard* sa eth Arist Ir^iii.12,14(17) Ir^gk=cod 1739mg Ephr^[see note 2] Eus

Acts xv. 29

B	D
..., ἀπέχεσθαι εἰδωλοθύτων	..., ἀπέχεσθαι εἰδωλοθύτων
καὶ αἵματος καὶ πνικτῶν	καὶ αἵματος
καὶ πορνείας·	καὶ πορνίας,

[1] For a more detailed discussion of the textual evidence, see Ropes, *Text*, pp. 265–9; Zahn, *Urausgabe*, pp. 154–66; Harnack, *Studien*, I, 4–17; A. C. Clark, *Acts*, pp. 360f.; W. G. Kümmel, 'Die älteste Form des Apostel- dekrets', *Spiritus et Veritas* (Eutin, 1953), pp. 85–9.

[2] Ephrem's text of the 'decree' does not have the 'golden rule', but he mentions it a little later when referring to the 'decree'.

ἐξ ὧν διατηροῦντες ἑαυτοὺς
εὖ πράξετε.

ἔρρωσθε.

καὶ ὅσα μὴ θέλετε ἑαυτοῖς
γείνεσθαι ἑτέρῳ μὴ ποιεῖν·
ἀφ' ὧν διατηροῦντες ἑαυτοὺς
εὖ πράξατε
φερόμενοι ἐν τῷ ἁγίῳ πνεύματι
ἔρρωσθε.

καὶ πνικτῶν] om D *d l* eth Cypr[test iii.119] Ir[iii. 12,14(17)] Ir[gk=cod 1739 mg]
Tert[pud 12] Ambr Ambst[gal 2, 2] Ful Aug Pac Ephr[(p426)] Hier[gal 5, 2]
καὶ ὅσα...ἑτέρῳ (-ροις *q* Ir) μὴ ποιεῖν (-εῖτε *cod.ard q* sa Ir Cypr) D
d 42 51 234 242 323 429 464 614 *l p q w*[2] *cod.ard* sa eth prov tepl
sy[h]* Cypr[test iii.119] Ir[iii. 12,14(17)] Ir[gk=cod 1739mg] Eus[adv. porph] (*secundum* cod
1739 mg); cf. Cl[strom ii. 22, 139]] *om cett* Tert[pud 12] Cl$\frac{2}{3}$ Pac Const.Apost
ἀφ' ὧν D, a quibus *d e* vg Ir[lat] Tert
πράξατε D 𝔓[74] C H L *cod.ard*] πράξετε *cett* cod 1 739mg
φερόμενοι... πνεύματι D *d l* Tert[pud 12] Ir[iii. 12,14(17)] Ir[gk=cod 1739 mg]
Cass Ephr[(p426)]] *om cett* Cl Pac Const.Apost
(ambulantes in spiritu sancto *l* Ir; vectante vos spiritu sancto Tert;
ferentes in s. sp. *d*)

Acts xxi. 25

B

περὶ δὲ τῶν πεπιστευκότων
ἐθνῶν

ἡμεῖς ἀπεστείλαμεν
κρείναντες

φυλάσσεσθαι αὐτοὺς
τό τε εἰδωλόθυτον καὶ αἷμα
καὶ πνικτὸν καὶ πορνείαν.

D

περὶ δὲ τῶν πεπιστευκότων
ἐθνῶν
οὐδὲν ἔχουσι λέγειν πρὸς σέ,
ἡμεῖς γὰρ ἀπεστείλαμεν
κρείνοντες μηδὲν τοιοῦτον
τηρεῖν αὐτοὺς εἰ μὴ
φυλάσσεσθαι αὐτοὺς
τὸ ε(ἰ)δωλόθυτον καὶ αἷμα
καὶ πορνείαν.

οὐδὲν...πρὸς σέ D *d gig* sa
γάρ D *d gig* sa] *om cett* Aug
κρείνοντες D* 103
μηδὲν...εἰ μή D *d* C E H L P S 614 383 *gig* arm (eth) geo sy[h] Aug
Chr[9, 387] Bede[retr 150]
καὶ πνικτόν] *om* D *d gig* geo Aug[ep 82. 9]

Most of the discussion of these variants has revolved around
the question of originality,[1] but this question is not of primary

---

[1] The literature on these variants is vast; that which is cited in Haenchen, *Apostelgeschichte*, pp. 382 f., 390, n. 5, and in Kümmel, 'Die älteste Form', p. 85, n. 4, covers the significant discussions. The following might be added:

importance for the present purpose; rather the interest is in the meaning of the D-text. Actually, very little need be said even on this point, for it is obvious that, while the 'apostolic decree' in the B-text has both a ceremonial part (εἰδωλόθυτα, αἷμα, and πνικτά) and a moral part (πορνεία), the 'decree' in the D-text has only the moral part (πνικτά, the specifically ceremonial part, is lacking, and εἰδωλόθυτα and αἷμα stand for idolatry and murder respectively) and the additional general ethical statement in the form of the negative[1] 'golden rule'. This ethical emphasis in the D-text, over against the largely ceremonial

Windisch in *Beginnings*, II, 324–6; F. C. Burkitt, *Christian Beginnings* (London, 1924), pp. 112–16 ff.; B. W. Bacon, 'Some "Western" Variants in the Text of Acts', *HTR*, XXI (1928), 128–35; G. B. King, 'The "Negative" Golden Rule', *JRel*, VIII (1928), 268–79; K. Lake, *The Earlier Epistles of St Paul* (London, 1930), pp. 48–60; J. A. Montgomery, 'On the Interpolation in Acts 15: 29', *JBL*, LII (1933), 261; Knox, *Church of Jerusalem*, pp. 234–6; Conzelmann, *Apostelgeschichte*, pp. 84 f.

[1] The negative form is the 'perfect equivalent' of the positive form, so that 'the meaning of the golden rule is not modified by its negative form in Acts. Its form is in harmony with the context' (Menoud, 'Western Text', p. 26). King, *JRel*, VIII (1928), 268–79, refers to a large number of forms of the golden rule, both negative and positive, Jewish and Christian, and concludes that the dispute as to the superiority of the positive or negative form should cease, for 'basically they are the same, in idea as in origin' (p. 277; cf. p. 271, n. 4. Thus also A. Dihle, *Die Goldene Regel* (Göttingen, 1962), pp. 10 f.). King (pp. 275–8) points out that the positive form of Jesus, over against the negative form in Tobit (iv. 15), Philo, Hillel, Akiba, etc., does not in itself imply that Jesus' teaching is of a higher nature, for Jesus also gave his teaching in a negative form: 'Judge not, that ye be not judged', etc.

Nor does the negative form necessarily imply a Jewish standpoint for this D-variant. King, p. 272, gives examples which show that 'positive forms of the rule have...had a place in Judaism'. Moreover, the negative form is found in other Christian sources (besides D), such as Aristides, Didache, Const.Apost (cf. Gospel of Thomas, 6) and many others (Dihle, p. 107, lists twenty examples), and may lie behind Rom. xiii. 10 (King, pp. 271 f.); it also may have been present in the Diatessaron, for it is found in Ephrem, Aphraates, and Philoxenus: for details, see R. H. Connolly, 'A Negative Form of the Golden Rule in the Diatessaron?', *JTS*, XXXV (1934), 351–7; O. E. Evans, 'The Negative Form of the Golden Rule in the Diatessaron', *ET*, LXIII (1951/2), 31 f. All of this would suggest that the positive and negative rules were regarded as identical in meaning (cf. King, p. 271, n. 4, who thus understands Didache's use of the negative form). Further, see H. Köster, *Synoptische Überlieferung bei den apostolischen Vätern* (Berlin, 1957), pp. 14, 167–70.

stress of B, is clear,[1] and shows that once again the D-text reveals its distance from the Judaizing viewpoint and, by so doing, its distance from the viewpoint of Judaism itself, at least in its ritual and ceremonial emphasis; and it was this emphasis, after all, which occasioned the 'apostolic decree' in the first place. There is, of course, nothing anti-Jewish or non-Jewish in the ethical precepts; the point concerns the emphasis of the B- and D-texts and the direction of the apostolic inquiry. There is, however, in the final statement of the apostolic letter ('If you keep yourselves from these, you will do well') additional D-material which 'attests the specific Christian value attached to the golden rule',[2] and that is the formal mention of the Holy Spirit: φερόμενοι ἐν τῷ ἁγίῳ πνεύματι (xv. 29). This D-phrase has too often been neglected in discussions of the 'decree'. W. G. Kümmel does refer to it as a 'Christianizing addition', and Harnack said it was most relevant to a statement of the general Christian ethic,[3] but notably it is P. H. Menoud who finds in this reading the indication of the chief intention of the D-text, namely, 'to emphasize the newness of the Christian faith as regards Judaism', and consequently he sees the whole D-version of the 'decree' in an anti-Judaic setting:

This golden rule becomes a standard of Christian belief and practice, so much so that this rule cannot be practised except in Christ or in

[1] Thus e.g. Harnack, *Studien*, I, 10; Idem, *Acts*, pp. 250–63; W. Sanday, 'The Apostolic Decree (Acts xv. 20–29)', *Theologische Studien Theodor Zahn*... *dargebracht* (Leipzig, 1908), pp. 8f.; Burkitt, *Christian Beginnings*, pp. 114f.; Bacon, *HTR*, XXI (1928), 128, 134f.; Ropes, *Text*, p. 269; Plooij, *BBC*, VI (1929), 15f.; Lake, *Earlier Epistles*, pp. 48ff.; Lietzmann, 'Der Sinn des Aposteldekretes und seine Textwandlung', *Amicitiae Corolla*,...*Essays Presented to James Rendel Harris* (London, 1933), pp. 204, 208; Dibelius, *Studies*, pp. 93, n. 2, 98, n. 12; Klijn, *Survey*, p. 19; Williams, *Alterations*, p. 74; Bruce, *Acts*'52, p. 299; Menoud, 'Western Text', pp. 25, 27; Fascher, *Textgeschichte*, p. 34; H. J. Cadbury, *The Book of Acts in History* (New York, 1955), p. 154; Haenchen, *Apostelgeschichte*, p. 390, n. 5; H. C. Snape, 'The Composition of the Lukan Writings: A Re-Assessment', *HTR*, LIII (1960), 43; H. J. Schonfield, 'Should "Things strangled" Be Omitted from Acts xv. 29?', *ET*, XLI (1929/30), 128f.; V. Taylor, *The Text of the New Testament. A Short Introduction*[2] (London, 1963), p. 100; Conzelmann, *Apostelgeschichte*, pp. 84f.; T. Boman, 'Das textkritische Problem des sogenannten Aposteldekrets', *NovTest*, VII (1964), 27–9.   [2] Menoud, 'Western Text', p. 27.

[3] Kümmel, 'Die älteste Form', pp. 88, 92; Harnack, *Studien*, I, 9; on the ethical force of the phrase, see Haenchen, *Apostelgeschichte*, p. 395; Conzelmann, *Apostelgeschichte*, p. 86.

the Spirit, and the actual possession of the Spirit is the God-given gift which separates Christianity from Judaism.[1]

The phrase, 'being sustained by the Holy Spirit', serves, then, to counteract any legalistic overtones which might accompany the apostolic letter as a result of the Judaizing controversy. This same interest would account for the supplementary words in xv. 32, where Judas and Silas, the oral bearers of the contents of the letter (see xv. 26–7), are described by Codex Bezae as πλήρεις πνεύματος ἁγίου, D d.

Thus, this ethical interpretation of the 'decree' and its pneumatic setting[2] in the 'Western' text not only reveal a distinctively Christian emphasis over against Judaism, but also minimize the seriousness of the Judaizing dispute[3] and, more important, nullify the Judaizing contentions, for the apostolic decision, understood in this way, yields nothing to their position and enjoins upon the Gentile Christians none of their demands.

The context of Acts xxi. 25 concerns the elders advising Paul as to how to avoid trouble with those of the Judaizing viewpoint who have heard that Paul inveighs against circumcision and the customs (xxi. 21). They will hear of Paul's arrival and, according to the D-text, will certainly gather (xxi. 22): δεῖ πλῆθος συνελθεῖν (D d H L P S 383; δεῖ συνελθεῖν πλῆθος $\mathfrak{P}^{74}$ ℵ A C² E minn gig vg Aug Hier] om 614 sy^{p,h} sa cett). This sentence probably should be translated 'A mob will congregate'[4] and be taken as an indication, according to the D-text, of a more hostile attitude toward Paul on this issue. The advice of the elders is that Paul prominently associate himself with pious Jews in their ceremonial acts and thus allay any suspicions about his adherence to the law, etc. (v. 24). Then comes v. 25. The μηδὲν τοιοῦτον τηρεῖν αὐτοὺς εἰ μή... of D emphasizes in a pointed way that the Gentile Christians are certainly not to follow these Mosaic customs and law: 'They are to observe nothing of the kind, except' the three restrictions of the 'decree'. The preceding οὐδὲν ἔχουσιν λέγειν πρός σε in D means, then, that these Jewish Christians would have nothing

---
[1] Menoud, 'Western Text', pp. 26f.
[2] Fascher, *Textgeschichte*, pp. 36f., stresses the pneumatic element in the D-text of Acts xv.
[3] Dibelius, *Studies*, p. 93, n. 2.
[4] See *Beginnings*, IV, 272, for the possibility of this translation.

to say against Paul about the Gentile Christians, for (γάρ D) the 'decree' was sufficient for them. This variant, consequently, points to the fact that the conflict of the Jewish Christians here was with Paul and Paul alone. The D-text has, then, reduced the Judaizing controversy to the 'decree' (*ethically conceived*) and to Paul personally (involving, of course, his alleged unorthodox teaching to Jews).

Continuing with the narrative in Acts xv, *v*. 33 in the B- and D-texts relates that Judas and Silas, after delivering the letter, were sent off in peace from Antioch to Jerusalem. The D-text, however, says in the additional *v*. 34:

ἔδοξε δὲ τῷ Σειλέᾳ ἐπιμεῖναι αὐτοῦ, μόνος δὲ 'Ιούδας ἐπορεύθη.

ἔδοξε...αὐτοῦ (αὐτούς D *d* C) D *d* C 33 614 383 minn *gig c l q w cod.ard* vg[cl] prov tepl sa bo[codd] eth arm geo arab[e] sy[h]* Cass Thphyl[b] Ephr[(p426)]
μόνος...ἐπορεύθη D *d gig l q w cod.ard* vg[cl] arm[osc] Cass Ephr[(p426)]]
+Jerusalem vg[cl] arm[osc]; +reversus est Hierosolymam *w*

The usual explanation for this variant is that the D-text sees the contradiction between the return of Silas to Jerusalem in *v*. 33 and his presence in Antioch again in *v*. 40.[1] This, however, is to prejudge the relationship of the B- and D-texts and does not allow the meaning of the D-text to be heard and understood on its own. It is, in fact, consistent with the account in the D-text to understand that Silas, as one sympathetic with Paul's position, viewed even these ethical demands as a concession to the Judaizing group, and that he preferred for this reason not to return to Jerusalem.[2] According to Fascher, this D-variant also explains why Paul, after his disagreement with and separation from Barnabas (xv. 37–9), chose (in *v*. 40) a Hellenistic Christian, Silas—that is, Silvanus,[3] rather than a Jerusalem-Jewish Christian for a companion.[4]

Paul, with Silas, then went through Syria and Cilicia, strengthening the churches (*v*. 41) and, says the D-text, 'delivering the charges of the apostles and elders' [παραδιδούς τε τὰς ἐντολὰς τῶν ἀποστόλων καὶ (*om* ἀποστόλων καί D *d* Cass)

---

[1] For this view and two other possibilities, see *Beginnings*, IV, 182.
[2] Fascher, *Textgeschichte*, p. 35, who suggests that Silas may have viewed the decrees as a βάρος (*v*. 28).
[3] See Williams, *Acts*, p. 184.   [4] Fascher, *Textgeschichte*, p. 35.

πρεσβυτέρων D *d gig c dem q w cod.ard* vg[s,cl] prov tepl arm sy[hmg] Cass; cf. Ephr[cat(p429)]]. The perspective in which the D-text sees this delivery of the 'decree' is revealed, however, by its variant reading in Acts xvi. 4:[1]

Acts xvi. 4

B	D
ὡς δὲ διεπορεύοντο τὰς πόλεις,	διερχόμενοι δὲ τὰς πόλεις ἐκήρυσσον καὶ
παρεδίδοσαν αὐτοῖς	παρεδίδοσαν αὐτοῖς μετὰ πάσης παρρησίας τὸν κύριον Ἰησοῦν Χριστὸν ἅμα παραδιδόντες καὶ
φυλάσσειν τὰ δόγματα τὰ κεκριμένα ὑπὸ τῶν ἀποστόλων καὶ πρεσβυτέρων τῶν ἐν Ἱεροσολύμοις.	τὰς ἐντολὰς ἀποστόλων καὶ πρεσβυτέρων των ἐν Ἱεροσολύμοις.

διερχόμενοι δέ (οὖν *gig*) D *d gig* sa
ἐκήρυσσον καὶ παρεδίδοσαν αὐτοῖς D *d* sy[p]] ἐκήρυσσον Ephr[(p428)]; κηρύσσοντες sy[hmg]
μετὰ πάσης...Χριστόν D *d* sy[hmg] (cf. Ephr[(p428n1)])
ἅμα...ἐντολάς D *d*
τῶν (*ante* ἀποστόλων)] *om* D*

The καὶ παρεδίδοσαν αὐτοῖς of D is clearly due to contamination from the B-text,[2] as shown by sy[hmg], which reads 'preaching with all forthrightness the Lord Jesus Christ'; thus, καὶ παρεδίδοσαν αὐτοῖς must not be regarded as part of the original 'Western' tradition.

The B-text in this verse is concerned with only one thing, the delivery of the decrees. Verse 5 (joined by μὲν οὖν) is to be interpreted, then, to mean that for the B-text the delivery of these decrees is the means whereby the churches are strengthened in the faith and increased in numbers. The D-text is quite different. Here, as Paul, Silas, and Timothy went through the cities, 'they *preached* with all forthrightness the Lord Jesus Christ, at the same time also delivering the charges of the apostles...', etc. For the D-text, the strengthening of the

[1] *Beginnings*, IV, 183, says that the D-text in xv. 41 intends to emphasize the fact that Paul enforced the apostolic decree. But this is inconsistent with D's clear emphasis in xvi. 4 (see below).
[2] Ropes, *Text*, pp. 150 f.

churches (D *d om* τῇ πίστει) is the result of the *preaching*, and the delivery of the ἐντολαί (rather than B's δόγματα) is introduced by ἅμα and *placed in a participial phrase as an appendix*.[1] This makes the delivery of the decrees clearly secondary to the preaching and shows a devaluation of the significance both of the 'decree' and of the disputation which occasioned it.

Another variant in this connection occurs in the context of the third account of the apostolic letter, Acts xxi. 25. Verse 19 tells of Paul's report of his ministry among the Gentiles, and the response of the Jerusalem elders follows (*v.* 20 B): θεωρεῖς, ἀδελφε, πόσαι μυριάδες εἰσὶν ἐν τοῖς 'Ιουδαίοις τῶν πεπιστευκότων, καὶ πάντες ζηλωταὶ τοῦ νόμου ὑπάρχουσιν. The D-text, however, in place of ἐν τοῖς 'Ιουδαίοις, reads ἐν τῇ 'Ιουδαίᾳ, D *d p* sa sy^p Aug^ep 82, 9 Hier ⅓.[2] Does this not reveal a desire in the D-text to limit the mass of believers who are 'zealous for the law' to Judea? The B-reading is capable of broad geographical interpretation—there are thousands of Jews everywhere who are believers and also adhere to the law. But the statement in the D-text provides a strict limitation to Judea only, circumscribing a much more narrow compass for this viewpoint and practice.

The whole verse, Acts xxviii. 29, is a 'Western' reading (though, as happens often, it has been taken into the Koine text). The B-text of xxviii. 17–28 tells of Paul's ministry in Rome, and it is a ministry only to Jews. There is, moreover, no indication in the B-text that Paul's ministry went beyond the Jews in xxviii. 30–1, though the statement is general enough to allow such an implication. The 'Western' text is different. What has been said in *v.* 25 (B and 'Western') is repeated in *v.* 29 ('Western'; D *def*): καὶ ταῦτα αὐτοῦ εἰπόντος ἀπῆλθον οἱ 'Ιουδαῖοι πολλὴν ἔχοντες ἐν ἑαυτοῖς συζήτησιν H L P S 614 383 *gig p c cod.ard* vg^s, cl (*w* prov tepl) sy^h* Cass. The presence, however, of this verse at this point shows that it is intended to round off the section on Paul's exclusive ministry to the Jews. This appears from the 'Western' variant in the next verse (xxviii. 30, D *def*): 'Paul welcomed all who came to him, *both Jews and Greeks*' ['Ιουδαίους τε καὶ Ἕλληνας 614 *gig p* vg^codd sy^h*

[1] Fascher, *Textgeschichte*, p. 36.
[2] Ἐν τοῖς 'Ιουδαίοις 𝔓^74 (*om* ἐν) A B C E minn vg bo eth Ambst^eph 3, 9 Spec; 'Ιουδαίων H L P 614 383 arm sy^h Chr Thdrt^1, 622 *et* 3, 1501 Thphyl; hominum *gig*] *om* ℵ.

THE JEWS, GENTILES, AND CHRISTIANITY

Ephr[(p452)] et cat[(p453)]; *praem* καὶ διελέγετο πρός, gig p (q) tepl], and preached to them. Thus, after his meeting with the Jews and their lack of response (see vv. 24–8), Paul, according to the 'Western' text, included Gentiles in his preaching ministry.

The same variant occurs in the D-text of Acts xx. 24. In xx. 18–22, Paul is represented as reviewing his ministry in Asia, especially Ephesus, and he concludes by saying that he testified both to Jews and Greeks. In xx. 22–4, Paul speaks of his impending journey to Jerusalem and concludes that he does not hold his life dear but seeks only to accomplish his ministry (D *et al.* add τοῦ λόγου), to testify to the gospel *both to Jews and to Greeks* ['Ιουδαίοις καὶ "Ελλησιν D d 𝔓[41] gig sa Lcf[241] Ephr[(p444)] et cat[(p445)]]. Much the same purpose is to be found for this reading here as for the one in xxviii. 30, that the D-text wanted no reader to think that in Jerusalem Paul's ministry would be limited to Jews; rather, even there Paul would minister both to Jews and Gentiles at whatever cost.

This section on 'The Jews, Gentiles, and Christianity' has shown that the D-text is anti-Judaic in that it not only minimizes the response of the Jews and the importance of Judaism and its institutions (notably the synagogue) to the new faith, but also diminishes the value of the customs and practices of Judaism itself, and especially their influence on and intrusion into Christianity. Moreover, this devaluation and by-passing of Judaism is developed in view of and in contrast to a clearly greater Gentile interest and a more distinctly emphasized universalism in D, and reveals itself markedly in the outreach of the new faith to the Gentiles.[1] Thus, there is here, as in the previous section, both a negative and a positive thrust: the D-text's anti-Judaic emphasis finds a complement in a positive accent on the Gentile element in early Christianity and on the universalism of the new faith, and in addition the D-text's downgrading of some of the distinctive elements in and features of Judaism finds its corollary in the D-text's greater stress on some of the distinctive elements in the new faith.

Apart from the strong Christological emphasis already noted, especially in the additional κύριος or Χριστός or both in the titles applied to Jesus, other special characteristics or new

---

[1] See Lagrange, *Critique textuelle*, p. 399.

emphases of Christianity, when viewed alongside Judaism, come to the forefront in the D-text's presentation. Very prominent, for example, is the more frequent mention of the Holy Spirit. In fact, the fuller and more immediate presence, availability, and activity of the Spirit, and the recognition of Jesus as Messiah and Lord are two important elements which distinguish Christianity from Judaism.[1] As to the former, W. D. Davies, for instance, emphasized the distinctiveness of the Holy Spirit in Christianity over against Judaism (though the evidence of the Dead Sea Scrolls later led him to modify this emphasis somewhat and to allow that there was one Jewish community which had 'a vivid awareness of the Spirit').[2]

The D-text, in referring to the Holy Spirit, seems to show preference for the formal expression, 'the Holy Spirit', as in Acts vi. 10 (see below), viii. 18 (τὸ ἅγιον D *d* 𝔓⁴⁵ 𝔓⁷⁴ A C E H L P S 614 vg bo arm geo eth sy^{p,h} Bas^{eth} Chr] *om* ℵ B sa Const. Apost), xi. 17 (see below), xv. 29 (see above), xv. 32 (see below), cf. viii. 39 (see below), xv. 7 sy^{hmg} (see below). Furthermore, the D-text emphasizes that:

(1) It was through the Holy Spirit that Jesus commanded the apostles to preach the gospel (i. 2). This is at least a plausible interpretation of the D-text here: taking the διὰ πνεύματος ἁγίου with ἐντειλάμενος, which in turn is explained in D by καὶ ἐκέλευσε κηρύσσειν τὸ εὐαγγέλιον (see the earlier discussion, pp. 65f.).

(2) The apostles *are about to receive* the Holy Spirit *on Pentecost* (i. 5): ὃ καὶ μέλλετε λαμβάνειν D* *d* gig *t* Aug^{abc et ep 256, 3 et de cons. evv. iv, 8 et c.petil 32 et c.cresc ii, 14(17) et serm 71} Ambst Hil^{964} Vig Max^{taur} Cass Ephr; ἕως τῆς πεντηκοστῆς D *d* sa cop^{G67} Aug^{ab et c.petil 2, 76 et c.cresc ii, 17} Cass Ephr^{eph iv. 10}.

(3) Stephen spoke 'in the Holy Spirit' (vi. 10: τῷ ἁγίῳ D *d* E gig g₂ *h p t* vg^{cod} eth cop^{G67} Ado Beder^{retr 124}) rather than in a spirited way (as B); Peter at the 'Jerusalem Council' spoke (xv. 7) ἐν πνεύματι (+ἁγίῳ 614 257 sy^{hmg} Cass) D* *d* 614 257 *l* sy^{hmg} Cass Tert^{pud 21} Ephr^{cat (p425)}] *om* Ir^{iii. 12, 14(17)}; and Paul, defend-

---
[1] Menoud, 'Western Text', p. 28; cf. Conzelmann, *Mitte der Zeit*⁴, p. 127; Eng. trans. p. 135 (quoted above, p. 64, n. 2).
[2] W. D. Davies, *Paul and Rabbinic Judaism*, pp. 215–17, 220; cf. Idem, 'Contemporary Jewish Religion', *Peake's Commentary on the Bible* (London/New York, 1962), p. 706 for the later view.

ing himself from Jewish charges before Agrippa, was 'consoled by the Holy Spirit' (xxvi. 1: sy^hmg [?Ephr^(p448)]).[1]

(4) Possibly Philip also 'was in the Spirit' when he explained the scripture to the eunuch (viii. 35), if cop^G67 can be taken to represent the 'Western' text in this passage, where, in fact, no other 'Western' witnesses are extant.

(5) The Holy Spirit fell on the eunuch after he was baptized (viii. 39, D *def*): πνεῦμα ἅγιον ἐπέπεσεν ἐπὶ τὸν εὐνοῦχον· ἄγγελος δὲ κυρίου ἥρπασεν τὸν Φίλιππον, supported wholly or partly by A minn *l p q w cod.ard* tepl cop^G67 arm geo sy^h* Aug $\frac{3}{4}$ Cyr^hr Didy Hier^c.lucif 9 *et* esai 63 = $\frac{2}{4}$ Cass Ephr^(p408)] *om* Aug^c Hier $\frac{2}{4}$.

(6) God gives the Holy Spirit to all who have believed, in this case to Cornelius and other Gentiles: (xi. 17): τοῦ μὴ δοῦναι αὐτοῖς πνεῦμα ἅγιον πιστεύσασιν D *d* (*p*) *q w cod.ard* vg^codd bohem prov tepl (cop^G67) sy^h* (Aug).

(7) The Jerusalem 'decree' should be performed φερόμενοι ἐν τῷ ἁγίῳ πνεύματι (xv. 29; see the earlier discussion of this above, pp. 108, 110f.).

(8) The oral bearers of this apostolic letter were (xv. 32) πλήρεις πνεύματος ἁγίου D *d* (see above, p. 111).

(9) Paul was directed in his journeys by the Holy Spirit (xix. 1): θέλοντος δὲ τοῦ Παύλου κατὰ τὴν ἰδίαν βουλὴν πορεύεσθαι εἰς Ἱεροσόλυμα εἶπεν αὐτῷ τὸ πνεῦμα ὑποστρέφειν εἰς τὴν Ἀσίαν D *d* 𝔓38 sy^hmg Ephr^cat (p441) Ado; and in xx. 3: εἶπεν δὲ τὸ πνεῦμα αὐτῷ D *d gig* sy^hmg Ephr^(p442); and cf. xvii. 15 in Ephr^(pp 382,432) *et* cat (p433): 'The Holy Spirit prevented him from preaching...' (this is discussed below, pp. 142 f.).

(10) While in the B-text of xix. 2 doubt is expressed as to the existence of the Holy Spirit by certain disciples in Ephesus (ἀλλ᾽ οὐδ᾽ εἰ πνεῦμα ἅγιον ἔστιν ἠκούσαμεν), there is no doubt on this point in D, but only doubt whether *any received* the Spirit: ἀλλ᾽ οὐδ᾽ εἰ (οὐδὲ D) πνεῦμα ἅγιον λαμβάνουσίν τινες ἠκούσαμεν D* *d* 𝔓38 𝔓41 sa sy^hmg.[2]

It is significant that mention is made of the Holy Spirit in D or the 'Western' text (1) when preaching the gospel is mentioned in a passage which, as shown above (pp. 65 f.), involves universalistic overtones (i. 2); (2) when Stephen was confuting the Jews (vi. 10); (3) when a *Gentile* is evangelized and baptized

---

[1] On Ephr, see *Beginnings*, IV, 314.
[2] On this passage, see Fascher, *Textgeschichte*, pp. 45 f.

(the eunuch in viii. 35 and viii. 39), and a second time in the D-text when Cornelius *et al.* believe (xi. 17); (4) when Peter speaks about the Gentile mission and against a strong Judaizing position (xv. 7); (5) when the compromising 'decree' is delivered (xv. 29, 32), as if to counteract any legalistic suggestion; (6) when Paul is in danger from Jewish plots against him (xx. 3; cf. xvii. 15 Ephr), and when he makes his defence against Jewish charges (xxvi. 1).

This list of references to the Holy Spirit, comprising nearly all of those peculiar to D and the 'Western' text in Acts, supports not only the anti-Judaic and pro-Gentile view adduced here for that text but also the contention that this important pneumatic element in Christianity was viewed by the D-text in its significance to the new faith over against Judaism.

Some other ideas prominent in early Christianity find added emphasis in the D-text. For example, in Acts xiii. 39 repentance is mentioned in a passage which has been shown to have a universalistic construction in D (see above, pp. 81 f.). There is also a stress on faith: (1) ii. 41, where the D-text, in place of B's ἀποδεξάμενοι, reads πιστεύσαντες (D *d*), or has the additional καὶ πιστεύσαντες following τὸν λόγον αὐτοῦ (*p r cod.ard* cop[G67] sy[p] sy[hmg] Aug[c et de mend]); (2) iv. 31, in a universalistic phrase, παντὶ τῷ θέλοντι πιστεύειν (see above, p. 82); (3) xvii. 12-13, where πιστεύειν occurs two additional times in D, and the opposite ἀπιστεῖν occurs once, in this anti-Judaic passage (see above, pp. 74f.); and (4) xviii. 8, where πιστεύοντες τῷ θεῷ διὰ τοῦ ὀνόματος τοῦ κυρίου ἡμῶν Ἰησοῦ Χριστοῦ, as noted earlier (pp. 87-90 above), is a passage showing Gentile interests and devaluing Judaism. In xviii. 27, D lacks τοῖς πεπιστευκόσιν (*om* D *d* 𝔓[38]), but has in its place ἐν ταῖς ἐκκλησίαις (D *d* 𝔓[38]), revealing another distinctively Christian interest of the D-text, the church. Here in xviii. 27 Apollos is described in the D-text as being very helpful *in the churches*, 'for [verse 28, B and D] he powerfully refuted the Jews in public [+ διαλεγόμενος καὶ D *d* 𝔓[38] 614 383] proving...that the Christ was Jesus'.[1] Notice ἐν τῇ ἐκκλησίᾳ in ii. 47 (D *d* E P S 614 383 462 minn cop[G67] sy[p, h] geo Chr Bede[retr]).

---

[1] On an ecclesiastical interest—an interest in churches rather than believers—here in the D-text of xviii. 27, see Zuntz, *Class et Med*, III (1940), 31.

There is in the D-text, moreover, a stress on preaching the word of God and on its influence: (1) Jesus' command to preach the gospel in i. 2D (see above, pp. 65f., 116f.); (2) the D-text in xiii. 43 says of Paul's ministry in Pisidian Antioch: ἐγένετο δὲ καθ' ὅλης τῆς πόλεως διελθεῖν τὸν λόγον τοῦ θεοῦ (see discussion above, pp. 83f.); (3) in xiv. 7, the D-text says of Lystra: καὶ ἐκεινήθη ὅλον τὸ πλῆθος ἐπὶ τῇ διδαχῇ D *d h p*² *q w* prov tepl Cass (E cop^G67 Bede⁶³); (4) in xiv. 4 those Iconians who sided with the apostles did so, according to the D-text, κολλώμενοι διὰ τὸν λόγον τοῦ θεοῦ, D *d* sy^hmg (cf. cop^G67 sy^p). It is significant that the first two of these variants occur in D-contexts involving overtones of universalism and the Gentile mission, while the latter two, as they stand in the D-text, are in contexts of Jewish opposition to the apostles (see below, pp. 138–42); (5) in xiv. 25, the D-text has an additional evangelization by the apostles in Attalia: εὐαγγελιζόμενοι αὐτούς (αὐτοῖς 383) D *d* 614 383 minn cop^G67 sy^h*; (6) in xvi. 4, Paul, Silas, and Timothy ἐκήρυσσον μετὰ πάσης παρρησίας τὸν κύριον Ἰησοῦν Χριστόν... (see above, pp. 113f., for the significance of this variant in the D-text); (7) the prohibition (by the Spirit in Ephr) against Paul preaching in Thessaly (xvii. 15D) was, according to Ephrem, due to danger from the Jews (see below, pp. 142f.); and (8) in xix. 14, the D-text repeats the statement, ...ἐν Ἰησοῦ ὃν Παῦλος...κηρύσσει, D *d* 𝔓³⁸ *w* tepl sy^hmg Cass Ephr^(p440). Note, finally, (9) that in xiv. 9D the cripple heard Paul *speaking*, ὑπάρχων ἐν φόβῳ D *d h*^(end of v.8).

Again, in this list of references to preaching which are peculiar to the D-text, two-thirds of them come in anti-Judaic or pro-Gentile contexts.

There is no need to pursue this trend at length. The accent on distinctive elements separating Christianity from Judaism or finding increased emphasis in Christianity and the emphasis on features especially germane to the new faith are clear, and their significance is enhanced by the frequency and poignancy with which they are emphasized precisely in those contexts which partake of an anti-Judaic flavour in the D-text.

C. THE JEWS AND THE APOSTLES

Many of the variants treated in the earlier sections have been concerned with the Jews and the apostles, but the special interest of this section is the Jews *versus* the apostles. This theme, too, has already appeared at certain points (for example, pp. 85f., 102f., 118), but in those cases the main thrust of the D-text made their earlier treatment more appropriate.

In Acts iv the Jewish leaders arrest Peter and John after the healing of the lame man and their preaching to the people (chapter iii):

Acts iv. 8*b*–9

B	D
Ἄρχοντες τοῦ λαοῦ	Ἄρχοντες τοῦ λαοῦ
καὶ πρεσβύτεροι,	καὶ πρεσβύτεροι τοῦ Ἰσραήλ,
εἰ ἡμεῖς σήμερον	9. εἰ ἡμεῖς σήμερον
ἀνακρεινόμεθα	ἀνακρεινόμεθα ἀφ' ὑμῶν
ἐπὶ εὐεργεσίᾳ	ἐπ' εὐεργεσείᾳ
ἀνθρώπου ἀσθενοῦς,...	ἀνθρώπου ἀσθενοῦς,...

τοῦ Ἰσραήλ D *d* E P S 614 (61 326 460) *h gig p** arm geo cop[G67] syh Cyprtest ii. 16 Iriii. 12, 4 Chr9, 94 *bis* Bederetr 116; τοῦ οἴκου Ἰσραήλ *p*² *q w* prov tepl syp

ἀφ' ὑμῶν D *d* E *h gig p* w* prov ethpp arab syp, h Cyprtest ii. 16 Iriii. 12, 4

Following ἀνακρεινόμεθα in Peter's statement (*v.* 9), D, with strong 'Western' support, has the prepositional phrase ἀφ' ὑμῶν, so that Peter says, 'If today we are being examined *by you* concerning a good deed done to a cripple...', placing emphasis on 'by you', i.e. on the ἄρχοντες τοῦ λαοῦ καὶ πρεσβύτεροι of *v.* 8. The D-text's ἀφ' ὑμῶν links the vocative, ἄρχοντες...καὶ πρεσβύτεροι, directly and unmistakably with ἀνακρεινόμεθα, whereas this connection is not so clearly demanded in B. Moreover, as if to leave no doubt as to who these rulers and elders were, the D-text reads τοῦ Ἰσραήλ (*v.* 8).[1] It is true that the D-text has given no new information about the situation, but the variants emphasize the fact that it is the rulers and elders of Israel who arrested the apostles and were now attempting legal

---

[1] The phrase πρεσβύτεροι τοῦ Ἰσραήλ does not occur elsewhere in NT, but is frequent in LXX.

THE JEWS AND THE APOSTLES

action against them, so that on them must fall the responsibility for the opposition to the apostles.¹

Acts iv. 13–15

B	D
θεωροῦντες δὲ τὴν τοῦ Πέτρου παρρησίαν καὶ Ἰωάννου, καὶ καταλαβόμενοι ὅτι ἄνθρωποι ἀγράμματοί εἰσιν καὶ ἰδιῶται, ἐθαύμαζον, ἐπεγείνωσκόν τε αὐτοὺς ὅτι σὺν τῷ Ἰησοῦ ἦσαν, τόν τε ἄνθρωπον βλέποντες σὺν αὐτοῖς ἑστῶτα τὸν τεθεραπευμένον οὐδὲν εἶχον ἀντειπεῖν. κελεύσαντες δὲ αὐτοὺς ἔξω τοῦ συνεδρίου ἀπελθεῖν συνέβαλλον πρὸς ἀλλήλους...	13. θεωροῦντες δὲ τὴν τοῦ Πέτρου παρρησίαν καὶ Ἰωάνου, καὶ καταλαβόμενοι ὅτι ἄνθρωποι ἀγράμματοί εἰσιν, ἐθαύμαζον, ἐπεγείνωσκον δὲ αὐτοὺς ὅτι σὺν τῷ Ἰησοῦ ἦσαν· 14. τὸν ἄνθρωπον βλέποντες σὺν αὐτοῖς ἑστῶτα τὸν τεθεραπευμένον οὐδὲν εἶχον ποιῆσαι ἢ ἀντιπεῖν. 15. κελεύσαντες αὐτοὺς ἔξω τοῦ συνεδρίου ἀπαχθῆναι συνέβαλον πρὸς ἀλλήλους...

14, line 2: αυτων
15, line 1: καιλευσαντες

13. θεωροῦντες δέ] ἀκούσαντες δὲ πάντες (om πάντες syᵖ) h syᵖ
    παρρησίαν] constantiam h (fiduciam d)
    καὶ ἰδιῶται h gig sa cett] om D d
    ἐπεγείνωσκον...ἦσαν post ἀντειπεῖν (v. 14) h (copᴳ⁶⁷)
14. τε] om D*
    ποιῆσαι ἤ D h
15. δέ d cett; tunc h copᴳ⁶⁷ syᵖ] om D eth
    ἀπαχθῆναι D h syᵖ
    συνέβαλον D E sa arm eth syʰ

Acts iv. 13–15
Codex h

13. cum au[diren]t autem omnes Petri constantiam et Joannis, [persu]asi quoniam homines inlitterati sunt et idio[tae, am]mirati sunt: 14. videntes autem et illum infirmū [cum ei]s stantem curatum, nihil potuerunt facere [aut co]ntradicere. quidam autem ex

¹ Lagrange, *Critique textuelle*, p. 392; Menoud, 'Western Text', p. 28; Williams, *Alterations*, p. 58.

121

ipsis agnosce[bant e]is, quoniam cum ihu conversabantur. 15. tunc [conlo]cuti jusserunt foras extra concilium adduci [Petru]m et Johanem: et quaerebant ab invicem...[1]

The textual situation in this passage is complicated by the fact that the 'Western' witnesses here (D and *h*) are divided on some readings. Unfortunately, Ir, Ephr, sy[hmg], etc., do not comment on these verses. It is necessary, therefore, to decide whether D or *h*, where they differ, best represents the 'Western' tradition. D here differs significantly from B at only three points: D lacks καὶ ἰδιῶται (*v.* 13); D has the additional ποιῆσαι (*v.* 14); and D has ἀπαχθῆναι for B's ἀπελθεῖν (*v.* 15). Codex *h* agrees with D on the last two readings, though not on the first. More important, *h* has a different order of happenings and has some additional variations. What seems decisively in favour of *h* as better representing the 'Western' text over against D is this: four readings[2] of the *h*-text, not found in D, are present in sy[p]; the origin of these readings would be hard to explain in a text (*h* sy[p]) which otherwise agrees with D two out of three times against the whole B-tradition, whereas D's agreements with B could have come into D from B by conflation.

D's first variant, the lack of καὶ ἰδιῶται, does not, then, represent the 'Western' text, at least on the basis of the present evidence regarding the whole passage, iv. 13-15. Taken by itself, the omission of καὶ ἰδιῶται could be defended as 'Western', since in this case conflation from the B-text could have affected *h*; the only other 'Western' witnesses with the reading are such mixed witnesses as *gig* sa, which cannot be decisive against D; thus, the choice comes to that between D and *h*. Since no editor of the 'Western' text of Acts has followed D at this point, it is preferable not to base anything on this omission as far as the viewpoint behind the D-text is concerned.

Parenthetically, it may be noted that if the reading of D were to be chosen over *h*, reasons for the absence of this reading in D could be worked out along the lines of the other D-variants in this context. The terms ἀγράμματος and ἰδιώτης overlap in meaning, and it is likely that the B-text simply means that Peter

---

[1] Text from Ropes, *Text*, p. 39. The second word in *v.* 15 could be *collocuti* or *adsecuti* (*ibid.* p. cccxiv).

[2] See Ropes, *Text*, p. 38, for these readings.

and John belong to the 'people of the land'.[1] Is it possible that D understood these terms in different senses and did not wish to represent the apostles as ἰδιῶται? Chrysostom on this passage distinguishes the two terms, but he does not explain how they differ (*In Acta Apost. Homil.* x, 3 (85): Migne, tome IX). The contrast in D's version between the apostles' openness, confidence, or forthrightness in speech (παρρησία) and the fact that they were ἀγράμματοι, understood in the sense of unversed in the learning of the schools—the opposite of the scribes before whom they stood[2]—was an acceptable contrast, for it presented the apostles in a more spectacular light, since they, though not lettered in the strict sense, could conduct a disputation with those who were. It is possible, moreover, that ἰδιώτης here had reference to a lack of eloquence.[3] D may have felt that the reference to the apostles' παρρησία in speaking (note that *h* has *cum* **audirent** *autem omnes Petri constantiam*... for the θεωροῦντες... of B and D) would be neutralized by a suggestion that they were not eloquent. Indeed, D has an additional παρρησία with reference to Stephen's disputations (vi. 10, D *d h* cop[G67] sy[hmg]), Paul and Silas' preaching (xvi. 4, D *d* sy[hmg]), and perhaps also Paul's preaching in ix. 20 (D *def*, but *h l* Ir[lat et gk] have it); it occurs also in the 'Western' text (though not D) of xiv. 19 in reference to Barnabas and Paul's discourse (see below, p. 141). D's omission of ἰδιῶται would mean, then, that while the apostles may be untrained, let no one think that they were unskilled or not eloquent.

The other, more clearly 'Western' variants are of greater significance. As already stated, the 'Western' text of *vv.* 13–15 presents another sequence of events in this scene. In the B-text the council's recognition that the apostles 'had been with Jesus' took place after they had marvelled at the forthrightness of these unlearned and common men. In the 'Western' text, however, it is only after they had, in addition, seen the healed man standing with the apostles and found themselves unable either to do or say anything against it that 'some of them recognized that they had been with Jesus'. Furthermore, it was

---

[1] See *Beginnings*, IV, 44; Haenchen, *Apostelgeschichte*, p. 177, n. 2.
[2] See Bruce, *Acts*'[52], p. 122; *Beginnings*, IV, 44; to the contrary, Haenchen, *Apostelgeschichte*, p. 177, n. 2.
[3] *Beginnings*, IV, 44, which refers to Justin, *Apol.* 39. 2.

after this (*v.* 15: *tunc h* cop^(G67)) that, in the 'Western' text, the apostles were led out from the council so that some decision could be made as to what might be done with them.

This 'Western' picture of the incident suggests that the combination of a healed man, an unlearned and common healer(s), and an audience much in sympathy with what had happened (see *vv.* 16–17, 21), reminded the council of Jesus, which reveals the intent of the 'Western' text: to draw a parallel between the life and work of Jesus and that of the apostles. The purpose of this parallel is to show that the apostles, like Jesus, were opposed, rejected, and maltreated by the Jewish leaders, here the supreme ruling council itself. Observe that in Acts, and especially in D, it is the Jews *and their leaders* who are responsible for killing Jesus (see, for example, Acts iii. 13–17; xiii. 27–31, where in both cases the rulers are specifically mentioned, and in D the excuse on grounds of ignorance is significantly toned down [see above, pp. 41–61]).

The ποιῆσαι ἤ of D (and *h*) in iv. 14 sharpens up the powerlessness of the Jewish rulers in the face of the apostles: 'They could *do or* say nothing against (it).'[1]

The use of a different verb by D (and *h*) in iv. 15 (κελεύσαντες αὐτοὺς **ἀπαχθῆναι** as opposed to ...ἀπελθεῖν in B) implies a harsher treatment of Peter and John in the legal inquiry: they *were taken out* under custody. A similar harshness is evident in the ἐκράτησαν αὐτούς (*h*, om D)[2] in iv. 3.

Further variants of the D-text in this context supplement this somewhat different conception of these council proceedings:

Acts iv. 18

B	D
	συνκατατιθεμένων δὲ αὐτῶν τῇ γνώμῃ
καὶ καλέσαντες αὐτοὺς παρήγγειλαν καθόλου μὴ φθέγγεσθαι...	φωνήσαντες αὐτοὺς παρήγγειλαν τὸ κατὰ τὸ μὴ φθέγγεσθαι...

---

[1] Menoud, 'Western Text', p. 28. Jacquier, *Actes*, p. 132, says D's variant must be a gloss, since the account following in Acts (iv. 16) shows that they could do something. But against this, see iv. 21.

[2] But see Zahn, *Urausgabe*, p. 254, who thinks the words are attested indirectly also by D, because of the καί which follows. Thus also Blass, *Acta*'95, p. 71. Zahn, Hilgenfeld, and Clark have the words in their texts.

συνκατατιθεμένων δὲ αὐτῶν (+πάντων d gig Lcf) τῇ γνώμῃ (om τῇ γνώμῃ gig vg^codΘ Lcf) D d h gig vg^codΘ cop^G67 sy^hmg Lcf232 φωνήσαντες αὐτούς D] om h τὸ κατὰ τό D[see note 1]

The D-text here provides information lacking in B, stating expressly that the council came to an official agreement regarding action against the apostles: 'And when they agreed to the decision....' (Συνκατατίθεσθαι occurs in the New Testament only in Lk xxiii. 51, where it is used of Joseph not *consenting* τῇ βουλῇ καὶ τῇ πράξει of the council, and in the additional material of D in Acts xv. 12, see above, pp. 83, 97f., 103. Γνώμη occurs nowhere else in the gospels and Acts except Acts xx. 3, where D, incidentally, does not read it, see above, p. 117, and below, pp. 143f.)

In Acts iv. 17 some 'Western' witnesses (though not D) picture somewhat differently the council's reasoning behind this decision. The B-text has ἀλλ' ἵνα μὴ ἐπὶ πλεῖον διανεμηθῇ εἰς τὸν λαόν, ἀπειλησώμεθα αὐτοῖς.... The subject of διανεμηθῇ, for this text, is σημεῖον (v. 16). However, h and some other witnesses have τὰ ῥήματα αὐτῶν (h: *verba istorum*) or τὰ ῥήματα ταῦτα (E gig sa sy^p Lcf232; cf. sy^hmg: διὰ τὰ ῥήματα ταῦτα) after λαόν; 'their words' then becomes the subject of διανεμηθῇ.[2] On this reading, the council feared the spread of the apostles' message,[3] and this was the basis for the decision upon which the council agreed (v. 18D). Such a portrayal of the council's action as opposed to the apostolic message reveals an anti-Judaic bias, which again has the Jewish leaders in view. The strong support for this additional phrase lends likelihood to its originality in the 'Western' tradition. (The reading of sy^hmg, though it leaves σημεῖον as subject of the verb, nevertheless emphasizes the function of the apostles' words as the chief factor in the dissemination which the council sought to deter.)

[1] Παρηγγείλαντο κατὰ τὸ μή (D) is probably a corruption of παρήγγειλαν τὸ καθόλου, which is found in 𝔓^74 A E 614 etc. (Blass, *Acta'95*, p. 75; Ropes, *Text*, p. 38).

[2] Blass, *Acta'95*, p. 75.

[3] Note that in iv. 1 D, with strong 'Western' support, is found, with reference to the sermon of Peter in Solomon's Portico (iii. 12-26), the reading τὰ ῥήματα ταῦτα D d h w arab sy^hmg Cass Thphyl^a43; ταῦτα τὰ ῥήματα E gig p q sy^p Lcf232. This favours the contention that the phrase in iv. 17 also emphasizes the message of the apostles.

Moreover, the real intent of the council, for the D-text, is expressed in the variant αἰτίαν in iv. 21: they had hoped to charge Peter and John with a crime for which they could be punished:

Acts iv. 21

B	D
οἱ δὲ προσαπειλησάμενοι	οἱ δὲ προσαπειλησάμενοι
ἀπέλυσαν αὐτούς,	ἀπέλυσαν αὐτούς,
μηδὲν εὑρίσκοντες	μὴ εὑρίσκοντες αἰτίαν
τὸ πῶς κολάσωνται αὐτούς,	τὸ πῶς κολάσωνται αὐτούς,
διὰ τὸν λαόν,...	διὰ τὸν λαόν,...

B reads κολάσωσιν, but ℵ cett read -ωνται

μὴ...αἰτίαν D d p*[et2] tepl bo sy[p] (nihil...causam d)
(Note: no other leading 'Western' witnesses are available at this point; Hilgenfeld, Zahn, and Clark read the D-variant in their texts.)

A comparison of D's text here with that of Acts xiii. 28 (B and D), μηδεμίαν αἰτίαν θανάτου εὑρόντες,[1] which refers to Jesus' treatment by the Jews and their rulers (the subject of εὑρόντες in xiii. 28 is οἱ κατοικοῦντες ἐν Ἱερουσαλὴμ καὶ οἱ ἄρχοντες αὐτῶν), suggests that the D-text in Acts iv. 21 is again paralleling the experience of the apostles with that of Jesus:[2] the Jewish rulers seek to make the apostles answerable for a crime,[3] just as they did Jesus; and the apostles, like him, are suffering innocently since no crime could be found. This parallelism gives to the D-text's representation a distinctive anti-Judaic flavour: not only is the Jewish opposition to the apostles heightened, but the leaders of the Jews are brought to the mind of the reader in their role as the murderers of Jesus. At the same time, the apostles are enhanced, for they now follow in the path of Jesus' sufferings.

[1] For other instances of the combination of εὑρίσκειν αἰτίαν and some form of the negative, cf. John xviii. 38; xix. 4, 6 (D def in these Johannine passages); Lk xxiii. 22 D. (See also Acts xxv. 18; xxviii. 18.)
[2] This parallelism is borne out by D's αἰτίαν in place of αἴτιον in Lk xxiii. 22: οὐδεμίαν αἰτίαν θανάτου εὑρίσκω.
[3] On the use of αἰτία in iv. 21 D, cf. D's use of ἀναίτιος of Paul and Silas in a similar situation in Acts xvi. 37 D (see the discussion below, p. 149). For both terms (or cognates), cf. Josephus, *War*, IV, 543; *Antiquities*, XVII, 174 (XVII, 6. 5).

The D-text in Acts iv. 24 offers a summarizing comment to this whole incident, characterizing the episode of the healing, and the praise of God by the people, and the resultant triumph of the apostles over the imprisonment and threats of the Jewish leaders as the working of God. The believers listened to the report of Peter and John, at which point the D-text says: καὶ ἐπιγνόντες τὴν τοῦ θεοῦ ἐνέργειαν... D *d* cop^G67] *om* Ir[iii. 12, 5] E *gig* sy[p, h] Lcf. Few 'Western' witnesses are available at this point, and the evidence calls for some caution in declaring this an early 'Western' reading, though Hilgenfeld and Clark include the reading in their editions of the 'Western' text, and cop^G67 ('when they understood that our strength was of God') strengthens the case. The use of ἐνέργεια in descriptions of divine deliverance is found in II Macc. iii. 29; III Macc. iv. 21; v. 12, 28. Note that in the last two cases the word δεσπότης is used of God, as it is in Acts iv. 24 *b*.[1] (It is of great interest, by the way, that J. Rendel Harris completely reversed himself regarding this variant of D in iv. 24—and also that in v. 39— when he noticed these parallels with Maccabees. He says that retranslations from Latin or Syriac are out of the question: 'The chances are infinitesimal that its peculiar turns of speech would have survived a pilgrimage through an adjacent language', and that 'a Montanist explanation, as suggested in my *Study of Codex Bezae*, is no longer to be thought of'.)[2]

The import of this variant is that the apostles are vindicated by God over against the Jewish leaders who opposed them; before God even the powerful ones are powerless.[3]

Observe at this point that even the few variants so far treated in this section clearly reveal an emphasis in the D-text on the leaders of the Jews. At the same time, there is just as clear an emphasis on the apostles, before whom even the Jewish leaders are powerless, for the apostles move in the stream of God's action. These two emphases find further illustration and confirmation as the discussion proceeds, but it is already evident that the D-text is playing these two groups off against each other as leaders and representatives of two contending viewpoints, Judaism and Christianity, and that this conflict was one of D's

---

[1] J. R. Harris, 'Two Important Glosses in Codex Bezae', *Exp*, VI, 2 (1900), 396.
[2] *Ibid.* pp. 399f. [3] Fascher, *Textgeschichte*, p. 30.

primary concerns. The D-text's apparent method is to accentuate, on the one hand, the hostility and opposition of the Jewish leaders to the apostles and, on the other hand, to enhance the dignity and deeds of the apostles themselves. The obvious aim is to demonstrate the superiority of the new faith through a portrayal of the greatness and power of its leaders in the face of adverse treatment by the opposing party—a sort of leaders *versus* leaders motif.

Apart from the variants already considered and some presently to be discussed, the D-text of a passage like Acts v. 34-5 reveals this preoccupation. The D-text here makes specific mention of both groups:

B: Γαμαλιὴλ... ἐκέλευσεν ἔξω βραχὺ τοὺς ἀνθρώπους ποιῆσαι,
35. εἶπέν τε πρὸς αὐτούς·
D: Γαμαλιὴλ... ἐκέλευσεν τοὺς ἀποστόλους ἔξω βραχὺ ποιῆσαι,
35. εἶπέν τε πρὸς τοὺς ἄρχοντας καὶ τοὺς συνεδρίους·

---

34. τοὺς ἀποστόλους D *d* E H P S 614 383 *gig h* sa eth sy[p, h] Chr[1, 771]
35. πρὸς... συνεδρίους D *d* sa; πρὸς ὅλον τὸ συνέδριον (ad totum concilium) *h*

Mere frequency of terminology is not in itself decisive, but is nevertheless of interest as part of the larger picture.[1]

Furthermore, it is worth asking at least whether the D-text's emphasis on the apostles' connection with Jerusalem shows an interest in more closely identifying the apostles, not only with the place of origin of the church, but with Jerusalem as the centre of Judaism—it was here that the conflict between them had its fountainhead. Notice, for example, that in D it is emphasized that after Pentecost the believers devoted themselves to the teaching of the apostles ἐν Ἱερουσαλήμ, D *d t* vg[cod] (Acts ii. 42);[2] that the apostles bravely remained in Jerusalem when the Jews brought persecution against the church there

---

[1] Note that D *d gig p q t w* sa sy[p] *add* ἀποστόλοις in Acts ii. 14; D *d* 614 *p* cop[G67] sy[h] Ambst *add* ἀπόστολοι in v. 41 (*h* has a lacuna here); *h* reads *apostolos* instead of *Paulum* in xiv. 9; but D *d h gig* sy[p] *om* οἱ ἀπόστολοι in xiv. 14; and in v. 29-30 D *d h* (*gig*) *om* οἱ ἀπόστολοι, but this is in the interest of enhancing the position of Peter (see below, p. 159).

[2] Though in the next verse (ii. 43) D, with B (and *d gig p** sa minn) lacks ἐν Ἱερουσαλήμ, which is read by 𝔓[74vid] ℵ A C E minn *p*² *q w* vg bo sy[p] etc.

THE JEWS AND THE APOSTLES

(viii. 1, see the discussion below, p. 134); that Herod, to please the Jews, persecuted certain ones of the church ἐν τῇ 'Ιουδαίᾳ D *d* 614 *p q w* vg^codR prov tepl sy^h*; in Jerusalem cop^G67 (xii. 1); that the Judaizers who harassed Paul were from Jerusalem (xv. 2, discussed above, pp. 97, 101 f.); that Paul wished to go to Jerusalem [xviii. 21: ...εἰς Ἱεροσόλυμα D *d* H L P S 614 383 *gig q w dem cod.ard* prov tepl eth dut sy^p,h Cass Chr^9,336 Thphyl, cf. Ephr^cat(p439); and xix. 1: ...εἰς Ἱεροσόλυμα D *d* 𝔓^38 vg^cod sy^hmg Ephr^cat(p441) Ado]; that Paul knew that bonds and afflictions awaited him in Jerusalem [xx. 23. ἐν Ἱεροσολύμοις D *d* 𝔓^41 614 *c gig* vg^s,cl tepl sa sy^h* Or Lcf^241, cf. Ephr^cat(p445)].

The theme of leaders *versus* leaders finds expression again in chapter v:

Acts v. 18–19*a*

B	D
καὶ ἐπέβαλον τὰς χεῖρας ἐπὶ τοὺς ἀποστόλους καὶ ἔθεντο αὐτοὺς ἐν τηρήσει δημοσίᾳ.	18. καὶ ἐπέβαλον τὰς χεῖρας ἐπὶ τοὺς ἀποστόλους καὶ ἔθεντο αὐτοὺς ἐν τηρήσει δημοσίᾳ· καὶ ἐπορεύθη εἷς ἕκαστος εἰς τὰ ἴδια.
ἄγγελος δὲ κυρίου διὰ νυκτός...	19. τότε διὰ νυκτὸς ἄγγελος κυρίου...

line 2: ηθεντο

καὶ ἐπορεύθη...ἴδια D *d* cop^G67] *om* E 614 383 *gig* Lcf Cass (Hilgenfeld, Zahn, and Clark include the D-reading in their texts) τότε D sy^p] δέ *d gig* Lcf *cett*

The council has just arrested the apostles and placed them in prison. At this point D has the additional words, καὶ ἐπορεύθη εἷς ἕκαστος εἰς τὰ ἴδια, which are followed by '*Then* by night an angel of the Lord opened the doors of the prison...'. The subject of D's καὶ ἐπορεύθη...εἰς τὰ ἴδια is ambiguous; does it mean that the members of the council each went to his own home (taking τὰ ἴδια in the way it is used in LXX Esther v. 10; John xvi. 32; xix. 27; Acts xxi. 6; and xiv. 18 in C 614 383 arm sy^hmg)? Or does it take its subject from the nearer preceding αὐτούς, i.e. the apostles? Erich Fascher states that, according to the context, the sentence can mean nothing but solitary confinement for the apostles: each went to his own place of confinement.

The D-text's τότε in *v.* 19 supports this by linking *v.* 19 more closely with D's *v.* 18: the council arrested and placed the apostles in prison; each then went to his own cell; *then* by night an angel of the Lord opened the doors. Fascher's interpretation is the more significant in that he states that he can find no motivation for this variant reading in D;[1] his interpretation, then, cannot be accused of arising out of bias. Once alerted to an anti-Judaic interest in the D-text, however, the variant, thus interpreted, is immediately seen as pointing to severe treatment of the apostles by the Jewish leaders; they are, for D, treated as bad criminals who must be locked in solitary prison confinement.

Observe also Acts v. 21, which relates that when the high priest came, and those with him, they called together the council, etc., and sent to the prison for the apostles. The D-text, however, reads ἐγερθέντες τὸ πρωΐ (D *d*, cf. bo Ephr[(p400)]] *om* E *gig*) with reference to the high priest and those with him. This variant may suggest a special preoccupation on the part of the leaders with the apostles' case, and an eagerness to expedite the legal proceedings against them.

When the apostles are found to have escaped during the night, they are apprehended again and brought before the council (v. 22–7). The council deliberation, especially the speech of Gamaliel (Acts v. 35–40), is of interest in this connection, notably *vv.* 38–9. In *v.* 38, where B reads

...ἀπόστητε ἀπὸ τῶν ἀνθρώπων τούτων καὶ ἄφετε αὐτούς,

D has

...ἀπόστητε ἀπὸ τῶν ἀνθρώπων τούτων καὶ ἐάσατε αὐτοὺς μὴ μιάναντες τὰς χεῖρας.

ἀπόστητε *post* τούτων *h*
ἐάσατε D E H P S 614 383 Chr[9, 129]
μὴ μιάναντες (μολύνοντες E Bede) τὰς χεῖρας (+ὑμῶν E *h* Bede) D *d* E 61 *h* cop[G67] Bede[retr 122]

According to the D-text, Gamaliel says that for the council to slay the apostles would be to defile their hands. The phrase, μιαίνειν τὴν χεῖρα, occurs only once in LXX: Eccles. vii. 19(18),

---

[1] Fascher, *Textgeschichte*, p. 28.

καί γε ἀπὸ τούτου μὴ μιάνῃς τὴν χεῖρά σου, and here it seems to be used in a moral sense, and it is likely that the phrase in Acts v. 38 also refers to a moral defilement by sin[1]—here the shedding of blood.

It is tempting to connect the phrase with the statement of the high priest in v. 28: ...καὶ βούλεσθε ἐπαγαγεῖν ἐφ' ἡμᾶς τὸ αἷμα τοῦ ἀνθρώπου ἐκείνου (τούτου 𝔓74 B d E p vg sy^{p,h} cett; ἐκείνου D gig h sa Lcf). Gamaliel would then be suggesting to the council that to slay the apostles would be to defile their hands with the blood also of Jesus whom the apostles preach. Action by the Jews against the apostles would be action against the Lord Jesus Christ. This is the implication of the D-text, and this high compliment to the apostolic office, along with the suggestion of possible divine sanction upon them, by a member of the opposition group not only enhances the apostles, but also reveals the seriousness of any further action against them.

Along the same line, notice v. 39:

Acts v. 39

B	D
εἰ δὲ ἐκ θεοῦ ἐστίν,	εἰ δὲ ἐκ θεοῦ ἐστίν,
οὐ δυνήσεσθε καταλῦσαι αὐτούς·	οὐ δυνήσεσθε κα(τα)λῦσαι αὐτοὺς οὔτε ὑμεῖς οὔτε βασιλεῖς οὔτε τύραννοι. ἀπέχεσθε οὖν ἀπὸ τῶν ἀνθρώπων τούτων
μή ποτε καὶ θεομάχοι εὑρεθῆτε.	μή ποτε θεομάχοι εὑρεθῆτε.

line 2: δυνησεσθαι
line 4: απεχεσθαι

εἰ...ἐστίν] si autem haec potestas ex di volū[tate est] = εἰ δὲ αὕτη ἡ ἐξουσία ἐκ θεοῦ θελήματός ἐστιν h (cop^{G67})
οὔτε...τύραννοι D d h cop^{G67} sy^{h}*; οὔτε ὑμεῖς οὔτε οἱ ἄρχοντες ὑμῶν E gig w dem cod.ard Bede^{retr 123}; οὔτε τύραννοι ὑμῶν sa
ἀπέχεσθε (ἀπόσχεσθε 614)...ἀνθρώπων (ἀνδρῶν 614 431) τούτων D d (326^{mg}) 431 614 h w dem cop^{G67} sy^{h}*
καί] om D* d 630 p cop sy^{p,h}

[1] Thus Bauer, Wörterbuch⁵, ad loc. It is also possible that 'defiling the hands' could have reference to ceremonial purity (see Cerfaux and Dupont, Actes, p. 69), as this formula is often used by the Rabbis with reference to holy books; see P. Billerbeck, Kommentar zum Neuen Testament aus Talmud und Midrasch (München, 1922–61), IV, 348, 426–34.

The D-text makes the statement of Gamaliel considerably stronger: if the apostles represent a movement[1] which is from God, not only will the council be unable to overthrow them, but even kings and tyrants *beyond Israel* cannot do so.[2] The D-text then repeats the warning to keep away from these men. For the D-text, the apostles and their work are invincible, and before them not only Jewish rulers are powerless, but others as well.

Stephen, as a figure of some importance in the book of Acts, may be treated along with the apostles:

Acts vi. 10–11

B	D
καὶ οὐκ ἴσχυον ἀντιστῆναι τῇ σοφίᾳ καὶ τῷ πνεύματι ᾧ ἐλάλει.	10. οἵτινες οὐκ ἴσχυον ἀντιστῆναι τῇ σοφίᾳ τῇ οὔσῃ ἐν αὐτῷ καὶ τῷ πνεύματι τῷ ἁγίῳ ᾧ ἐλάλει, διὰ τὸ ἐλέγχεσθαι αὐτοὺς ἐπ' αὐτοῦ μετὰ πάσης παρρησίας.
	11. μὴ δυνάμενοι οὖ(ν) ἀντοφθαλμεῖν τῇ ἀληθείᾳ,
τότε ὑπέβαλον ἄνδρας...	τότε ὑπέβαλον ἄνδρας...

10. οἵτινες D *d h t*
τῇ οὔσῃ ἐν αὐτῷ D *d* E *h* cop[G67] Bede[retr 124]
τῷ ἁγίῳ D *d* E *gig g₂ h p t* vg[cod] cop[G67] eth Ado Bede[retr 124]
διὰ τὸ ἐλέγχεσθαι αὐτοὺς (διότι ἠλέγχοντο E) ὑπ' (ἐπ' D*) αὐτοῦ...παρρησίας D *d* E *h t w cod.ard* vg[codd] tepl bohem cop[G67] sy[hmg] Bede[retr] (cf. Ephr[(p402)])
11. μὴ δυνάμενοι...ἀληθείᾳ D *d h* sy[hmg]; ἐπειδὴ οὐκ ἐδύναντο ἀντιλέγειν τῇ ἀληθείᾳ E *t w* vg[codΘ] tepl bohem cop[G67] Bede[retr]

In the D-text here, at one and the same time, Stephen is enhanced and the Jews come off in a poorer light. Notice, first of all, that in the D-text there is no doubt that Stephen is inspired in speech: τῷ ἁγίῳ *post* πνεύματι. The additional

---
[1] Notice that *h* speaks of *haec potestas* in both v. 38 and 39; cf. iii. 12; iv. 7.
[2] See Fascher, *Textgeschichte*, p. 28. Notice the parallel in Wisdom xii. 14, which, says Harris, *Exp*, VI, 2 (1900), 399f., is concerned with the same question as in Acts v. 39, whether it is safe to oppose God: οὔτε βασιλεύς ἢ τύραννος ἀντοφθαλμῆσαι δυνήσεταί σοι περὶ ὧν ἐκόλασας. Τύραννος is not in NT. Note that *h* (*ac*) corresponds to the βασιλεύς ἤ of Wisdom (Harris, p. 400). For the contrary view, that Acts v. 39 has nothing to do with Wisdom xii. 14, see Harnack, *TLZ*, XXXII (1907), 400.

material in D gives the reason for the Jews'[1] inability to withstand his wisdom and inspired speech: 'Because they were refuted by him with all forthrightness.' The D-text also makes clear their reason for obtaining false witnesses against him: 'Not being able, therefore, to face (or withstand) the truth....'[2] Ἐλέγχειν is frequent in the New Testament, but it occurs in Lk–Acts only in Lk iii. 19. This is illuminating for the present occurrence, for Lk iii. 19 refers to John the Baptist reproving Herod (ἐλεγχόμενος ὑπ' αὐτοῦ), and John the Baptist and Stephen shared the same fate. Observe also the use of διακατελέγχεσθαι in Acts xviii. 28 (its only occurrence) in the context of refuting the Jews: the text concerns Apollos: εὐτόνως γὰρ τοῖς Ἰουδαίοις διακατηλέγχετο... (B and D).

Reference may be made incidentally to the κατὰ αὐτοῦ *post* ἔστησαν μάρτυρας ψευδεῖς in Acts vi. 13, D *d h* (eth), which reinforces the already obvious hostility of the Jews *against* Stephen. Note, too, that the D-text in vi. 15 makes Stephen the centre of the scene: ἐστῶτος ἐν μέσῳ αὐτῶν D *d h t* cop[G67] Ephr[cat (p405)]. This was suggested by P. Corssen in answer to J. Rendel Harris's well-known explanation that this D-phrase was a misplaced description of the high priest and belonged to the next verse.[3] The case of ἐστῶτος is against Harris, but if Harris's view were to be adopted, it would provide an interesting additional instance of the D-text's paralleling of leading figures in Acts with Jesus, since Harris's view equates Stephen before the high priest with Jesus before Caiaphas (cf. Mark xiv. 60).

Although D reads κράξαντες δὲ φωνῇ μεγάλῃ... with B in Acts vii. 57, *h* (sa) have *tunc populus exclama[vit voce] magna*.... If *h* represents the 'Western' text[4] and D has been conformed to

[1] Whether these were Jews from one synagogue or from as many as five is a difficult question: see *Beginnings*, IV, 66–8; Bruce, *Acts*'[52], pp. 155–7; Haenchen, *Apostelgeschichte*, p. 223, n. 3.

[2] Ἀντοφθαλμεῖν occurs in NT only in Acts xxvii. 15.

[3] Corssen, *GGA*, CLVIII (1896), 434f.; Harris, *Four Lectures*, pp. 70–3; Idem, *ET*, XXXIX (1927/8), 380f.; Idem, *BBC*, VIII (1930), 6f. Supporting Corssen is Williams, *Alterations*, p. 57; Harris's view was accepted in *Beginnings*, IV, 69.

[4] Zahn follows *h* for his 'Western' text and also asks whether *d*'s reading, *et cum exclamasset*, may not have 'people' as its subject: Zahn, *Urausgabe*, p. 260. Wordsworth–White take Stephen as subject in *d*.

B here, then the 'Western' text may have conceived of Stephen's death as a mob lynching rather than as an execution by the council, a point left in doubt in the B-text.[1] If the 'Western' text is given this interpretation, the role of the Jewish leaders is minimized, but the frenzied violence of the hostile Jewish crowd receives stress.

Acts viii. 1 tells of the great persecution (B: διωγμὸς μέγας; D *d h* sa dut: διωγμὸς μέγας καὶ θλῖψις; cf. Acts xiii. 50D) which arose on the day of Stephen's death, and of the scattering of the church, with the exception of the apostles. Here D* *d gig* g_2 *h t* prov[mg] cop[G67] sa eth Ephr[cat(p407)] Aug[c et serm 315] Bede[retr] have the additional words οἳ ἔμειναν ἐν Ἱερουσαλήμ. These words could be understood in several ways,[2] but the comment in Ephr[cat (p407)], which must have come from Ephrem,[3] gives an attractive interpretation:

> The apostles however because they desired thus to draw the Jews to themselves, did not quit the city, but in other cities also furnished cause for being bold enough to preach the word of life.

That the apostles remained in Jerusalem was clearly a brave act, done in the hope of winning the Jews, who in fact had launched 'a great persecution and affliction' against them. That this is the point here is confirmed by the explicit mention that the persecution came ἐπὶ τὴν ἐκκλησίαν τὴν ἐν Ἱεροσολύμοις (B and D) and that the D-text specifies that the apostles remained ἐν Ἱερουσαλήμ.

The 'Western' text of Acts ix. 20 and 22 (D *def*), relating to Paul's first preaching after his conversion, tells how he confounded the Jews:

Acts ix. 22

B	D-text
Σαῦλος δὲ μᾶλλον ἐνεδυναμοῦτο	Σαῦλος δὲ μᾶλλον ἐνεδυναμοῦτο ἐν τῷ λόγῳ,
καὶ συνέχυννεν Ἰουδαίους	καὶ συνέχυννεν Ἰουδαίους
τοὺς κατοικοῦντας ἐν Δαμασκῷ,	τοὺς κατοικοῦντας ἐν Δαμασκῷ,

---

[1] *Beginnings*, IV, 84; cf. 85–7; Haenchen, *Apostelgeschichte*, pp. 243–7.

[2] Several views are given in *Beginnings*, IV, 87. That these words in the D-text are not superfluous is pointed out by Zahn, *Apostelgeschichte*, I, 269, n. 99, who remarks that the apostles could have gone to other cities, such as Pella or Damascus.

[3] Ropes, *Text*, p. 407, n. 4.

THE JEWS AND THE APOSTLES

συμβιβάζων   συμβιβάζων καὶ λέγων
ὅτι οὗτός ἐστιν ὁ Χριστός.   ὅτι οὗτός ἐστιν ὁ Χριστός,
                                    ἐν ᾧ εὐδόκησεν ὁ θεός.

ἐν (om C 467) τῷ λόγῳ   C E 467 h l p cop[G67]
καὶ λέγων   E l p r
ἐν ᾧ (in quem h p) εὐδόκησεν ὁ θεός   gig h l p

    The 'Western' reading, ἐν τῷ λόγῳ, specifies that Paul's increase in strength referred to his preaching (rather than physical strength, as would be inferred from ix. 19), and that this was how he confounded the Jews of Damascus. The καὶ λέγων reinforces this idea. Compare with these readings the D-reading of xx. 24, where Paul defines his ministry as a ministry τοῦ λόγου D d gig dem vg[s etc1] Amhr Lcf Eph[r(p444) et cat(p445)].

    The variants of ix. 20 (D def) fit into this context of verbal dispute with the Jews. The 'Western' text says that Paul entered (εἰσελθών h p q w cop[G67] Spec, cf. prov) the synagogues of the Jews (τῶν Ἰουδαίων h p w sy[p] sa cop[G67] Spec) and, with all boldness (μετὰ πάσης παρρησίας h Ir[iii.12,9(11)etcat]; sim l Spec), proclaimed Jesus, that he is ὁ Χριστός (441 h l t sa cop[G67] Ir[iii.12,9(11)etcat] Spec Thphyl[b]), the son of God. The τῶν Ἰουδαίων and ὁ Χριστός only reveal further the preoccupation of the 'Western' text with the Jews.

    The conflict of Paul and the Jews recurs almost as soon as he begins his first journey. For example, Bar-Jesus, a *Jewish* false prophet, sought to turn Sergius Paulus from the faith, and the D-text reveals the reason why (xiii. 8): ἐπειδὴ ἥδιστα ἤκουεν αὐτῶν D* d cop[G67] sy[h*] (E Bede[retr 139]: ὅτι ἡδέως αὐτῶν ἤκουεν). When this Jewish opponent of Paul, Bar-Jesus (or Ἐλύμας B; Ετ[.]ιμας D), is blinded, the proconsul ἐπίστευσεν (xiii. 12), but according to D he

ἐθαύμασεν καὶ ἐπίστευσεν τῷ θεῷ.

ἐθαύμασεν καί   D d E gig eth (sy[p]) Lcf[235] Vigil Ephr[(p382)]
τῷ θεῷ   D d (cf. eth: τῷ κυρίῳ)

    When Paul and his company arrive in Pisidian Antioch, they are invited to speak in the synagogue (xiii. 15: B: εἴ τις ἔστιν ἐν ὑμῖν λόγος παρακλήσεως...; D: εἴ τις ἔστιν λόγος **σοφίας** ἐν ὑμεῖν παρακλήσεως...). After Paul's sermon (discussed above, pp. 79–84), the D-text reports (xiii. 43): ἐγένετο δὲ καθ' ὅλης τῆς πόλεως διελθεῖν τὸν λόγον [D d (+τοῦ θεοῦ D, domini d) and with variations E p q w vg^codd prov tepl cop^G67 sy^hmg Bede^retr [142]], certainly reason enough for the Jews' reaction in xiii. 45 and 50:

Acts xiii. 45

B
ἰδόντες δὲ οἱ Ἰουδαῖοι
τοὺς ὄχλους
ἐπλήσθησαν ζήλου καὶ ἀντέλεγον
τοῖς ὑπὸ Παύλου λαλουμένοις

βλασφημοῦντες.

D
..., καὶ ἰδόντες οἱ Ἰουδαῖοι
τὸ πλῆθος
ἐπλήσθησαν ζήλου καὶ ἀντέλεγον
τοῖς λόγοις ὑπὸ τοῦ Παύλου
λεγομένοις
ἀντιλέγοντες καὶ βλασφημοῦντες.

καί D d sy^p
τὸ πλῆθος D sa arm (sy^p); turbam d
λόγοις D d E 35* gig sy^p
τοῦ D C E L P S 81 Chr^9, 256
λεγομένοις D C L P S 614 383 Chr
ἀντιλέγοντες καί D d P S 181 614 383 p* sy^h Chr Thphyl; ἐναντιούμενοι καί E 35*; resistentes et gig

While the additional ἀντιλέγοντες may seem to be little more than tautological, the picture of Jewish opposition is nevertheless intensified in the D-text.[1]

This heightened opposition becomes more explicit in the D-version of v. 50:

Acts xiii. 50

B
οἱ δὲ Ἰουδαῖοι
παρώτρυναν τὰς σεβομένας
γυναῖκας τὰς εὐσχήμονας
καὶ τοὺς πρώτους τῆς πόλεως
καὶ ἐπήγειραν

διωγμὸν ἐπὶ τὸν Παῦλον
καὶ Βαρνάβαν,...

D
οἱ δὲ Ἰουδαῖοι
παρώτρυνον τὰς σεβομένας
γυναῖκας τὰς εὐσχήμονας
καὶ τοὺς πρώτους τῆς πόλεως
καὶ ἐπήγειραν
θλῖψιν μεγάλην καὶ
διωγμὸν ἐπὶ Παῦλον
καὶ Βαρνάβαν,...

line 6: θλειψειν
line 7: επει

---

[1] Lagrange, Critique textuelle, p. 392. The textual problem is discussed by Wilcox, Semitisms, pp. 135f.

THE JEWS AND THE APOSTLES

παρώτρυνον D*
θλῖψιν μεγάλην (om μεγάλην E) καί D d E; cf. Ephr[(p418)] et cat[(p419)] et comm on IITim iii. 11[(p419n1)]
τόν] om D

The persecution stirred up by the Jews against Paul and Barnabas appears in the D-text as a *great affliction and* persecution. The D-text's additional καὶ θλῖψις after the διωγμὸς μέγας (B) in Acts viii. 1 has already been mentioned (above, pp. 129, 134). A similar situation developed in Iconium:

Acts xiv. 2

B	D
οἱ δὲ ἀπειθήσαντες Ἰουδαῖοι	οἱ δὲ ἀρχισυνάγωγοι τῶν Ἰουδαίων καὶ οἱ ἄρχοντες τῆς συναγωγῆς
ἐπήγειραν	ἐπήγαγον αὐτοῖς διωγμὸν κατὰ τῶν δικαίων,
καὶ ἐκάκωσαν τὰς ψυχὰς τῶν ἐθνῶν κατὰ τῶν ἀδελφῶν.	καὶ ἐκάκωσαν τὰς ψυχὰς τῶν ἐθνῶν κατὰ τῶν ἀδελφῶν. ὁ δὲ κύριος ἔδωκεν ταχὺ εἰρήνην.

ἀρχιυυνάγωγοι D d sy[hmg]; seniores Ephr[(p418)]
τῶν Ἰουδαίων D d
καὶ οἱ ἄρχοντες D d sy[hmg]
τῆς συναγωγῆς D d
ἐπήγαγον D] ἐπήγειραν cett d sy[hmg]
αὐτοῖς D] om d sy[hmg]
διωγμόν D d E 614 383 gig w cod.ard sy[h] sy[hmg] Ephr[(p418)]
κατὰ τῶν δικαίων D d Ephr[(p418)]] om sy[hmg]
ὁ δὲ κύριος (θεός E Bede) ἔδωκεν (ἐποίησεν E cod.ard Bede) ταχὺ (om ταχύ E Bede) εἰρήνην D d E gig p q w dem cod.ard vg[8 Paris MSS] prov tepl cop[G67] sy[hmg] Cass Bede[exp 63]

The possibility that the τῶν Ἰουδαίων and τῆς συναγωγῆς of D may not have been part of the 'Western' text[1] does not greatly affect the meaning; the emphasis in the D-text upon the Jewish rulers is clear. Lake and Cadbury thought that οἱ ἄρχοντες referred to the Iconian rulers,[2] but J.-B. Frey said that the author of the D-variants had an exact knowledge of the situation and clearly distinguished the ἀρχισυνάγωγοι (not officials, but persons of rank) from the ἄρχοντες, thereby

---
[1] Ropes, *Text*, p. 128. [2] *Beginnings*, iv, 161.

indicating perhaps an important knowledge of internal Jewish conditions.[1] All of this does not prove that D represents the 'Western' text, but at the least it favours the view that both terms refer to Jewish leaders. Thus, whereas in the B-text 'the unbelieving Jews stirred up and poisoned the minds of the Gentiles against the brethren', in D the Jewish *leaders* themselves brought upon (ἐπήγαγον) the apostles (αὐτοῖς)[2] a persecution against the righteous, in addition to evil-affecting the Gentiles against them.

A further interest here is the final sentence of the D-text: ὁ δὲ κύριος ἔδωκεν ταχὺ εἰρήνην. The effect of this statement is at once evident: the D-text sees two distinct persecutions at Iconium.[3] This D-reading marks the end of the first persecution, after which the apostles remained for a long time (xiv. 3). Soon, however, the people of the city became divided (xiv. 4, B and D): καὶ οἱ μὲν ἦσαν σὺν τοῖς 'Ιουδαίοις οἱ (ἄλλοι D) δὲ σὺν τοῖς ἀποστόλοις. From this point D continues: κολλώμενοι διὰ τὸν λόγον τοῦ θεοῦ D *d* sy[hmg] (cf. cop[G67] sy[p]). This last phrase certifies that those who sided with the apostles did so, not on the superficial level of personalities, etc., but from higher motives: 'for the sake of the word of God'.

The second persecution occurs in xiv. 5, and it is explicitly so designated in cop[G67] and sy[hmg]: καὶ πάλιν ἐπήγειραν διωγμὸν ἐκ δευτέρου, and in Ephr: *post anteriorem tribulationem*..., (though not in D). That D here has undoubtedly been assimilated to B appears from a comparison of the last part of *v*. 5 in B D *d h* cop[G67] Ephr and sy[hmg]:

Acts xiv. 5

B: ὡς δὲ ἐγένετο ὁρμὴ τῶν ἐθνῶν τε καὶ 'Ιουδαίων σὺν τοῖς ἄρχουσι αὐτῶν ὑβρίσαι καὶ λιθοβολῆσαι αὐτούς,...

D: ὡς δὲ ἐγένετο ὁρμὴ τῶν ἐθνῶν καὶ τῶν 'Ιουδαίων σὺν τοῖς ἄρχουσιν αὐτῶν ὑβρίσαι καὶ λιθοβολῆσαι αὐτούς,...

[1] J.-B. Frey, *Corpus Inscriptionum Judaicarum* (Rome/Paris, 1936), I, xcviii, n. 1; thus also W. M. Ramsay, *The Church in the Roman Empire* (London, 1893), pp. 45f., 480; Klijn, *Survey*, p. 21. On the meaning of the two groups in D, see further Fascher, *Textgeschichte*, p. 30.

[2] Torrey, *Documents*, p. 125, thinks αὐτοῖς is simply the 'usual ethical dative of the Aramaic text'; so also Wilcox, *Semitisms*, p. 131. See also Ropes, *Text*, pp. 128, 138.

[3] Harris, *Four Lectures*, p. 23; Zahn, *Urausgabe*, p. 357.

d: ut autem factum est impetus gentilium et judaeorum cum magistr(at)ibus ipsorum et injuriaverunt et lapidaverunt eos....
h: [...(*def*)...]runt eos et lapidaverunt,...
cop[G67]: But when they again raised trouble about them a second time, namely the Jews and the Gentiles with their rulers to insult and stone them, hearing of it they left the city.[1]
Ephr (Comm on II Tim. iii. 11):[2] Iconii autem post anteriorem tribulationem suscitarunt persecutionem Iudaei et gentiles et lapidantes eum ac Barnabam ejecerunt illos a civitate.
sy[hmg]: καὶ πάλιν ἐπήγειραν διωγμὸν ἐκ δευτέρου οἱ 'Ιουδαῖοι σὺν τοῖς ἔθνεσιν, καὶ λιθοβολήσαντες ἐξέβαλον αὐτοὺς ἐκ τῆς πόλεως,...

In sy[hmg] the subject of ἐπήγειραν διωγμόν is οἱ 'Ιουδαῖοι σὺν τοῖς ἔθνεσιν, which makes the Jews the primary instigators, with the Gentiles only secondarily so.[3] In *d h* sy[hmg] and Ephr, the apostles are actually stoned (cf. also *e*: *et contumeliis adficerunt eos et lapidarent*), whereas B (and D) speak only of a hostile movement under way for the purpose of molesting and stoning them. Only in sy[hmg] and Ephr, however, is this idea consistently carried through, for both *d* and *h* begin *v*. 6 with *intellexerunt et fugerunt*... (*h def* for the last two words), but sy[hmg] and Ephr say that after stoning them, they (i.e. the Jews) cast them out of the city, καὶ φυγόντες ἦλθον εἰς τὴν Λυκαονίαν... (*v*. 6), thus lacking the συνιδόντες (*intellexerunt*) of the other texts [B and D: συνιδόντες (+καὶ D) κατέφυγον...].

The contradictory Latin readings suggest that fragments of a version like that of sy[hmg] have survived there, and that D has been entirely conformed to the B-text. Whether sy[hmg] can be taken to represent the 'Western' text in every detail is, of course, not certain either, but the conclusion cannot be doubted that the 'Western' text of xiv. 5 shows a more direct and violent persecution of the apostles, and perhaps also a more distinctly *Jewish* responsibility for this opposition. Moreover, sy[hmg] and Ephr make it quite clear that the apostles were ejected from the city, rather than that they fled it. Once out, it does say that they fled to the cities of Lycaonia, but notice the variant, attested only by *h*, which explains this action (xiv. 6 *h*): *sicut ihs dixerat eis*

---

[1] Translation of Petersen, *CBQ*, XXVI (1964), 241.
[2] The text is given in Ropes, *Text*, p. 419, n. 1.
[3] Thus also Corssen, *GGA*, CLVIII (1896), 444.

LX[XII].[1] The flight, then, was not out of fear of persecution, but in response to the command of Jesus, when persecuted in one city, to flee to another.[2] And, as if further to vindicate this change of locality, the D-text reads in xiv. 7:

καὶ ἐκεινήθη ὅλον τὸ πλῆθος ἐπὶ τῇ διδαχῇ. ὁ δὲ Παῦλος καὶ Βαρνάβας διέτριβον ἐν Λύστροις.

καὶ...διδαχῇ D *d h* (...omne genus... *h*) p^2 *q w* vg^s vg^{cod} prov tepl Cass (E Bede[exp 63]: καὶ ἐξεπλήσσετο πᾶσα ἡ πολυπληθία ἐπὶ τῇ διδαχῇ αὐτῶν; cop^{G67}: and all the people drew near to their teaching)

ὁ δὲ Παῦλος...Λύστροις D *d* E *h p q w* vg^s prov tepl cop^{G67} Bede[exp 63]

The reading of *h* is of interest: ...*ut motum est omne genus in doctri[na eorum]*. Zahn says this represents ὅλον τὸ ἔθνος, which was the Greek text which lay before the copyists of D and E.[3] If Zahn is correct in this conclusion, the 'Western' text here attributed an even wider influence to Paul's preaching: the whole Lycaonian countryside was moved by it, in spite of the efforts of the Jews against him.

As the narrative proceeds in chapter xiv, the eye of one reading the D-text is drawn from the...διέτριβον... of xiv. 7 D to the διατριβόντων αὐτῶν καὶ διδασκόντων of xiv. 19 D (D *d* C E 81 minn *h* arm arab geo cop^{G67} sy^{hmg} Cass Bede[retr 142]). These statements, 'Now Paul and Barnabas spent some time at Lystra' (*v.* 7), and 'While they were spending some time and teaching...' (*v.* 19), show that what intervenes (*vv.* 8–18, the healing of a cripple) is parenthetical to the main interest of this text here, which is the conflict between the apostles and the Jews. Verse 19 tells of the stoning of Paul by people stirred up by the Jews (D says **τινὲς** 'Ιουδαῖοι)[4] from Iconium and Antioch,

---

[1] Zahn, *Urausgabe*, includes this reading in his text. D. DeBruyne, 'Quelques documents nouveaux pour l'histoire du texte africain des Évangiles', *RBén*, xxvii (1910), 434, n. 1, thought this reading in *h* was a marginal gloss by a devout reader, which was incorporated in the text. Proof for or against is lacking.

[2] Though the words ὅταν δὲ διώκωσιν ὑμᾶς ἐν τῇ πόλει ταύτῃ, φεύγετε εἰς τὴν ἑτέραν (Matt. x. 23) were spoken to the Twelve, not to the 70 (72). Zahn, *Urausgabe*, pp. 356f., suggests that this may read 72 (in *h*) because Paul and Barnabas did not belong to the Twelve.

[3] Zahn, *Urausgabe*, pp. 151f. See his evidence.

[4] τινές D E *h* vg cop^{G67} Cass Bede[retr 142]] om *d* sy^{hmg}.

and the 'Western' text (though not D) of v. 19 has the following additional information about these certain Jews (post '...Jews from Antioch and Iconium'):

καὶ διαλεγομένων αὐτῶν παρρησίᾳ ἔπεισαν τοὺς ὄχλους ἀποστῆναι ἀπ' αὐτῶν λέγοντες ὅτι οὐδὲν ἀληθὲς λέγουσιν, ἀλλὰ πάντα ψεύδονται.

καὶ...παρρησίᾳ (+τὸν λόγον τοῦ θεοῦ h) ἔπεισαν τοὺς ὄχλους (ἀνθρώπους h) C 1739 minn h arm geo cop^G67 sy^hmg] om D d sa Cass cett
ἀποστῆναι ἀπ' αὐτῶν C 1739 minn arm geo cop^G67 sy^hmg; μὴ πιστεύειν αὐτοῖς διδάσκουσιν h] om D d sa Cass cett
λέγοντες ὅτι...ψεύδονται C 1739 minn h arm geo cop^G67 sy^hmg] om D d sa Cass cett

No further comment is necessary; the anti-Judaic emphasis of this 'Western' variant is obvious.

Immediately following this, the D-text reads καὶ ἐπισείσαντες τοὺς ὄχλους (D d h e gig sy^p sy^hmg) for B's καὶ πείσαντες τοὺς ὄχλους. That D's reading is not simply a corruption of B is shown by the wide support for this variant, which represents a survival, in D, of the 'Western' text in v. 19,[1] and which shows more clearly the anti-Judaic motivation for the stoning of Paul which ensued.

Moreover, the 'Western' text (though not D) of xiv. 20 indicates that the disciples ('brethren' cop^G67) had to surround Paul in order to prevent further attack[2] and that only when the crowd had left and when evening had come did Paul dare to get up and enter the city of Lystra: *tunc circumdederunt eum di(s)centes, et [cum disce]ssisset populus vespere, levavit se, et intro[ivit civit]atem Lystrum h, sim* cop^G67 ('...the crowd left. But when evening had come...'). *Vespere* is attested also by sa; cf. Ephr^(p420) et cat (p421).

The evidence of cop^G67 is decisive in taking this version as the 'Western' text and in indicating that D has been conformed to the B text at this point, with only Λύστραν (D d h) remaining in D as a possible fragment of the 'Western' text. The reading of cop^G67 is decisive also in confirming the restoration of *cum discessisset* in *h*. This was the reading of Blass (1895) and of Buchanan, Zahn, Ropes, and A. C. Clark, but it was not taken up by Wordsworth and White (who followed Berger) and was

[1] Ropes, *Text*, p. 134. [2] *Beginnings*, IV, 167.

questioned by Lake and Cadbury. Thus, in xiv. 20 cop[G67] shows the way to the restoration of *h*, clarifies the 'Western' text of the passage, and leads to the disclosure of a heightened opposition against Paul by the Jews.

This general picture of Jewish opposition to Paul is confirmed by the D-text of Acts xv. 26. The letter sent out after the 'Jerusalem Council' commends Barnabas and Paul (B: 'our beloved'; D: 'your beloved', *v.* 25) to the Gentile Christians in Antioch, Syria, and Cilicia by characterizing them as 'men who have devoted their lives to the name of the Lord Jesus Christ', but D continues: εἰς πάντα πειρασμόν D *d* E 614 383 *l* sy[hmg] Bede[retr 143]] *om gig* Ir[iii.12,14(17)] Const.Apost[vi.12,15]. What is striking about this variant is that πειρασμός occurs only one other time in Acts, and that is xx. 19, where the context is most illuminating for the meaning of the D-text in xv. 26. In Acts xx. 19 Paul is recounting his stay at Ephesus to the elders there (B and D):

..., δουλεύων τῷ κυρίῳ μετὰ πάσης ταπεινοφροσύνης καὶ δακρύων καὶ **πειρασμῶν τῶν συμβάντων** μοι **ἐν ταῖς ἐπιβουλαῖς τῶν 'Ιουδαίων**.

These πειρασμοί, then, came upon Paul *by the plots of the Jews*, and what better way for the D-text to emphasize this than by having the apostles and elders in Jerusalem refer to the devotion of Barnabas and Paul *in every* **πειρασμός**?[1] The D-text, furthermore, prefaces this statement with the words (xx. 18) not found in B, ὡς τριετίαν ἢ καὶ πλεῖον (D *d*). Although the primary reference of this temporal phrase is to Paul's stay in Ephesus, it nevertheless implies that his trials extended over this period of time as well.

An interesting reading, though not strongly attested, occurs in Acts xvii. 15 in the text of Ephrem. In the preceding verses in Acts, the Jews from Thessalonica had stirred up the people in Beroea (notice that D *d* arab[e] sy[p] in *v.* 13 read οὐ διελίμπανον stirring up and troubling...), so that the brethren sent Paul away ἐπὶ τὴν θάλασσαν (D; B reads ἕως ἐπὶ τὴν θάλασσαν, *v.* 14). From there Paul went to Athens (*v.* 15), and here the D-text has the following additional material: παρῆλθεν δὲ τὴν Θεσσαλίαν, ἐκωλύθη γὰρ εἰς αὐτοὺς κηρύξαι τὸν λόγον D *d*,

[1] In NT the phrase πᾶς πειρασμός occurs only in Acts xv. 26D and Lk iv. 13 (B and D), both times in the same form: πάντα πειρασμόν.

THE JEWS AND THE APOSTLES

which Ephr^(pp382, 432) *et* cat (p433) read as, 'But the Holy Spirit prevented him from preaching, lest perhaps they should slay him'. This reading of Ephrem, though it may not necessarily represent the 'Western' text, gives a plausible meaning to D's ἐκωλύθη...λόγον: Paul could not preach at Θεσσαλία (is this Thessaly, or Thessalonica as in Ephrem, or θάλασσα?)[1] because the Jews would have killed him.

Another D-reading concerned with a Jewish plot against Paul and with the Holy Spirit occurs in Acts xx. 3:

Acts xx. 3

B	D
..., ποιήσας τε μῆνας τρεῖς γενομένης ἐπιβουλῆς αὐτῷ ὑπὸ τῶν Ἰουδαίων μέλλοντι ἀνάγεσθαι εἰς τὴν Συρίαν ἐγένετο γνώμης τοῦ ὑποστρέφειν διὰ Μακεδονίας.	..., ποιήσας δὲ μῆνας γ̄ καὶ γενηθείσ(ης) αὐτῷ ἐπιβουλῆς ὑπὸ τῶν Ἰουδαίων ἠθέλησεν ἀναχθῆναι εἰς Συρίαν, εἶπεν δὲ τὸ πνεῦμα αὐτῷ ὑποστρέφειν διὰ τῆς Μακεδονίας.

δέ D *d e* minn bo
καὶ γενηθείσης D *d gig*
αὐτῷ ἐπιβουλῆς D *d* H L P S 614 383 vg sy^h Chr^(9, 362)] ἐπιβουλῆς αὐτῷ *cett*
ἠθέλησεν ἀναχθῆναι εἰς Συρίαν D *d* sy^hmg Ephr^(p442) *et* cat (p443)
εἶπεν δὲ (τε *d*) τὸ πνεῦμα αὐτῷ D *d gig* sy^hmg Ephr^(p442) *et* cat (p443)
τῆς D

Here both B and D speak of a plot of the Jews against Paul in Greece. In B Paul was about to set sail for Syria when this occurred, but the Jewish plot made him change his mind and 'he determined to go through Macedonia' instead, that is, he decided to travel by land rather than by sea, which implies that a sea voyage would entail danger from the Jews. The D-text is different; here Paul's desire to go to Syria is occasioned by the plot of the Jews, and the change to a land journey is attributed to the instruction of the Holy Spirit.[2] The only point to be noted

---
[1] For the last view, see Ropes, *Text*, pp. 164f.; but see A. C. Clark, *Acts*, p. 367.
[2] Ropes, *Text*, p. 190; *Beginnings*, IV, 253. For a contrary view, that there is not a great difference between the two forms of the text here, see Zuntz, *Class et Med*, III (1940), 44.

143

ANTI-JUDAIC TENDENCIES IN ACTS

is that in the D-text here, as in the previous case (xvii. 15 Ephr), the Holy Spirit directs Paul in order to protect him from the Jews. It is this recurring juxtaposition in the D-text of Jewish hostility and the activity of the Holy Spirit which is of significance.

The occasion for Paul's appearance before Gallio is differently formulated in D:

Acts xviii. 12-13a

B	D
Γαλλίωνος δὲ ἀνθυπάτου ὄντος τῆς Ἀχαΐας κατεπέστησαν οἱ Ἰουδαῖοι ὁμοθυμαδὸν τῷ Παύλῳ καὶ ἤγαγον αὐτὸν ἐπὶ τὸ βῆμα, λέγοντες...	12. Γαλλίωνός τε ἀνθυπάτου ὄντος τῆς Ἀχαΐας κατεπέστησαν ὁμοθυμαδὸν οἱ Ἰουδαῖοι συνλαλήσαντες μεθ' ἑαυτῶν ἐπὶ τὸν Παῦλον, καὶ ἐπιθέντες τὰς χεῖρας ἤγαγον αὐτὸν ἐπὶ τὸ βῆμα, 13. καταβοῶντες καὶ λέγοντες...

τε D d sy[p]] δέ cett h
συνλαλήσαντες μεθ' ἑαυτῶν D d h
ἐπὶ τὸν Παῦλον D; de Paulo d h
καί B D cett] om h
ἐπιθέντες τὰς χεῖρας D d; ἐπέθηκαν αὐτῷ τὰς χεῖρας h sa sy[h]*
ἐπὶ τὸ βῆμα] πρὸς τὸν ἀνθύπατον h sy[h]* Ephr[cat (p437)]
καταβοῶντες καί D d h; cf. Ephr[cat (p437)]

Little comment is necessary here. The B-text indicates quite simply that 'the Jews rose up together against Paul and led him to the tribunal'. In D, however, συνλαλήσαντες μεθ' ἑαυτῶν shows that the action of the Jews against Paul was deliberate and premeditated, and not mere mob action; καὶ ἐπιθέντες τὰς χεῖρας specifies that for the D-text there was a seizure or arrest of Paul by the Jews; and καταβοῶντες indicates a high degree of emotional excitement and points to a heightened hostility *against* (κατα-) Paul on the part of the Jews.[1]

In connection with ἐπιθέντες τὰς χεῖρας, notice D's variant in xii. 3:

[1] It should be noted that D also has κράζοντες in xvi. 22 and ἐπικράζοντες in xvi. 39, both with reference, presumably, to Gentile mobs.

THE JEWS AND THE APOSTLES

Acts xii. 3

B
ἰδὼν δὲ ὅτι ἀρεστόν ἐστιν
τοῖς Ἰουδαίοις

προσέθετο συλλαβεῖν
καὶ Πέτρον,...

D
καὶ ἰδὼν ὅτι ἀρεστόν ἐστιν
τοῖς Ἰουδαίοις
ἡ ἐπιχείρησις αὐτοῦ
ἐπὶ τοὺς πιστοὺς
προσέθετο συνλαβεῖν
καὶ Πέτρον,...

line 3: επιχειρη]σεις

καὶ ἰδών D d H L P S 614 383 gig sa eth sy[p,h] Lcf[187] Chr[9,225txt]
ἡ ἐπιχείρησις ἐπὶ τοὺς (+ἁγίους καὶ p* vg[cod]) πιστοὺς D d p*
vg[codR] sy[hmg]

In B it is the execution of James by Herod Agrippa I which is pleasing to the Jews; in D the action referred to is broader: the arrest of believers pleases the Jews, and this D-variant in xii. 3 illuminates that in xviii. 12 D, which shows the Jews themselves undertaking such action.

Observe the D-text's version of the death of Herod Agrippa I:

Acts xii. 23

B
παραχρῆμα δὲ ἐπάταξεν αὐτὸν
ἄγγελος κυρίου ἀνθ' ὧν οὐκ
ἔδωκεν τὴν δόξαν τῷ θεῷ,
καὶ
γενόμενος σκωληκόβρωτος
ἐξέψυξεν.

D
παραχρῆμα δὲ αὐτὸν ἐπάταξεν
ἄγγελος κυρίου ἀνθ' ὧν οὐκ
ἔδωκεν δόξαν τῷ θεῷ,
καὶ καταβὰς ἀπὸ τοῦ βήματος,
γενόμενος (σ)κωληκόβρωτος
ἔτι ζῶν καὶ οὕτως ἐξέψυξεν.

τήν] om D E H L P S 614 383 Chr[9,235]
καταβὰς...βήματος D d (cop[G67]) Ephr[(pp382, 416)]
ἔτι ζῶν καὶ οὕτως D d

Regarding the B-text, it is clear that Luke 'intended the readers to see in the death of Agrippa divine punishment for his cruelty to the apostles'.[1] The D-text, however, makes the death, and therefore the punishment, an even more horrible one than appears in B. D has καταβὰς ἀπὸ τοῦ βήματος γενόμενος σκωληκόβρωτος ἔτι ζῶν. In view of the fact that Agrippa was

[1] Beginnings, IV, 139.

well liked by the Jews,[1] and that his 'seizure of the faithful' (D-text) was pleasing to the Jews, the more severe picture of his death in the D-text can only be interpreted as revealing a greater animosity toward one who persecuted the believers and the apostles, especially when that was done to please the Jews.

The text of Acts xviii. 17 in D is defective at points, but the 'Western' text is clear from other witnesses:

Acts xviii. 17

B	D
ἐπιλαβόμενοι δὲ πάντες	[ἀ]πολαβόμενοι δὲ πάντες
	οἱ Ἕλληνες [...]
Σωσθένην τὸν ἀρχισυνάγωγον	Σωσθένην τὸν ἀρχεισυνάγωγον
ἔτυπτον ἔμπροσθεν τοῦ βήματος·	ἔτυπτον ἔνπροσθεν τοῦ βήματος·
καὶ οὐδὲν τούτων τῷ Γαλλίωνι	τ[.........].
ἔμελεν.	

d: tunc Gallio fingebat eum non videre
h: et Gallio simulabat [se non vi]dere
Cf. Ephr[cat (p437)]: he became as one not seeing

ἀπολαβόμενοι D*] ἐπιλαβόμενοι *cett*; adpraehendentes *d*; cō[prehen]derunt *h*
πάντες] *om h* Ephr[cat (p437)]
οἱ Ἕλληνες D *d* E H L P S 614 383 minn *gig h cod.ard* sa arm eth sy[p, h] Chr[9, 329 (but not com 331)] Bede[retr 147] cf. geo] οἱ πεπιστευκότες Ἕλληνες Ephr[cat (p437)]; (some MSS read οἱ Ἰουδαῖοι)

The natural meaning of the B-text is that the πάντες who seized Sosthenes and beat him in the presence of Gallio were Jews; there is nothing in the context to indicate otherwise.[2] The obscurity of Sosthenes' identity clouds the issue; is he the leader of the Jewish delegation opposing Paul,[3] and is he beaten because he mismanaged the case?[4] Or, is he (like Crispus, xviii. 8) an adherent of Paul, who is beaten by the Jews to take vengeance on a prominent Jew attracted to Christianity?[5] (This view finds

[1] M. S. Enslin, *Christian Beginnings* (New York, 1938), pp. 76f. See the references there to Josephus.
[2] But Haenchen, *Apostelgeschichte*, p. 473, rejects this view; cf. Conzelmann, *Apostelgeschichte*, p. 107. *Beginnings*, IV, 228, defends the beating as by both Jews and Greeks.
[3] Haenchen, *Apostelgeschichte*, p. 473.   [4] See *Beginnings*, IV, 228.
[5] See C. S. C. Williams, *A Commentary on the Acts of the Apostles* (New York, 1957), p. 212.

support in identifying this Sosthenes with the one in I Cor. i. 1, a doubtful procedure.)[1] In this case, however, would they dare to beat Sosthenes but not Paul? Rather, the fact that 'Gallio was not concerned at all about these things' suggests that the beating of Sosthenes was, like questions about their own law (v. 15), an internal affair of the Jews. The B-text, then, can be taken as it stands: Sosthenes was a leading Jew (ἀρχισυνάγωγος) who was beaten by his own people for his failure to obtain a judgement against Paul.

The D-reading, πάντες οἱ Ἕλληνες, has the Greeks beating Sosthenes. (The reading indicated in Ephr[cat], 'the believing Greeks', has no other support, against the strong evidence for οἱ Ἕλληνες.)[2] The natural meaning here (assuming again that Sosthenes is the leader of the Jewish party) is that an anti-Judaic reaction set in, encouraged by Gallio's snubbing of the Jews.[3] The 'Western' reading in v. 17b fits this situation: 'Gallio pretended not to see', which suggests that what was happening was something not ordinarily permitted. The D-text is content to portray such a demonstration of anti-Judaic sentiment and makes it clear that the Roman proconsul, who had just acted in Paul's favour, knowingly condones such an action.

This attitude of Gallio raises the question as to the attitude of the D-text toward the Roman officials, as evidenced by its variant readings. Some indications follow.

The D-text of Acts xvi. 39 has been dealt with above (pp. 50f.), where it was shown that the Roman magistrates were allowed the excuse of ignorance for their actions against the apostles. The context in xvi. 35–9 deserves further attention. The situation of Paul and Silas here is similar to that of Peter and John in Acts iv. In both cases the apostles have been arrested and are about to be released by the officials in charge. The D-text in chapter iv, as already shown (above, pp. 120–7), not only portrays a harsher treatment of the apostles by the Jews, especially by their leaders, but also insists on their powerlessness before the apostles (iv. 14D). This last emphasis finds

[1] Haenchen, *Apostolgeschichte*, p. 473, n. 2.
[2] Though it is possible (but not certain) that Ephr thought that 'Greeks' here meant Jews who spoke Greek: see Ropes, *Text*, p. 437, n. 3.
[3] Bruce, *Acts*[57], p. 348. See also A. Resch, *Agrapha. Ausscrcanonische Schriftfragmente* (Leipzig, 1906), p. 350, n. 1.

a parallel in chapter xvi in that the magistrates are afraid when they learn the apostles are Romans (xvi. 38) and are forced to apologize to them and beg them to leave the city (xvi. 39B): ...καὶ ἐλθόντες παρεκάλεσαν αὐτούς, καὶ ἐξαγαγόντες ἠρώτων ἀπελθεῖν ἀπὸ τῆς πόλεως. Both of these elements of fear and apology appear more strongly in the D-text, but also with a significant difference. The D-text in xvi. 35 provides an additional and prior occasion of fear on the part of the magistrates, a fear due to the earthquake of the preceding night: συνῆλθον... ἐπὶ τὸ αὐτὸ εἰς τὴν ἀγορὰν καὶ ἀναμνησθέντες τὸν σεισμὸν τὸν γεγονότα ἐφοβήθησαν D *d* sy[hmg] Cass Ephr [(p430) et cat (p431)]. It was in the market-place that the apostles had been brought the day before by their accusers, and according to D the magistrates, meeting here, saw some mysterious connection between the earthquake and the apostles. This is shown by their command to 'release those men *whom you took into custody yesterday*' (οὓς ἐχθὲς παρέλαβες D *d* 614 383 sy[h] geo; [ἐχθές Ephr[(p430) et cat (p431)]]). Thus, in D the release is motivated by superstitious fear. (Notice Ephr[(p430) et cat (p431)] on this incident: 'The astaritae the optimates of the city were appalled and terrified by the earthquake, and learning the truth knew that this earthquake was really on their account, but they did not choose to admit it. They sent secretly to liberate them....') Can the Romans be blamed if this fear is later intensified by the realization that they have wrongly treated Roman citizens? The D-text, then, gives to the Romans an additional *and less culpable* basis for the fear which they felt.

How different this release in chapter xvi is from that in chapter iv! In chapter iv the decision (iv. 18D) to release Peter and John included a strong prohibition against teaching in the name of Jesus, revealing a severe opposition to the apostles' message (see the discussion on the 'Western' text of iv. 17 above, p. 125), but here in chapter xvi (D) the release is occasioned by an awesome natural phenomenon.

As for the apology in xvi. 39, this is quite clear in B, where there is at least a polite request to leave (RSV translates 'apologized to them'), but the D-text is clearer, stating that the magistrates came μετὰ φίλων πολλῶν εἰς τὴν φυλακήν,[1] and

[1] D *d*; note that 614 383 vg[codR2] sy[h*] read εἰς τὴν φυλακήν, though not μετὰ φίλων πολλῶν.

THE JEWS AND THE APOSTLES

said, Ἡγνοήσαμεν τὰ καθ' ὑμᾶς ὅτι ἐστὲ ἄνδρες δίκαιοι D d 614 383 vg[codR²]sy[h]* Ephr[(p432)] et cat [(p433)]. The excuse here in D on the basis of ignorance has already been discussed. It is necessary only to remark that in chapter iv the Jewish rulers were still seeking to charge Peter and John with some crime (αἰτία, iv. 21 D, see discussion above, p. 126) when they already knew they could not hold them. In contrast with D's αἰτία in iv. 21, notice the D-text's version of xvi. 37:

Acts xvi. 37

B	D
	Ἀναιτείους
Δείραντες ἡμᾶς δημοσίᾳ	δείραντες ἡμᾶς δημοσίᾳ
ἀκατακρίτους,	ἀκατακρίτους,
ἀνθρώπους Ῥωμαίους ὑπάρχοντας,	ἀνθρώπους Ῥωμαίους ὑπάρχοντας
ἔβαλαν εἰς φυλακήν.	ἔβαλαν εἰς φυλακήν.

ἀναιτείους *ante* δείραντες D d(anetios) sy[p] geo; *post* Ῥωμαίους sa Cass [Clark places it *post* δημοσίᾳ; Hilgenfeld and Zahn follow D] ἀκατακρίτους] *om* sa sy[p] Cass

The fact that all the witnesses (except geo) which attest D's ἀναιτείους omit ἀκατακρίτους makes it clear that the 'Western' text lacked the latter term, which came into D later by conflation. The D-text's ἀναιτείους would then be parallel to B's ἀκατακρίτους.[1] (Ἀκατάκριτος = not yet tried; ἀναίτιος = innocent, guiltless.)

Can the D-text's reading of the two terms, αἰτία and ἀναίτιος, in these two chapters be mere coincidence? The Jewish officials sought to charge Christian apostles with an αἰτία, while, in a similar situation before Romans, Christian apostles are described as ἀναίτιοι (with neither term appearing in B in these passages); and, though the Romans imprisoned such men, they are excused for doing so. This is striking evidence that the D-text was hard on the Jewish officials, but was willing to wink at the Romans.[2]

One final comparison of B and D in chapter xvi involves the

[1] Ropes, *Text*, p. 159; Blass, *Acta*[95], p. 184.
[2] A further evidence that chapters iv and xvi are parallel, especially in D, is the similar reading which D has at the conclusion of each; in iv. 24 D reads καὶ ἐπιγνόντες τὴν τοῦ θεοῦ ἐνέργειαν (discussed above, pp. 11, 127), and in xvi. 40 D has διηγήσαντο ὅσα ἐποίησεν κύριος αὐτοῖς D d cod. ard Cass.

149

last part of *v.* 39. B reads simply καὶ ἐξαγαγόντες ἠρώτων ἀπελθεῖν ἀπὸ τῆς πόλεως. D, however, gives the reason for the request to leave the city:

καὶ ἐξαγαγόντες παρεκάλεσαν αὐτοὺς λέγοντες· Ἐκ τῆς πόλεως ταύτης ἐξέλθατε μήποτε πάλιν συνστραφῶσιν ἡμεῖν ἐπικράζοντες καθ' ὑμῶν.

καὶ ἐξαγαγόντες...λέγοντες D *d*
ἐκ τῆς πόλεως...ἐξέλθατε (-ετε 614 383) D *d* 614 383 sy^h* Ephr^(p432) *et* cat(p433); +καί *ante* ἐκ 614 383
μήποτε (μή πως 614 383) πάλιν συστραφῶσιν (ἐπιστραφῶσιν πάλιν 614 383) ἡμῖν (*om* ἡμῖν; *add* οἱ 614 383 sy^h*) ἐπικράζοντες (-άξαντες 614 383 sy^h*) καθ' ὑμῶν D *d* 614 383 sy^h* Ephr^(p432) *et* cat(p433)

The D-text tempers the request to leave the city with an explanation: the officials do not want another scene of disorder in the city—'Depart...lest those who cried out against you assemble (*or* conspire) against us again.' Fascher sees in this D-variant an acknowledgement of the officials' blamelessness, for they desired only to avoid another mob-scene, an unpleasant thing for both parties.[1] This motivation would relieve the officials of any thought of opposition to the apostles as such, and again it excuses them, for their action was only in the interest of preserving public order, with no reflection at all upon the apostles' message or mission.

The result is obvious: the D-text, which elsewhere emphasizes the opposition of the Jews to the apostles and Jesus and stresses their culpability, is able to provide excuses for the Romans for similar treatment of the apostles. Moreover, this deference toward the Romans in such cases serves to accentuate the opposite feeling expressed toward the Jews.

The 'Western' text of Acts xxii. 29 (D *def*), incidentally, has the Roman tribune release Paul as soon as he discovers he is a Roman: καὶ παραχρῆμα ἔλυσεν αὐτόν (*post* δεδεκώς) 614 1611 sy^h* sa. In the B-text Paul is not released until the next day. (Note that the 'Western' text apparently read ἔπεμψεν for the ἔλυσεν of xxii. 30.[2] The sa omits the ἔλυσεν αὐτόν καί in *v.* 30, which has become superfluous in the 'Western' text in view of

[1] Fascher, *Textgeschichte*, p. 38.
[2] Ropes, *Text*, p. 215.

THE JEWS AND THE APOSTLES

its reading in v. 29.) This is another case in which the Jews were accusing Paul, but in which the Roman official is portrayed as more lenient in the 'Western' text.

Does the 'Western' text pay the Roman governor, Felix, a compliment when, in Acts xxiv. 10 (D *def*), it reads κριτὴν δίκαιον for B's κριτήν? (δίκαιον E Ψ minn 614 sy[h] Chr[9,418 et com] = ⅔ Thphyl Ishodad.)[1]

As is the case with the last two variants treated, a number of readings relevant to this section on the Jews and the apostles occur in those chapters of Acts where D is lacking. They are of significance both as additional 'Western' evidence and as a point of comparison with the picture presented by the D-readings proper (see above, p. 34).

The additional words in the 'Western' text of Acts xxiii. 15, ἐὰν δέῃ καὶ (+ ἡμᾶς *h*) ἀποθανεῖν 614 2147 *h* sy[hmg], which are included in the 'Western' version of the vow of certain of the Jews[2] (v. 12) who pledged themselves to kill Paul, shows a greater devotion to this malevolent cause and, consequently, a greater hostility on their part toward Paul. In short, it characterizes their fanaticism.[3] (Note also the τὸ καθόλου [*in totum*] in xxiii. 14, *gig h* Lcf.)

The ever-present danger to Paul's life at the hands of these Jews is referred to an additional time in the 'Western' text of Acts xxiii. 24;[4] the tribune is speaking: ἐφοβήθη γὰρ μήποτε ἁρπάσαντες αὐτὸν οἱ Ἰουδαῖοι ἀποκτείνωσιν καὶ αὐτὸς μεταξὺ ἔγκλησιν ἔχῃ ὡς ἀργύριον εἰληφώς (𝔓[48]) 614 (2147) *gig p*² *c w cod.ard* vg[cl] prov tepl sy[h*] Cass; *sim* arm[osc]; (*h def* after 24*a*).

In the letter of the tribune to Felix (Acts xxiii. 26–30), the 'Western' text has the tribune say that he was barely able to rescue Paul from the hostile Jewish mob (xxiii. 29): ἐξήγαγον αὐτὸν μόλις τῇ βίᾳ 614 2147 *gig* sy[h*]. When Tertullus presents the case for the Jews (xxiv. 2–8), the 'Western' text repeats this idea (xxiv. 7): παρελθὼν δὲ Λυσίας ὁ χιλίαρχος μετὰ πολλῆς βίας ἐκ τῶν χειρῶν ἡμῶν ἀπήγαγεν... E Ψ 614 minn *gig p*² *c dem cod.ard* vg[cl] tepl arm eth sy[p, h] Cass Thphyl Chr[9, 418] Bede[exp 87].

---

[1] Zahn, *Urausgabe*, p. 375, calls this a strongly attested reading.
[2] Acts xxiii. 12: τινὲς τῶν Ἰουδαίων 𝔓[48] H L P S 383 minn *gig h* vg sa sy[p] Lcf Thphyl[a]) οἱ Ἰουδαῖοι *cett.* Cf. a similar variant in xiv. 19 D; see above, p. 140.   [3] Fascher, *Textgeschichte*, p. 42.
[4] Thus also Corssen, *GGA*, CLVIII (1896), 444.

151

To say the least, the Jews, according to the 'Western' text, were very reluctant to give up Paul; they wanted to deal with him themselves: compare the 'Western' text of xxiv. 6: ...καὶ κατὰ τὸν ἡμέτερον νόμον ἠθελήσαμεν κρῖναι (same attestation as for the 'Western' reading in *v.* 7). Is it not significant that this same desire was observed in the D-text of Acts xiii. 28-9, only there with reference to Jesus? (See above, p. 58.)

The reasons given for Paul's seizure by the Jews in Jerusalem were that he taught against the people, the law, and the temple, and had defiled the temple by bringing Gentiles into it (xxi. 28). (Hence the outcry when Paul in his defence mentioned that God had sent him to the Gentiles, xxii. 21.) After this, until Tertullus appears (xxiv. 2-8), there is no statement of the charges against Paul except the general statement of xxiii. 29, 'that he was accused about questions of their law'. The 'Western' text follows this with the words, Μωσέως καὶ 'Ιησοῦ τινός, (𝔓⁴⁸?) 614 2147 *gig* sy^hmg. This is the only time that charges involving Paul's Christian faith have been made explicit in the whole proceedings, and this report of the 'Western' text that Paul was accused about 'questions of the law of Moses and of a certain Jesus', shows that this text viewed the Jews as hostile toward his teachings about Jesus, in addition to his Jewish unorthodoxy. Fascher says that in this reading the decisive reproach against Paul first becomes clear.[1]

The part played in Paul's trial by Drusilla, Felix's wife, who was a Jewess, is interesting in its 'Western' version (xxiv. 24, 27). In *v.* 24 the 'Western' text reports that it was she 'who requested to see Paul and to hear the word. Then, since he wished to grant her a favour', Felix summoned Paul. [ἥτις ἠρώτησεν ἰδεῖν τὸν Παῦλον καὶ ἀκοῦσαι τὸν λόγον (*om* τὸν λόγον bohem) bohem sy^hmg; θέλων οὖν χαρίζεσθαι αὐτῇ sy^hmg.] What makes this significant, however, is that in xxiv. 27, where the B-text reads θέλων τε χάριτα καταθέσθαι τοῖς 'Ιουδαίοις ὁ Φῆλιξ κατέλιπε τὸν Παῦλον δεδεμένον, the 'Western' text reads instead τὸν δὲ Παῦλον εἴασεν ἐν τηρήσει διὰ Δρούσιλλαν, 614 2147 sy^hmg.

Thus, whereas the B-text implicates Felix as one who at Paul's expense would please the Jews, the 'Western' text places the direct blame for Paul's prolonged imprisonment upon a *Jewess*!

[1] Fascher, *Textgeschichte*, p. 42.

THE JEWS AND THE APOSTLES

Felix is, of course, still in the picture here in the 'Western' text, but his direct responsibility is obscured and the motivation differently construed. This different reason again shows the 'Western' text to be more reserved in its attitude toward Roman officials, while not minimizing its hostility toward the Jews. The 'Western' text of Acts xxviii. 19 again varies in its reference to the Jews' part in Paul's trial:

Acts xxviii. 19

B	D-text
ἀντιλεγόντων δὲ τῶν Ἰουδαίων	ἀντιλεγόντων δὲ τῶν Ἰουδαίων καὶ ἐπικραζόντων· Αἶρε τὸν ἐχθρὸν ἡμῶν,
ἠναγκάσθην ἐπικαλέσασθαι Καίσαρα, οὐχ ὡς τοῦ ἔθνους μου ἔχων τι κατηγορεῖν.	ἠναγκάσθην ἐπικαλέσασθαι Καίσαρα, οὐχ ὡς τοῦ ἔθνους μου ἔχων τι κατηγορεῖν, ἀλλ' ἵνα λυτρώσωμαι τὴν ψυχήν μου ἐκ θανάτου.

καὶ ἐπικραζόντων...ἡμῶν 614 minn sy^h *
ἀλλ' ἵνα...θανάτου 614 minn *gig p q c* sy^h * prov tepl] *om s cett*

No comment is necessary; the greater hostility of the Jews toward Paul and the severe danger from them is obvious in the 'Western' text.

Observe, finally, that in Acts xxvi. 1, when Paul made his defence against the charges of the Jews, the 'Western' text describes him as 'confident and consoled by the Holy Spirit', sy^hmg (cf. *fiducialiter* Ephr^(p448)), which may represent παρρησια-σάμενος καὶ τῷ πνεύματι τῷ ἁγίῳ παρακληθείς[1] or θαρρῶν καὶ ἐν πνεύματι ἁγίῳ παράκλησιν λαβών.[2] As noted earlier, this is only one of several instances where D or the 'Western' text makes mention of the Holy Spirit in circumstances involving Jewish opposition to the apostles or other anti-Judaic overtones (see above, pp. 117f., 143f.). Paul speaks against Jewish accusations under the tutelage of the Holy Spirit!

One contention of this section on 'The Jews and the Apostles', that the D-text plays off against one another the leaders of the Jews and the leaders of the new faith, finds support in the additional emphasis which the D-text places upon the apostles,

[1] *Beginnings*, IV, 314.   [2] A. C. Clark, *Acts*, p. 159.

first, by enhancing them and their deeds in general, and, secondly, by giving Peter and Paul in particular a greater prominence than they receive in the B-text. These points have been illustrated throughout, and those examples already given, plus some additional instances, may be summarized as follows:

(a) General

(1) Acts i. 16. The D-text understands the Psalm passages (quoted in i. 20) to refer to the necessity of electing a successor to Judas rather than to the fate of the betrayer.[1] This is indicated by the present tense δεῖ (D* *d gig p t* vg Ir[iii.12,1; ii.20,2(32,1)] Aug[b] Vigil), for which B reads ἔδει (B *cett* D[A] Or Eus Hier). For the D-text, 'it *is* necessary for this[2] scripture...to be fulfilled' in order to complete the broken circle of apostleship (cf. δεῖ in *v.* 21). (Notice that cop[G67] [cf. vg[codG]ᶜ] has an additional 'and the apostleship' following 'ministry' in *v.* 17; cf. *v.* 25.)

(2) iv. 14. The Jewish leaders were powerless before the apostles (see above, p. 124).

(3) iv. 24. The D-variant, καὶ ἐπιγνόντες τὴν τοῦ θεοῦ ἐνέργειαν (see above, pp. 11, 127), ascribes divine protection to Peter and John.[3]

(4) v. 38-9. The work of the apostles Peter and John has divine sanction and is invincible (see above, pp. 130-2).

(5) iv. 21; v. 38. As developed above (pp. 126, 130f.), the D-text parallels events in the apostles' experience to that of Jesus; the result is an enhancing of the apostles.

(6) xvi. 37. Whereas the ἀκατακρίτους of B describes Paul and Silas as uncondemned or as not yet tried, D's ἀναιτείους affirms their innocence (see above, p. 149).

(b) Variants concerned with the apostles' speech or preaching

(1) ii. 37. The D-text's ὑποδείξατε ἡμεῖν serves to heighten the effect of Peter's words on the hearers (see above, p. 73).

---

[1] Conzelmann, *Apostelgeschichte*, p. 23; Haenchen, *Apostelgeschichte*, p. 124, n. 5.

[2] ταύτην D *d* C³E S minn *gig p t* geo Ir[iii.12,1; ii.20,2(32,1)]; istam Aug[b]] om ℵ A B C *al* vg sa Or Eus Hier Vigil.

[3] J. Crehan, 'Peter according to the D-Text of Acts', *ThSt*, xviii (1957), 600.

(2) xiii. 41. Similarly, the D-text's καὶ ἐσείγησαν may emphasize the effect of Paul's speech on his audience (see above, pp. 82f.).

(3) xiii. 8. The proconsul *heard* Paul, Barnabas, and John Mark *with great pleasure* and, in xiii. 12, *marvelled* at their deeds (see above, p. 135).

(4) xiv. 9. The lame man heard Paul speaking and *was in fear*: ὑπάρχων ἐν φόβῳ D *d h*(end of v.8) (see above, p. 119). [Cf. xvi. 35 D, where the Roman magistrates were in fear because of the earthquake (see above, pp. 147f.); 'their respect for the apostles is enhanced by the word ἐφοβήθησαν'.][1]

(5) xv. 7; vi. 10. Peter and Stephen were inspired in speech by the Holy Spirit (see above, pp. 116, 132). [Note also that Stephen is made the centre of the scene in vi. 15 D (see above, p. 133).] In viii. 35 D Philip explained the scriptures 'in the Spirit' (see above, p. 117).

(6) xix. 8. According to the D-text, Paul spoke in the synagogue *with great power*: ἐν δυνάμει μεγάλῃ D *d* sy^hmg.

(7) xiv. 7; xiii. 43. The apostles' preaching had great effect and influence (see above, pp. 136, 140).

(8) xiv. 19. The διαλεγομένων αὐτῶν παρρησίᾳ (see above, p. 141) refers to Barnabas and Paul *speaking openly* or possibly *boldly refuting* the Jews even while the latter were influencing the crowd against the apostles. The phrase does not refer to the Jews as, for example, *h* (*Judaei*...[*qui*] *palam disputabant verbum dei*) has taken it.[2]

(c) *Variants concerned with miracles and the apostles' ministry*

(1) iii. 3–5. In the B-text it is Peter and John who 'look intently at' (ἀτενίζειν) the lame man, but in D the lame man 'looks intently at' the apostles from the outset, and the strong word, ἀτενίζειν, is used throughout of his attention to them, which may indicate a more awesome status and a higher regard for the apostles in their role as miracle workers:

Verse 3
B: ὃς ἰδὼν Πέτρον καὶ Ἰωάνην...
D: οὗτος ἀτενίσας τοῖς ὀφθαλμοῖς αὐτοῦ καὶ ἰδὼν Πέτρον καὶ Ἰωάνην...
D *d h*

---
[1] Williams, *Alterations*, p. 57. [2] See Ropes, *Text*, p. 134.

ANTI-JUDAIC TENDENCIES IN ACTS

Verses 4-5a
B: ἀτενίσας δὲ Πέτρος εἰς αὐτὸν σὺν τῷ 'Ιωάννῃ εἶπεν· Βλέψον εἰς ἡμᾶς. ὁ δὲ ἐπεῖχεν αὐτοῖς...
D: ἐμβλέψας δὲ ὁ Πέτρος εἰς αὐτὸν σὺν 'Ιωάνῃ καὶ εἶπεν· 'Ατένεισον εἰς ἡμᾶς. ὁ δὲ ἀτενείσας αὐτοῖς...

ἐμβλέψας D *d h p*² vg
ἀτένεισον D
ἀτενείσας D *d*(adtendebat) cop

In a similar way the 'Western' reading of ix. 34 (D *def*) could mean that Aeneas fixed his gaze on Peter before he was healed: the B-text has καὶ εἶπεν αὐτῷ ὁ Πέτρος, while the 'Western' text reads *intendens autem in eum Petrus dixit ei, p* sa. Ropes states that this doubtless is the true 'Western' text.[1] On the view just mentioned, *intendens* would have to modify Aeneas, as C. S. C. Williams takes it,[2] but in this case it is more likely that *intendens* goes with Peter and that the 'Western' phrase here is used to draw a parallel between Peter's cure of Aeneas and Paul's curse of Elymas in xiii. 9: ἀτενίσας εἰς αὐτὸν εἶπεν....[3]

(2) v. 15-16. Acts v. 15 refers to the believers who brought the sick (+ αὐτῶν D *d p* Cass) so that Peter's shadow might fall on some of them, and following this the D-text has

ἀπηλλάσσοντο γὰρ ἀπὸ πάσης ἀσθενίας ὡς εἶχεν ἕκαστος αὐτῶν.

ἀπηλλάσσοντο... αὐτῶν D (*d*) (*p*) cop^G67; καὶ ῥυσθῶσιν ἀπὸ πάσης ἀσθενείας ἧς εἶχον E, *sim gig c dem cod.ard cor.vat** vg^(s et cl) dut Lcf

To understand this D-variant, one must read κἂν (*v*. 15, B and D) as intensifying ἄν: 'if perchance'. The B-text implies that the healing then results if the circumstances permit (see *v*. 12).[4] The additional sentence in D makes it clear that the D-text does not conceive merely of a possibility of healing through the shadow, but all are healed from whatever sickness they had.[5]

[1] Ropes, *Text*, p. 91.   [2] Williams, *Alterations*, p. 57.
[3] See Crehan, *ThSt*, XVIII (1957), 599.
[4] Fascher, *Textgeschichte*, p. 27.
[5] *Ibid.* J. M. Wilson, *The Acts of the Apostles* (London, 1923), pp. 20f., 50 n., says that D's εἰῶντο (ἰᾶσθαι) in v. 16 means 'cured', while B's ἐθεραπεύοντο strictly means 'treated' (medically). If this distinction can be maintained [the terms are, however, used often as synonyms in NT], the D-reading in *v*. 15 would be confirmed by this variant in *v*. 16.

156

Observe also that this D-reading in v. 15 is obviously intended to show Peter in a parallel light with Paul in xix. 12 (B and D), which refers to handkerchiefs brought from Paul to the sick: ...καὶ ἀπαλλάσσεσθαι ἀπ' αὐτῶν τὰς νόσους....[1]

(3) ix. 40. In the account of the raising of Tabitha by Peter, the 'Western' text (D *def*) reports that when Peter said, 'Tabitha, arise ἐν τῷ ὀνόματι τοῦ κυρίου ἡμῶν Ἰησοῦ Χριστοῦ' (see above, p. 62), she opened her eyes *immediately* (παραχρῆμα E *gig p r* sa eth cop[G67] Spec).

Ropes's designation of this variant as a 'Western' reading and its inclusion in the 'Western' texts of Hilgenfeld, Blass, and Clark are now supported by the presence of the reading in cop[G67]. [Cf. the additional παραχρῆμα also in the 'Western' text (D *def*) of ix. 18, which indicates that Paul received his sight *immediately* (C² E L 614 minn *h p* tepl sy[h] Chr[9,173]).]

(d) Variants singling out or enhancing either Peter or Paul

(1) Several of the variants just mentioned would fit here as well, notably those in xv. 7 and v. 15 with reference to Peter, and xix. 8 referring to Paul.

(2) xiii. 44. The B-text says that σχεδὸν πᾶσα ἡ πόλις συνήχθη ἀκοῦσαι τὸν λόγον τοῦ θεοῦ, but D *d* have σχεδὸν ὅλη ἡ πόλις συνήχθη ἀκοῦσαι **Παύλου**! The only other 'Western' witness extant here, cop[G67], does not follow D in the reading 'Paul', but it does agree with D in the immediately following material: πολύν τε λόγον ποιησαμένου περὶ τοῦ κυρίου D *d*; 'But Paul spoke lengthily in the discourse concerning the Lord Jesus' cop[G67].

(3) Note a similar variant concerning Peter in the words of Cornelius in x. 33:

B: νῦν οὖν πάντες ἡμεῖς ἐνώπιον τοῦ θεοῦ πάρεσμεν ἀκοῦσαι πάντα...
D: νῦν (ἰ)δοὺ πάντες ἡμεῖς ἐνώπιόν **σου**, ἀκοῦσαι βουλόμενοι παρά σου...

ἐνώπιόν σου D* *d c l p* vg tepl sa eth arm[osc] sy[p] sy[msK(vid)]
βουλόμενοι D* *d gig l t* tepl sy[p] sy[msK]
παρά σου D *d gig* (sy[msK]??)

(4) i. 23. In connection with choosing a successor to Judas, B says καὶ ἔστησαν δύο, Ἰωσήφ... καὶ Ματθίαν. The D-text,

---

[1] *Beginnings*, IV, 55; Crehan, *ThSt*, XVIII (1957), 599.

however, puts the verb in the singular, an obvious reference to Peter: καὶ ἔστησεν δύο D *d gig* Aug[ab]. Thus it is Peter who presents or nominates the two candidates, showing an anxiety in the D-text to accentuate the role of Peter in the church government.[1] Ropes remarks that the attesting witnesses show ἔστησεν to be no accidental variant of D alone,[2] and the fact that Aug[ab] (though not D) also reads *et precatus dixit*... in *v.* 24 for καὶ προσευξάμενοι εἶπαν... gives added weight to the 'Western' assumption of Peter's prominence in this scene.

(5) ii. 14.

Acts ii. 14

B	D
	τότε
σταθεὶς δὲ ὁ Πέτρος	σταθεὶς δὲ ὁ Πέτρος
σὺν τοῖς ἕνδεκα	σὺν τοῖς δέκα ἀποστόλοις
ἐπῆρεν	ἐπῆρεν πρῶτος
τὴν φωνὴν αὐτοῦ	τὴν φωνὴν αὐτοῦ
καὶ ἀπεφθέγξατο αὐτοῖς.	καὶ εἶπεν.

τότε   D sy[p]
δέκα   D* *d* *
ἀποστόλοις   D *d gig p q r t w* vg[cod] tepl sa sy[p] (discipulis Aug[c])
πρῶτος   D* *d* (primus); prior *p*[2] *w* vg[codΘ] prov tepl; πρότερον *post* αὐτοῦ E *e* (prior)] *om* Aug[c]
εἶπεν   D *d gig p r t*] ἀπεφθέγξατο αὐτοῖς *cett* Aug[c]

In the D-text Peter becomes the first to speak to the crowd. Crehan characterizes this minute variant as:

a fussy addition by someone who is anxious to show the reader that, although in 2: 6 the glossolalia is quite general on the part of the Twelve, and although Peter then stands up to speak with the rest, he is heard first, and then the others have their turn.[3]

Commentators on Acts seem anxious to make it clear that ἀποφθέγγεσθαι in ii. 14 implies that Peter here gave an *inspired* utterance, and that it was 'in quite articulate language',[4] apparently to avoid any misunderstanding from the use of ἀποφθέγγεσθαι in ii. 4, where, though it need not mean

---
[1] *Beginnings,* IV, 14; Cerfaux and Dupont, *Actes,* p. 40; cf. Conzelmann, *Apostelgeschichte,* p. 25.   [2] Ropes, *Text,* p. 10.
[3] Crehan, *ThSt,* XVIII (1957), 597.
[4] *Beginnings,* IV, 21; cf. Haenchen, *Apostelgeschichte,* p. 141, n. 4.

THE JEWS AND THE APOSTLES

ecstatic speech,[1] its association with the glossolalia might convey such an impression. The D-text has anticipated modern commentators, reading the simple εἶπεν for ἀπεφθέγξατο.

It is worth asking whether the D-text's additional ἀποστόλοις suggests that Peter stood out from the other apostles, as though there were two ranks, Peter and then the apostles. This is clearer in D's version of Acts ii. 37, where those who are cut to the heart spoke πρὸς τὸν Πέτρον καὶ τοὺς λοιποὺς ἀποστόλους... (B), but D *d* 241 *gig r* Aug^c(*et ler*) lack λοιπούς. This would remove Peter from an equation with the apostles in general. The other instances where Peter is spoken of in connection with the larger group bear out this conclusion. In the listing of the Eleven (Acts i. 13), Peter, of course, comes first (B and D), and in i. 15 Peter is said to have stood up in the midst of the brethren (B) or, as D has it, the disciples. Neither of these, however, makes specific mention of the 'apostles'. The only instance remaining is Acts v. 29–30, where B reads ἀποκριθεὶς δὲ Πέτρος καὶ οἱ ἀπόστολοι εἶπαν.... The D-text, however, lacks any reference to the apostles in the sentence: ὁ δὲ Πέτρος εἶπεν πρὸς αὐτούς (*v.* 30), which is attested by D *d h gig cod.ard* vg^codΘmg, so that no identification with the apostles remains, but Peter stands alone. (Though cop^G67 appears to be conflated, since it presents both readings.)

(The textual problem in v. 29–30 is actually more complicated than this, though the picture is unchanged. D has probably dropped out the words corresponding to the B-sentence quoted above, but *h* has preserved them: [*v.* 29] *respondens autem Petrus dixit ad il[lum]*.... [*v.* 30] *et dixit Petrus ad eum*.... In this case the apostles also are lacking from the 'Western' text, though the corresponding phrase is now in *v.* 29, as in B. The textual problem of B and D has other complications, but these do not pertain to the present point. The text of *gig*, like that of cop^G07, gives a conflate version, including both the B- and 'Western' elements.)[2]

(6) viii. 24. At the end of this verse the D-text has these additional words concerning Simon: ὃς πολλὰ κλαίων οὐ

---

[1] See Haenchen, *Apostelgeschichte*, p. 132, n. 2, who says it does not; but cf. *TWNT*, I, 448, which refers to its use with reference to spirit-filled Christians, ecstatically excited.

[2] On the whole question, see Ropes, *Text*, pp. 50f.

διελίμπανεν D* cop^G67 sy^hmg Tert^anima 34 Ephr^cat (p409); cf. Chr. The point is that in the D-text Peter reduced Simon Magus to tears;[1] 'the intention to glorify Peter is quite plain'.[2] The D-text has insisted on what was not clearly expressed in B, namely, the repentance of Simon[3] which occurred through the agency of Peter.

(7) x. 24b-25, 33.

Acts x. 24b-25

B

ὁ δὲ Κορνήλιος
ἦν προσδοκῶν αὐτοὺς
συγκαλεσάμενος τοὺς συγγενεῖς
αὐτοῦ καὶ τοὺς ἀναγκαίους
φίλους.

ὡς δὲ ἐγένετο τοῦ εἰσελθεῖν
τὸν Πέτρον,

συναντήσας αὐτῷ ὁ Κορνήλιος
πεσὼν ἐπὶ τοὺς πόδας
προσεκύνησεν.

D

ὁ δὲ Κορνήλιος
ἦν προσδεχόμενος αὐτούς, καὶ
συνκαλεσάμενος τοὺς συνγενεῖς
αὐτοῦ καὶ τοὺς ἀναγκαίους
φίλους
περιέμεινεν.

25. προσεγγίζοντος δὲ
τοῦ Πέτρου
εἷς τὴν Καισαρίαν προδραμὼν
εἷς τῶν δούλων διεσάφησεν
παραγεγονέναι αὐτόν.
ὁ δὲ Κορνήλιος ἐκπηδήσας καὶ
συναντήσας αὐτῷ
πεσὼν πρὸς τοὺς πόδας
προσεκύνησεν αὐτόν.

24, line 4: B reads αυτους, but ℵACD cett read αυτου

προσδεχόμενος D] προσδοκῶν cett E 614 383
καί D d
περιέμεινεν D d (sustinuit d) p* sy^hmg
25. προσεγγίζοντος (εἰσελθόντος sy^p) δὲ τοῦ Πέτρου D d gig sy^p sy^hmg
εἰς τὴν Καισαρίαν D d p q t w prov tepl cop^G67 sy^hmg
προδραμὼν...αὐτόν D d gig (cop^G67) sy^hmg
ὁ δὲ Κορνήλιος...αὐτῷ D d sy^hmg; cf. cop^G67, and l p t: processit
πρός D
αὐτόν D* d l^vid p dem t w cod.ard cor.vat* vg^codd tepl sa geo cop^G67

In the B-text Cornelius, with his friends and relatives, awaits Peter's arrival and greets him at the door of his house. In the D-text there is the additional mention of the expectant waiting

[1] Williams, *Alterations*, p. 57. Note that διαλιμπάνειν occurs in Tobit x. 7 with reference to weeping. It does not occur in NT, outside of D, but is found again in D at Acts xvii. 13 (see above, p. 142).
[2] Crehan, *ThSt*, XVIII (1957), 599. [3] Jacquier, *Actes*, pp. 264f.

for Peter (περιέμεινεν), and Cornelius posts a slave to watch for Peter's coming; when Peter's approach to the city is reported and before he is actually on the scene, Cornelius 'leaps up' (ἐκπηδήσας) and meets him, falling at his feet, etc. The D-text thus indicates that the meeting and Cornelius's προσκύνησις took place in the street, in public.[1] Dibelius thought that the 'Western' text was a rewriting of the incident due to the impossibility of the καὶ συνομιλῶν αὐτῷ (v. 27) in the situation in the B-text. The proof of this, he said, was that these words are omitted by the 'Western' text.[2] It is not, however, so certain as it apparently was to Dibelius that these words were not part of the 'Western' text, since they are lacking only in D d, but occur in E 614 383 gig l p cop[G67] sy[p,h] sa, etc., and need not, says Ropes, be regarded as a 'Western non-interpolation'.[3] Thus, though Dibelius was correct in his assessment of the meaning of the D-text here, his explanation of its motivation is doubtful. Rather, the D-text betrays an emphasis on the greater importance of Peter, expressed through the portrayal of Cornelius's more eager anticipation of his arrival and more demonstrative, public reception.

This subordination of Cornelius to Peter is reinforced by the D-text's version of x. 33, where Cornelius says that he sent for Peter, παρακαλῶν ἐλθεῖν πρὸς ἡμᾶς (D d p q cop[G67] sa[cod (vid)][4] prov sy[h*] sy[msK]), where he commends Peter for coming ἐν τάχει (D d sy[msK]), and says:

B: νῦν οὖν πάντες ἡμεῖς ἐνώπιον τοῦ θεοῦ πάρεσμεν ἀκοῦσαι πάντα τὰ προστεταγμένα σοι ὑπὸ τοῦ κυρίου.
D: νῦν (ἰ)δοὺ πάντες ἡμεῖς ἐνώπιόν σου, ἀκοῦσαι βουλόμενοι παρά σου τὰ προστεταγμένα σοι ἀπὸ τοῦ θεοῦ.

ἰδού D; καὶ ἰδού sy[p]; οὖν ἰδού sa (sy[msK] def)
ἐνώπιόν σου] D* d e l p vg tepl sa eth arm[osc] sy[p] sy[msK (vid)]
πάρεσμεν] om D* d gig sa sy[p] sy[msK]

---

[1] Dibelius, Studies, p. 113 (Aufsätze, p. 99); Crehan, ThSt, XVIII (1957), 597; according to Zahn, Apostelgeschichte, I, 351 f., they met (in D) on the road outside the city gate.
[2] Dibelius, Studies, p. 113 (Aufsätze, p. 99).
[3] Ropes, Text, p. 96. They are included in the texts of Blass, Hilgenfeld, Zahn and Clark.
[4] See Ropes, Text, p. cxliii; A. C. Clark, Acts, p. 330.

βουλόμενοι D* *d gig l t* tepl sy^p sy^msK
παρά σου D *d gig* (sy^msK??)
πάντα] om D *d* 460 618 sa
θεοῦ D *d* 𝔓^74 H L P S 383 minn *p* sa sy^p sy^msK Chr

Observe the repeated stress on Peter himself: ἐνώπιόν **σου** (instead of B's ἐνώπιον τοῦ θεοῦ!)[1] and ἀκοῦσαι βουλόμενοι παρά **σου**. Williams says this last phrase indicates 'a docile and receptive attitude on the part of Cornelius'.[2]

(8) xi. 17. Peter may be enhanced in the D-text by the implied suggestion that he might have prevented God from bestowing the Holy Spirit on the Gentiles who believed: the B-text reads simply, '...Who was I that I could withstand God?' The D-text has '...Who was I that I could prevent God from giving the Holy Spirit to them when they have believed?' [τοῦ μὴ δοῦναι αὐτοῖς πνεῦμα ἅγιον πιστεύσασιν D *d* (*p*) *q w cod.ard* vg^codd bohem prov tepl (cop^G67) sy^h* (Aug)].[3]

(9) xii. 5. Peter is kept in prison *by the cohort of the king*: a *cohorte regis p** vg^codR cop^G67 sy^h*.

Although in 1925 W. L. Knox could say that 'in general D shows no particular interest in S. Peter',[4] his opinion must now be regarded as totally unfounded. Lagrange and Williams[5] have listed a number of D-variants which revealed a special emphasis on Peter, and more recently Crehan has collected and discussed these instances at greater length.[6] The question is, what was the purpose of the D-text in thus enhancing Peter? Crehan takes it to be, quite simply, to glorify Peter. He points to at least three instances, however, where the D-text draws or could be taken as drawing parallels between Peter and Paul in Acts, though he insists that even if this is the case the intention

[1] G. D. Kilpatrick, 'An Eclectic Study of the Text of Acts', *Biblical and Patristic Studies in Memory of Robert Pierce Casey* (Freiburg, 1963), p. 73, suggests that confusion of ΣΟΥ and ΤΟΥΘΥ accounts for the variant (though he does not venture to say which was original), but his suggestion is not convincing: cf. Epp, *JBL*, LXXXIV (1965), 174.

[2] Williams, *Alterations*, p. 58.

[3] On D's interest in the Spirit being given through an apostle, see Knox, *Church of Jerusalem*, p. xix; contrast *Beginnings*, IV, 98.

[4] Knox, *Church of Jerusalem*, p. xxiv.

[5] Lagrange, *Critique textuelle*, p. 391; Williams, *Alterations*, pp. 57 f.

[6] Crehan, *ThSt*, XVIII (1957), 596–603. However, not all the instances referred to in the preceding pages have been noticed by Lagrange, Williams, or even Crehan.

to glorify Peter is plain.[1] But in view of the fact that the D-text tends also to accentuate Peter *and* John, as well as Paul, Barnabas, and Silas, etc., it is easier to see in the D-text an intention to stress the apostles in general, and to emphasize in particular the two leading figures in Acts, Peter and Paul. These two leaders then represent the new faith over against the Jewish leaders. The book of Acts, however, is so much more concerned with Paul than with Peter that the D-text heightens Peter in order more nearly to balance these two great figures, and several times draws parallels between them, not (as Crehan thinks) primarily to glorify Peter,[2] but rather to place them more on the same level, as the two outstanding figures in Christianity who represent the strong, united church over against the stubborn and hostile Jewish leaders. This paralleling may be summarized as follows:

(1) xi. 2 D with xv. 1–5 (see above, pp. 104 f.), or xi. 2 D with xv. 41–xvi. 1,[3] or xi. 2D with xix. 1 D (D-readings in bold type):

xi. 2 D: ὁ μὲν οὖν Πέτρος διὰ ἱκανοῦ χρόνου ἠθέλησε πορευθῆναι εἰς Ἱεροσόλυμα.

xix. 1 D: θέλοντος δὲ τοῦ Παύλου κατὰ τὴν ἰδίαν βουλὴν πορεύεσθαι εἰς Ἱεροσόλυμα.

(2) v. 15 D with xix. 12 (see above, p. 157).

(3) viii. 24 D, where Peter reduced Simon to unceasing tears (see above, pp. 159 f.), may correspond to the effect of Paul's words on Elymas in xiii. 9–11.[4]

(4) iii. 6 D with xiv. 10 D (D-readings in bold type):

iii. 6 D

6. εἶπεν δὲ ὁ Πέτρος...
ἐν τῷ ὀνόματι Ἰησοῦ Χριστοῦ τοῦ Ναζοραίου
περιπάτει.
7. ...καὶ παραχρῆμα...

xiv. 10 D

εἶπεν μεγάλῃ φωνῇ·
Σοί λέγω ἐν τῷ ὀνόματι τοῦ κυρίου Ἰησοῦ Χριστοῦ,
ἀνάστηθι ἐπὶ τοὺς πόδας σου ὀρθὸς καὶ περιπάτει.
καὶ εὐθέως παραχρῆμα...

---

[1] Crehan, *ThSt*, XVIII (1957), 598, 599.
[2] Since Paul is also enhanced in D (as noted above, pp. 154, 155, 157), there is no trace of an anti-Pauline bias in D (see Menoud, 'Western Text', p. 29). Snape, *HTR*, LIII (1960), 44, points to Pauline interests in the 'Western' text, though much of his evidence cannot *exclusively* demand such an interpretation for the D-readings.
[3] Crehan, *ThSt*, XVIII (1957), 598.
[4] *Ibid.* p. 599.

(5) Perhaps also the following: ix. 34 'Western' with xiii. 9 (see above, p. 156); ii. 37 D with xiii. 41 D (see above, pp. 154f.); xiii. 44 D with x. 33 D (see above, p. 157). Note, too, that the D-text makes Peter preach the Pauline gospel in ii. 17 (see above, p. 69).

This section on 'The Jews and the Apostles' has shown the D-text's emphasis on an increased hostility toward and an intensified persecution of the apostles by the Jews, with an added emphasis on the role of the Jewish leaders in these actions. On the positive side, the D-text clearly enhances the apostles themselves as leaders of the church over against the opposing Jews. Not only are the apostles' deeds heightened in splendour or influence, but sometimes the Holy Spirit is depicted as guiding and protecting the apostles from the malevolence of the Jews, and at other times the Jewish leaders are shown to be powerless before the apostles, and so forth.

Finally, in contrast to the D-text's handling of the Jews and the Jewish leaders, the Roman officials are treated with reserve and, on occasion, are freed from blame with reference to the difficulties of the apostles.

CHAPTER III

CONCLUSION

For generations the striking text which Codex Bezae presents has been the object of extensive study, has evoked considerable controversy, has occasioned several novel theories,[1] and has remained, all the while, at the centre of the yet unsolved mystery of the 'Western' text. The researcher approaching this enigmatic area of New Testament textual criticism does so under the almost ominous words of B. H. Streeter, who said that many a scholar '...has met his Waterloo in the attempt to account for, or explain away, the existence of the Bezan text'.[2] The present investigation, however, has had a somewhat more modest goal: simply to *understand* the D-text of Acts on its own terms without reference to the questions of origin or originality.

By applying to Codex Bezae a theological approach to textual criticism—an approach which recognizes that textual variants may conceal (and reveal) dogmatic bias or other tendencies— a clear and unmistakable conclusion emerges: Codex Bezae in Acts, where it represents (as is so often the case) the distinctive 'Western' text, shows a decidedly heightened anti-Judaic attitude and sentiment. This same bias is also evident in and supported by the 'Western' variants outside of Codex Bezae.

The anti-Judaic tendency in the D-text of Acts is disclosed in the following manner:

(1) The D-text portrays the Jews and their leaders as more hostile toward Jesus and assigns to them a greater responsibility for his death than does the B-text. A positive emphasis on Jesus as Lord and Messiah accentuates Jesus over against Judaism and stresses the heinousness of the Jews' action against him.

(2) The D-text minimizes the response of the Jews and the

[1] For example, Blass's theory of two editions by Luke himself; Harris's theory of Latinization; Chase's theory of Syriac origin; Torrey's of Aramaic; and A. C. Clark's theory that the D-text was abbreviated to form the B-text.

[2] B. H. Streeter, 'Codices 157, 1071 and the Caesarean Text', *Quantulacumque, Studies Presented to Kirsopp Lake* (London, 1937), p. 150.

165

importance of Judaism and its institutions to the new faith and diminishes the value of the customs and practices of Judaism itself, and especially their influence on and intrusion into Christianity. This devaluation and by-passing of Judaism is developed in view of and in contrast to a clearly greater Gentile interest and a more distinctly emphasized universalism and reveals itself markedly in the outreach of the new faith to Gentiles. A positive stress on certain features (notably the Holy Spirit) which tend to distinguish Christianity from Judaism appears frequently in contexts which, in the D-text, are anti-Judaic or pro-Gentile.

(3) The D-text portrays the Jews, and especially their leaders, as more hostile toward the apostles and as persecuting them more vigorously. At the same time, the D-text emphasizes the apostles themselves as the leaders of the church over against the Jews who oppose them, revealing a 'leaders *versus* leaders' motif—Jewish leaders *versus* Christian leaders, the former oppressing the latter, but the latter triumphing over the former. Moreover, contrary to the D-text's treatment of the Jews and their leaders, the Roman officials are handled with reserve and now and again are relieved of blame for the apostles' difficulties.

In short, the Jews come out rather poorly in the D-text.

Obviously, the notion of anti-Judaic tendencies in the 'Western' text of Acts is not new; Peter Corssen, for example, in 1896 mentioned nine D- or 'Western' variants in Acts as anti-Jewish in character (xiv. 5; xiv. 19; xvii. 12; xviii. 4; xix. 9; xxiii. 24; xxiv. 5; and probably ii. 47; iv. 31).[1] What is striking, however, is the discovery that this anti-Judaic bias is as widespread and as evident on so large a scale as the foregoing pages have demonstrated, and that such a large number of D-variants can be seen as directly or indirectly supporting this trend in the D-text. The position of Ropes (see above, p. 4) can no longer be accepted; evidence of a special point of view in the 'Western' text is not lacking or elusive, at least as far as Acts is concerned.

The significance of this result is increased by the fact that those earlier studies which did recognize a certain anti-Judaic element in the 'Western' text of Acts found so little evidence of it: Corssen's nine passages have been mentioned; Ropes himself

[1] Corssen, *GGA*, CLVIII (1896), 444.

CONCLUSION

(1926) referred to 'one or two passages' which stressed the hostile attitude of the Jews or emphasized universalism, etc. (xiv. 5; xxiv. 5; ii. 17; ii. 47; xviii. 4; possibly xx. 21; xvi. 15),[1] though he mostly reproduces Corssen's instances; D. Plooij (1931) listed 'dogmatically also a stronger anti-Judaism' as one special characteristic of the 'Western' text, though he cited no specific passages or evidence;[2] Lagrange (1935) listed some ten passages under the joint category of manifestations of the evil disposition of the Jews and universalism (ii. 17; ii. 39; ii. 47; iv. 9; iv. 12; vi. 1; xiii. 45; xiii. 50; xiv. 2; xviii. 12–13; xv. 20, 29);[3] Klijn (1949) refers only to the possibility that 'there may be something of an anti-judaistic spirit';[4] and even Menoud (1951), who went the farthest in tracing out the anti-Judaic evidence in the 'Western' text of Acts, cited only nine passages directly related to this bias (iii. 17; iv. 9; iv. 14; v. 38; v. 39; vi. 11; xiii. 45; xiv. 2–7; xviii. 12–13).[5] Many of the passages in these lists overlap; hence the total number previously recognized is rather small. (Note that Torrey and Ehrhardt could speak of a *pro*-Jewish interest in the 'Western' text!)[6]

Thus, whereas in the past only a limited amount of evidence could be marshalled for an anti-Judaic attitude in the D-text of Acts, the present study demonstrates that a very large number[7]

[1] Ropes, *Text*, p. ccxxxiii.
[2] Plooij, *BBC*, IX (1931), 13. He does discuss ii. 17 at length in 'Ascension', p. 43 (see above, pp. 68–70).
[3] Lagrange, *Critique textuelle*, pp. 392f. Note that only ii. 17 and xv. 20, 29 receive any discussion; he simply lists the others. His example from iv. 12 cannot be considered a 'Western' variant (see above, p. 71). Williams, *Alterations*, p. 58, reproduces Lagrange's references and adds xiv. 5 sy^{hmg}.
[4] Klijn, *Survey*, p. 21.
[5] Menoud, 'Western Text', p. 28. He stresses also the 'newness of the Christian faith' over against Judaism, as shown by emphasis on the Holy Spirit and on Jesus as Christ and Lord, etc., pp. 25f.
[6] Torrey, *Documents*, *passim* in pp. 124–33; A. Ehrhardt, 'The Construction and Purpose of the Acts of the Apostles', *StudTheol*, XII (1958), 45.
[7] Any statistical tabulation is problematic because of the difficulty of defining a 'variant'. However, a count of the variants printed in dark type in A. C. Clark's edition of Acts shows that about 40 per cent have been utilized in this study in support of the anti-Judaic bias as it is developed here. This count involved variation-units [cf. now E. C. Colwell and E. W. Tune, 'Variant Readings: Classification and Use', *JBL*, LXXXIII (1964), 254 f.], i.e. both a single word and a lengthy, connected variant were each regarded as one variant. If number of variant words were to be considered, the

of the D- or 'Western' variants either reveal this tendency directly, are contributory to it, or at least comport with such a viewpoint. There are, in fact, no D-variants which contradict it. (Those which appear to be opposed, or have been alleged as pro-Jewish, and so forth, have been treated in the text or footnotes above; see, for example, pp. 68f. on Acts ii. 33.)

'Western' readings in Acts frequently have been regarded as free and often unnecessary additions and expansions. J. H. Ropes, for instance, spoke of the colourlessness, empty naïveté, and the virtual lack in the 'Western' text of anything new—of anything which could not be inferred from the B-text,[1] while W. L. Knox, perhaps representing an extreme position, is harshly critical of the 'Western' tradition of Acts. In evaluating the D-readings, he characterizes them as follows (taking only passages used in the present study): 'a clumsy compilation' (xi. 2; cf. on xv. 5; xiii. 43); 'meaningless' (xiii. 38); 'amazing insertion' and 'nonsense' (xix. 1); 'unnecessary and clumsy' (iv. 18); 'a typically unnecessary explanation' (viii. 1; cf. on xvi. 35; xvii. 12; xviii. 12); 'makes confusion worse confounded' (xiii. 27); 'a good instance of D's lack of intelligence' (xx. 3); 'no new information; details...not worth recording' (x. 25); and finally Knox refers in general to D's 'own quite unique stupidity'.[2]

By way of contrast, compare the value of the anti-Judaic percentage of D-variants supporting the anti-Judaic viewpoint would be very much higher.

A large number of the variants not employed in this study consist of place indications (about twenty-five) and time references (more than thirty, including 'immediately', etc., but not τότε, which occurs about thirteen additional times in D in Acts). See Harnack, *Acts*, pp. 44–8, for a list of about fifteen chronological variants found in D. There are also about fifty simple synonyms constituting variants in D over against B. Some other categories of variants apparently not connected with the anti-Judaic theme are those concerned with (1) the ascension (i. 2, 9, 11; cf. Lk xxiv. 51); (2) name changes (e.g. i. 23; iv. 6; xiii. 8; xv. 22; xviii. 7; xviii. 24); (3) women (e.g. i. 14; xvii. 12, 34; xviii. 3, 26); and (4) apocalyptic (e.g. ii. 17; ii. 19, 20; xvii. 31; cf. xxviii. 31). The variants in these categories are not, however, either numerous or significant enough to affect the thesis; they do, of course, deserve further study. One question, for example, is the possibility of an anti-feminist tendency in D (see above, p. 75, n. 3).

[1] Ropes, *Text*, pp. ccxxivf., ccxxxif.
[2] Knox, *Church of Jerusalem*, pp. xviii–xxvii.

CONCLUSION

frame of reference for illuminating a great many of the distinctive variants of the D-text; these many readings now become meaningful and significant when this anti-Judaic bias is recognized, and they fall naturally into place in their contexts against this tendentious background.

The contribution, then, of this investigation is clear: the relatively few D-variants previously recognized as distinctly anti-Judaic have been vastly expanded so that a clear and consistent tendency comes boldly into view. For example, in the first section, 'The Jews and Jesus', the πονηρόν of iii. 17 was taken as anti-Judaic by Menoud (see above, p. 44), but the D-text's *consistently* anti-Judaic treatment of passages concerned with the 'ignorance motif', as well as the supporting evidence from the context of these passages, has not previously been observed. In fact, apart from this interpretation of πονηρόν and a few remarks of E. Fascher on xiii. 28–9 (see above, pp. 56–8), the whole of the section involves a new understanding of the D-text's formulation of the passages discussed there.

In the second section, 'The Jews, Gentiles, and Christianity', not so many of the variants find an entirely new interpretation here, for the Gentile interest and universalistic stress of a number of them have been earlier recognized. About one-half do, however, find a place within an anti-Judaic framework for the first time, while the others have been collected and newly formulated as evidence for this tendency, a tendency which frequently finds fresh confirmation in the D-context of these passages. Finally, while the D-text's emphasis on the Holy Spirit has been observed by many, its frequency in universalistic and anti-Judaic passages has not been noticed.

In the last section, 'The Jews and the Apostles', only about 15 per cent of the variants have been identified previously as anti-Judaic in character, and this includes such obvious ones as xiii. 50 and xiv. 2. Moreover, the thematic notion of the D-text, that it plays off against one another the leaders of the Jews and the leaders of Christianity, is a new formulation.

Finally, several other points are worthy of mention: (1) A careful assessment of the smaller, less conspicuous variants of the D-text, especially in the contexts of the larger, more obvious readings which are anti-Judaic in tenor, shows that these smaller variants provide strikingly frequent and significant confirmation of that bias. Examples appear in the treatment of Acts iii. 17 and its larger context (above, pp. 42–6, 51–6); xiii. 27 and its context (above, pp. 46–8, 56–8); ii. 17 and its context (above, pp. 66–74, 76–9); chapter xiii (above, pp. 79–84); xviii. 4–8 (above, pp. 84–94); and chapter xv (above, pp. 96–8, 100–4, 107–12), and so forth.

(2) The D-text is both considerably more consistent in delineating its special viewpoint and somewhat more abundant in its evidence than might reasonably be expected of an aberrant textual tradition (see above, pp. 37–40). Apart from the consistency in Acts xv. 20, 29, and xxi. 25 (above, pp. 107–12) and in the passages concerning the 'ignorance motif' (above, pp. 41–51), there is, for example, a consistently favourable handling of the Roman officials (e.g. see above, pp. 50f., 147–53), to say nothing of the general consistency evident in the overall attitude toward the Jews—the main thesis itself—which is a rather remarkable show of consistency on a large scale.

(3) It is often said that the speeches in Acts show fewer textual variants than do the narrative portions,[1] and there is no reason to doubt this judgement from a quantitative standpoint. Considering variants which reveal theological tendency, however, there is good reason to assign the variants in speeches a more important place, qualitatively, than this statement would grant them. Witness the discussion of the speeches in Acts ii, iii, and xiii above (pp. 41–8, 51–61, 66–72, 79–84). When Menoud then says that the 'Western' variants are *both* fewer and *less striking* in the speeches,[2] his statement is open to suspicion. It is true that in the longest speech in Acts, that of Stephen in chapter vii, there are few anti-Judaic D-variants, but this speech in any text is already strongly anti-Judaic (cf. vii. 51–3). Observe, however, that precisely in the anti-Judaic climax of the speech the D-text offers an expression which confirms this anti-Judaic thrust (see above on vii. 52 D, pp. 95f.). Furthermore, the famous variants in the apostolic 'decree' in two of their three occurrences appear in speeches (xv. 20; xxi. 25), as do a number of other theologically significant readings (e.g. iv. 9; v. 38–9).

---

[1] E.g. Cadbury in *Beginnings*, v, 416, n. 1; Nock, *Gnomon*, xxv (1953), 502; Menoud, 'Western Text', p. 21. (To the contrary, A. C. Clark, *Acts*, p. xlviii.)   [2] Menoud, 'Western Text', p. 21.

CONCLUSION

These considerations by no means distinguish all of the new and old elements in this investigation, but they indicate its general relationship to past assessments of theologically significant variants in the D-text of Acts. The study itself does, in fact, point to the small amount of such work previously done. The unmistakable result—a clearly anti-Judaic tendency in the D-text of Acts—admittedly leaves unanswered many of the traditional text-critical questions regarding the 'Western' text, but, though the 'Western' text is still an enigma, perhaps the approach taken here will contribute to its solution.

BIBLIOGRAPHY

A. REFERENCE WORKS

Aland, K. *Kurzgefasste Liste der griechischen Handschriften des Neuen Testaments.* Vol. I. *Gesamtübersicht.* (Arbeiten zur neutestamentlichen Textforschung, 1; Berlin, 1963).

Bauer, W. *Griechisch-deutsches Wörterbuch,* 5th ed. (Berlin, 1958).

[Bauer, W.], Arndt, W. F. and Gingrich, F. W. *A Greek–English Lexicon of the New Testament and Other Early Christian Literature* (Chicago, 1957).

Hatch, E. and Redpath, H. A. *A Concordance to the Septuagint,* 2 vols. (Oxford, 1897).

Kittel, Gerhard and Friedrich, G. (eds.). *Theologisches Wörterbuch zum Neuen Testament* (Stuttgart, 1933–).

Kraft, B. *Die Zeichen für die wichtigeren Handschriften des griechischen Neuen Testaments,* dritte Auflage (Freiburg, 1955).

Liddell, H. G. and Scott, R. *A Greek–English Lexicon,* 9th ed. revised H. S. Jones (Oxford, 1940).

Lowe, E. A. (ed.). *Codices Latini Antiquiores. A Palaeographical Guide to Latin Manuscripts Prior to the Ninth Century* (Oxford, 1934–).

Metzger, B. M. *Annotated Bibliography of the Textual Criticism of the New Testament, 1914–1939* (Studies and Documents, 16; Copenhagen, 1955).

Moulton, J. H. *A Grammar of New Testament Greek.* Vol. I. *Prolegomena,* 3rd ed. (Edinburgh, 1908).

Moulton, J. H. and Howard, W. F. *A Grammar of New Testament Greek.* Vol. II. *Accidence and Word-Formation* (Edinburgh, 1929).

Moulton, W. F. and Geden, A. S. *A Concordance to the Greek Testament,* 3rd ed. (Edinburgh, 1926).

Yoder, J. D. *Concordance to the Distinctive Greek Text of Codex Bezae* (New Testament Tools and Studies, 2; Leiden, 1961).

B. EDITIONS

(Including collations and publications of manuscripts)

Berger, Samuel. *Un ancien texte latin des Actes des Apôtres retrouvé dans un manuscrit provenant de Perpignan* (Paris, 1895).

Blass, F. *Acta Apostolorum sive Lucae ad Theophilum liber alter, secundum formam quae videtur Romanam* (Leipzig, 1896).

—— *Acta Apostolorum sive Lucae ad Theophilum liber alter. Editio philologica* (Göttingen, 1895). [Abbreviated Blass, *Acta'95*.]

BIBLIOGRAPHY

—— *Evangelium secundum Lucam sive Lucae ad Theophilum liber prior, secundum formam quae videtur Romanam* (Leipzig, 1897).
—— 'Neue Texteszeugen für die Apostelgeschichte', *TSK*, LXIX (1896), 436–71.
Bornemann, Fr. A. *Acta Apostolorum ab Sancto Luca conscripta ad Codicis Cantabrigiensis...* (Grossenhain, 1848).
Clark, A. C. *The Acts of the Apostles* (Oxford, 1933).
Codex Bezae Cantabrigiensis quattuor Evangelia et Actus Apostolorum complectens Graece et Latine. Phototypice repraesentatus (Cambridge, 1899).
Coleman, A. M. *The Biblical Text of Lucifer of Cagliari (Acts)* (Welwyn, Herts. 1927).
Corssen, P. *Der Cyprianische Text der Acta Apostolorum* (Berlin, 1892).
Fischer, B. 'Ein neuer Zeuge zum westlichen Text der Apostelgeschichte', *Biblical and Patristic Studies in Memory of Robert Pierce Casey*, ed. J. N. Birdsall and R. W. Thomson (Freiburg, 1963), pp. 33–63.
Funk, F. X. *Didascalia et Constitutiones Apostolorum* (Paderborn, 1905).
Garitte, G. *L'ancienne version géorgienne des Actes des Apôtres d'après deux manuscrits du Sinaï* (Bibliothèque du *Muséon*, 38; Louvain, 1955).
Harvey, W. W. *Sancti Irenaei ep. Lugdunensis libr. quinque adversus haereses*, 2 vols. (Cambridge, 1857).
Hilgenfeld, Adolf. *Acta Apostolorum Graece et Latine secundum antiquissimos testes* (Berlin, 1899).
Kasser, R. (ed.). *Papyrus Bodmer XVII. Actes des Apôtres. Épîtres de Jacques, Pierre, Jean et Jude* (Cologny–Genève, 1961).
Klijn, A. F. J. 'A Medieval Dutch Text of Acts', *NTS*, I (1954/5), 51–6.
Koole, J. L. 'Die koptischen Übersetzungen der Apostelgeschichte', *BBC*, XII (1937), 65–73.
Laistner, M. L. W. (ed.). *Bedae Venerabilis Expositio Actuum Apostolorum et Retractatio* (Cambridge, Mass., 1939).
Lake, K. and New, S. (eds.). *Six Collations of New Testament Manuscripts* (Harvard Theological Studies, 17; Cambridge, Mass., 1932).
Martin, V. and Kasser, R. (eds.). *Papyrus Bodmer XIV–XV. Évangiles de Luc et Jean* (Cologny–Genève, 1961).
Montgomery, J. A. 'The Ethiopic Text of Acts of the Apostles', *HTR*, XXVII (1934), 169–205.
Muncey, R. W. *The New Testament Text of Saint Ambrose* (Texts and Studies, n.s. 4; Cambridge, 1959).
Nestle, Eberhard, Nestle, Erwin, and Aland, K. (eds.). *Novum Testamentum Graece*, 25th ed. (Stuttgart, 1963).

BIBLIOGRAPHY

Perrot, Ch. 'Un fragment christo-palestinien découvert à Khirbet Mird (Actes des Apôtres, x, 28-29; 32-41)', *RB*, LXX (1963), 506-55.
Petersen, T. C. 'An Early Coptic Manuscript of Acts: An Unrevised Version of the Ancient So-called Western Text', *CBQ*, XXVI (1964), 225-41.
Ropes, J. H. *The Text of Acts*. Vol. III of *The Beginnings of Christianity*. Part I. *The Acts of the Apostles*, ed. F. J. Foakes Jackson and Kirsopp Lake, 5 vols. (London, 1920-1933, vol. III, 1926).
Sanday, W. and Turner, C. H. (eds.). *Novum Testamentum Sancti Irenaei Episcopi Lugdunensis* (Old Latin Biblical Texts, 7; Oxford, 1923).
Sanders, H. A. 'A Papyrus Fragment of Acts in the Michigan Collection', *HTR*, XX (1927), 1-19.
Scrivener, F. H. *Bezae Codex Cantabrigiensis, Being an Exact Copy in Ordinary Type* (Cambridge, 1864).
Septuaginta. Societatis Scientiarum Gottingensis auctoritate edidit A. Rahlfs. Vol. X. *Psalmi cum Odis* (Göttingen, 1931).
—— *Vetus Testamentum Graecum* auctoritate Societatis Litterarum Gottingensis editum. Vol. XIII. *Duodecim prophetae*. Edidit Joseph Ziegler (Göttingen, 1943).
Soden, H. von. *Die Schriften des Neuen Testaments in ihrer ältesten erreichbaren Textgestalt hergestellt auf Grund ihrer Textgeschichte*, zweite unveränderte Ausgabe, 2 parts in 4 vols. (Göttingen, 1911-13).
Tischendorf, Constantinus. *Novum Testamentum Graece*. Editio octava critica maior. Vols. I and II (Leipzig, 1869-72); vol. III: Prolegomena, C. R. Gregory (Leipzig, 1894).
Valentine-Richards, A. V. *The Text of Acts in Codex 614 (Tisch. 137) and its Allies* (Cambridge, 1934).
Westcott, B. F. and Hort, F. J. A. *The New Testament in the Original Greek*. 2 vols. (I. Text; II. Introduction, Appendix; London, 1881-2).
Wordsworth, J. and White, H. J. *Novum Testamentum Domini Nostri Iesu Christi Latine*, 3 vols. (Oxford, 1889-1954).
Zahn, Th. *Die Urausgabe der Apostelgeschichte des Lucas*. (Forschungen zur Geschichte des neutestamentlichen Kanons und altkirchlichen Literatur, IX. Teil; Leipzig, 1916).

C. COMMENTARIES

Bauernfeind, O. *Die Apostelgeschichte* (Theologischer Handkommentar zum Neuen Testament; Leipzig, 1939).
Billerbeck, P. *Kommentar zum Neuen Testament aus Talmud und Midrasch*, 6 vols. in 7 (München, 1922-61).

BIBLIOGRAPHY

Bruce, F. F. *The Acts of the Apostles. The Greek Text with Introduction and Commentary*, 2nd ed. (London, 1952). [Cited as Bruce, *Acts*'[52].]

—— *Commentary on the Book of Acts* (London, 1954). [Cited as Bruce, *Acts*'[54].]

Cerfaux, L. and Dupont, J. *Les Actes des Apôtres* (La Sainte Bible, traduite en français sous la direction de l'École Biblique de Jérusalem; Paris, 1953).

Conzelmann, H. *Die Apostelgeschichte* (Handbuch zum Neuen Testament, 7; Tübingen, 1963).

Creed, J. M. *The Gospel according to St Luke* (London, 1930).

Haenchen, E. *Die Apostelgeschichte*, 13. durchgesehene und erweiterte Auflage (Kritisch-exegetischer Kommentar über das Neue Testament, 3; Göttingen, 1961).

Jacquier, F. *Les Actes des Apôtres* (Études Bibliques; Paris, 1926).

Knowling, R. J. *The Acts of the Apostles* (The Expositor's Greek Testament, vol. II; New York, 1900).

Lake, K. and Cadbury, H. J. *Translation and Commentary*, vol. IV, and *Additional Notes*, vol. V, of *The Beginnings of Christianity*, ed. F. J. Foakes Jackson and K. Lake, 5 vols. (London, 1920–33).

Preuschen, E. *Die Apostelgeschichte* (Handbuch zum Neuen Testament; Tübingen, 1912).

Wettstein, J. J. Η ΚΑΙΝΗ ΔΙΑΘΗΚΗ. *Novum Testamentum Graecum*, 2 vols. (Amsterdam, 1751–2).

Williams, C. S. C. *A Commentary on the Acts of the Apostles* (Harper's New Testament Commentaries; New York, 1957).

Zahn, Th. *Die Apostelgeschichte des Lucas*, 2 vols. (I, 1922³; II, 1927³⁻⁴; Leipzig, 1922, 1927).

D. BOOKS AND ARTICLES

Aland, K. 'The Position of New Testament Textual Criticism', *Studia Evangelica* (Texte und Untersuchungen, 73; Berlin, 1959), pp. 717–31.

Bacon, B. W. 'Some "Western" Variants in the Text of Acts', *HTR*, XXI (1928), 113–45.

Belser, J. *Beiträge zur Erklärung der Apostelgeschichte auf Grund der Lesarten des Codex D und seiner Genossen* (Freiburg, 1897).

Bieder, W. 'Der Petrusschatten, Apg. 5,15', *TZ*, XVI (1960), 407–9.

Black, M. *An Aramaic Approach to the Gospels and Acts*, 2nd ed. (Oxford, 1954).

Blackman, E. C. *Marcion and his Influence* (London, 1948).

Blass, F. *Philology of the Gospels* (London, 1898).

BIBLIOGRAPHY

Blass, F. 'Zu Codex D in der Apostelgeschichte', *TSK*, LXXI (1898), 539–42.
Bludau, A. *Die Schriftfälschungen der Häretiker. Ein Beitrag zur Textkritik der Bibel* (Münster i. W. 1925).
Boman, T. 'Das textkritische Problem des sogenannten Aposteldekrets', *NovTest*, VII (1964), 26–36.
Bulletin of the Bezan Club. 12 numbers. (For private circulation.) (Leyden, 1925–37.)
Bultmann, R. 'Zur Frage nach den Quellen der Apostelgeschichte', *New Testament Essays. Studies in Memory of Thomas Walter Manson, 1893–1958*, ed. A. J. B. Higgins (Manchester, 1959), pp. 68–80.
Burgon, J. W. and Miller, E. (ed.). *The Causes of the Corruption of the Traditional Text of the Holy Gospels* (London, 1896).
—— *The Traditional Text of the Holy Gospels Vindicated and Established* (London, 1896).
Burkitt, F. C. *Christian Beginnings* (London, 1924).
—— 'The Date of Codex Bezae', *JTS*, III (1901/2), 501–13.
Cadbury, H. J. *The Book of Acts in History* (New York, 1955).
Casey, R. P. 'Two Notes: (1) Dickinson's Collation of Codex Bezae...', *HTR*, XVI (1923), 392–4.
Cerfaux, L. 'Citations scripturaires et tradition textuelle dans le Livre des Actes', *Aux sources de la tradition Chrétienne, Mélanges offerts à M. Maurice Goguel...* (Neuchâtel, 1950), pp. 43–51. Also in *Recueil Lucien Cerfaux*, II, 93–103 (q.v.). [Page citations according to former.]
—— *Recueil Lucien Cerfaux*, 3 vols. (Gembloux, 1954–62).
Chapman, J. 'The Order of the Gospels in the Parent of Codex Bezae', *ZNW*, VI (1905), 339–46.
Chase, F. H. *The Old Syriac Element in Codex Bezae* (London, 1893).
—— 'The Reading of Codex Bezae in Acts 1, 2', *Exp*, IV, 9 (1894), 314–17.
—— *The Syro-Latin Text of the Gospels* (London, 1895).
Cheetham, F. P. 'Acts ii. 47: ἔχοντες χάριν πρὸς ὅλον τὸν λαόν', *ET*, LXXIV (1962/3), 214–15.
Clark, K. W. 'The Effect of Recent Textual Criticism upon New Testament Studies', *The Background of the New Testament and its Eschatology*, ed. W. D. Davies and D. Daube (Cambridge, 1956), pp. 27–51.
—— 'The Manuscripts of the Greek New Testament', *New Testament Manuscript Studies*, ed. M. M. Parvis and A. P. Wikgren (Chicago, 1950), pp. 1–24.
—— 'Textual Criticism and Doctrine', *Studia Paulina in honorem Johannis De Zwaan septuagenarii* (Haarlem, 1953), pp. 52–65.

BIBLIOGRAPHY

—— 'The Textual Criticism of the New Testament', *Peake's Commentary on the Bible*, ed. M. Black and H. H. Rowley (London/New York, 1962), pp. 663–70.

Colwell, E. C. 'Method in Locating a Newly-Discovered Manuscript within the Manuscript Tradition of the Greek New Testament', *Studia Evangelica* (Texte und Untersuchungen, 73; Berlin, 1959), pp. 757–77.

Colwell, E. C. and Tune, E. W. 'Variant Readings: Classification and Use', *JBL*, LXXXIII (1964), 253–61.

Connolly, R. H. 'A Negative Form of the Golden Rule in the Diatessaron?', *JTS*, XXXV (1934), 351–7.

—— 'A Negative Golden Rule in the Syriac Acts of Thomas', *JTS*, XXXVI (1935), 353–6.

Conybeare, F. C. 'Three Early Doctrinal Modifications of the Text of the Gospels', *HibbJ*, I (1902/3), 96–113.

Conzelmann, H. *Die Mitte der Zeit* (Tübingen, 1954¹, 1957², 1960³, 1962⁴). Eng. trans. *The Theology of St Luke* (London, 1960).

Coppieters, H. *De historia textus Actorum Apostolorum* (Louvain, 1902).

Corssen, P. 'Acta Apostolorum ed. F. Blass', *GGA*, CLVIII (1896), 425–48.

Creed, J. M. 'The Text and Interpretation of Acts i. 1–2', *JTS*, XXXV (1934), 176–82.

Crehan, J. 'Peter according to the D-Text of Acts', *ThSt*, XVIII (1957), 596–603.

Dahl, N. A. '"A People for His Name" (Acts xv. 14)', *NTS*, IV (1957/8), 319–27.

Daube, D. '"For they know not what they do": Luke 23, 34', *Studia Patristica*, vol. IV. Papers Presented to the Third International Conference on Patristic Studies held at Christ Church, Oxford, 1959. Part II. Biblica, Patres Apostolici, Historica. Ed. F. L. Cross (Texte und Untersuchungen, 79; Berlin, 1961), pp. 58–70.

Davies, W. D. *Paul and Rabbinic Judaism* (London, 1955²).

—— 'Contemporary Jewish Religion', *Peake's Commentary on the Bible*, ed. M. Black and H. H. Rowley (London/New York, 1962), pp. 705–11.

DeBruyne, D. 'Quelques documents nouveaux pour l'histoire du texte africain des Évangiles', *RBén*, XXVII (1910), 273–324, 433–46.

Dibelius, M. *Aufsätze zur Apostelgeschichte*, ed. H. Greeven (Göttingen, 1951, 1961⁴). Eng. trans., *Studies in the Acts of the Apostles* (London, 1956).

—— 'Der Text der Apostelgeschichte', *Aufsätze zur Apostelgeschichte*, pp. 76–83. Eng. trans., 'The Text of Acts: An Urgent Critical Task', *Studies in the Acts of the Apostles*, pp. 84–92.

BIBLIOGRAPHY

Dihle, A. *Die Goldene Regel. Eine Einführung in die Geschichte der antiken und frühchristlichen Vulgärethik* (Studienhefte zur Altertumswissenschaft, 7; Göttingen, 1962).
Duplacy, J. 'Bulletin de critique textuelle du Nouveau Testament', *RSR*, L (1962), 242–63, 564–98; LI (1963), 432–62.
—— 'Où en est la critique textuelle du Nouveau Testament?', *RSR*, XLV (1957), 419–41; XLVI (1958), 270–313, 431–62. (Reprinted Paris, 1959.)
Dupont, J. *Les problèmes du Livre des Actes d'après les travaux récents* (Louvain, 1950).
Ehrhardt, A. 'The Construction and Purpose of the Acts of the Apostles', *StudTheol*, XII (1958), 45–79. Reprinted in Ehrhardt, *The Framework of the New Testament Stories* (Manchester, 1964), pp. 64–102.
Eisentraut, E. *Studien zur Apostelgeschichte. Kritische Untersuchung der von Th. v. Zahn rekonstruierten 'Urausgabe der Apostelgeschichte des Lucas'* (Würzburg, 1924).
Enslin, M. S. *Christian Beginnings* (New York, 1938).
Epp, E. J. 'Coptic Manuscript G 67 and the Rôle of Codex Bezae as a Western Witness in Acts', *JBL*, LXXXV (1966), 197–212.
—— 'The "Ignorance Motif" in Acts and Anti-Judaic Tendencies in Codex Bezae', *HTR*, LV (1962), 51–62.
—— 'Some Important Textual Studies', *JBL*, LXXXIV (1965), 172–5.
Evans, O. E. 'The Negative Form of the Golden Rule in the Diatessaron', *ET*, LXIII (1951/2), 31–2.
Fascher, E. 'Gott und die Götter', *TLZ*, LXXXI (1956), 279–308.
—— *Textgeschichte als hermeneutisches Problem* (Halle (Saale), 1953).
Findlay, J. A. 'On Variations in the Text of d and D', *BBC*, IX (1931), 10–11.
Frede, H. J. *Altlateinische Paulus-Handschriften* (Vetus Latina... Aus der Geschichte der lateinischen Bibel, 4; Freiburg, 1964).
Frey, J.-B. *Corpus Inscriptionum Judaicarum*. Vol. I. Europe (Rome/Paris, 1936).
Gard, D. H. *The Exegetical Method of the Greek Translator of the Book of Job* (*JBL* Monograph Series, 8; Philadelphia, 1952).
Gärtner, B. *The Areopagus Speech and Natural Revelation* (Acta Seminarii Neotestamentici Upsaliensis, 21; Uppsala, 1955).
Gerhardsson, B. *Memory and Manuscript. Oral Tradition and Written Transmission in Rabbinic Judaism and Early Christianity* (Acta Seminarii Neotestamentici Upsaliensis, 22; Uppsala, 1961).
—— *Tradition and Transmission in Early Christianity* (Coniectanea neotestamentica, 20; Lund/Copenhagen, 1964).
Glaue, P. 'Der älteste Text der geschichtlichen Bücher des Neuen Testaments', *ZNW*, XLV (1954), 90–108.

BIBLIOGRAPHY

—— 'Einige Stellen, die die Bedeutung des Codex D charakterisieren', *NovTest*, II (1958), 310–15.

Glombitza, O. 'Akta XIII. 15–41. Analyse einer Lukanischen Predigt vor Juden', *NTS*, V (1958/9), 306–17.

Goguel, M. *Le texte et les éditions du Nouveau Testament grec* (Paris, 1920).

Greenlee, J. H. *Introduction to New Testament Textual Criticism* (Grand Rapids, 1964).

Greeven, H. 'Erwägungen zur synoptischen Textkritik', *NTS*, VI (1959/60), 281–96.

Gregory, C. R. *Canon and Text of the New Testament* (Edinburgh, 1907).

Grosheide, F. W. 'Acts 18: 27, A Test Case', *BBC*, VIII (1930), 18–20.

Grosheide, F. W. and P[looij], D. 'Acts 15: 29 par., A Suggestion', *BBC*, VI (1929), 15–16.

Haenchen, Ernst. 'Schriftzitate und Textüberlieferung in der Apostelgeschichte', *ZTK*, LI (1954), 153–67.

—— 'Tradition und Komposition in der Apostelgeschichte', *ZTK*, LII (1955), 205–25.

—— '"We" in Acts and the Itinerary', *Journal for Theology and the Church*, 1. *The Bultmann School of Biblical Interpretation: New Directions?* Ed. R. W. Funk. Tübingen/New York, 1965. Pp. 65–99.

—— 'Zum Text der Apostelgeschichte', *ZTK*, LIV (1957), 22–55.

Harnack, A. (von). *The Acts of the Apostles* (London, 1909).

—— '[Review of] Blass, *Professor Harnack und die Schriften des Lukas–Papias bei Eusebius*...', *TLZ*, XXXII (1907), 396–401.

—— *Studien zur Geschichte des Neuen Testaments und der alten Kirche*. Vol. I. *Zur neutestamentlichen Textkritik* (Berlin, 1931).

Harris, J. Rendel. 'The Acts of the Apostles', *BBC*, XI (1936), 5–9.

—— *Codex Bezae, A Study of the So-called Western Text of the New Testament* (Texts and Studies, II, 1; Cambridge, 1891).

—— 'A Curious Bezan Reading Vindicated', *Exp*, VI, 5 (1902), 189–95.

—— *Four Lectures on the Western Text of the New Testament* (London, 1894).

—— 'The Mentality of Tatian', *BBC*, IX (1931), 8–10.

—— 'New Points of View in Textual Criticism', *Exp*, VIII, 7 (1914), 316–34.

—— 'A New Witness for a Famous Western Reading', *ET*, XXXIX (1927/8), 380–1.

—— *Side-Lights on New Testament Research* (London, 1908).

—— 'Two Important Glosses in Codex Bezae', *Exp*, VI, 2 (1900), 394–400.

BIBLIOGRAPHY

Harris, J. Rendel. 'Was the Diatessaron Anti-Judaic?', *HTR*, XVIII (1925), 103–9.

Hatch, W. H. P. *The 'Western' Text of the Gospels* (Evanston, 1937).

Howard, W. F. 'The Influence of Doctrine upon the Text of the New Testament', *LQHR*, X (1941), 1–16.

Karnetzki, M. 'Textgeschichte als Überlieferungsgeschichte', *ZNW*, XLVII (1956), 170–80.

Kenyon, F. G. *Handbook to the Textual Criticism of the New Testament*, 2nd ed. (London, 1912).

—— *Recent Developments in the Textual Criticism of the Greek Bible* (Schweich Lectures, 1932; London, 1933).

—— *The Text of the Greek Bible*, new ed. (London, 1949).

—— 'The Western Text in the Gospels and Acts', *ProcBrAc*, XXIV (1938), 287–315.

Kerschensteiner, J. 'Beobachtungen zum altsyrischen Actatext', *Biblica*, XLV (1964), 63–74.

Kilpatrick, G. D. 'Atticism and the Text of the Greek New Testament', *Neutestamentliche Aufsätze. Festschrift für Prof. Josef Schmid zum 70. Geburtstag*, ed. J. Blinzler, O. Kuss and F. Mussner (Regensburg, 1963), pp. 125–37.

—— 'Codex Bezae and Mill', *JTS*, VI (1955), 235–8.

—— 'An Eclectic Study of the Text of Acts', *Biblical and Patristic Studies in Memory of Robert Pierce Casey*, ed. J. N. Birdsall and R. W. Thomson (Freiburg, 1963), pp. 64–77.

—— 'A Theme of the Lucan Passion Story and Luke xxiii. 47', *JTS*, XLIII (1942), 34–6.

King, G. B. 'The "Negative" Golden Rule', *JRel*, VIII (1928), 268–79.

Klijn, A. F. J. 'Stephen's Speech—Acts vii. 2–53', *NTS*, IV (1957/8), 25–31.

—— *A Survey of the Researches into the Western Text of the Gospels and Acts* (Utrecht, [1949]).

—— 'A Survey of the Researches into the Western Text of the Gospels and Acts (1949–1959)', *NovTest*, III (1959), 1–27, 161–73.

Knox, W. L. *St Paul and the Church of Jerusalem* (Cambridge, 1925).

Köster, H. *Synoptische Überlieferung bei den apostolischen Vätern* (Texte und Untersuchungen, 65; Berlin, 1957).

Kraft, R. A. *Barnabas and the Didache* (The Apostolic Fathers. A New Translation and Commentary, 3. Ed. R. M. Grant) Toronto/New York/London, 1965.

Kümmel, W. G. 'Die älteste Form des Apostelkrets', *Spiritus et Veritas* [Festschrift für K. Kundsin], edidit Auseklis Societas

Theologorum Universitatis Latviensis (Eutin, 1953), pp. 83–98. Reprinted in Kümmel, *Heilsgeschehen und Geschichte. Gesammelte Aufsätze 1933–1964* (Marburg, 1965), pp. 278–88.

—— 'Textkritik und Textgeschichte des Neuen Testaments 1914–1937', *TRu*, X (1938), 206–21, 292–327; XI (1939), 84–107.

Lagrange, M.-J. *Critique textuelle.* Vol. II. *La critique rationnelle* (Études Bibliques; Paris, 1935).

—— 'Les Papyrus Chester Beatty pour les Évangiles', *RB*, XLIII (1934), 5–41.

Lake, K. *The Earlier Epistles of St Paul*, 2nd ed. (London, 1930).

—— *The Influence of Textual Criticism on the Exegesis of the New Testament* (Oxford, 1904).

—— *The Text of the New Testament*, 4th ed. (London, 1908); 6th ed. revised by Silva New, 1928. [Sixth edition quoted unless otherwise specified.]

Lake, K., Blake, R. P. and New, Silva. 'The Caesarean Text of the Gospel of Mark', *HTR*, XXI (1928), 207–404.

Lietzmann, H. 'Der Sinn des Aposteldekretes und seine Textwandlung', *Amicitiae Corolla, ...Essays Presented to James Rendel Harris*, ed. H. G. Wood (London, 1933), pp. 203–11. Reprinted in Lietzmann, *Kleine Schriften*, II (Texte und Untersuchungen, 68; Berlin, 1958), pp. 292–8.

Lowe, E. A. 'A Note on the Codex Bezae', *BBC*, IV (1927), 9–14.

McHardy, W. D. 'The Text of Acts in James of Edessa's Citations and in the Cambridge Add. MS. 1700', *JTS*, L (1949), 186–7.

Massaux, E. 'État actuel de la critique textuelle du Nouveau Testament', *NouvRevThéol*, LXXV (1953), 703–26.

Menoud, P. H. 'The Western Text and the Theology of Acts', *Studiorum Novi Testamenti Societas*, Bulletin II (1951), 19–32. Reprinted in *Bulletin of the Studiorum Novi Testamenti Societas*, nos. I–III (Cambridge, 1963).

Merk, A. 'Der heilige Ephraem und die Apostelgeschichte', *ZKT*, XLVIII (1924), 460–5.

Metzger, B. M. 'The Evidence of the Versions for the Text of the New Testament', *New Testament Manuscript Studies*, ed. M. M. Parvis and A. P. Wikgren (Chicago, 1950), pp. 25–68.

—— 'A Survey of Recent Research on the Ancient Versions of the New Testament', *NTS*, II (1955/6), 1–16.

—— *The Text of the New Testament. Its Transmission, Corruption, and Restoration* (New York and London, 1964).

Montgomery, J. A. 'On the Interpolation in Acts 15: 29', *JBL*, LII (1933), 261.

Munck, J. *Paulus und die Heilsgeschichte* (Copenhagen, 1954). Eng. trans., *Paul and the Salvation of Mankind* (Richmond, Va., 1959).

Nestle, Eberhard. 'Einige Beobachtungen zum Codex Bezae', *TSK*, LXIX (1896), 102–13.
—— *Introduction to the Textual Criticism of the Greek New Testament* (London, 1901).
—— 'Some Observations on the Codex Bezae', *Exp*, v, 2 (1895), 235–40.
Nock, A. D. '[Review of] Martin Dibelius: Aufsätze zur Apostelgeschichte. Göttingen, 1951', *Gnomon*, XXV (1953), 497–506.
O'Neill, J. C. 'The Use of "Kyrios" in the Book of Acts', *SJT*, VIII (1955), 155–74.
Parvis, M. M. 'The Nature and Tasks of New Testament Textual Criticism: An Appraisal', *JRel*, XXXII (1952), 165–74.
—— 'New Testament Criticism in the World-Wars Period', *The Study of the Bible Today and Tomorrow*, ed. H. R. Willoughby (Chicago, 1947), pp. 52–73.
Parvis, M. M. and Wikgren, A. P. (eds.). *New Testament Manuscript Studies* (Chicago, 1950).
Plooij, D. 'The Ascension in the "Western" Textual Tradition', *MKAWA*, 67, A, 2 (1929), 39–58.
—— 'The Bezan Problem', *BBC*, IX (1931), 12–17.
—— *A Further Study of the Liège Diatessaron* (Leyden, 1925).
—— *Tendentieuse Varianten in den Text der Evangeliën* (Leiden, 1926).
—— 'The Apostolic Decree and its Problems', *Exp*, XXV (1923), 81–100, 223–38.
Porter, C. L. 'Papyrus Bodmer XV (P75) and the Text of Codex Vaticanus', *JBL*, LXXXI (1962), 363–76.
Ramsay, W. M. *The Church in the Roman Empire* (London, 1893).
Raphelius, Georgius. *Annotationes philologicae in Novum Testamentum ex Polybio & Arriano collectae*. Hamburg, 1715.
Reicke, Bo. *Glaube und Leben der Urgemeinde* (Zürich, 1957).
Resch, A. *Agrapha. Aussercanonische Schriftfragmente*, zweite Auflage (Texte und Untersuchungen, 15: 3/4; Leipzig, 1906).
Riddle, D. W. 'Textual Criticism as a Historical Discipline', *AngThR*, XVIII (1936), 220–33.
Riesenfeld, H. 'The Gospel Tradition and its Beginnings', *Studia Evangelica* (Texte und Untersuchungen, 73; Berlin, 1959), pp. 43–65.
—— 'The Meaning of the Verb ἀρνεῖσθαι', *Coniect.neotest*, XI (1947), 207–19. (=*In honorem Antonii Fridrichsen sexagenarii*.)
Robertson, A. T. *An Introduction to the Textual Criticism of the New Testament* (Nashville, 1925).
Ropes, J. H. 'Three Papers on the Text of Acts. I. The Reconstruction of the Torn Leaf of Codex Bezae', *HTR*, XVI (1923), 163–8; '...III. The Greek Text of Codex Laudianus', *ibid*. pp. 175–86.

BIBLIOGRAPHY

Ropes, J. H. and Hatch, W. H. P. 'The Vulgate, Peshitto, Sahidic, and Bohairic Versions of Acts and the Greek Manuscripts', *HTR*, XXI (1928), 69–95.
Sanday, W. 'The Apostolic Decree (Acts XV. 20–29)', *Theologische Studien Theodor Zahn...dargebracht...* (Leipzig, 1908), pp. 317–38. [Separately printed, Leipzig, 1908, 22 pp.]
Sanders, H. A. 'An Early Papyrus Fragment of the Gospel of Matthew in the Michigan Collection', *HTR*, XIX (1926), 215–26.
—— 'The Egyptian Text of the Four Gospels and Acts', *HTR*, XXVI (1933), 77–98.
—— 'On the New Editions of the Acts of the Apostles', *BBC*, XI (1936), 12–15.
Saunders, E. W. 'Studies in Doctrinal Influences on the Byzantine Text of the Gospel', *JBL*, LXXI (1952), 85–92.
Schäfer, K. T. 'Die Zitate in der lateinischen Irenäusübersetzung und ihr Wert für die Textgeschichte des Neuen Testamentes', *Vom Wort des Lebens. Festschrift für Max Meinertz...*, ed. Nikolaus Adler (Neutestamentliche Abhandlungen, 1. Ergänzungsband; Münster, 1951).
Schonfield, H. J. 'Should "Things strangled" Be Omitted from Acts xv. 29?', *ET*, XLI (1929/30), 128–9.
Seeligmann, I. L. *The Septuagint Version of Isaiah* (Leiden, 1948).
Simon, M. *St Stephen and the Hellenists in the Primitive Church* (London, 1958).
Smothers, E. R. 'Les Papyrus Beatty de la Bible grecque', *RSR*, XXIV (1934), 12–34.
—— 'Les Papyrus Beatty. Deux leçons dans les Actes', *RSR*, XXIV (1934), 467–72.
Snape, H. C. 'The Composition of the Lukan Writings: A Re-Assessment', *HTR*, LIII (1960), 27–46.
Sneyders de Vogel, K. 'Le codex Bezae est-il d'origine sicilienne?', *BBC*, III (1926), 10–13.
Souter, A. *The Text and Canon of the New Testament*, revised by C. S. C. Williams (London, 1954).
Stendahl, K. *The School of St Matthew* (Acta Seminarii Neotestamentici Upsaliensis, 20; Uppsala, 1954).
Stone, R. C. *The Language of the Latin Text of Codex Bezae* (Illinois Studies in Language and Literature, 30: 2/3; Urbana, Illinois, 1946).
Streeter, B. H. 'Codices 157, 1071 and the Caesarean Text', *Quantulacumque, Studies Presented to Kirsopp Lake* (London, 1937), pp. 149–50.
—— *The Four Gospels. A Study of Origins* (London, 1924).
Studia Evangelica. Papers presented to the International Congress on

'The Four Gospels in 1957' held at Christ Church, Oxford, 1957, ed. K. Aland, F. L. Cross, J. Daniélou, H. Riesenfeld and W. C. van Unnik (Texte und Untersuchungen, 73; Berlin, 1959).

Taylor, V. *The Text of the New Testament. A Short Introduction*, 2nd ed. (London, 1963).

Thiele, W. 'Ausgewählte Beispiele zur Charakterisierung des "westlichen" Textes der Apostelgeschichte', *ZNW*, LVI (1965), 51–63.

—— 'Eine Bemerkung zu Act 1. 14', *ZNW*, 53 (1962), 110–11.

—— *Die lateinischen Texte des 1. Petrusbriefes* (Vetus Latina... Aus der Geschichte der lateinischen Bibel, 5; Freiburg, 1965).

Titus, E. L. 'The Motivation of Changes Made in the New Testament Text by Justin Martyr and Clement of Alexandria: A Study in the Origin of New Testament Variation', unpublished Ph.D. thesis, University of Chicago, 1942.

Torrey, C. C. *Documents of the Primitive Church* (New York, 1941).

Turner, C. H. 'Historical Introduction to the Textual Criticism of the New Testament', *JTS*, X (1908–9), 13–28, 161–82, 354–74; XI (1909–10), 1–27, 180–210.

—— 'A Textual Commentary on Mk 1', *JTS*, XXVIII (1926/7), 145–58.

Vogels, H. J. 'Codex Bezae als Bilingue', *BBC*, II (1926), 8–12.

—— 'Der Einfluss Marcions und Tatians auf Text und Kanon des Neuen Testaments', *Synoptische Studien, Alfred Wikenhauser zum siebzigsten Geburtstag*... (München, 1953), pp. 278–89.

—— *Handbuch der Textkritik des Neuen Testaments*, zweite Auflage (Bonn, 1955).

—— *Die Harmonistik im Evangelientext des Codex Cantabrigiensis* (Texte und Untersuchungen, 36: 1a; Leipzig, 1910).

Vööbus, A. *Early Versions of the New Testament* (Papers of the Estonian Theological Society in Exile, 6; Stockholm, 1954).

—— 'New Data for the Solution of the Problem Concerning the Philoxenian Version', *Spiritus et Veritas* [Festschrift für K. Kundsin] (Eutin, 1953), pp. 169–86.

Warfield, B. B. *An Introduction to the Textual Criticism of the New Testament* (New York, 1887).

Weiss, B. *Die Apostelgeschichte. Textkritische Untersuchungen und Textherstellung* (Texte und Untersuchungen, 9: 3/4; Leipzig, 1893).

—— *Der Codex D in der Apostelgeschichte. Textkritische Untersuchung* (Texte und Untersuchungen, 17: 1; Leipzig, 1897).

Wensinck, A. J. 'The Semitisms of Codex Bezae and their Relation to the Non-Western Text of the Gospel of Saint Luke', *BBC*, XII (1937), 11–48.

Wilckens, U. *Die Missionsreden der Apostelgeschichte* (Wissenschaftliche

Monographien zum Alten und Neuen Testament, 5; Neukirchen-Vluyn, 1963²).
Wilcox, M. *The Semitisms of Acts* (Oxford, 1965).
Williams, C. S. C. *Alterations to the Text of the Synoptic Gospels and Acts* (Oxford, 1951).
Wilson, J. M. *The Acts of the Apostles. Translated from the Codex Bezae* (London, 1923).
Wright, L. E. *Alterations of the Words of Jesus* (Cambridge, Mass., 1952).
Yoder, J. D. 'The Language of the Greek Variants of Codex Bezae Cantabrigiensis', unpublished Th.D. thesis, Princeton Theological Seminary, 1958, 624 pp.
—— 'The Language of the Greek Variants of Codex Bezae', *NovTest*, III (1959), 241–8.
—— 'Semitisms in Codex Bezae', *JBL*, LXXVIII (1959), 317–21.
Zuntz, G. *The Text of the Epistles* (Schweich Lectures, 1946; London, 1953).
—— 'A Textual Criticism of Some Passages of the Acts of the Apostles', *Class et Med*, III (1940), 20–46.

ADDENDA

The following works appeared while the present volume was in the final stages of production

Aland, K., Black, M., Metzger, B. M. and Wikgren, A. (eds.). *The Greek New Testament* (New York/London/Edinburgh/Amsterdam/Stuttgart, 1966). [Contains a full citation of textual evidence for a limited number of variants.]
Clark, K. W. 'The Theological Relevance of Textual Variation in Current Criticism of the Greek New Testament', *JBL*, LXXXV (1966), 1–16.
Hanson, R. P. C. 'The Provenance of the Interpolator in the "Western" Text of Acts and of Acts itself', *NTS*, XII (1965/66), 211–30.
Klijn, A. F. J. 'In Search of the Original Text of Acts', *Studies in Luke–Acts*, ed. L. E. Keck and J. L. Martyn (Nashville, 1966), pp. 103–10.

INDEX OF SUBJECTS

Note. Page numbers in italic following textual witnesses (manuscripts, versions, patristic sources) indicate citation in textual apparatus

Acts of Perpetua and Felicitas, xiv, 67
Ado, xiii, *92, 99, 116 f., 129, 132*
Agrippa, *see under* Herod
Akiba, 109 n. 1
Ambrose, xiii, *62 f., 68, 72, 96, 98, 107 f., 135*
Ambrosiaster, xiii, *33, 43, 63, 95, 107 f., 114 n. 2, 116, 128 n. 1*
Andover-Harvard Theological Library, 30
Anti-Judaic, the term, 23 f., 96 n. 1
Anti-Judaic bias in Gospel of Luke, 2, 41 f., 45
Anti-Judaic tendencies in Acts, 3, 23 f., 41–171
Antioch of Pisidia, 46, 79, 89, 119, 135, 140 f.
Antioch of Syria, 96 f., 99, 101 f., 105, 112, 142
Antiochian text, relation to Codex Bezae, 10
Anti-Semitism, 23
Aphraates, 109 n. 1
Apollos, 118, 133
Apostles, 16, 22, 41, 43, 97, 116–19, 120–64, 159
  enhancement of in 'Western' text, 126–8, 131, 153–63
  innocence of, 51, 126, 149
  as leaders of the church, 127–32, 153–64, 166; *see also* Jews, leaders of
  versus Jewish leaders, 127–32, 153 f., 164, 166, 169
  paralleled with Jesus, 51, 124, 126, 131, 133, 154
  paralleled with one another, 147–9, 156 f., 162–4
  persecution of, by the Jews, *see* Jews, opposition to the apostles; by the Romans, 51
  preaching/message of, 63, 120, 123, 125, 128, 134, 148, 150, 155; *see also* Paul, preaching of; Peter, preaching of
  as Roman citizens, 148–50
  signs/healings done by, 63, 120, 124, 127, 155 f., 164
  triumph over Jewish leaders, 127, 132, 147, 154, 166
Apostolic Constitutions, xiii, 31, *100, 108,* 109 n. 1, *116, 142*
Apostolic 'decree', 100 f., 107–14; *see also* Acts xv. 20, 29; xxi. 25
Aquila, 91–3
Arabic version (arab), xii, *63, 68, 94, 100, 112, 120, 125* n. 3, *140, 142*
Aramaic influence on 'Western' text, 26, 52 f.
  Black on, 3, 24, 43 n. 1
  Torrey's theory of, 3, 24, 52, 77, 138 n. 2, 165 n. 1
  Wensinck's theory of, 3, 24 f.
  Wilcox on, 53 n. 2, 58 n. 2, 138 n. 2
  see also Hebrew influence; Semitic influence; Syriac influence
Aristides, xiii, *107,* 109 n. 1
Armenian version (arm), xii f., 33, *62 f., 67, 72, 84, 88, 91, 94 f., 101, 108, 112 f., 114* n. 2, *116 f., 120 f., 129, 136, 140 f., 146, 151, 157, 161*
Assimilation, *see* Scribal activity
Athenians/Athens, 49, 142
Augustine, xiii, 29, *43, 52, 62–5, 67 f., 70, 72 f., 81 f., 98–100, 107 f., 111, 114, 116–18, 134, 154, 158 f., 162;* see also *Speculum*
Autographs, 13, 17

Baptism, 117
  in the name of the Lord Jesus Christ, 63, 68, 88
  for the remission of sins, 63
Barabbas, 53, 57
Bar-Jesus, *see* Elymas
Barnabas, 79, 82, 96 f., 101–3, 112, 123, 136 f., 140, 142, 155, 163
Basil, xiii, *53* n. 7, *62, 72, 116*
Bede, xiii, *31, 59, 62–4, 66, 73, 80, 82 f., 94, 98, 101, 108, 116, 118–20, 125* n. 3, *130–2, 134–7, 140, 142, 146, 151*

INDEX OF SUBJECTS

Beza, Theodore, 12
Bezae, Codex, *see* Codex Bezae
'Bezan text', the term, 1 n. 1
Bohairic, *see* Coptic versions, Bohairic
Bohemian version (bohem), xiii, 32 f., 57, *117*, *132*, *152*, *162*
B-text, *see* 'Neutral' text
Byzantine text, 14, 19 n. 4, 37, 114

Cassiodorus, xiii, 33, *62 f.*, *96*, *103*, *108*, *112–14*, *116 f.*, *119*, *129*, *137*, *140 f.*, *148 f.*, *151*, *156*
Christianity, and Judaism, *see* Judaism, and Christianity
Christology, *see* Jesus, as Christos
Chrysostom, xiii, 31, *44*, *54*, *59*, *62 f.*, *67*, *72*, *84*, *91*, 123, *129 f.*, *136*, *143*, *145 f.*, *151*, *157*, *160*, *162*
Church, 22, 118
  at Antioch, 99, 102
  at Jerusalem, 97–103, 128 f., 134
  strengthening of, 113 f.
  unity of in 'Western' text, 97–100, 102, 163
Circumcision, 100–2, 105 f., 111
Clement of Alexandria, xiii, 19 n. 4, *108*
Codex Bezae (D)
  conformation to other texts, 9 f., 28, 34 f., 65, 72, 85 f., 88 n. 2, 113, 122, 133 f., 138 f., 149
  correctors of, xiv, 9, *43*, *45 f.*, *54*, *67*, *69*, *95*, *154*
  date, of the manuscript, xi, 7, 10; of its text, 5, 8, 10–12, 27
  description and character, 7–12, 28, 38 f.
  eschatology of, 67 n. 2, 167 n. 7
  homogeneity of its text, *see* Codex Bezae, textual strata in
  lacunae in, 8, 34
  language of, 12 n. 2
  Latin side (*d*), xi, 8–10; conformation to 'Neutral' text, 9; language of, 12 n. 2; relation to Greek side, 8–10, 25
  Montanized, 2, 13, 21, 127
  omissions in, 24, 34, 39, *45*, *54*, *64*, *67 f.*, *70*, *91*, *101*, *105–8*, *113 f.*, *118*, *121–5*, *138*, *141*, *145*, *161 f.*; *see also* Codex Bezae, lacunae in
  originality of text/readings in, 12 f.; *see also* 'Western' text and 'Neutral' text, question of originality
  orthography of, 12 n. 1
  relation to Antiochian text, 10
  relation to cop^{G67}, ix, 10 f., 29 f.
  relation to $\mathfrak{P}^{38}$, 27, 31
  relation to 'Western' text, 9–12, 22 f., 27 f., 31, 34, 47, 65, 69, 71, 91–3, 99, 122, 133 f., 138 f., 141, 149, 158 f., 161, 165
  scribal errors in, 10, 24, 27, 71, 95, 125 n. 1
  Semitisms in, 12 n. 2; *see also* Semitic influences on 'Western' text
  singular readings of, 10 f., 34, *49 f.*, *52*, *55* n. 2, *56 f.*, *67–9*, *71*, *74*, *76*, *80*, *88*, *91*, *95*, *111*, *113*, *118*, *125*, *135*, *137*, *142*, *145 f.*, *148* n. *1*, *150*, *156–8*, *160*
  textual strata in, 10 f., 27 f., 34, 71, 90; *see also* Codex Bezae, date of its text; Codex Bezae, conformation to other texts
Codex Teplensis (tepl), xiii, 33, *63*, *68*, *73*, *83 f.*, *99*, *101*, *105*, *107 f.*, *112–15*, *117*, *119 f.*, *126*, *129*, *132*, *136 f.*, *140*, *151*, *153*, *157 f.*, *160–2*
Codex Thomae, xii, 30 f.; *see also* Syriac versions, Harclean margin
Constitutiones Apostolorum, *see* *Apostolic Constitutions*
Coptic Manuscript G67, ix, xii, 10 f., 29–31, *43*, *46*, *57*, *58* n. *3*, *61–3*, *65*, *72 f.*, *80–3*, *91*, *95*, *99*, *101*, *105*, *107*, *116–21*, *123–5*, *127*, *128* n. *1*, *129–42*, *145*, *154*, *156 f.*, *159–62*
Coptic version
  Bohairic (bo), xii, 33 n. 1, *45*, *62 f.*, *67*, *95*, *112*, *114* n. *2*, *116*, *126*, *128* n. *2*, *130*, *143*; included in cop, *54*, *56*, *131*, *156*
  Crispus, 87 f. 146
  Sahidic (sa), xii, 33, *44 f.*, *49*, *54*, *59*, *62–5*, *67 f.*, *72 f.*, *81*, *88*, *96*, *100*, *107 f.*, *111–17*, *121 f.*, *125*, *128 f.*, *131*, *133–6*, *144–6*, *149–51*, *154* n. *2*, *156–8*, *160–2*; included in cop, *54*, *56*, *62*, *91*, *114* n. *2*, *131*, *156*
Corinth/Corinthians, 87 f., 90, 93
Cornelius, 61, 66, 69, 117 f., 157, 160–2
Cosmas Indicopleustes, xiii, *59*, *95*
Cyprian, xiii, 29, *62*, *64*, *70–2*, *98*, *108*, *120*; see also *Liber de rebaptismate*
Cyril of Alexandria, xiii, *53* n. *7*, *49*, *59*, *62 f.*, *72*
Cyril of Jerusalem, xiii, *62*, *67*, *72 f.*, *117*

INDEX OF SUBJECTS

Dead Sea Scrolls/Qumran, 19 n. 4, 25, 116
Diatessaron, 2 n. 1, 109 n. 1; Liège, 73 f.
Didache, 109 n. 1
Didascalia Apostolorum, xiii, 31, *100*
Didymus the Blind, xiii, *62*, *117*
Dogmatic variants, *see* Tendentious variants
Drusilla, 152
Dutch version (Medieval) (dut), xiii, *62*, *72*, *105*, *129*, *134*, *156*

Egyptian versions, *see* Coptic versions
Elymas, 135, 156, 163
Ephesus, 92, 115, 117, 142
Ephrem of Syria, xiii, 30, *43*, 45 n. 1, *50*, *52*, *54*, *62 f.*, *65*, *73*, *82*, *97*, *101–4*, *107 f.*, 109 n. 1, *112 f.*, *115–17*, *119*, *122*, *129 f.*, *132–5*, *137–9*, *141–50*, *153*, *160*
Epiphanius, xiv, *62*, *72*
Eschatology, in Codex Bezae, 67 n. 2, 167 n. 7
Ethiopic version (eth), xiii, 33, *54*, *56*, *62–4*, *67*, *72*, *85*, *91*, *93*, *101*, *107 f.*, *112*, *114* n. 2, *116*, *120 f.*, *128 f.*, *132–5*, *145 f.*, *151*, *157*, *161*
Eusebius, xiv, *59*, *71*, *107 f.*, *154*
Evil, 43–5
Excuse
 of the Jews, 41–9, 51, 53, 55, 124
 of the Romans, 51, 147–53, 164, 166, 170

Faith, 63, 90, 118; *see also* πιστεύω κτλ.
Fear, 50, 76, 119, 148, 151, 155
Felix, 151–3
Forgiveness, 45, 63 f., 72, 81
Fulgentius, xiv, *108*

Gallio, 144, 146 f.
Gamaliel, 128, 130–2
Gaudentius, xiv, *62*, *107*
Gentile interest in the 'Western' text, 23, 65–119 (*especially* 66, 69 f., 75, 80, 82–4, 86 f., 92–5, 102, 111, 115, 118), 166, 169; *see also* Universalism
Gentile mission, 66, 69, 75, 79, 83 f., 96, 103–7, 114 f., 118 f.
Gentiles, 41, 49, 59, 74 f., 76, 138 f., 152, 162; Gentile converts, relationship to Judaism, 96, 98 f., 101, 103, 105–7, 111 f.; *see also* Judaizers

Georgian version (geo), xiii, 33, *49*, *54*, *56*, *62 f.*, *71*, *84 f.*, *95*, *100 f.*, *108*, *112*, *116–18*, *120*, *140 f.*, *146*, *148 f.*, *154* n. 2, *160*
German version, *see* Codex Teplensis
Glossolalia, 158 f.
'Golden Rule', 50 n. 1, 107–11
Gospel, response of the Jews to, *see* Jews, unbelief of
Greek manuscripts, uncials
 Codex Alexandrinus (A), xi, 36 n. 6, *49*, *54*, *63*, *67 f.*, *71*, *81*, *91*, *95 f.*, *111*, *114* n. 2, *116 f.*, *125* n. 1, *128* n. 2, *154* n. 2, *160*
 Codex Angelicus (L), xi, *49*, *62*, *83* n. 3, *84*, *91*, *94*, *96*, *100 f.*, *108*, *111*, *114*, *116*, *129*, *136*, *143*, *145 f.*, *151* n. 2, *157*, *162*
 Codex Athous (S), xi, *49*, *62*, *67*, *72*, *83* n. 3, *84*, *94*, *96*, *100 f.*, *108*, *111*, *114*, *116*, *118*, *120*, *128–30*, *136*, *143*, *145 f.*, *151* n. 2, *154* n. 2, *162*
 Codex Athous Laurae (Ψ), xi, *101*, *151*
 Codex Bezae, *see* Codex Bezae
 Codex Claromontanus, 26
 Codex Ephraemi rescriptus (C), xi, 36 n. 6, *54*, *59*, *62 f.*, *67 f.*, *71*, *81*, *95 f.*, *101*, *108*, *111 f.*, *114* n. 2, *116*, *128* n. 2, *129*, *135 f.*, *140 f.*, *154* n. 2, *157*, *160*
 Codex Laudianus (E), xi, 32, *43*, *46*, *49*, *54*, *59*, *62–4*, *67 f.*, *72 f.*, *82 f.*, *89*, *91*, *94–6*, *98*, *100 f.*, *108*, *111*, *114* n. 2, *116*, *118–21*, *125* nn. 1, 3, *127–32*, *135–7*, *139* *43*, *145 f.*, *154* n. 2, *156–8*, *160 f.*
 Codex Mutinensis (H), xi, *49*, *62*, *84*, *91*, *94*, *96*, *100 f.*, *108*, *111*, *114*, *116*, *128–30*, *143*, *145 f.*, *151* n. 2, *162*
 Codex Porphyrianus (P), xi, *49*, *54*, *59*, *62*, *67*, *72*, *83* n. 3, *84*, *91*, *94–6*, *100 f.*, *108*, *111*, *114*, *116*, *118*, *120*, *129 f.*, *136*, *143*, *145 f.*, *151* n. 2, *162*
 Codex Sinaiticus (ℵ), xi, 36, *45*, *49*, *53* n. 7, *54*, *59*, *62 f.*, *67 f.*, *81*, *91*, *95 f.*, *111*, *114* n. 2, *116*, *126*, *128* n. 2, *154* n. 2, *160*
 Codex Vaticanus (B), xi, 36 f., *et saepe*
Greek manuscripts, minuscules
 383, xi, 31, *49 f.*, *54*, *59*, *62 f.*, *68*, *72*, *74*, *91*, *93 f.*, *99*, *91*, *94–7*, *100 f.*, *108*, *111 f.*, *114*, *118 f.*, *128–30*, *136 f.*, *142 f.*, *145 f.*, *148–50*, *151* n. 2, *160–2*

INDEX OF SUBJECTS

Greek Manuscripts (cont.)
614, xi, 31, 49 f., 54, 56, 59, 62 f., 68, 72, 74, 81 f., 88, 91, 94–7, 100 f., 103, 108, 111 f., 114, 116, 118–20, 125 n. 1, 128–31, 136 f., 142 f., 145 f., 148–53, 157, 160 f.
1739, xi, 107 f., 141
Greek papyri, xi, 3, 8, 28
𝔓²⁹, xi, 28
𝔓³⁸, xi, 27, 31, 63, 117–19, 129; relation to Codex Bezae, 27; importance as a 'Western' witness, 31
𝔓⁴¹, xi, 28, 49, 115, 117, 129
𝔓⁴⁵, 116
𝔓⁴⁸, xi, 28, 151 f.
𝔓⁷⁴, xi, 49, 54, 63, 91, 95 f., 108, 111, 114 n. 2, 116, 125 n. 1, 128 n. 2, 131, 162
𝔓⁷⁵, xi, 36 n. 4, 45
Greeks, 74 f., 86 f., 95, 114 f., 146 f.; see also Gentiles

Harmonization, see Scribal activity
Hebrew influence on 'Western' text, 52 f., 77 f.; see also Aramaic influence; Semitic influence; Syriac influence
Hellenists, 95
Hermeneutic, 15–21, 25, 39 f.; see also Tendentious variants; Scribal activity
Herod, Agrippa I, 129, 145; Agrippa II, 117; Antipas, 133
Hilary of Poitiers, xiv, 33, 62, 67, 80, 116
Hillel, 109 n. 1
Holy Spirit, 64 n. 2, 65, 68, 80 n. 3, 96, 107 in the 'Western' text, 23, 63, 68–70, 80 n. 3, 110 f., 116–18, 132, 143 f., 153, 155, 162, 164, 166, 169

Iconium/Iconians, 89, 119, 137–41
'Ignorance motif', 38, 41–51, 55, 124, 169
ignorance as guilt, 44, 46, 48 n. 2
Irenaeus, xiv, 29 f., 43, 49, 52, 54, 59, 61–4, 67 f., 71–3, 82, 95, 99, 101, 103 f., 107 f., 116, 120, 122 f., 127, 135, 142, 154
Ishodad, 151
Israel, 47, 70, 74, 76 f., 120, 132

James the Apostle, 145
James the Just, 103 f.
Jerome, xiv, 54, 62 f., 68, 72, 107 f., 111, 114, 117, 154

Jerusalem, 65 f., 74, 77, 96–9, 101–6, 112, 114 f., 116 f., 128 f., 134, 142, 152; see also Ἱερουσαλήμ
'Jerusalem Council', 116, 142; see also Apostolic 'decree'; Judaizers
Jesus, 41–64, 83, 109 n. 1, 123 f., 126, 133, 140, 152; see also Apostles, paralleled with Jesus
ascension of, 167 n. 7, cf. 63; see also Acts i. 2
as Christos, 23, 43, 47 f., 55 f., 63 f., 80 n. 3, 90, 115 f., 118, 135, 165, 167 n. 5
crucifixion/death of, 24, 41 f., 44 f., 48 f., 51, 53, 56–61, 66 n. 3, 124, 131, 165
innocence of, 44, 51, 57, 126
ipsissima verba of, 18
name of, 54 f., 62–4, 84, 86, 88, 90, 142, 148, 157, 163; see also ὄνομα
prayer from the cross, 45
resurrection of, 63, 80
as Son of God, 64 f., 80, 135
treatment by the Jews, 41–64, 66 n. 3, 124, 126, 165, 169
trial of, 56–8, 126, 133
Jewish Christians/Christianity, 96–114; see also Judaizers
Jews
Council of, 58, 122–6, 129–32
guilt of, 41 f., 44, 46, 48, 55 f., 58 f., 61, 64, 66 n. 3
leaders of, 24, 42 f., 48, 59, 124–32, 137–9, 149, 153 f., 164–6; Jewish leaders versus Christian leaders, 127–32, 153 f., 164, 166, 169
opposition to/persecution of the apostles, 79, 85 f., 94 f., 102 f., 111, 116–19, 120–64 (especially 120 f., 124, 126–30, 133–5, 137–45, 149–53, 163 f.), 166
opposition to Christianity, 75, 94 f., 138, 167
and Paul, 85–7, 92–5, 111, 114–18, 134–44, 146–53; see also Jews, opposition to the apostles
treatment of Jesus, 41–64, 66 n. 3, 124, 126, 165, 169
unbelief of, 22, 74 f., 79, 82, 87 f., 94, 96, 115
John the Apostle, 120 f., 124, 126 f., 147–9, 154 f., 163
John the Baptist, 76, 133

190

INDEX OF SUBJECTS

Judaism, 22–4, 64–119
  by-passing/minimizing of by 'Western' text, 69 f., 73, 75, 77, 86 f., 90, 94, 97, 102 f., 110 f., 115, 118, 165 f.
  and Christianity, 43, 64–119 (*especially* 75, 90, 110 f., 115 f.), 127 f., 166, 167 n. 5
  exclusivism of, 23, 66, 87; *compare* Gentile interests in the 'Western' text; Universalism
Judaizers/Judaizing, 95–8, 100–15, 118, 129, 152
Judas Iscariot, 154, 157
Judea, 96, 101 f., 105–7, 114, 129

Latinization
  in Codex Bezae, 8 f., 25, 52, 127
  in 'Western' text, 8 f., 24 f., 52 f., 58 n. 2, 78, 127
  Harris's theory of, 3, 8 f., 24 f., 52, 78, 127, 165 n. 1
Latin manuscripts
  Codex Ardmachanus (*cod.ard*), xii, 32, *43, 46, 54, 62 f., 65*, 68, *71, 73, 80–2, 84 f., 95, 100, 108, 112–14, 117 f., 129, 131 f., 137, 146, 149* n. 2, *151, 156, 159 f., 162*
  Codex Bezae, Latin side (*d*), *see* Codex Bezae, Latin side
  Codex Bobbiensis (*s*), xii, 32, *153*
  Codex Colbertinus (*c*), xi, 32, *62*, 68, *84 f., 94, 112–14, 129, 151, 153, 156 f.*
  Codex Demidovianus (*dem*), xi, 32, *69*, 68, *81, 84 f., 94, 105, 107, 113, 129, 131, 135, 137, 151, 156, 160*
  Codex Dublinensis, *see* Codex Ardmachanus
  Codex Floriacensis (*h*), xi, 29 f., 32, *43, 54, 62–4, 84 f., 87 f., 91–3, 95 f., 116, 119–25, 128, 130–5, 138–41, 144, 146, 151, 155–7, 159*
  Codex Gigas (*gig*), xi, 10, *31–3, 43, 46, 49, 53* n. 7, *54, 56 f., 62–5, 67 f., 72 f., 80 f., 84 f., 89, 91, 94 f., 100 f., 105, 107 f., 111–17, 120–2, 125, 127–31, 134–7, 141–3, 145 f., 151–4, 156–62*
  Codex Laudianus, Latin side (*e*), *see under* Greek manuscripts
  Codex Paris. 343 (*q*), xii, 32, *43, 62–4, 69, 79, 81* 4, *99, 101, 105, 107 f., 112 f., 115, 117, 119 f., 125* n. 3, *128* nn. 1 f., *129, 135–7, 140, 153, 158, 160–2*

Codex Perpinianus (*p*), xii, 31–3, *43, 54, 61–4, 67 f., 70, 72 f., 83, 91, 99, 100, 105, 107 f., 114–20, 125* n. 3, *126, 128* nn. 1 f., *129, 131 f., 135–7, 140, 145, 151, 153 f., 156–8, 160–2*
Codex Wernigerodensis (*w*), xii, 32, *43, 62 f., 73, 82–5, 95, 99, 101, 105, 107 f., 112–14, 117, 119 f., 125* n. 3, *128* nn. 1 f., *129, 131 f., 135–7, 140, 151, 158, 160, 162*
Correctorium vaticanum (*cor.vat*), xii, *46, 69, 156, 160*
Lectionary, Fragmenta Mediolanensia (*g*₂), xi, 31, *62, 116, 132, 134*
Lectionary, Liber comicus (*t*), xii, 32, *46, 56, 61–3, 65, 68, 72 f., 81, 96, 116, 128, 132–5, 154, 157 f., 160, 162*
Lectionary, Schlettstadt, Stadtbibliothek 1093 (*r*), xii, 32, *54, 62 f., 68, 72 f., 82, 94, 118, 135, 157–9*
León palimpsest (*l*), ix, xi, 32, *61–4, 89, 103, 105, 107 f., 112, 116 f., 123, 135, 142, 157, 160–2*
Latin versions, Old Latin
  importance to 'Western' text, 28, 31–3
  and Irenaeus, 29
Latin versions, Vulgate (*vg*), xii, 32 f., *46, 49, 54, 56 f., 62 f., 68, 72, 89, 91, 108, 111, 114* n. 2, *116, 128* n. 2, *131, 140* n. 4, *154, 156 f., 161*
  vg^(s and/or cl) cited, *62*, 68, *84 f., 94 f., 112–14, 129, 135, 140, 151, 156*
  vg codices cited, *43, 46 f., 50, 62 f., 68, 81 f., 84, 99, 101, 105, 114, 116 f., 125, 128, 132, 136 f., 140, 145, 148* n. 1, *149, 154, 158–60, 162*
Law of Moses, 81, 100–3, 111, 114, 152; *see also* Judaizers
Lectionaries, 18, 37; *see also* Latin manuscripts
Liber de rebaptismate (Pseudo-Cyprian), xiv, 33, *67, 70, 72*
Liber promissionum et praedictorum dei, xiv, 73
Liège Diatessaron, 73 f.
Local texts, 15
Lucifer of Cagliari, xiv, *32, 62–4, 72, 115, 125, 127, 129, 131, 135, 145, 151, 156*
Luke (author of Luke-Acts)
  style of, 79, 82 f.
  theology of, 39, 41 f., 48 n. 2, 59, 66, 69, 79, 96, 145; Lucan emphases in

191

INDEX OF SUBJECTS

Luke (author of Luke–Acts) (cont.)
  the 'Western' text, 41–5, 66 and n. 3, 79, 95, 170; see also Gentile interests in the 'Western' text; Holy Spirit in the 'Western' text; Universalism
  two versions of Luke–Acts, 3, 165 n. 1
Luke, Gospel of in 'Western' text, 2, 44 f., 51, 53 n. 7, 82 n. 1, 83 n. 1, 126 nn. 1 f., 167 n. 7; anti-Judaic bias in, 2, 41 f., 45, 66 n. 3
Lystra, 89, 119, 140 f.

Marcion, 1, 15, 19 n. 4, 25, 36; Marcionite influence on 'Western' text, 2
Maximus of Turin, xiv, *116*
Montanists, 2, 13, 21, 127
Moses, see Law of Moses

Nestle Greek Testament, 36, 173
'Neutral' text (B-text), 2, 36 f.
  relation to the 'Western' text, see 'Western' text and 'Neutral' text
  a revision, 6, 36

Old Latin, see Latin versions
Old Syriac, see Syriac versions
Old Testament, 19 n. 4, 21 nn. 1 f., 69 n. 4, 76, 82 n. 2, 83, 86; see also Septuagint
Origen, xiv, *67*, *80*, *129*, *154*
'Original' text/reading, 13–21 *passim*, 36, 45, 79, 80 n. 3, 92, 108, 165; see also 'Western' text and 'Neutral' text

Pacianus, xiv, *108*
Papyri, see Greek papyri
Paul, 69, 76, 82, 126 n. 3
  arrest, trial, imprisonment, 50 f., 147–50, 152 f.
  enhanced in the 'Western' text, 154–7, 163
  and the Holy Spirit, 116–19, 142–4, 153
  and the Jews, see Jews, and Paul; Judaizers
  and the Judaizers, 96 f., 101–3, 111–14, 129
  missionary activity, 76, 79, 84, 86, 92–5, 114 f., 152
  preaching/speeches of, 46, 48, 58, 76, 82, 94, 113 f., 119, 123, 134 f., 140, 143, 155
  as Roman citizen, 50 f., 148–50
  theology of, 39, 48 n. 2
Pentecost, 66 f., 116, 128
People of God, 70, 76–8; see also Israel
Peshitta, see Syriac versions, Peshitta
Peter, 21, 53, 73, 76, 105–7, 126 f., 147–9
  enhanced in the 'Western' text, 128 n. 1, 154–64
  and the Gentile mission, 67–70, 75, 103–7, 116, 118, 162; Peter a Paulinist in the 'Western' text, 69, 103 f.; see also Universalism
  and the Holy Spirit, 68–70, 103 f., 116–18, 162
  preaching/speeches of, 42–4, 48 n. 2, 61, 66–9, 75, 83, 103 f., 116, 118, 120, 125 n. 3
Petilianus, xiv, *63*
Philip, 117, 155
Philippi, 50, 89
Philo of Alexandria, 49 n. 2, 109 n. 1
Philoxenus, 33, 109 n. 1; see also Syriac versions, Philoxenian
Pilate, 42, 54, 56–8, 61
Priscillian, xiv, *67*
Prophetiae ex omnibus libris collectae, xiv, *99*
Proselytes, 67, 90
Provençal version (prov), xiii, 32 f., *43*, *62 f.*, *67 f.*, *73*, *83–5*, *99*, *101*, *105*, *107 f.*, *112–13*, *117*, *119 f.*, *129*, *134–7*, *140*, *151*, *153*, *158*, *160–2*

Rabbinic hermeneutic, 25
Repentance, 73, 81, 118, 160
Roman officials
  attitude toward in the 'Western' text, 51, 147–53, 155, 164, 166, 170
  treatment of the apostles, 147–53, 164, 166
Rome/Romans, 45 n. 2, 56, 59, 114

Sahidic version, see Coptic versions, Sahidic
Scribal activity
  assimilation, conflation, conformation to other texts, 9 f., 24, 28, 34 f., 38, 50, 65, 71, 85 f., 88 n. 2, 91, 113, 122, 133 f., 138 f., 149
  conservative generally, 38 f.
  error, 2, 10, 17 n. 1, 24, 27, 35; see also Codex Bezae, scribal errors in

192

INDEX OF SUBJECTS

Scribal activity (*cont.*)
  falsification, 1 f., 16 f., 45
  harmonization, 24, 26, 36, 38, 44 f.
  improvement, embellishment, 17, 20, 24, 36, 39
  theological motivation, 15–20, 24 f., 35, 78
  see also Tendentious variants; 'Western' text, character of; Codex Bezae, conformation to other texts, etc.
Scriptures, 16 f., 25, 46–8, 86, 90, 117
  fulfilment of, 46–8, 57 f.
Semitic influence on 'Western' text, 3, 12 n. 2, 24, 52 f., 77 f.
  mistranslation, 24 f., 52 f.
  see also Aramaic influence; Hebrew influence; Syriac influence
Septuagint (LXX), 21 n. 1, 49 n. 2, 53 n. 7, 66 f., 69, 79 f., 82, 120 n. 1, 129 f.
Sergius Paulus, 88, 135
Silas, 50 f., 84 f., 111–13, 119, 123, 126 n. 3, 147 f., 154, 163
Simon Magus, 159 f., 163
Sosthenes, 146 f.
Speculum (Pseudo-Augustine), xiv, 33, 62 f., 114 n. 2, 135, 157
Speeches in Acts, 26, 41 f., 95 f., 170; *see also* Paul, preaching/speeches of; Peter, preaching/speeches of
Stephen, 55 n. 1, 95 f., 116 f., 123, 132–4, 155, 170
  boldness in speech, 123, 133
  death, 134
  inspired, 116, 132, 155
  and the Jews, 96, 117, 132–4
Synagogue, 86–90, 92–4, 115, 133 n. 1, 135, 137, 155
Syriac fragment from Khirbet Mird (sy^{msK}), ix, xii, 30, 61, 157, 161 f.
Syriac influence on 'Western' text, 3, 24–6, 53, 60 n. 1, 68, 127
  Chase's theory of, 3, 24 f., 53, 60 n. 1, 68, 77 f., 165 n. 1
  Harvey on, 53
  Zuntz on, 3
  see also Aramaic influence; Hebrew influence; Semitic influence
Syriac versions
  Harclean (sy^h), xii, 30, 33, 49, 54, 55 n. 1, 59, 62 f., 68, 72, 88, 91, 95, 100 f., 108, 111, 114 n. 2, 116, 118,
  120 f., 127–9, 131, 136 f., 143, 145 f., 148, 151, 157, 161
  Harclean margin (sy^{hmg}), xii, 30 f., 43, 54, 57, 58 n. 3, 62–5, 68, 73, 80 f., 83–5, 91–3, 97, 100–3, 113, 116–19, 122 f., 125, 129, 132, 136–43, 145, 148, 151–3, 155, 160
  Harclean with asterisk (sy^{h*}), xii, 30 f., 50, 56, 61–3, 81 f., 85, 88, 94–7, 101, 103, 105, 107 f., 112, 114, 117, 119, 129, 131, 135, 144, 148 n. 1, 149–51, 153, 161 f.
  Peshitta (sy^p), xii, 33, 46, 49, 54, 56, 61–3, 65, 67 f., 72, 78, 85, 88, 91, 94 f., 101, 103 f., 111–14, 116, 118–22, 125 n. 3, 126–9, 131, 135 f., 138, 141 f., 144–6, 149, 151, 157 f., 160–2
  Philoxenian, 30 n. 5, 33
Syriac witnesses, importance to the 'Western' text, 28, 31

Tatian, 15, 19 n. 4, 26, 73
Tendentious variants, 1–40
  consistency of/in, 38–40, 50 f., 170
  deliberate falsification in, 1, 16, 45
  early date of, 37
  frequency of, 1 f., 37 f.
  importance/significance of, 14, 37–40
  motivation for, *passim*, *see especially* 19 f., 23–5, 165–9
  in 'Western' text, *passim*, *see especially* 2–4, 12, 21–4, 34
  view of Hort on, 1 f., 13, 45
  view of Ropes on, 4, 12, 38, 166
Tertullian, xiv, 29, 63, 65, 67, 71, 80, 103, 108, 116, 160
Tertullus, 151 f.
Text-types, development of, 5 f.
Textual criticism
  and church history, 12 f., 15–19, 40
  and Form-criticism, 16 18
  as a historical discipline, 18, 40; *see also* Textual criticism and church history
  purposes of, 13–21
  and *Redaktionsgeschichte*, 39 f.
  theological approach to, *passim*, *see especially* 14–29, 35–40, 165
Textual transmission
  history of, 13–20, 25
  nature of, 5–7, 16 f., 35, 37–40, 44 f.
  view of K. W. Clark, 18 f.; view of Fascher, 19 f., 39; view of Parvis,

INDEX OF SUBJECTS

Textual transmission (*cont.*)
   17 f., 39; view of Riddle, 16–18, 39; view of Riesenfeld and Gerhardsson, 16 f.
Textual variants, ambiguity in comparison of, 35–7
Theodoret of Cyrus, xiv, *62 f.*, *72*, *114 n. 2*
Theodotus of Ancyra, xiv, *59*
Theological tendency, *see* Tendentious variants
Theophylact of Bulgaria, xiv, *62 f.*, *85*, *91*, *95*, *100 f.*, *112*, *114 n. 2*, *125 n. 3*, *129*, *135 f.*, *151*
Thessalonica, 74, 142 f.
Thomas of Harkel, xii, 30, 33; *see also* Syriac versions, Harclean
Timothy, 84 f., 119
Tyrannus, 94

Universalism, 66–119 (especially 66, 69 f., 75, 77, 79 f., 82, 94, 115, 117–19), 166 f., 169; *see also* Gentile interest in the 'Western' text; Gentile mission

Versions, *see* Coptic; Latin; Syriac, etc.
Vigilius of Thapsus, xiv; *Contra Varimadum* (Pseudo-Vigilius), xiv, 33, *62*, *65*, *72*, *116*, *135*, *154*

'We'-passages, 99
'Western non-interpolation', 161
'Western' text
   character of, 5, 7, 16, 168 f.; paraphrastic, 3, 73 f., 168
   conformation to other texts, *see* Codex Bezae, conformation; 'Western' text and 'Neutral' text
   consistency in, 38, 50, 72 n. 2, 170
   date of, 5, 8, 11 f., 27
   homogeneity of, 4–7, 16 n. 2, 34
   Latinization of, *see* Latinization
   Marcionite influence on, 2
   Montanized, *see* Codex Bezae, Montanized
   and 'Neutral' text, 5, 22, 28, 112 f., 122, 133 f., 138 f., 165 n. 1; question of originality, 3, 5 n. 1, 6, 45, 79, 108, 165
   paralleling technique, 44, 51, 104 f., 124, 126, 133, 154, 157, 162–4
   reconstruction of, 4, 6, 7; *see also* Blass; A. C. Clark, Hilgenfeld, Zahn
   reviser/revision of, 4–6, 70, 77; Kenyon's view, 6; Ropes's view, 4–6, 9, 47
   Semitic influence on, *see* Semitic influence on 'Western' text
   the term 'Western' text, 1 n. 1
   textual strata in, *see* Codex Bezae, textual strata in
   witnesses to, 5 f., 8, 27–34; 'pure' witnesses to, ix, 7, 10–12, 27–31, 34; mixed witnesses to, 31–4, 91 n. 2
   see also Codex Bezae, relation to 'Western' text
'Western' text of the Gospels, 28 n. 1; *see also* Luke, Gospel of, 'Western' text of
Women, 75, 90, 167 n. 7
   anti-feminist bias in Codex Bezae, 75 n. 3, 167 n. 7

Zeno of Verona, xiv, *98*

INDEX OF AUTHORS

Adler, N., 183
Aland, K., 14 nn. 1 f., 172 f., 175, 184
Arndt, W. F., 51 n. 3, 172

Bacon, B. W., 22, 104, 105 n. 1, 108 n. 1, 110 n. 1, 175
Bauer, W., 51 n. 3, 131 n. 1, 172
Bauernfeind, O., 106 n. 3, 174
Belser, J., 175
Berger, S., 141, 172
Bieder, W., 89 n. 2, 175
Billerbeck, P., 131 n. 1, 174
Birdsall, J. N., 173, 180
Black, M., 3, 12 n. 1, 16 n. 4, 24 f., 43 n. 1, 53 n. 2, 175, 177
Blackman, E. C., 19 n. 4, 175
Blake, R. P., 15 n. 2, 181
Blass, F., 2 f., 6, 32, 43, 46 n. 1, 52, 77 n. 3, 91 f., 93 nn. 2 f., 124 n. 2, 125 nn. 1 f., 141, 157, 161 n. 3, 165 n. 1, 172 f., 175–7, 179
Blinzler, J., 180
Bludau, A., 19 n. 4, 176
Boman, T., 110 n. 1, 176
Bornemann, F. A., 57, 173
Bruce, F. F., 52 n. 4, 53, 55 n. 4, 56 n. 5, 59 nn. 3 f., 69 n. 4, 75 nn. 3 f., 82 n. 5, 83 n. 3, 86 n. 1, 89 nn. 2, 5, 90 n. 1, 92, 110 n. 1, 123 n. 2, 133 n. 1, 147 n. 3, 175
Buchanan, E. S., 141
Bultmann, R., 99, 176
Burgon, J. W., 2, 176
Burkitt, F. C., 7, 108 n. 1, 110 n. 1, 176

Cadbury, H. J., 5 n. 1, 22, 60, 67, 71, 110 n. 1, 137, 142, 170 n. 1, 175 f.
Casey, R. P., 8 n. 1, 162 n. 1, 173, 176, 180
Cerfaux, L., 21, 70, 80 n. 3, 104 n. 2, 131 n. 1, 158 n. 1, 175 f.
Chapman, J., 7, 176
Chase, F. H., 3, 24–6, 46 n. 1, 53, 60 n. 1, 68, 77, 78 n. 1, 165 n. 1, 176
Cheetham, F. P., 77 n. 5, 176

Clark, A. C., 1 n. 1, 3, 5 n. 3, 6–9, 10 nn. 1, 3, 12 n. 1, 27 f., 29 n. 2, 30–3, 36 n. 6, 46 n. 1, 47, 53 n. 7, 57, 58 n. 1, 65 n. 1, 85, 92, 99, 107 n. 1, 124 n. 2, 126 f., 129, 141, 143 n. 1, 149, 153 n. 2, 157, 161 nn. 3 f., 165 n. 1, 167 n. 7, 170 n. 1, 173
Clark, K. W., 14 nn. 1 f., 18 f., 36 nn. 3 f., 176, 177
Coleman, A. M., 32, 173
Colwell, E. C., 21 n. 1, 26, 167 n. 7, 177
Connolly, R. H., 109 n. 1, 177
Conybeare, F. C., xiii, 2 n. 1, 30, 177
Conzelmann, H., 4 n. 1, 41 f., 46 f., 59, 64 n. 2, 66 n. 3, 69 n. 2, 108 n. 1, 110 nn. 1, 3, 116 n. 1, 146 n. 2, 154 n. 1, 158 n. 1, 175, 177
Coppieters, H., 177
Corssen, P., 3, 9 n. 3, 29, 65, 75, 77 n. 5, 85, 92 n. 2, 94 n. 3, 133, 139 n. 3, 151 n. 4, 166 f., 173, 177
Creed, J. M., 65 n. 1, 66 n. 2, 175, 177
Crehan, J., 21, 154 n. 3, 156 n. 3, 157 n. 1, 158, 160 n. 2, 161 n. 1, 162 f., 177
Cross, F. L., 177, 184

Dahl, N. A., 76 n. 1, 77 n. 2, 177
Daniélou, J., 184
Daube, D., 176 f.
Davies, W. D., 116, 176 f.
DeBruyne, D., 140 n. 1, 177
Dibelius, M., 5 n. 1, 47, 49 n. 1, 97 n. 2, 102 n. 2, 110 n. 1, 111 n. 3, 161, 177, 182
Dihle, A., 109 n. 1, 178
Duplacy, J., 5 n. 3, 7 n. 2, 11 n. 3, 178
Dupont, J., 104, 131 n. 1, 158 n. 1, 175, 178

Ehrhardt, A., 167, 178
Eisentraut, E., 178
Enslin, M. S., 146 n. 1, 178
Epp, E. J., 11 n. 2, 30 n. 1, 32 n. 4, 162 n. 1, 178
Evans, O. E., 109 n. 1, 178

INDEX OF AUTHORS

Fascher, E., 6 n. 1, 17, 19 f., 21, 39, 48 n. 2, 58, 86 n. 2, 90, 92 nn. 4, 6, 102 n. 1, 103 n. 1, 104 n. 1, 110 n. 1, 111 n. 2, 112, 114 n. 1, 117 n. 2, 127 n. 3, 129 f., 132 n. 2, 138 n. 1, 150, 151 n. 3, 152, 156 n. 4, 169, 178
Findlay, J. A., 9, 178
Fischer, B., 32, 173
Foakes Jackson, F. J., 174 f.
Frede, H. J., 7, 178
Frey, J. B., 137, 138 n. 1, 178
Friedrich, G., xvi, 172
Funk, F. X., 31, 173
Funk, R. W., 179

Gard, D. H., 21 n. 1, 178
Garitte, G., 173
Gärtner, B., 48 n. 2, 49 nn. 1 f., 178
Geden, A. S., 172
Gerhardsson, B., 16, 178
Gingrich, F. W., 51 n. 3, 172
Glaue, P., 3, 178 f.
Glombitza, O., 47 n. 2, 179
Goguel, M., 2 n. 1, 14 n. 2, 19 n. 2, 35, 37, 176, 179
Grant, R. M., 180
Greenlee, J. H., 13 n. 5, 179
Greeven, H., 26 n. 2, 177, 179
Gregory, C. R., xiv, 1 n. 3, 174, 179
Grosheide, F. W., 4 n. 3, 179

Haenchen, E., 6 n. 1, 9 n. 2, 11 n. 2, 47 n. 1, 48 n. 2, 55 n. 4, 56 nn. 2, 4, 58 n. 2, 59 nn. 2, 4, 67 n. 2, 68 nn. 1 f., 4, 70 n. 3, 73, 80 n. 3, 82 nn. 2, 5, 85 n. 2, 89 n. 2, 92 n. 2, 94 n. 2, 99, 108 n. 1, 110 nn. 1, 3, 123 nn. 1 f., 133 n. 1, 134 n. 1, 146 nn. 2 f., 147 n. 1, 154 n. 1, 158 n. 4, 159 n. 1, 175, 179
Harnack, A. (von), 2 n. 1, 19 n. 4, 36, 43–5, 60 n. 1, 76, 77 n. 1, 82 n. 3, 91 n. 2, 107 n. 1, 110, 132 n. 2, 167 n. 7, 179 f.
Harris, J. R., 2 f., 8 f., 13, 15, 21, 22 n. 1, 24–6, 45, 52 f., 74 n. 1, 78, 91, 92 n. 3, 127, 132 n. 2, 133, 138 n. 3, 165 n. 1, 179 f.
Harvey, W. W., 53, 173
Hatch, E., 172
Hatch, W. H. P., 6, 33 nn. 1, 3, 36 n. 4, 38 n. 1, 180, 182

Higgins, A. J. B., 176
Hilgenfeld, A., 6, 46 n. 1, 47, 92, 99, 124 n. 2, 126 f., 129, 149, 157, 161 n. 3, 173
Hort, F. J. A., 1 f., 4 f., 6 n. 1, 12 n. 1, 13, 15, 36 nn. 4, 6, 45, 174
Howard, W. F., 2 n. 1, 12 n. 1, 19 n. 2, 172, 180

Jacquier, E., 5 n. 3, 47 n. 3, 55 n. 3, 75 n. 1, 82, 88 n. 1, 106 nn. 1 f., 124 n. 1, 160 n. 3, 175
Jones, H. S., 55 n. 5, 172

Karnetzki, M., 20 n. 1, 180
Kasser, R., 173
Kenyon, F. G., 4–6, 8 n. 6, 13 n. 4, 36 nn. 4 f., 39 n. 3, 80, 180
Kerschensteiner, J., 180
Kilpatrick, G. D., 8 n. 1, 37, 51 n. 3, 162 n. 1, 180
King, G. B., 108 n. 1, 109 n. 1, 180
Kittel, G., xvi, 172
Klijn, A. F. J., 2 n. 2, 3 n. 2, 5, 6 nn. 1 f., 9 n. 2, 11 f., 14, 19 n. 4, 20 n. 1, 24 n. 1, 25, 35 n. 1, 36, 37 n. 2, 53 n. 4, 95 n. 2, 110 n. 1, 138 n. 1, 167, 173, 180
Knowling, R. J., 175
Knox, W. L., 52 n. 4, 82 n. 4, 97 n. 1, 108 n. 1, 162, 168, 180
Koole, J. L., 173
Köster, H., 109 n. 1, 180
Kraft, B., 172
Kraft, R. A., 96 n. 1, 180
Kümmel, W. G., 6 n. 3, 12 n. 1, 107 n. 1, 108 n. 1, 110, 180 f.
Kuss, O., 180

Lagrange, M.-J., 22, 24 n. 1, 26, 28 n. 3, 69 f., 71 n. 1, 72 n. 3, 115 n. 1, 121 n. 1, 136 n. 1, 162, 167, 181
Laistner, M. L. W., 173
Lake, K., 2 n. 1, 14 n. 1, 15, 22, 26, 27 n. 1, 28, 37 f., 60, 67, 71, 108 n. 1, 110 n. 1, 137, 142, 173–5, 181
Liddell, H. G., 53 n. 7, 55 n. 5, 172
Lietzmann, H., 110 n. 1, 181
Loisy, A., 106 n. 1
Lowe, E. A., 7, 172, 181

McHardy, W. D., 105 n. 2, 181
MacKenzie, R. S., 10 n. 1

INDEX OF AUTHORS

Martin, V., 173
Massaux, E., 181
Menoud, P. H., 21–3, 38 n. 2, 44 n. 2, 45 n. 1, 64, 69 f., 75 n. 3, 97 n. 2, 109 n. 1, 110, 111 n. 1, 116 n. 1, 121 n. 1, 124 n. 1, 163 n. 2, 167, 169 f., 181
Merk, A., 52 nn. 1 f., 181
Metzger, B. M., 18 n. 1, 33 n. 2, 95 n. 1, 172, 181
Miller, E., 2, 176
Montgomery, J. A., 33, 108 n. 1, 173, 181
Moulton, J. H., 12 n. 1, 52 n. 3, 172
Moulton, W. F., 172
Muncey, R. W., 173
Munck, J., 69 n. 4, 181
Mussner, F., 180

Nestle, E. (= Eberhard), 3, 52 f., 77, 78 n. 1, 173, 182
Nestle, Erwin, 173
New, S., 15 n. 2, 173, 181
Nock, A. D., 5 n. 1, 39 n. 1, 170 n. 1, 182

O'Neill, J. C., 67 n. 2, 90 n. 3, 182

Parvis, M. M., 14 n. 1, 17 f., 20, 39, 176, 181, 182
Perrot, Ch., 30, 174
Petersen, T. C., 11, 12 n. 1, 29 f., 139 n. 1, 173
Plooij, D., 2 n. 1, 8 n. 5, 26, 68, 70, 71 n. 1, 73, 74 n. 1, 110 n. 1, 167, 179, 182
Porter, C. L., 36 n. 4, 182
Pott, A., 19 n. 4, 36
Preuschen, E., 175

Rahlfs, A., 174
Ramsay, W. M., 138 n. 1, 182
Raphelius, G., 60, 182
Redpath, H. A., 172
Reicke, B., 48 n. 1, 182
Resch, A., 147 n. 3, 182
Riddle, D. W., 6 n. 3, 13, 14 n. 1, 15–18, 20, 39, 182
Riesenfeld, H., 16, 52 n. 5, 182, 184
Robertson, A. T., 1 n. 3, 182
Ropes, J. H., xiii, 1 n. 1, 2 n. 2, 3 n. 2, 4–12, 22, 27–31, 32 nn. 1 f., 33 nn. 1–3, 36, 38, 45 n. 1, 46 n. 1, 47, 53, 57 n. 1, 50 nn. 1–3, 65 n. 1, 68 n. 1, 69 n. 2, 72, 75 n. 3, 77 nn. 4, 6, 80 n. 1, 85 nn. 1–3, 87 n. 1, 88 n. 2, 90 n. 3, 91 n. 2, 92, 94 n. 1, 99 n. 2, 100 n. 1, 102 n. 1, 106 n. 5, 107 n. 1, 110 n. 1, 113 n. 2, 122 nn. 1 f., 125 n. 1, 134 n. 3, 137 n. 1, 138 n. 2, 139 n. 2, 141, 143 nn. 1 f., 147 n. 2, 150 n. 2, 155 n. 2, 156, 158, 159 n. 2, 161, 166, 168, 174, 182
Rowley, H. H., 177

Sanday, W., 29 n. 1, 110 n. 1, 174, 183
Sanders, H. A., 4 n. 3, 6 n. 1, 11 n. 2, 15 n. 3, 27 f., 34 n. 1, 174, 183
Saunders, E. W., 19 n. 4, 183
Schäfer, K. T., 29, 183
Schonfield, H. J., 110 n. 1, 183
Schrenk, G., 53 n. 7
Scott, R., 53 n. 7, 55 n. 5, 172
Scrivener, F. H., 7 f., 12 n. 1, 46 n. 1, 69 n. 1, 91, 92 n. 1, 174
Seeligmann, I. L., 21 n. 1, 39 n. 2, 183
Simon, M., 69 n. 4, 183
Smothers, E. R., 4 n. 3, 80 n. 1, 183
Snape, H. C., 110 n. 1, 163 n. 2, 183
Sneyders de Vogel, K., 7, 183
Soden, H. von, 10 n. 3, 14, 24 n. 1, 174
Souter, A., 13 n. 5, 29 n. 1, 183
Stendahl, K., 19 n. 4, 24 n. 2, 183
Stone, R. C., 12 n. 2, 183
Streeter, B. H., 45 n. 2, 165 n. 2, 183

Taylor, V., 110 n. 1, 184
Thiele, W., 75 n. 3, 184
Thomson, R. W., 173, 180
Tischendorf, C., xiv, 72 n. 1, 174
Titus, E. L., 19 n. 4, 184
Torrey, C. C., 3, 5 n. 3, 6 n. 1, 11 n. 3, 24, 52, 53 n. 1, 58 n. 3, 59 n. 3, 77, 106, 138 n. 2, 165 n. 1, 167, 184
Tune, E. W., 167 n. 7, 177
Turner, C. H., 15 n. 3, 28 n. 1, 29 n. 1, 36 n. 4, 174, 184

Unnik, W. C. van, 184

Valentine-Richards, A. V., 31, 174
Vogels, H. J., 2 n. 1, 9 nn. 2, 4, 19 n. 4, 24 n. 1, 31 n. 3, 37, 78, 184
Vööbus, A., 30 n. 5, 31 n. 3, 33 nn. 1 f., 4, 184

Warfield, B. B., 1 n. 3, 184

INDEX OF AUTHORS

Weiss, B., 4, 10 n. 3, 12, 13 n. 1, 36 n. 4, 44, 184
Wensinck, A. J., 3, 24 f., 184
Westcott, B. F., 1, 4, 6 n. 1, 12 n. 1, 13, 15, 36 nn. 4, 6, 45 n. 4, 174
Wettstein, J. J., 60 n. 2, 175
White, H. J., 133 n. 4, 141, 174
Wikgren, A. P., 176, 181 f.
Wilckens, U., 184
Wilcox, M., 3, 24, 53 n. 2, 58 n. 2, 136 n. 1, 138 n. 2, 185
Williams, C. S. C., 3, 21 f., 52 n. 8, 72 n. 3, 78 n. 5, 97, 100 n. 1, 102 n. 1, 110 n. 1, 112 n. 3, 121 n. 1, 133 n. 3, 146 n. 5, 155 n. 1, 156, 160, 162, 175, 185
Willoughby, H. R., 182

Wilson, J. M., 156 n. 5, 185
Windisch, H., 108 n. 1
Wood, H. G., 181
Wordsworth, J., 133 n. 4, 141, 174
Wright, L. E., 2 n. 1, 19 n. 4, 37 n. 3, 39 n. 2, 185

Yoder, J. D., 12 n. 2, 36 n. 6, 172, 185

Zahn, T., 3, 6, 43 n. 2, 46 f., 52 n. 1. 59 n. 1, 60 n. 1, 91 n. 4, 99, 107 n. 1, 124 n. 2, 126, 129, 133 n. 4, 134 n. 2, 138 n. 3, 140 f., 149, 151 n. 1, 161 nn. 1, 3, 174 f., 183
Ziegler, J., 174
Zuntz, G., 3, 14 nn. 1 f., 21 n. 1, 89 nn. 4 f., 118 n. 1, 143 n. 2, 185

INDEX OF PASSAGES

THE OLD TESTAMENT

Esther			xlix. 6		80
v. 10		129	lii. 13		86
Psalms			Ezekiel		
ii. 1 f.		76	xxvii. 25		53 n. 7
ii. 7 f.		79 f.			
ii. 7		83	Joel		
ii. 8		80	ii. 28		66 f., 70 n. 3
Ecclesiastes			Nahum		
vii. 19 (18)		130 f.	iii. 15		53 n. 7
Isaiah			Habakkuk		
xlii. 1		83, 86	i. 5		82

THE APOCRYPHA OF THE OLD TESTAMENT

Tobit			II Maccabees		
iv. 15		109 n. 1	iii. 29		127
x. 7		160 n. 1	ix. 9		53 n. 7
Wisdom			III Maccabees		
xii. 14		132 n. 2	iv. 21		127
			v. 12, 28		127

THE NEW TESTAMENT

Note. Page numbers in italic indicate text-critical discussions

Matthew			xiv. 41		59
i. 21		78	xiv. 60		133
ix. 4		44 f.	xv. 34		24
x. 23		140 n. 2	xvi. 15		79
xvi. 26		79			
xxii. 18		45	Luke		
xxvi. 13		79	i. 77		72
xxvi. 28		72 n. 1	ii. 10		77, 78 n. 2
xxvii. 19		51 n. 2	ii. 32		66
xxvii. 24		51 n. 2	ii. 38		73
xxvii. 25		79	iii. 3		72 n. 1
			iii. 19		133
Mark			iv. 13		142 n. 1
i. 4		72 n. 1	v. 22		*44 f.*
viii. 36		79	ix. 25		79
xi. 22		88 n. 3	ix. 36		83
xii. 24		46	xviii. 39		83 n. 1
xiv. 9		79	xix. 40		*83 n. 1*

INDEX OF PASSAGES

Luke (cont.)
xx. 23	*45*
xx. 26	*83*
xxi. 34	*53 n. 7*
xxii. 37	*59*
xxii. 59	101 n. 1
xxiii. 22	*126 nn. 1 f.*
xxiii. 34	*45*
xxiii. 41	*44 f.*
xxiii. 47	*51*
xxiii. 51	125
xxiv. 20	56
xxiv. 43–53	65
xxiv. 46 f.	66
xxiv. 47–52	65
xxiv. 47–9	65
xxiv. 47	66, *82 n. 1*
xxiv. 51	*167 n. 7*

John
viii. 2	79
xiv. 1	88 n. 3
xvi. 32	129
xviii. 20	78
xviii. 31	58, 60 n. 1
xviii. 38	126 n. 1
xix. 4	126 n. 1
xix. 6	60 n. 1, 126 n. 1
xix. 27	129

Acts
i. 1–12	65
i. 2	3 n. 2, *65 f., 116 f.*, 119, *167 n. 7*
i. 4 f.	65
i. 5	*116*
i. 8	65
i. 9	*167 n. 7*
i. 11	*167 n. 7*
i. 13	*159*
i. 14	*75 n. 3, 167 n. 7*
i. 15	*159*
i. 16	*154*
i. 17	*154*
i. 20	*154*
i. 21	*54, 62 f., 154*
i. 23	*157 f., 167 n. 7*
i. 24	*158*
i. 25	*154*
ii. 4	*159*
ii. 5	67
ii. 6	*158*
ii. 10	67
ii. 14–40	66

Acts (cont.)
ii. 14–36	75
ii. 14	67, 71, *128 n. 1, 158*
ii. 17	*66–72, 164, 167 f., 170*
ii. 18	67, *70*
ii. 19	*167 n. 7*
ii. 20	*67 n. 2, 167 n. 7*
ii. 22	*67, 71*
ii. 23	*59–61*
ii. 33	*68 f., 168*
ii. 36	*58 n. 5*
ii. 37	*73 f., 86, 154, 159, 164*
ii. 38	*54, 62 f., 68, 72*
ii. 39	69 n. 4, *70 f., 167*
ii. 41	*118*
ii. 42	*128*
ii. 43	*128 n. 2*
ii. 47	*25, 68, 76–9, 118, 166 f.*
iii. 3–5	*155 f.*
iii. 6	*29, 163*
iii. 12–26	*42, 125 n. 3*
iii. 12	132 n. 1
iii. 13–18	47
iii. 13–17	*124*
iii. 13–15	*42*
iii. 13 f.	*56*
iii. 13	*52, 54–6, 63, 71*, 95
iii. 14	*51–3*, 55
iii. 15	*43, 71*
iii. 17	*38, 42–51, 53, 55, 167, 169 f.*
iii. 18	43, 48, 55
iii. 20	*54 n. 1*, 55
iii. 22	*71*, 95
iii. 25	*71*, 95
iii. 26	55
iv. 1	*125 n. 3*
iv. 3	*124*
iv. 6	*167 n. 7*
iv. 7	132 n. 1
iv. 8–12	29
iv. 8 f.	*120 f.*
iv. 9	*167, 170*
iv. 10	58 n. 5, *64*
iv. 11	*71*
iv. 12	*71, 167*
iv. 13	*121–4*
iv. 14	*121–4, 147, 154, 167*
iv. 15	*121–4*
iv. 16	*124* f.
iv. 17	*124, 125, 148*
iv. 18	*124 f., 148, 168*
iv. 21	*124, 126, 149*
iv. 24	*11, 127, 149 n. 2, 154*

200

INDEX OF PASSAGES

Acts (cont.)		Acts (cont.)	
iv. 25	76	viii. 24	*159*, *163*
iv. 27	55, 76	viii. 35	54, 62 f., 117 f., 155
iv. 30	55	viii. 37	55 n. 1, 63
iv. 31	82, 118, 166	viii. 39	116–18
iv. 32	98	ix. 17	63
iv. 33	54, 62 f.	ix. 18	*157*
v. 4	44 f.	ix. 19	*135*
v. 8	11	ix. 20	63, *123*, 134 f.
v. 12	*156*	ix. 22	64, 134 f.
v. 14	89	ix. 31	*100*
v. 15	156 f., *163*	ix. 34	*156*, *164*
v. 16	*156*	ix. 40	54, 62 f., *157*
v. 18	11, 129 f.	ix. 42	89
v. 19	129 f.	x. 24 f.	160 f.
v. 21	*130*	x. 25	*168*
v. 22–7	*130*	x. 27	*161*
v. 28	*131*	x. 28	49 n. 4
v. 29 f.	128 n. 1, *159*	x. 33	*157*, *160–2*, *164*
v. 30	95	x. 39	*61*, *71*
v. 31	64, 72 n. 2	x. 42 f.	66
v. 34 f.	*128*	x. 43	72 n. 2, 89 n. 3
v. 35–40	*130*	x. 48	54, 62 f.
v. 37	76	xi. 1	104–6, *107*
v. 38	130 f., 132 n. 1, *154*, *167*, *170*	xi. 2	11, 104–7, *163*, *168*
v. 39	*127*, *130–2*, *154*, *167*, *170*	xi. 3	105 f.
v. 41	128 n. 1	xi. 17	89 nn. 1, 3, 116–18, *162*
v. 42	54, 62 f.	xi. 18	*107*
vi. 1	95, *167*	xi. 20	54, 62 f.
vi. 8	54, 62 f.	xi. 24	89 n. 2
vi. 10	116 f., *123*, 132 f., *155*	xi. 27	99
vi. 11	132 f., *167*	xi. 28	99
vi. 13	*133*	xii. 1	*129*
vi. 15	*133*, *155*	xii. 2	144 f.
vii. 4	95	xii. 5	*162*
vii. 11 f.	95	xii. 15	101 n. 1
vii. 12	95	xii. 17	83 n. 1
vii. 15	95	xii. 23	145 f.
vii. 31	11	xiii. 8	*135*, *155*, 167 n. 7
vii. 32	95	xiii. 9–11	*163*
vii. 38	71, 95	xiii. 9	*156*, *164*
vii. 39	95	xiii. 12	88, 89 n. 2, *135*, *155*
vii. 44	95	xiii. 13	85
vii. 45	71, 95	xiii. 14	89
vii. 51–3	*170*	xiii. 15	*135*
vii. 51	96	xiii. 16	89
vii. 52	51 n. 2, 95 f., *170*	xiii. 17	95
vii. 54	11	xiii. 25	47
vii. 55	55, 63	xiii. 26	47, 71
vii. 57	*133*	xiii. 27–31	*124*
viii. 1	128 f., *131*, *137*, *168*	xiii. 27	38, 45 n. 1, 46–8, 49 n. 2, 50, 55–7, 58 n. 1, *168*, *170*
viii. 16	54, 62 f.	xiii. 28	47, 56–8, *126*, *152*, *169*
viii. 18	*116*		

INDEX OF PASSAGES

Acts (cont.)		Acts (cont.)	
xiii. 29	*11, 47*, 48, *56–8, 152, 169*	xv. 22	*167 n. 7*
xiii. 32	48, 80, *95*	xv. 24	*100 f.*
xiii. 33	48, *54, 62 f., 79 f.*	xv. 25	*71*, 142
xiii. 38	*72* n. 2, *81 f., 168*	xv. 26 f.	111
xiii. 39	*81 f., 118*	xv. 26	*142*
xiii. 41	*82 f., 155, 164*	xv. 28	*71*
xiii. 42–4	89	xv. 29	*38, 50* n. *1, 107–11, 116–18, 167*
xiii. 43	*83 f., 119, 136, 155, 168*	xv. 32	*111, 116–18*
xiii. 44	*11*, 83, *157, 164*	xv. 33	112
xiii. 45–7	79	xv. 34	*112*
xiii. 45	*136, 167*	xv. 37–9	112
xiii. 47	66, 80, 84	xv. 37	85
xiii. 49	83	xv. 40	*112*
xiii. 50	*134, 136 f., 167, 169*	xv. 41	89, 112, *113* n. *1*, 163
xiv. 1	89	xvi. 1	*163*
xiv. 2–7	*167*	xvi. 4	54, 62, *113 f., 119, 123*
xiv. 2	*51* n. 2, *137 f., 167, 169*	xvi. 10	*99*
xiv. 3	138	xvi. 13	*89*
xiv. 4	*119, 138*	xvi. 14	*90*
xiv. 5	*138–40, 166 f.*	xvi. 15	*89 f., 167*
xiv. 6	*139 f.*	xvi. 31 f.	*93*
xiv. 7	*119, 140, 155*	xvi. 31	54, *62 f.*, 89 n. *3*
xiv. 8–18	140	xvi. 34	88, 89 n. 2
xiv. 9	*119, 128* n. *1, 155*	xvi. 35–9	*147*
xiv. 10	*54, 62 f., 163*	xvi. 35	*148, 155, 168*
xiv. 14	*128* n. *1*	xvi. 37	*126* n. *3, 149, 154*
xiv. 16	49 n. 3	xvi. 38	*148*
xiv. 17	68	xvi. 39	48, *50 f., 51* n. *1, 147–50*
xiv. 18	129	xvi. 40	*149* n. 2
xiv. 19	*123, 140 f., 151* n. 2, *155, 166*	xvii. 11	*74*
xiv. 20	*141 f.*	xvii. 12	*74 f.*, 86, *118, 166, 167* n. *7, 168*
xiv. 22 f.	89		
xiv. 25	*119*	xvii. 13	*118, 142, 160* n. *1*
xv. 1–5	105, 163	xvii. 15	*117–19, 142–4, 147*
xv. 1–3	*96*	xvii. 17	*142*
xv. 1	97, *100, 102*	xvii. 23	48 f.
xv. 2	97, *101–3, 129*	xvii. 28	*71*
xv. 3	29 f.	xvii. 30	*38, 48–50, 55*
xv. 4	*96 f.*	xvii. 31	*55* n. *1, 63, 167* n. *7*
xv. 5	97, 100, *102, 168*	xvii. 34	*167* n. *7*
xv. 7–11	83, 103	xviii. 2	*92*
xv. 7	43 n. 4, *71, 103 f., 116, 118, 155, 157*	xviii. 3	*167* n. *7*
		xviii. 4–8	84, *94*
xv. 9	98 f.	xviii. 4–6	*84–7, 90*
xv. 10	*95*	xviii. 4 f.	*92*
xv. 11	54, *62 f.*	xviii. 4	*55* n. *1, 63, 84–7, 166 f.*
xv. 12	83, *97 f., 103, 125*	xviii. 5	54, *62 f., 84–6*
xv. 13	83 n. *1, 104*	xviii. 6 f.	*93*
xv. 14	76, 77 n. *1*, 83	xviii. 6	*84 f.*, 87, *92* n. 2, *93*
xv. 19	*104*	xviii. 7	*91–3, 167* n. *7*
xv. 20	22, *38, 50* n. *1, 107–11, 167, 170*	xviii. 8	54, *62 f., 87 f.*, 89, *90, 118,* 146

202

INDEX OF PASSAGES

Acts (*cont.*)		Acts (*cont.*)	
xviii. 10	76	xxiii. 24	*151, 166*
xviii. 12	*144 f., 167 f.*	xxiii. 26–30	151
xviii. 13	*144, 167*	xxiii. 29	*151 f.*
xviii. 17	*146 f.*	xxiv. 2–8	151 f.
xviii. 18 f.	92	xxiv. 5	*166 f.*
xviii. 21	*129*	xxiv. 6	*58, 152*
xviii. 24	*167* n. 7	xxiv. 7	*151 f.*
xviii. 26	92, *167* n. 7	xxiv. 10	*151*
xviii. 27	*4* n. *3, 118*	xxiv. 24	89 n. 3, *152 f.*
xviii. 28	118, 133	xxiv. 27	*152*
xix. 1	*117, 129, 163, 168*	xxv. 10	126 n. 1
xix. 2	*117*	xxvi. 1	*117 f., 153*
xix. 4	76	xxvi. 6	95
xix. 5	*54, 63, 72* n. 2	xxvi. 17	76
xix. 8	*155, 157*	xxvi. 18	72 n. 2
xix. 9	*94 f., 166*	xxvi. 23	76
xix. 12	157, *163*	xxvii. 15	133 n. 2
xix. 14	55 n. *1, 63, 119*	xxvii. 25	89
xix. 25	43 n. 4	xxviii. 17–28	114
xx. 3	*117 f., 125, 143 f., 168*	xxviii. 17	76, 114
xx. 12	55 n. 2	xxviii. 18	126 n. 1
xx. 18–22	115	xxviii. 19	*153*
xx. 18	*142*	xxviii. 24–8	115
xx. 19	142	xxviii. 24	75 n. 1, 115
xx. 21	*54, 63, 89* n. *3, 90* n. *4, 167*	xxviii. 25	95, 114
xx. 22–4	115	xxviii. 26	76
xx. 23	*129*	xxviii. 27	*53* n. *7,* 76
xx. 24	*115, 135*	xxviii. 29	114
xx. 25	55 n. *1, 64*	xxviii. 30	*114 f.*
xx. 27	*71*	xxviii. 31	55 n. *1, 63,* 114, *167* n. 7
xxi. 6	129		
xxi. 13	*54, 63*	**Romans**	
xxi. 19	114	i. 8	79
xxi. 20	107, *114*	iii. 19	79
xxi. 21	111	xiii. 10	109 n. 1
xxi. 22	*111*	xv. 11	79
xxi. 24	111		
xxi. 25	*38, 50* n. *1, 107* 12, 114, *170*	**I Corinthians**	
		i. 1	147
xxi. 28	152	ii. 8	45 n. 1
xxi. 40	83 n. 1	vii. 14	68
xxii. 4	95		
xxii. 14	*51* n. *2*	**Colossians**	
xxii. 19	89	i. 6	79
xxii. 21	152		
xxii. 29	30, *150 f.*	**II Timothy**	
xxii. 30	*150*	iii. 11	137, 139
xxiii. 5	76		
xxiii. 12	*151*	**Hebrews**	
xxiii. 14	*151*	v. 5	55
xxiii. 15	*151*	ix. 19	79

203

INDEX OF PASSAGES

I John			Revelation	
ii. 2	79		xiii. 7	79
v. 19	79		xiv. 6	79

OTHER ANCIENT WRITINGS

Acts of John
    22   62

Chrysostom
    Homilies on Acts x, 3 (85)   123

Epistle of Barnabas
    ii. 9 f.   96
    iii. 6   96
    iv. 6 f.   96
    v. 9   65
    viii. 7   96
    ix. 6   96
    x. 12   96
    xiii. 1, 3   96
    xiv. 4 f.   96

Gospel of Peter
    3   60 n. 1

Gospel of Thomas
    6   109 n. 1

Homer
    Iliad v, 664   53 n. 7

Josephus
    Antiquities
        VI, 13. 9 (= VI, 316)   61
        XVII, 6. 5 (= XVII, 174)   126 n. 3
    The Jewish War
        IV, 9. 8 (= IV, 543)   126 n. 3

Justin
    Apology XXXIX, 2   123 n. 3

Polybius
    Histories XXVI, 2. 13 (= XXIV, 9. 13 Loeb)   60 f.

INDEX OF GREEK WORDS

ἀγαλλίασις, 99
ἄγγελος, 117, 129, 145
ἅγιος, 51, 55, 145; *see also* πνεῦμα
ἀγνοέω, 46–51, 149
ἄγνοια, 42–4, 46, 48 f., 51
ἄγνωστος, 49
ἀγορά, 148
ἀγράμματος, 121–3
ἄγω, 47, 144
ἀδελφός, 42 f., 71, 73, 81, 100, 105, 114, 137
αἷμα, 107–9, 131
αἰνέω, 76
αἵρεσις, 100
αἴρω, 153
αἰτέω, 51 f., 56 f., 80
αἰτία, 56, 126, 149
αἴτιος, 126 n. 2
ἀκατάκριτος, 149
ἀκούω, 68, 73, 88, 117, 135, 152, 157, 161 f.
ἀλήθεια, 132
ἀληθής, 141
ἀλίσγημα, 107
ἅμα, 113 f.
ἁμαρτία, 66, 72, 81, 82 n. 1
ἁμαρτωλός, 59
ἀναβαίνω, 97, 101 f., 105
ἀναγινώσκω, 46
ἀναγκάζω, 153
ἀναγκαῖος, 160
ἀνάγω, 143
ἀναίρεσις, 56–8
ἀναιρέω, 56 f., 58 n. 2, 59, 61
ἀναίτιος, 126 n. 3, 149
ἀνακρίνω, 120
ἀναλαμβάνω, 65
ἀναμιμνήσκω, 148
ἀνασκευάζω, 100
ἀνήρ, 42 f., 50 f., 73 5, 81, 131 f., 149
ἀνθίστημι, 132
ἄνθρωπος, 49, 51, 120 f., 128, 130 f., 141, 149
ἀνθύπατος, 144
ἀνίστημι, 103 f., 163

ἄνομος, 59–61
ἀντεῖπον, 121
ἀντιλέγω, 132, 136, 153
ἀντιτάσσω, 84–6
ἀντοφθαλμέω, 132, 133 n. 2
ἀπαγγέλλω, 49, 105
ἀπάγω, 121 f., 124, 151
ἀπαλλάσσω, 156 f.
ἀπαρνέομαι, 52, 54
ἀπειθέω, 94, 137
ἀπειλέω, 125
ἀπέρχομαι, 50, 91 n. 4, 114, 121 f., 124, 148, 150
ἀπέχω, 107, 131
ἀπιστέω, 74 f., 118
ἀποδέχομαι, 118
ἀποδοκιμάζω, 61
ἀποθνῄσκω, 151
ἀποκρίνομαι, 159
ἀπόκρισις, 83
ἀποκτείνω, 60 f., 151
ἀπολαμβάνω, 146
ἀπολύω, 54, 56 f., 126
ἀποστέλλω, 55, 108
ἀπόστολος, 65, 73, 96, 101, 112 f., 128 f., 138, 158 f.
ἀποφθέγγομαι, 158 f.
ἀργύριον, 151
ἀρεστός, 145
ἀρνέομαι, 51–4
ἁρπάζω, 117, 151
ἀρχιερεύς, 55
ἀρχισυνάγωγος, 87, 137, 146 f.
ἄρχομαι, 66
ἄρχων, 42, 46, 120, 126, 128, 131, 137 f.
ἀσθένεια, 156
ἀσθενής, 120
ἀτενίζω, 155 f.
ἄτοπος, 44
ἄφεσις, 66, 72, 81, 82 n. 1
ἀφίημι, 45, 130
ἀφίστημι, 94, 130, 141

βάλλω, 149

βαπτίζω, 72, 88
βαρέω, 53 n. 7
βάρος, 112 n. 2
βαρύνω, 51–3
βασιλεύς, 131, 132 n. 2
βῆμα, 144–6
βία, 151
βλασφημέω, 84, 86, 136
βλέπω, 68, 121, 156
βουλή, 59, 117, 125, 163
βούλομαι, 131, 157, 161 f.

γενεά, 49 n. 3
γεννάω, 80
γῆ, 80
γίνομαι, 55, 83 f., 86, 101, 107 f., 119, 136, 138, 143, 145, 148, 160
γνώμη, 124 f., 143
γνωστός, 81
γραφή (αἱ γραφαί), 46, 48, 84, 86
γράφω, 56 f., 79
γυνή, 74 f., 136

δάκρυον, 142
δεῖ, 101, 111, 151, 154
δεξιός, 55 n. 1
δέρω, 149
δεσπότης, 127
δεύτερος, 79 f., 138 f.
δέω, 150, 152
δῆμος, 76
δημόσιος, 129, 149
διακατελέγχομαι, 133
διακονία, 95
διάκονος, 95
διακρίνω, 99, 105
διάκρισις, 98
διαλέγομαι, 84, 115, 118, 141, 155
διαλιμπάνω, 142, 160
διαλογίζομαι, 44
διαμαρτύρομαι, 84 f.
διανέμω, 125
διαπορεύομαι, 113
διασαφέω, 160
διαστέλλω, 100 f.

INDEX OF GREEK WORDS

διατάσσω, 100
διατηρέω, 108
διατρίβω, 140
διδάσκω, 100, 105, 140 f.
διδαχή, 119, 140
δίδωμι, 80, 89 n. 1, 117, 137 f., 145, 162
διερμηνεύω, 84–6
διέρχομαι, 83, 113, 119, 136
διηγέομαι, 149 n. 2
διϊσχυρίζομαι, 101
δίκαιος, 50 f., 55, 137, 149, 151
δικαιόω, 81
διωγμός, 134, 136–9
διώκω, 96, 140 n. 2
δόγμα, 113 f.
δοκέω, 89, 112
δόξα, 55 n. 1, 145
δοξάζω, 54 f., 105, 107
δουλεύω, 142
δοῦλος, 70, 160
δύναμαι, 81, 100, 131 f.
δύναμις, 155
δυνατός, 89 n. 1
δῶρον, 68

ἐάω, 49 n. 3, 130, 152
Ἑβραῖος, 95
ἐγείρω, 130
ἔγκλησις, 151
ἔθνος, 49 n. 3, 66, 80, 83 n. 3, 87, 94, 108, 137–40, 153
ἔθος, 100
εἶδον, 55 n. 1, 136, 145, 152, 155
εἰδωλόθυτος, 107–9
εἴδωλον, 107
εἶπον, 50, 83 f., 97, 103 f., 114, 117, 128, 143, 156, 158 f., 163
εἰρήνη, 100, 137 f.
εἰσέρχομαι, 91, 93, 135, 160
εἰσπορεύομαι, 84
ἐκβάλλω, 139
ἔκδοτος, 59–61
ἐκκλησία, 96, 100, 118, 134
ἐκλέγομαι, 65
ἐκπηδάω, 160 f.
ἐκπλήσσω, 140

ἐκταράσσω, 100
ἐκτινάσσω, 84
ἐκχέω, 67 f.
ἐκψύχω, 145
ἐλέγχω, 132 f.
Ἕλλην, 74 f., 84, 114 f., 146 f.
Ἑλληνίς, 74 f.
ἐμβλέπω, 156
ἐναντιόομαι, 136
ἐνδυναμόω, 134
ἐνέργεια, 127, 149 n. 2, 154
ἐντέλλω, 65, 116
ἐντίθημι, 63, 84, 86
ἐντολή, 112–14
ἐνυπνιάζομαι, 67
ἐνύπνιον, 67
ἐξάγω, 50, 148, 150 f.
ἐξέρχομαι, 50, 105, 150
ἐξουσία, 131
ἐπαγγελία, 70
ἐπάγω, 131, 137 f.
ἐπαίρω, 158
ἐπεγείρω, 136–9
ἐπέχω, 156
ἐπιβάλλω, 129
ἐπιβουλή, 142 f.
ἐπιγινώσκω, 121, 127, 149 n. 2, 154
ἐπικαλέω, 63, 153
ἐπικράζω, 50, 144 n. 1, 150, 153
ἐπιλαμβάνομαι, 146
ἐπιμένω, 112
ἐπισείω, 141
ἐπίσταμαι, 42 f.
ἐπιστέλλω, 107
ἐπιστηρίζω, 105
ἐπιτάσσω, 145
ἐπιτίθημι, 144
ἐπιτυγχάνω, 56 f.
ἐπιχείρησις, 145
ἔρχομαι, 50, 91, 93, 97, 101, 139, 148, 161
ἐρωτάω, 50, 148, 150, 152
ἔσχατος, 66 f.
εὐαγγελίζω, 119
εὐαγγέλιον, 65 f., 116
εὐγενής, 74
εὐδοκέω, 135
εὐεργεσία, 120
εὐνοῦχος, 117

εὑρίσκω, 56, 126, 131
εὐσχήμων, 74 f., 136
εὐτόνως, 133
ἐχθές, 148
ἐχθρός, 153
ἔχω, 76 f., 88 n. 3, 100, 108, 111, 114, 121, 151, 153, 156

ʒάω, 145
ʒῆλος, 136
ʒηλωτής, 114
ʒήτημα, 101
ʒήτησις, 101

ἡδέως, 135
ἡμεῖς, ἡμῶν, ἡμῖν, 70 f., 95 f. et passim
ἡμέρα, 65–7, 99

θάλασσα, 142 f.
θάνατος, 56, 126, 153
θαρρέω, 153
θαυμάζω, 83, 88, 121, 135
θέλημα, 131
θέλω, 54, 56, 82, 105–8, 117 f., 143, 152, 163
θεομάχος, 131
θεός, 47–9, 54 f., 59, 62 f., 66, 76, 81 f., 83 n. 2, 88–91, 95, 99, 105, 107, 118 f., 127, 131, 135–8, 141, 145, 149 n. 2, 154, 157, 161 f.
θεραπεύω, 121, 156 n. 5
θεωρέω, 114, 121, 123
θλῖψις, 134, 136 f.
θυγάτηρ, 67

ἰάομαι, 156 n. 5
ἰδιώτης, 121–3
Ἱερουσαλήμ, Ἱεροσόλυμα, 46, 61, 66, 74, 96 f., 99, 101, 105, 113, 117, 126, 128 f., 134, 163
Ἰησοῦς, 47, 54 f., 62–4, 68, 84–6, 119, 121, 152; ὁ κύριος Ἰησοῦς Χριστός (or sim), 55, 62–4, 68, 72, 84 f., 88, 89 nn. 1, 3, 90 n. 4, 113, 118 f., 157, 163
ἱκανός, 74 f., 105, 163

206

INDEX OF GREEK WORDS

ἱμάτιον, 84
'Ιουδαία, 100, 114, 129
'Ιουδαῖος, 61, 84 f., 114 f., 133-40, 142-6, 151-3
'Ισραήλ, 47, 74, 120
ἵστημι, 55 n. 1, 121, 133, 157 f.
ἰσχύω, 132

καθαιρέω, 56 f.
καθαρός, 87
καθόλου, 124, 125 n. 1, 151
κακολογέω, 94
κακόω, 137
καλέω, 124
καρδία, 44, 68, 73, 98
καταβαίνω, 145
καταβοάω, 144
καταγγέλλω, 81
καταλαμβάνω, 121
καταλείπω, 152
καταλύω, 131
καταντάω, 105
κατανύσσομαι, 73
κατάσχεσις, 80
κατατίθημι, 152
καταφεύγω, 139
κατέρχομαι, 84, 99 f.
κατεφίσταμαι, 144
κατηγορέω, 153
κατοικέω, 46, 126, 134
κελεύω, 65 f., 116, 121, 124, 128
κηρύσσω, 65 f., 113, 116, 119, 142
κινέω, 119, 140
κλαίω, 159
κληρονομία, 80
κολάζω, 126, 132 n. 2
κολλάω, 119, 138
κόσμος, 25, 76-9
κράζω, 133, 144 n. 1
κρατέω, 124
κρεμάννυμι, 61
κρίμα, 56
κρίνω, 46 f., 54, 56, 58 n. 1, 89, 101 f., 108, 113, 152
κρίσις, 54 f.
κριτήριον, 54
κριτής, 151
κύριος, 55 n. 1, 60 n. 1,

62-4, 66 f., 68, 81, 84-90, 115, 117, 129, 135, 137 f., 142, 145, 149 n. 2, 157, 161; see also 'Ιησοῦς
κωλύω, 89 n. 1, 142 f.

λαλέω, 78, 82, 93, 132, 136
λαμβάνω, 59-61, 116 f., 151, 153
λαός, 25, 76-9, 120, 125 f.
λέγω, 50, 66, 100 f., 104, 108, 111, 135 f., 141, 144, 150, 163
λιθοβολέω, 138 f.
λόγος, 47, 82-6, 100, 105 f., 115, 116 f., 134-6, 138, 141-3, 152, 157
λοιπός, 73, 159
λυτρόω, 153
λύω, 150

μάρτυς, 43, 133
μεγάλως, 96 f.
μέγας, 134, 136 f., 155, 163
μέλλω, 116, 143
μέλω (μέλει), 146
μένω, 101, 134
μεταβαίνω, 91-3
μετανοέω, 49, 72
μετάνοια, 66, 81 f.
μεταστρέφω, 67 n. 2
μήν, 143
μιαίνω, 130 f.
μνημεῖον, 56 f.
μόλις, 151
μολύνω, 130
μυριάς, 114

νεανίσκος, 55 n. 2, 67
νομίζω, 89
νόμος, 81, 101, 114, 152
νόσος, 157
νύξ, 129

ξύλον, 56 f., 61

ὁδός, 49 n. 3, 94
οἶδα, 40 f., 15
οἰκία, 91-3
οἶκος, 87, 91-3, 120

ὀλίγος, 74 f.
ὁμοθυμαδόν, 144
ὄνομα, 91; τὸ ὄνομα τοῦ κυρίου 'Ιησοῦ Χριστοῦ (or sim), 63, 66, 68, 72, 84, 86, 88, 118, 157, 163
ὅρασις, 67
ὁράω, 67
ὁρίζω, 59
ὁρμή, 138
ὀφθαλμός, 155
ὄχλος, 76, 77 n. 2, 136, 141

παῖς, 54 f.
πάλιν, 50, 56-8, 138 f., 150
πανταχοῦ, 49
παραγγέλλω, 49, 97, 101 f., 124, 125 n. 1
παραγίνομαι, 50, 84, 96, 160
παραδέχομαι, 96
παραδίδωμι, 54-9, 112 f.
παρακαλέω, 50, 83 n. 3, 148, 150, 153, 161
παράκλησις, 135, 153
παραλαμβάνω, 148
παραχρῆμα, 145, 150, 157, 163
παρεῖδον, 48 f.
πάρειμι, 157, 161
παρέρχομαι, 142, 151
παροίχομαι, 49 n. 3
παροτρύνω, 136 f.
παρρησία, 82, 113, 119, 121, 123, 132, 135, 141, 155
παρρησιάζομαι, 153
πατήρ, 45, 51, 95 f.
παχύνω, 53 n. 7
πείθω, 84, 141
πειρασμός, 142
πέμπω, 150
πέρας, 80
περιμένω, 160 f.
περιπατέω, 100, 163
περιτέμνω, 100 f.
περιτομή, 105
πίμπλημι, 136
πίπτω, 117, 160
πιστεύω, 63, 74 f., 81 f.,

207

INDEX OF GREEK WORDS

πιστεύω (*cont.*)
  87–90, 93, 98, 100 f.,
  108, 114, 117 f., 135,
  141, 146, 162
πίστις, 88 n. 3, 89 n. 3,
  90 n. 4, 114
πιστός, 89, 145
πλῆθος, 76, 83, 94, 98,
  103, 111, 119, 136, 140
πλήρης, 111, 117
πληρόω, 46–8
πνεῦμα, 67, 84, 103 f.,
  132, 143; τὸ πνεῦμα τὸ
  ἅγιον (or *sim*), 65,
  89 n. 1, 103 f., 108,
  110 f., 116 f., 132, 153,
  162
πνικτός, 50 n. 1, 107–9
ποιέω, 44 f., 73, 105–8,
  121 f., 124, 128, 137,
  143, 149 n. 2, 157
πόλις, 50, 83, 113, 119,
  136, 139 f., 148, 150,
  157
πολυπλήθεια, 140
πολύς, 50, 74 f., 84–8,
  105 f., 114, 125, 142,
  148, 151, 157, 159
πονηρία, 45
πονηρός, 42–5, 49, 169
πορεύομαι, 49 n. 3, 87, 150
  f., 112, 117, 129, 163
πορνεία, 107–9
πούς, 160, 163
πρᾶγμα, 44
πρᾶξις, 125
πράσσω, 42, 44, 108
πρεσβύτερος, 67, 83, 96 f.,
  101–3, 113, 120
πρόγνωσις, 59
προσαπειλέω, 126
προσδέχομαι, 160
προσδοκάω, 160
προσεγγίζω, 160
προσευχή, 89 n. 5
προσεύχομαι, 158
προσκυνέω, 160
προσκύνησις, 161
προσπήγνυμι, 59
προστάσσω, 161
προστίθημι, 89 n. 2, 145
προσφωνέω, 105
πρόσωπον, 54
πρότερος, 158

προφητεύω, 67
προφήτης, 46 f., 96, 99
προχειρίζομαι, 55
πρωΐ, 130
πρῶτος, 79 f., 136, 158

ῥῆμα, 125
ῥύομαι, 156
ῥώνυμι, 108

σάββατον, 46, 83 n. 3, 84
σάρξ, 67, 69 f.
σέβομαι, 75 n. 4, 90–2,
  136
σεισμός, 148
σημεῖον, 125
σήμερον, 80, 120
σιγάω, 82 f., 103, 155
σκληρύνω, 94
σκωληκόβρωτος, 145
σοφία, 132, 135
στάσις, 101
σταυρόω, 56–8
συγγενής, 160
συγκαλέω, 160
συγκατατίθημι, 83, 97,
  103, 124 f.
συγχέω/συγχύννω, 134
συζητέω, 114
συλλαλέω, 144
συλλαμβάνω, 145
συμβαίνω, 142
συμβάλλω, 121
συμβιβάζω, 135
συνάγω, 83, 157
συναγωγή, 84, 137
συναντάω, 160
συνέδριον; σύνεδρος, 121,
  128
συνέρχομαι, 73 f., 111, 148
συνέχω, 84 f.
συνίημι, 46–8
συνομιλέω, 161
συνοράω, 139
συστρέφω, 50, 99, 150
σχεδόν, 83, 157
σώζω, 78, 93, 100
σωτήρ, 47
σωτηρία, 47

ταπεινοφροσύνη, 142
τάσσω, 101 f.
ταχύς, 137 f., 161
τέκνον, 68, 70

τελέω, 56 f.
τηρέω, 101, 108, 111
τήρησις, 129, 152
τίθημι, 44, 56 f., 129
τίς, 73–5, 94, 101, 140,
  151 n. 2, 152
τότε, 73 f., 84, 94, 129 f.,
  132, 158, 167 n. 7
τρέχω, 160
τύπτω, 146
τύραννος, 131, 132 n. 2

ὑβρίζω, 138
υἱός, 62 f., 67, 80
ὑμεῖς, ὑμῶν, ὑμῖν, 42–4,
  67–71, 95 f. *et passim*
ὑπάρχω, 114, 119, 149,
  155
ὑπερεῖδον, 48, 49 n. 1
ὑποβάλλω, 132
ὑποδείκνυμι, 73, 154
ὑποστρέφω, 117, 143

φέρω, 108, 110, 117
φεύγω, 139 f.
φθέγγομαι, 124
φίλος, 50, 148, 160
φοβέω, 148, 151, 155
φόβος, 119, 155
φονεύς, 51
φυλακή, 50, 148 f.
φυλάσσω, 108, 113
φωνέω, 124 f.
φωνή, 46–8, 133, 158,
  163

χαρίζομαι, 51, 152
χάρις, 76, 77 n. 5, 105,
  152
χείρ, 59–61, 129–31,
  144, 151
χιλίαρχος, 151
Χριστός, 43, 47 f., 54–6,
  62 f., 68, 115, 135;
  see also Ἰησοῦς
χρόνος, 48 f., 105, 163
χώρα, 61, 105 f.
χωρισμός, 98

ψαλμός, 79
ψεύδομαι, 141
ψυχή, 98, 100, 137, 153

ὥρα, 95

INDEX OF LATIN WORDS

abeo, 91
abnego, 54
accusatio, 98
adduco, 122
admiror, 121
afficio, 139
aggravo, 52
agnosco, 122
ago, 49
ambulo, 108
anterior, 138 f.
apprehendo, 146
assequor, 122 n. 1
attendo, 156
audio, 121, 123

causa, 126
Christus, 46 f., 54 n. 1, 88
circumdo, 141
civitas, 139, 141
cohors, 162
colloquor, 122
comprehendo, 146
concilium, 122, 128
confirmo, 104
constantia, 121, 123
contradico, 85, 121
contumelia, 139
converso, 122
curo, 121

deus, 62, 131, 155
dico, 85, 139, 156, 158 f.
dies, 65
discedo, 141
discipulus, 158
disco, 141
discrimen, 98
disputo, 85, 155
doctrina, 140
dominus, 62, 83 n. 2, 85, 89, 136

ejecto, 139
eligo, 65
evangelium, 65

exclamo, 133
excutio, 85

facio, 85, 121, 139
fero, 108
fiducia, 121
fiducialiter, 153
filius, 62
fingo, 146
fugo, 139

gens, 87
gentilis, 139
genus, 140
Graeci, 85, 95
gravo, 52

homo, 121

idiota, 121
Iesus, 46 f., 54 n. 1, 62, 81, 85, 88, 122, 139
ignoro, 46
illiteratus, 121
impetus, 139
infirmus, 121
inhonoro, 52 n. 1
iniquitas, 43
iniquus, 44
injurior, 139
intelligo, 46, 139
intendo, 156
interficio, 57
interpono, 85
interpretor, 85
introeo, 85, 91, 141

jubeo, 122
Judaei, 61, 85 f., 139, 155
judico, 104

lapido, 139
levo, 141

magistratus, 139
maledico, 85

malum, 43 f.
moveo, 140

nego, 52, 54
nequam, 43
nomen, 85, 88

onero, 52

paenitentia, 49
palam, 155
persecutio, 139
persuadeo, 121
populus, 133, 141
possum, 121
potentia, 104
potestas, 131, 132 n. 1
praecipio, 65
praedico, 65
precor, 158
prior, 158
procedo, 160

quaero, 122

recedo, 93
resisto, 136
respondeo, 159
reverto, 112
rex, 162

sabbatum, 85
scelus, 43
scientia, 43
scio, 43
scribo, 57
scriptura, 85
senex, 137
separatio, 98
simulo, 146
sperno, 52
spiritus sanctus, 65, 108
sto, 104, 121
suadeo, 85
supervenio, 84 f.
suscipio, 139
sustineo, 160

INDEX OF LATIN WORDS

synagoga, 85

tribulatio, 138 f.
tunc, 84 f., 122–4, 133, 141, 146
turba, 136

vado, 87
vecto, 108
verbum, 85, 104, 125, 155
vesper, 141

vestis, 85
video, 121, 146
vidua, 95
voluntas, 131
vox, 133